Beginning SUSE Linux

From Novice to Professional

KEIR THOMAS

Beginning SUSE Linux: From Novice to Professional

Copyright © 2005 by Keir Thomas

ISBN (pbk): 1-59059-458-4

Printed and bound in the United States of America 9 8 7 6 5 4 3 2 1

Lead Editor: Chris Mills
Technical Reviewer: Frank Pohlmann
Editorial Board: Steve Anglin, Dan Appleman, Ewan Buckingham, Gary Cornell, Tony Davis, Jason Gilmore, Chris Mills, Dominic Shakeshaft, Jim Sumser
Assistant Publisher: Grace Wong
Project Manager: Emily K. Wolman
Copy Manager: Nicole LeClerc
Copy Editor: Marilyn Smith
Production Manager: Kari Brooks-Copony
Production Editor: Kelly Winquist
Compositor: Susan Glinert
Proofreader: Elizabeth Berry
Indexer: Valerie Perry
Artist: Kinetic Publishing Services, LLC
Cover Designer: Kurt Krames
Manufacturing Manager: Tom Debolski

Distributed to the book trade in the United States by Springer-Verlag New York, Inc., 233 Spring Street, 6th Floor, New York, NY 10013, and outside the United States by Springer-Verlag GmbH & Co. KG, Tiergartenstr. 17, 69112 Heidelberg, Germany.

In the United States: phone 1-800-SPRINGER, fax 201-348-4505, e-mail orders@springer-ny.com, or visit http://www.springer-ny.com. Outside the United States: fax +49 6221 345229, e-mail orders@springer.de, or visit http://www.springer.de.

For information on translations, please contact Apress directly at 2560 Ninth Street, Suite 219, Berkeley, CA 94710. Phone 510-549-5930, fax 510-549-5939, e-mail info@apress.com, or visit http://www.apress.com.

*Dedicated to my parents, Raymond and Freda Thomas,
in thanks for a lifetime of encouragement.*

Contents at a Glance

PART ONE ▬▬▬ Introducing the World of Linux

PART TWO ▬▬▬ Installing SUSE Linux

PART THREE ▬▬▬ The No-Nonsense Getting Started Guide

PART FOUR ■■■ The Shell and Beyond

PART FIVE ■■■ Multimedia

PART SIX ■■■ Office Tasks

PART SEVEN ■■■ Keeping Your System Running

PART EIGHT ■■■ Appendixes

Contents

PART ONE ■■■ Introducing the World of Linux

PART TWO ■■■ Installing SUSE Linux

PART THREE ■■■ The No-Nonsense Getting Started Guide

PART FIVE ■■■ Multimedia

PART SEVEN ■■■ Keeping Your System Running

PART EIGHT ▪▪▪ Appendixes

About the Author

 **KEIR THOMAS** has been writing about computing for a decade. He has edited several best-selling computer magazines, such as *LinuxUser & Developer*, *PC Utilities*, and *PC Extreme*; written for many others, including *Computer Buyer*, *PC Direct* and *IT Week*; and also written for several IT web sites.

After graduating from the University of Glamorgan with a First Class degree, Keir set about combining his love of computers with his passion for writing. This naturally led him to a career in IT journalism. Throughout his career, his aim has been to explain advanced and confusing technology in ways that the average person can understand.

Keir lives in Derbyshire in the north of Britain. Weekends find him walking the local mountains. He also plays the piano and the tin whistle, and is slowly but surely learning French in his spare time.

About the Technical Reviewer

 **FRANK POHLMANN** has been a committed Linux user since January 1996. He installed Slackware and, surprisingly, it worked. He started writing about Unix and Linux systems two years later, working for companies as varied as AT&T and SUSE. He became technical editor of the UK-based *LinuxUser & Developer* magazine in 2002 and refuses to stop writing about free software. He is a much-published writer on open-source issues, and has a deep and sustained interest in the history of computer science.

In a previous life, he worked on a PhD on early Persian literature; text-editing problems led him to Perl, and ultimately he "interrupted" his PhD. Frank threatened his supervisor with resuming his pursuit of this PhD, an event that led him to become a full professor in Germany. Frank lives in the UK and India, and has hobbies that usually involve languages and a lot of food.

Acknowledgments

Books such as the one you're holding now take an enormous amount of effort on behalf of many people. To this end, I'd like to thank Chris Mills and Emily Wolman at Apress for their considerable help getting this book written. This includes not only the practical work of processing my copy but also their encouragement when the going got tough. My thanks also go to the many other people at Apress who work behind the scenes to turn this book into reality.

I'd also like to thank the technical editor, Frank Pohlmann, for his insightful suggestions and his unerring ability to point out my many mistakes, no matter how small or trivial. His help was invaluable, and this book wouldn't be what it is without his comments.

Finally, I'd like to thank Christian Egle at SUSE for his help in organizing the DVD-ROM of SUSE Linux, which we have included with this book. Christian's willingness to help and handle the matter with SUSE HQ is appreciated.

Introduction

Linux has come a long way in a short time. Computing itself is still relatively young by any standard; if the era of modern computing started with the invention of the microchip, it's still less than 50 years old. But Linux is a youngster compared even to this; it has been around for only 13 of those years.

In that brief time span, a one-time student's personal project has grown and gone on to run a great deal of the world's computers. It has rampaged through the computing industry, pushing aside alternatives from the likes of Microsoft Corporation and toppling long-held beliefs about the way things should be done. This is all by virtue of the fact that Linux is simply better than every other choice out there. It's more secure, faster, and—the kicker for most people—free of charge. Yes, that's right. It doesn't have to cost a penny. It is one of the computing industry's best-kept secrets.

I was bitten by the Linux bug in the mid to late 1990s. I was introduced to it by a friend who sold it to me as a kind of alternative to DOS. At that time, I tapped a few commands at the prompt and was greeted by error messages. I must admit that I was put off. But shortly afterwards, I revisited Linux and quickly became hooked.

Yet getting used to Linux wasn't easy. I read as many books as I could but, in my opinion, all of them fell significantly short. They were usually overly complicated or simply irrelevant. To start off, I didn't want to know how to create a program that could parse text files. I just wanted to know how to copy and delete files. I didn't want to set up a web server with PHP functions. I just wanted to know how to play my MP3 tracks and browse the Web.

This book is my answer to that need for a fundamental, authoritative, and down-to-earth guide to Linux, done in the context of one of the most popular flavors of Linux in existence today. It's a book that is desperately needed in our modern world, especially as Linux becomes more and more popular and enters homes and workplaces.

Beginning SUSE Linux purely and simply focuses on what you need to know to use Linux. It's concise and to the point, aiming to re-create under Linux all the stuff you used to do under Windows. But don't think that this means *Beginning SUSE Linux* cuts corners. Wherever justified, we spend time examining the things you need to know in order to gain a complete and comprehensive understanding. For example, you'll find a hefty chapter looking at the command-line prompt—arguably the heart of Linux and the element that gives Linux most of its power. There's also an entire chapter discussing (and illustrating) how to initially install SUSE Linux on your computer. *Beginning SUSE Linux* really is the complete guide.

About SUSE Linux

Most versions of Linux are broadly similar, but in this book, we focus specifically on SUSE Linux. This is one of the premier distributions of Linux available today. Some would go further and say that it's the absolute best. It's a professional product, which delivers the best of the Linux world to its users.

Novell bought SUSE GmbH in 2003, giving SUSE Linux the kind of push that only a multi-national corporation allows. SUSE Linux is being snapped up around the world for use in corporate and home environments. SUSE partners with IBM, Hewlett-Packard, and many other computer manufacturers around the world as one of their distributions of choice.

This isn't without reason. SUSE Linux has managed to pull off the seemingly impossible feat of being both easy to use and also extremely powerful. It overcomes one of the standard criticisms of Linux—that it's hard to configure—by providing the YaST2 tool. Uniquely in the Linux world, this offers access to just about every aspect of Linux configuration, from setting up your printer to installing new software, and much more besides. Users of Windows might think of it as being like the Control Panel on steroid-enhancing drugs. But Windows doesn't even come close to providing an alternative.

The comparison with Windows is apt because SUSE Linux manages to pull off another seemingly impossible feat: it's easy to use for those coming from Windows, yet retains its own independent look and feel. Virtually everyone in the Linux world agrees that SUSE Linux has the best user interface around, and this is clearly something SUSE Linux's software engineers spent a long time developing. SUSE Linux is a luxury product in the often rough-and-ready world of Linux.

These same engineers were also aware of what most users need. Out of all the versions of Linux currently available, SUSE Linux is the best at handling multimedia such as video and audio. Its hardware support is also excellent, meaning that installing it is a breeze. It's ideal for every level of user, and the desktop user in particular.

What You'll Find in This Book

Beginning SUSE Linux is split into seven parts, each of which contains chapters looking at a certain aspect of SUSE Linux use. These individual parts of the book (and the chapters within them) can be read in sequence, or you can dip in and out of them at will. Whenever a technical term is mentioned, a reference is made to the chapter where this term is explained.

Part One of the book looks at the history and philosophy behind the Linux operating system. I aim to answer many of the common questions about Linux. Such knowledge is considered to be as important, if not more so, than understanding the technical details on how Linux works. But while these chapters should be read sooner rather than later, they contain no technical information that absolutely needs to be ingested to get started.

Those wanting to start using SUSE Linux immediately should head to Part Two, which covers installing SUSE Linux on your computer. An illustrated guide is provided, and all installation choices are explained in depth. Additionally, you'll find a problem-solving chapter to help just in case anything goes wrong.

Part Three of the book focuses on getting started with SUSE Linux. It covers setting up the Linux system so that it's ready to use. One chapter is dedicated to setting up common hardware devices, such as printers and modems, and another explains how you can secure your system. Other chapters in this part explore the desktop, explaining what you need to know to begin using SUSE Linux on a daily basis.

In Part Four, we take a look at how the underlying technology behind Linux functions. You'll be introduced to the command-line prompt and learn how the file system works. It's in these chapters that you'll *really* master controlling Linux!

Part Five covers the powerful multimedia functions built into SUSE Linux, which let you watch movies and play back music. We also take a look at the image-editing software built into SUSE Linux.

Part Six moves on to explain how typical office tasks can be accomplished under SUSE Linux. We investigate OpenOffice.org, the complete office suite built into SUSE Linux. After an introduction to OpenOffice.org, separate chapters explore its word processor, spreadsheet, and presentations package. Another chapter is devoted to the database component built into SUSE Linux.

Part Seven carries on from Part Four, taking an even more in-depth look at the underlying technology behind SUSE Linux. This time, the emphasis is on giving you the skills you need to keep your system running smoothly. You'll learn how to install software, manage users, optimize your system, back up essential data, and schedule tasks.

Finally, at the back of the book, you'll find two vital appendixes. The first is a glossary of Linux terms used not only in this book, but also in the Linux and Unix world. The second appendix is a quick reference to commands typically used at the command-line prompt under Linux. Both appendixes should prove invaluable for future reference.

Conventions Used in This Book

The goal when writing *Beginning SUSE Linux* was to make it as readable as possible while providing the facility for readers to learn at their own pace.

Throughout the book, you'll find various types of notes and sidebars complementing the regular text. These are designed to provide handy information to help further your knowledge. They also make reading the book a bit easier.

Note A note is designed to provide an important piece of information that you should know and that will help your understanding of the topic being discussed.

Tip A tip is something that will help when you need to perform the task being described. Alternatively, it might be something that can make your life easier when using SUSE Linux.

Caution A caution is something you should certainly pay attention to because it warns of a hidden danger or particular caveat that applies to the topic being discussed.

In the sidebars, I take a few moments out from the main body of the book to explain something that you should know, but that isn't vital to an understanding of the main topic being discussed. You don't need to read the sidebars there and then; you can return to them later if you wish.

The SUSE Linux DVD-ROM

Included with this book is a DVD-ROM containing the full hard disk installation of SUSE Linux 9.1. This is the version of Linux used during the writing of this book, and all references made throughout *Beginning SUSE Linux* refer to it specifically.

Just as we were finishing production of this book, SUSE released version 9.2 of SUSE Linux. This mostly polishes SUSE Linux and isn't very different from 9.1. Practically everything described in this book applies equally well to SUSE Linux 9.2 as it does to 9.1.

At the time of writing, a "live eval" version of SUSE Linux 9.2 is available from the SUSE FTP site. A live eval version lets you boot SUSE Linux 9.2 from CD without installing anything to the hard drive. The download address is `ftp://ftp.suse.com/pub/suse/i386/live-cd-9.2/`. If you wish, you can download one of the ISO images (you can choose from a GNOME or KDE CD version, or a DVD that includes both desktop GUI possibilities), then burn a CD/DVD from that image, and then put it in your drive!

Additionally, SUSE usually makes available a special download version of its latest distribution from its web site (`www.suse.com`). Readers of *Beginning SUSE Linux* might consider upgrading to this version when they've finished reading the book.

Support from Apress

Finally, a word about the online help offered by Apress, the publishers of this book. When you visit `www.apress.com`, you can click a link on the left side of the page to visit the forums. Here, you'll be able to make comments about this book and find help with any issues it raises.

PART ONE

Introducing the World of Linux

## CHAPTER 1

Welcome!

If you're an avid computer user, there's a good chance that you've heard of Linux. You might have read about it, or perhaps you've seen television ads that refer to it.

One of the odd things about Linux is that the more you learn about it, the more questions you have. For instance, it's generally thought that Linux is free of charge, but this then raises the question of how, in our modern world, something like an entire computer operating system can cost nothing. Who pays the programmers?

Over the following introductory chapters, I'm going to try and answer some of these questions. In this chapter, I'll explain what Linux is and its benefits compared to Windows.

What Is Linux?

There are two ways of looking at a PC. The first is to see it as a magical box, which lets you do cool stuff like browse the Internet or play games. Seen in this way, it's like a VCR—put in a tape, press a button, and a picture appears on your TV. On your PC, you click the Internet Explorer icon, type a web address, and a web site somehow appears. The astonishing technical complexity behind these simple procedures isn't important to most people.

The other way of looking at a PC is as a collection of components that are made by various manufacturers. You might be familiar with this way of thinking if you're ever tried to upgrade your PC's hardware. In that case, you'll know that your PC consists of a CPU, a hard disk, a graphics card, and so on. You can swap any of these out to put in newer and better components that upgrade your PC's performance or allow more data storage.

What almost no one realizes is that the operating system is just another component of your PC. It, too, can be swapped out for a better replacement. Windows doesn't come free of charge, and Microsoft isn't performing a public service by providing it. Around $50 to $100 of the price you pay for a PC goes straight into Microsoft's pocket. Bearing in mind that hundreds of millions of PCs are made each year, it's not hard to see why Microsoft is one of the world's richest corporations.

It would be difficult to question this state of affairs if Microsoft gave us our money's worth. But it often falls far short. Its products are full of serious security holes, which at best inconvenience us and at worst make us lose data. And that's before we consider the instability of Microsoft products—hardly a day goes by without something unexpected happening. One of the first things people are taught when attending Windows training is how to use the Ctrl+Alt+Delete keyboard combination, which resets the computer after a crash!

Microsoft became rich, and maintains its wealth, by a virtual monopoly over PC manufacturers. While the intelligent computer buyer can choose between components to make for a better PC—deciding between an AMD or Intel processor, for example—you usually have little choice but to buy Windows with a new PC. Try it now. Phone your favorite big-name computer retailer. Say that you want a PC but you *don't* want Windows installed. Then listen as the salesperson on the other end of the phone struggles to understand.

■**Note** Some PC manufacturers actually will sell you a PC without Windows installed on it. All you have to do is ask, although you might need to speak to a senior salesperson to get through to somebody who understands your request. Smaller local companies, in particular, will be more than willing to sell you a PC without Windows. Some retailers, such as Wal-Mart, even sell PCs with Linux preinstalled. These are usually inexpensive, largely because of the savings made when you don't pay the Microsoft tax!

Wouldn't it be terrific if you could get rid of Windows? Would you like to finally say goodbye to all those security holes and not have to worry about virus infections anymore, yet not lose out on any features or need to make sacrifices or compromises?

There is an alternative. Welcome to the world of Linux.

Linux is an operating system, which is to say that it's a bit like Windows. It's the core software that runs your computer and lets you do stuff on it. By the strictest definition of the term, an *operating system* is the fundamental software that's needed to make your PC work. Without an operating system installed on your PC, it would merely be an expensive doorstop. When you turned it on, it would beep in annoyance—its way of telling you that it can't do much without a whole set of programs to tell it what to do next.

An operating system allows your PC's hardware to communicate with the software you run on it. It's hundreds of programs, system libraries, drivers, and more, all tightly integrated into a whole. In addition, an operating system lets programs talk to other programs and, of course, communicate with you, the user. In other words, the operating system runs everything and allows everything to work.

■**Note** Some companies and individuals, including Microsoft, define an operating system as much more than this fundamental software. They add in the basic tools you run on an operating system, such as web browsers and file management programs.

Linux consists of a central set of programs that run the PC on a low level, referred to as the *kernel*, and hundreds (if not thousands) of additional programs provided by other people and various companies. Technically speaking, the word *Linux* refers explicitly just to the core kernel program. However, most people generally refer to the entire bundle of programs that make up the operating system as *Linux*.

GNU/LINUX

Although most of us refer to Linux as a complete operating system, the title "Linux" hides a lot of confusing but rather important details. Technically speaking, the word *Linux* refers merely to the kernel file: the central set of programs that lie at the heart of the operating system. Everything else that comes with a typical version of Linux, such as programs to display graphics on the screen or let the user input data, is supplied by other people, organizations, or companies. The Linux operating system is the combination of many disparate projects. (I'll explain how this works in the next chapter.)

The GNU organization, in particular, supplies a lot of vital programs and also system library files, without which Linux wouldn't run. These programs and files were vital to the acceptance of Linux as an operating system in its early days. Because of this, and the fact that Linux completed a long-running goal of the GNU project to create a Unix-like operating system, some people choose to refer to Linux as GNU/Linux.

A fierce debate rages over the correct way to refer to the Linux operating system and whether the GNU prefix should be used. For what it's worth, an equally fierce debate rages over how we should define an operating system. It can all get very confusing. It's also very easy to accidentally offend somebody by not using the correct terminology!

It's not the purpose of this book to get involved in this debate. Suffice it to say that I acknowledge the vital input of the GNU project into the operating system many people refer to simply as Linux, as well as that of other vital projects. However, readers should note that when I refer to *Linux* throughout this book, I mean the entire operating system. If I intend to refer simply to the kernel programs, I will make that clear.

The Age of Linux

At the time of writing this book, Linux is a little over 13 years old. It has gone from a hobbyist project maintained by just one man to a professional and corporate-sponsored solution for virtually every level of computer user.

Linux has also gone from being a server operating system, designed for central computers that hand out files and other computer resources to other computers, to becoming a full-fledged graphical desktop operating system like Windows. In fact, it's gone even further. Today, it's very likely that you'll find Linux running your digital video recorder and other computerized household gadgets.

Getting technical for a moment, Linux is a 32-bit and 64-bit, multitasking, multiuser operating system. This is a complicated way of saying that it's pretty darn powerful. Linux is as capable of running supercomputers as it is of running a desktop PC. Linux builds on the foundation laid by Unix, which itself was based on Multics, which was one of the first modern computer operating systems. It's not an exaggeration to say that Linux can trace its family tree all the way back to the pioneering days of computing.

CORRECT PRONUNCIATION

What most people refer to as the Linux operating system takes its name from the kernel program, one of its most important system components. This, in turn, was named after its creator, Linus Torvalds.

The name Linus is commonly pronounced "Lie-nus" in many English-speaking countries, but Torvalds speaks Swedish. He pronounces his name "Leen-us" (imagine this spoken with a gentle Scandinavian lilt, and you've got it about right).

Because of this, he pronounces Linux as "Lin-ux" and most people copy this pronunciation. You can hear this spoken by Torvalds himself by visiting www.paul.sladen.org/pronunciation/.

Some people refer to the Linux operating system by its full title of GNU/Linux. In this case, GNU is pronounced as in the name of the animal, with a hard *G*: "G-noo." The full pronunciation is therefore "G-noo Lin-ux."

Finally, the DVD that comes with this book includes a version of Linux called SUSE Linux. SUSE is a German acronym and is normally pronounced "Sooz-eh."

The Problems with Windows

The world's most popular operating system is Windows, which is made by the Microsoft Corporation. Linux has no links with Windows at all. Microsoft doesn't contribute anything to Linux and, in fact, is rather hostile toward it because it threatens Microsoft's market dominance. This means that installing Linux can give you an entirely Microsoft-free PC. How enticing does *that* sound?

Windows is used on 91% of the world's desktop computers. In other words, it must be doing a good job for it to be so popular, right?

Let's face facts. Windows is not without problems, and that's putting it mildly. It's stunningly insecure, and virtually every day a new security hole is uncovered. This leads to the creation of worms by malevolent programmers. *Worms* are small programs that exploit security holes within operating systems, leaping from computer to computer and spreading like wildfire via the Internet. Examples include Sasser (as well as its variations), which causes your computer to crash and shut down as soon as you go online.

Then there are the viruses—hundreds and hundreds of them. This has led to an entire industry that creates antivirus programs, which are additional pieces of software. Antivirus software is vital if you want to use Windows without losing data or running the risk of your files being stolen!

Some argue that Windows is hit by so many viruses merely because it's so popular. But consider that many of these viruses are simple programs that merely take advantage of security holes in Windows. For example, the Melissa virus took advantage of a bug in such a way that just viewing an e-mail message caused the virus to infect your computer! And we're *paying* for this quality of software?

■**Note** Although I'm being disparaging about Windows here, unlike many books, *Beginning SUSE Linux* doesn't ignore Windows. Throughout its pages, you'll find frequent references to Windows and the software that runs under it. You'll find direct comparisons with actual Windows programs. The intention is that anyone with prior experience will be able to get started with SUSE Linux much more quickly.

And how about the speed at which Windows runs? It's just dandy when your PC is brand new. But after just a few months, it seems like someone has opened up the case and poured molasses inside. It takes quite a few seconds for My Computer to open, and there's time for a coffee break while Internet Explorer starts up.

So is Linux the solution to these problems? Most would agree that it's a step in the right direction, at the very least. Linux doesn't have antivirus programs, because there are virtually no Linux-specific viruses. As with all software, security holes are occasionally discovered in Linux, but the way it is built means exploiting those holes is much more difficult.

Note There have been a couple of viruses for Linux, but they're no longer "in the wild" (that is, they are no longer infecting PCs). This is because the security holes they exploit were quickly patched, causing the viruses to die out. This happened because the majority of Linux users update their systems regularly, so any security holes that viruses might exploit are patched promptly. Compare that to Windows, where most users aren't even aware they can update their systems, even when Microsoft gets around to issuing a patch (which has been known to take months).

There's also the fact that Linux encourages you to take control of your computer, as opposed to treating it like a magical box. As soon as you install Linux, you become a power user. Every aspect of your PC is under your control, unlike with Windows. This means fixing problems is a lot easier, and optimizing your system becomes part and parcel of the user experience. You no longer have to take poor performance lying down. You can do something about it!

WINDOWS COMPATIBLE?

One of the biggest questions asked by most newcomers to Linux is whether it can run Windows software. The answer is yes... and no.

Linux is completely different from Windows on a fundamental technical level. Its creators based it on Unix, an industrial-strength operating system, and deliberately steered clear of emulating Windows. This means that Linux isn't a swap-in replacement for Windows. You cannot take the installation CD of a Windows program and use it to install that program on Linux, in the same way that you cannot install an Apple Mac program on Windows. However, several current projects let you run Windows programs on Linux. Wine (www.winehq.com) is an example of such a project. You can also use programs like VMware (www.vmware.com) to create a "virtual PC" running on Linux. Then you can install the Windows operating system and, therefore, any Windows software you like.

In most cases, however, you'll find that there's a Linux equivalent of your favorite Windows software. Frequently, you'll find that this Linux version is actually superior to the Windows program you've been using. We discuss many of these in Chapter 11.

The Benefits of Linux

People have been known to exaggerate about Linux when singing its praises, and there's certainly some hyperbole around. But there are a couple of cast-iron facts about its benefits.

Crash-Free

A primary benefit of Linux is that it doesn't crash. In years and years of using Linux, you will never experience your mouse cursor freezing on screen. A strange error box won't appear and not go away until you reboot. It's possible to leave a Linux system running for years without ever needing to reboot (although most desktop SUSE Linux users shut down their PC when they won't be using it for a while, just like the rest of us).

Of course, programs that run on top of Linux sometimes crash, but they don't take the rest of the system down with them, as can happen under Windows. Instead, you can clean up after a crash and just carry on.

Note Actually, very few programs under Linux crash. Because Linux programmers use a different method of bug testing than used by Microsoft developers, there are arguably fewer bugs, and those that are discovered are fixed very quickly.

Security

The next benefit is that Linux is far, far more secure than Windows. Linux is based on years or proven computer science research. It works on the principle of users who have permissions to undertake various tasks on the system. If you don't have the correct permission, then you cannot, for example, access a particular piece of hardware. Additionally, privacy can be ensured because the files on the PC are "owned" by individual users, who can permit or deny others access to those files.

Free and Shareable

Another big benefit is that Linux can be obtained free of charge. Once it's installed, the latest updates for all your programs are also free of charge. Not only that, but if you want any new software, it will also usually be free of charge (and normally just a download away). Is this starting to sound attractive yet?

Because the software is free, you can share it with friends. Suppose that you find a really great image editor. You mention it to a friend, and he asks for a copy. Under Windows, copying the program is strictly illegal—to do so turns you into a software pirate! Unless that image editor is freeware, your friend will need to buy the software himself. Under Linux, sharing software is normally entirely legal. In fact, it's encouraged! I'll explain why in Chapter 2.

Compatible with Older Hardware

Another benefit of Linux is that it works very well on older hardware and doesn't require a cutting-edge PC system. The latest version of Windows XP requires high-powered hardware, to the extent that upgrading to that operating system usually means buying a new PC, even if your old one still works fine!

In contrast, Linux works on computers dating back as far as the early 1990s. This book is largely being written on a five-year-old Pentium II 450 MHz notebook, running SUSE Linux 9.1. There's virtually no waiting around for programs to start. On the same machine, Windows 2000 (which came installed on the computer) grinds and churns, and using it can be a frustrating experience.

With Linux, there's software for just about every type (or age) of computer. For example, you'll find stripped-down graphical user interfaces (GUIs) that are designed specifically for old computer hardware. Linux encourages an attitude of both recycling and making the most of what you have, rather than constantly upgrading and buying new hardware.

In other words, you can pull out that "old" PC and bring it back to life by installing Linux. You might even be able to give it away to a family member or friend who does not have a PC. Perhaps it's time for grandma to get online, or perhaps you can give the kids their own PC so they will stop using yours.

Alternatively, you might consider turning old hardware into a server. Linux is capable of just about any task. As well as running desktop computers, it also runs around 60% of the computers that make the Internet work. Linux is extremely flexible. You could turn an old PC into a web, e-mail server, or firewall that you can attach to a broadband Internet connection. If you were to do this with Microsoft software, it would cost hundreds of dollars, not to mention requiring an advanced computer. It's free with Linux.

The Linux Community

So we've established that Linux is powerful, secure, and flexible. But we've saved the best for last. Linux is more than a computer operating system. It's an entire community of users spread across the globe. When you start to use Linux, you become part of this community (whether you like it or not!).

One of the benefits of membership is that you're never far from finding a solution to a problem. The community likes to congregate online around forums and newsgroups, which you can join in order to find help.

Your placement in the ranks of the community is "newbie." This is a popular way of describing somebody who is new to Linux. Although this sounds derisory, it will actually help when you talk to others. Advertising your newbie status will encourage people to take the time to help you. After all, they were newbies once upon a time!

There's another reason not to be disheartened by your newbie tag: you'll outgrow it very quickly. By the time you reach the end of this book, you'll have advanced to the other end of the spectrum—"guru." You'll be one of those giving out the advice to those poor, clueless newbies, and you'll be 100% confident in your skills.

■**Tip** One of the best ways to learn about Linux is under the auspices of a knowledgeable friend. It's very beneficial to have your own guru to help you along when you get stuck—someone who is just an e-mail message or phone call away. If you have a friend who uses Linux, consider taking him or her out for a drink and getting more friendly!

But being part of a community is not just about getting free technical support. It's about sharing knowledge. Linux is as much about a political ideal as it is about software. It was created to be shared among those who want to use it. There are no restrictions, apart from one: any changes you make must also be made available to others.

The spirit of sharing and collaboration has been there since day one. One of the first things Linus Torvalds did when he produced an early version of Linux was to ask for help from others. And he got it. Complete strangers e-mailed him and said they would contribute their time, skills, and effort to help his project. This has been the way Linux has been developed ever since. Hundreds of people around the world contribute their own small pieces, rather than there being one overall company in charge. And the same concept applies to knowledge of Linux. When you learn something, don't be afraid to share this knowledge with others. "Giving something back" is a very important part of the way of Linux.

To understand why Linux is shared, you need to understand its history, as well as the history of what came before it. This is the topic of Chapter 2.

Summary

This chapter provided an introduction to Linux. It explained what Linux can be used for and also its many advantages when compared to Microsoft Windows. It also introduced the community surrounding Linux, which adds to its benefits. You should be starting to realize what makes millions of people around the world use Linux as the operating system of choice.

The next chapter covers the history of Linux. It also discusses another curious aspect: the political scene that drives the operating system forward.

■ ■ ■

## CHAPTER 2

A History and Politics Lesson

Linux is more than just software. It's an entire community of users, and as such, there's a detailed social history behind it. In this chapter, we'll look at the origins of Linux, both in terms of where it came from and the people who make it.

You might be tempted to skip this chapter and move on to the information about installing SUSE Linux. To be fair, there's nothing of vital technical importance mentioned here. But it's important that you read this chapter at some stage, because Linux is more than simply the sum of its parts. It's far more than simply a set of computer programs.

If nothing else, this chapter explains the fundamental philosophies behind Linux and attempts to answer some of the often-baffling questions that arise when Linux is considered as a whole.

In the Beginning

Linux was created a little over a decade ago, in 1991. A decade is considered a lifetime in the world of computing, but Linux actually harks back even further, into the early days of modern computing in the mid-1970s.

Linux was created by a Finnish chap named Linus Torvalds. At the time, he was studying in Helsinki and had bought a desktop PC. His new computer needed an operating system. Torvalds's operating system choices were limited: there were various versions of DOS and something called Minix. It was the latter that Torvalds decided to use.

Minix was a freely available clone of the popular Unix operating system. Unix was used on huge computers in businesses and universities, including those at Torvalds's university. Unix was created in the early 1970s and has evolved since then to become what many considered the cutting edge of computing. Unix brought to fruition a large number of computing concepts in use today and, many agree, got almost everything just right in terms of features and usability.

Versions of Unix were available for smaller computers like Torvalds's PC, but they were considered professional tools and were very expensive. This was in the early days of the home computer craze, and the only people who used IBM PCs were business people and hobbyists.

■Note Linux is a pretty faithful clone of Unix. If you were to travel back in time 20 or 30 years, you would find that using Unix on those old mainframe computers, complete with their teletype interfaces, would be similar to using Linux on your home PC. Many of the fundamental concepts of Linux, such as the file system hierarchy and user permissions, are taken directly from Unix.

Torvalds liked Unix because of its power, and he liked Minix because it was free and ran on his computer. Minix was created by Andrew Tanenbaum, a professor of computing, to demonstrate the principles of operating system design to his students. Because Minix was also a learning tool, people could also view the *source code* of the program—the original listings that Tanenbaum had entered to create the software.

Minix was lacking in some significant areas. Many people, including Torvalds, found using it very frustrating. Torvalds decided to create from scratch his own version of Minix, but to make it better, avoiding what many considered the pitfalls of Minix. He managed to produce version 0.01 of Linux in just over half a year.

■Note Most clones or implementations of Unix are named so that they end in an *x*. One story has it that Torvalds wanted to call his creation Freax, but a containing directory was accidentally renamed Linux on an Internet server. The name stuck.

From day one, Torvalds intended his creation to be shared among everyone who wanted to use it. He encouraged people to copy it and give it to friends. He didn't charge any money for it, and he also made the source code freely available. The idea was that people could take the code and improve it.

This was a master stroke. Many people contacted Torvalds, offering to help out. Because they could see the program code, they realized he was onto a good thing. Soon, Torvalds wasn't the only person developing Linux. He became the leader of a team that used the fledgling Internet to communicate and share improvements.

■Note The popular conception of Linux is that it is created by a few hobbyists who work on it in their spare time. This might have been true in the very early days. Nowadays, in addition to these "bedroom programmers," Linux is programmed by hundreds of professionals around the world, many of whom are employed specifically for the task. Torvalds adds to the effort himself and also coordinates the work.

It's important to note that when we talk here about Linux, we're actually talking about the kernel—the central program that runs the PC hardware and keeps the computer ticking. This is all that Torvalds initially produced back in 1991. It was an impressive achievement, but needed a lot of extra add-on programs to take care of even the most basic tasks. Torvalds's kernel needed additional software so that users could enter data, for example. It needed a way for users to be able to enter commands so they could manipulate files, such as deleting or copying them. And that's before you even consider more complicated stuff like displaying graphics on the screen or printing documents.

Linux itself didn't offer these functions. It simply ran the computer's hardware. Once it booted up, it expected to find other programs. If they weren't present, then all you saw was a blank screen.

LINUS TORVALDS

Linus Benedict Torvalds was born in Helsinki, Finland, in 1969. A member of the minority Swedish-speaking population, he attended the University of Helsinki from 1988 to 1996, graduating with a Masters degree in Computer Science.

He started Linux, not through a desire to give the world a first-class operating system, but with other goals in mind. Its inspiration is in part due to Helsinki winters being so cold. Rather than leave his warm flat and trudge through the snow to the university's campus in order to use its powerful minicomputer, he wanted to be able to connect to it from home! He also wanted to have a platform to use to experiment with the properties of the Intel 386, but that's another story. Torvalds needed an operating system capable of such tasks. Linux was born.

It took Torvalds the better part of a year to come up with the very first version of Linux, during which he worked alone in a darkened room. In 1991, he announced his creation to the world, describing Linux as "just a hobby," and saying it would never be big. It wouldn't be until 1994 that it reached version 1.0.

In the early days, Torvalds's creation was fairly primitive. He was passionate that it should be free for everyone to use, and so he released it under a software license that said that no one could ever sell it. However, he quickly changed his mind, adopting the GNU Public License.

Torvalds was made wealthy by his creation, courtesy of the dot.com boom of the late 1990s, even though this was never his intention; he was driven by altruism. Nowadays, he lives in Portland, Oregon, with his wife and children, having moved to the United States from Finland in the late 1990s.

Initially, Torvalds worked for Transmeta, developing CPU architectures as well as overseeing kernel development, although this wasn't part of his official work. He still programs the kernel, but currently he oversees the Open Source Development Lab, an organization created to encourage open source adoption in industry and which is also referred to as the home of Linux.

The GNU Project

Around the time Linus created Linux, there was another project in existence, called GNU. This project team also hoped to create an operating system that used Unix as its inspiration, although avoiding some of the pitfalls that had blighted that operating system, both technically and in terms of its licensing. GNU is a so-called recursive acronym that stands for "GNU's Not Unix," a play on words favored by computer programmers.

GNU's parent organization, the Free Software Foundation (FSF), had been formed eight years prior to Torvalds's effort, and since that time, had produced the majority of the core software that Linux desperately needed. However, as luck would have it, FSF lacked the essential functionality of the kernel. The developers were in the process of creating their own kernel, but it had not come to fruition.

The GNU software was distributed for free to anyone who wanted it. The source code was also made available so users could adapt and change the programs to meet their own needs (in fact, Torvalds had used the GNU model when deciding how to distribute Linux).

Richard Stallman is the man behind GNU and, along with Linus Torvalds, is the second accidental hero in our story. Stallman had been around since the Dark Ages of computing, back when wardrobe-sized computers were "time-shared" among users who used small desktop terminals to access them. Like Torvalds, Stallman started GNU as a personal project, but then found others who were more than willing to join his cause.

Note Stallman created the Emacs text editor and the GNU C Compiler (GCC). Together, they allow the creation of yet more software, so it's no surprise that one of the very first programs Torvalds used in the early days to create Linux was Stallman's GCC.

Back in Stallman's day at the legendary Massachusetts Institute of Technology (MIT), computer software was shared. If you came up with a program to perform a particular task, you offered it to practically anyone who wanted it. Alternatively, if you found an existing program wasn't adequate or had a bug, you improved it yourself, and then made the resulting program available to others. People might use your improved version, or they might not; it was up to them.

This way of sharing software was disorganized and done on an ad hoc basis, but came about of its own accord. Nobody questioned it, and it seemed the best way of doing things. There certainly wasn't any money involved, any more than there would be money involved in one friend explaining an idea to another.

RICHARD STALLMAN

Richard Matthew Stallman, usually referred to as RMS, was born in 1953 in Manhattan. He comes from the old school of computing forged during the 1970s and was a member of MIT's legendary Artificial Intelligence Lab. Seemingly destined for a life in academia, Stallman left MIT in 1984 to found the GNU Project. This was as a reaction to the increasing commercialization of computer software. Whereas once all hackers (that is, programmers) had shared ideas and program code, the trend in the 1980s was toward proprietary, nonshared code, as well as legal contracts, which forced programmers to keep secrets from one another.

Stallman is a not inconsiderable programmer and is considered a genius by many observers. He single-handedly created many essential programming tools in his initial efforts to get GNU off the ground. Many of these find a home in Linux.

Stallman is also widely applauded for the creation of the GNU Public License. This is a legal document that lets people share software. It introduces the concept of *copyleft* and is opposed to the legal concept of copyright, which attempts to limit the freedom of individuals when using a piece of software (or any other creative work). Nowadays, the concept of copyleft has been applied to literature, music, and other arts in an attempt to avoid restricting who can and cannot access various items, as well as to encourage a collaborative working environment.

Proprietary Software and the GPL

In the 1980s, everything changed. The world became more corporate, and with the rise of the desktop PC, the concept of proprietary software became prevalent. More and more companies started to sell software. They reasoned that this was impossible to do if they shared it with everybody else, so they kept it secret. Microsoft led this charge and did very well with its proprietary software.

To Stallman, this "trade secrets" approach to software was anathema. He had nothing against software being sold for a profit, but he hated the fundamental ideas behind software being kept secret. He felt passionately that sharing software and being able to understand how it worked was akin to free speech—necessary and vital for the furthering of technology, and therefore society itself. How could the new generation of programmers improve on the previous generation's work if they were unable to see how it worked? It was absurd to need to create software from scratch each time, rather than taking something that already existed and making it better.

Because of his beliefs, Stallman resigned from his job in the MIT Artificial Intelligence Lab and founded GNU. His aim initially was to produce a complete clone of Unix that would be shared in the ways he knew from the early days of computing. This software would be available for everyone to use, to study, and to adapt. It would be free, in the same sense as free speech— shared and unrestricted. This gave rise to the vital concept of "free software" and soon GNU, and the FSF, became not just a programming venture, but also a political movement.

■**Note** A very common misconception of "free software" is that it is always free of charge. This isn't correct. The word *free* is used here in its political sense, as in "free speech." Many companies and individuals make a healthy profit from selling free software and, in fact, selling free software is encouraged by the GNU Project.

To protect the rights of people to share and adapt the GNU software, Stallman came up with the GNU Public License (GPL). Various drafts of this license were produced over time, until it became a completely watertight legal contract, which furthered the concept of free software.

Most software you buy comes with a license agreement—that big chunk of text you must agree to when installing software (in the case of Windows desktop software, it's frequently referred to as the End-User License Agreement, or EULA). The license agreement usually says that you cannot copy the software or share it with friends. If others want to use the software, they must buy their own version.

The GPL turns this on its head. Rather than restricting what people can do with the software, it gives them permission to share the software with whomever they wish. However, if they modify the program in any way, and then distribute it to others, the program they come up with must also be licensed under the GPL. In other words, people cannot make changes to a program that has a GPL, and then sell the modified program, keeping their improvements secret.

■**Note** An interesting side note is that the actual wording of the GPL says that any changes you make should be shared with others *only if the software is redistributed*. This means that if you modify some GPL software and don't give it to anyone else, there's no need for you to publish your changes or make others aware of those changes.

GNU and Linux Together

The Linux kernel, developed by Torvalds, and the GNU software, developed by Stallman, were a perfect match. It's important to note that this doesn't mean the two projects joined forces. It simply means that the Linux project took some of the GNU software and gave it a good home. This was done with Stallman's blessing, but there wasn't any official union between the two groups. Remember that Stallman had intended everyone to freely share and use the GNU tools. Linux represented a set of people doing just that. GNU is still working on its own kernel, called Hurd, which may provide an alternative to using Torvalds's Linux kernel.

■**Note** Hurd was first planned back in the 1980s and, at the time of writing, still has yet to see the light of day (although testing versions are available). Hurd is a hugely ambitious project and will set a gold standard when it is released.

GNU and Linux together formed a complete operating system, which mimicked the way Unix operated. Other projects and individuals spotted the success of Linux and came onboard, and it wasn't long before Linux realized the potential for a graphical user interface (GUI), the fundamentals of which were provided by the XFree86 Project. A lot of additional software was also provided by individuals and organizations, all using the same "share and share alike" example set by Stallman, with the GNU tools, and Torvalds, with his kernel.

Many people refer to Linux as GNU/Linux. This gives credit to the GNU Project that provided the majority of tools vital to making Linux into a usable operating system. However, like the majority of people in the computing world, I use the term *Linux* throughout this book to avoid confusion.

Different Flavors of Linux

All the pieces of GNU software were available for free download and were therefore free of charge. But this brought its own problems. Not everyone had the know-how to put all the bits and pieces together into a complete operating system. Those who could do this didn't necessarily have the time for it.

Because of this, a number of companies stepped in to do the hard work. They put together versions of Linux, complete with all the software from the GNU Project, which they then sold for a fee on floppy disks, CDs, or DVDs. They also added in bits of their own software, which made it possible to install Linux easily onto a computer's hard disk, for example. They produced their own manuals and documentation, too, and did other things such as bug testing to ensure it all worked well.

What they came up with became known as *distributions* of Linux, or *distros* for short. Examples of these companies include Red Hat, SUSE, Mandrake, and many others around the world. Additionally, a number of hobbyists got together and formed organizations to create their own distros, such as Debian and Slackware.

Modern distros are very advanced. They make it easy to install Linux on your PC, and they usually come with everything you need, so you can get started immediately. Additionally, they have their own look and feel, as well as unique ways of working and operating. This means that SUSE Linux is not the same as Red Hat Linux, for example, although they share a lot of common features and, of course, they all share the core GNU software.

Linux Today

Nowadays, Linux is a thoroughly modern and capable operating system, considered cutting edge by many. It also runs on many different types of computer hardware, including Apple Macintosh computers, Sun SPARC machines, and the humble desktop PC. One of the ironies is that, although Linux was based on Unix, it has slowly come to dominate the computer operating system market. According to industry sources, Linux is on its way to making commercial varieties of Unix redundant. Companies that sell their own versions of Unix, such as Hewlett Packard and IBM, have added Linux to their traditional product range.

Recent innovations in the latest versions of the kernel mean that it finds uses on the smallest computers in the world, as well as on the biggest. Several of the top supercomputers in the world run Linux and, ironically, it can also be used on handheld PDAs or even digital watches! You'll even find it running things like digital video recorders or other household goods, where it sits invisibly in the background and makes everything work. Remember that one of the fundamental principles of Linux is that you can use it for whatever you want. You don't need to ask for permission first or tell anyone what you're doing.

Linux initially found mainstream use by software developers, and on server computers, such as those that run the Internet. However, in recent years, it has become increasingly popular on desktop computers. This is the area where experts suggest it will see massive growth over the coming years.

Modern Linux Development

Nowadays, Linux is developed not only by Torvalds, who manages the huge project, but also by hundreds of volunteers and corporations who contribute resources. Most recently, IBM and Novell have gotten involved and contribute hundreds of people to the effort of creating Linux. Sun contributes the OpenOffice.org office suite and sells its own version of Linux (which is based on SUSE Linux, as supplied on the DVD-ROM with this book). Corporations like Computer Associates contribute their own software, too.

These companies have realized that the best way of producing software is to share and share alike, rather than develop their own proprietary software and keep it secret. The proprietary ways of the 1980s are starting to seem like an ill-conceived flash in the pan.

Most recently, Novell found that by embracing Linux, it could massively enhance the functions of its aging NetWare product, yet without needing to return to the drawing board and start from scratch. It could just take what it wanted from the pile of Linux software. This shows the philosophy of Linux in action.

Linux has software for just about every need, ranging from simply receiving e-mail to running a huge e-mail server. There are databases, office suites, web browsers, video games, movie players, audio tools, and more, as well as thousands of pieces of specialized software used in various niches of industry (and too boring to mention here). Most of this software is available to anyone who wants it, free of charge.

What more could you want?

Summary

This chapter has detailed the history of Linux and explained where it came from. It also explained *why* Linux came into being. We looked at how Linux formed one of the building blocks of a political movement geared toward producing software that can be shared.

We discussed the creator of Linux, Linus Torvalds. We've also looked at the massive input the GNU Project has made and, in particular, that of its philosopher king, Richard Stallman.

In the next chapter, we move on to look at what you can practically expect from day-to-day use of Linux.

## CHAPTER 3

The Realities of Running Linux

So now that you've learned about the politics, history, and personalities behind Linux, only one question remains: what's Linux actually like when used day to day? What should the average user expect from the experience?

These are the questions I hope to answer in this brief chapter.

Learning to Use Linux

What should you expect from Linux once you've installed it? Well, it's a little like running Windows, except there are no viruses, no crashes, and no inexplicable slowdowns.

In addition, you have complete control over the system. This doesn't mean Linux is necessarily complicated. It's just that you have the control if you wish to make use of it. We'll look into this in the latter half of this book.

Most software you use under Windows has at least one equivalent under SUSE Linux. In many cases, you'll find that the program comes preinstalled. It's unlikely that you'll need to download any additional programs and, even if you do, you'll probably find they're available for free.

In most cases, the Linux swap-ins are at least as powerful and easy to use as their Windows alternatives. Tabbed browsing in the Konqueror web browser lets you visit more than one site at once, for example, but without needing to have a lot of Internet Explorer instances running. Kmail has a search routine that lets you look through your e-mail messages quickly for a variety of criteria, and it puts the features in a similar Microsoft product to shame.

Does this sound too good to be true? There is just one caveat. Linux isn't a clone of Windows and doesn't aim to be. It has its own way of doing certain things and sometimes works differently compared to Windows. This means that many experience a learning curve when first using Linux. However, none of this will cause a problem for the experienced computer user. It's certainly no more difficult than the move from Windows 3.1 to Windows 95 (if you can remember back that far!). It's ultimately worth it.

■**Note** There are several Linux distributions that aim to mimic Windows pretty faithfully. For example, Xandros, Lycoris/lx, and Linspire copy the look and feel of Windows to the extent that (allegedly) some people are unable to tell the difference.

In just a few weeks after your move to Linux, everything will start to seem entirely normal. Most of the time, you won't even be aware you're running Linux. Of course, some patience is required during those initial few weeks. Linux can be illogical and frustrating; on the other hand, so can Windows. We simply got used to it.

Who Uses Linux?

Who uses Linux? The myth from the old days is that it's only for techies and power users. When you needed to put everything together by hand, this was clearly true. But modern distributions make Linux accessible to all. It's no exaggeration to say that you could install Linux on a computer Luddite's PC and have that person use it in preference to Windows.

Up until quite recently, Linux was largely seen as a developers' tool and a server operating system. It was geared toward programmers or was destined for a life running backroom computers, serving data, and making other computer resources available to users.

To this end, Linux continues to run a sizable proportion of the computers that make the Internet work, largely because it provides an ideal platform for the Apache web server, as well as various databases and web-based programming languages. This has lead to the LAMP acronym, which stands for Linux, Apache (a web server), MySQL (a database), and PHP or Perl (two programming languages that can be used in an online environment).

Despite its technical origins, recent years have seen a strong push for Linux on desktop computers. Linux has stepped out of the dark backrooms, with the goal of pushing aside Microsoft Windows and Mac OS in order to dominate the corporate workstation and home user market.

Running Linux on the desktop has always been possible, but the level of knowledge required was often prohibitively high, putting Linux out of the reach of most ordinary users. It's only comparatively recently that the companies behind the distributions of Linux have taken a long, hard look at Windows and attempted to mirror its user-friendly approach. In addition, the configuration software in distributions like SUSE Linux has progressed in leaps and bounds. Now, it's no longer necessary to know arcane commands in order to do something as simple as switch the screen resolution or configure a printer. The situation has also been helped by the development of extremely powerful office software, such as OpenOffice.org and Koffice.

Is Linux for you? There's only one way of finding out, and that's to give it a go. Linux doesn't require much of you except an open mind and the will to learn new ways of doing things. You shouldn't see learning to use Linux as a chore. Instead, you should see it as an adventure—a way of finally getting the most from your PC and not having to worry about things going wrong for reasons outside your control.

Linux puts you in charge of your PC. You're the mechanic of the car as well as its driver, and you'll be expected to get your hands dirty every now and then. Unlike with Windows, Linux doesn't hide any of its settings or stop you from doing things for your own protection; everything is available to tweak. Using Linux requires commitment and the realization that there are probably going to be problems, and they're going to need to be overcome.

However, using Linux should be enjoyable. In his initial newsgroup posting announcing Linux back in 1992, Linus Torvalds said that he was creating Linux "just for fun." This is what it should be for you.

Getting Hold of Linux

Getting hold of Linux is easy. You'll already have spotted that there is a version of SUSE Linux packaged with this book. SUSE Linux is the main focus of this book, and I consider it to be one of the very best versions of Linux out there.

SUSE is one of the most well-established Linux distributions. It's ideal for both beginners and power users, and it really does match the functionality offered in Windows. It includes the unique YaST2 configuration tool, which makes changing your system settings a breeze. It's also a very good-looking distribution. You'll find your friends and colleagues "wowing" when they happen to pass by and glance at your PC!

There are actually quite a number of Linux distributions available. If you want to explore other Linux distributions as well as SUSE, by far the most fuss-free method of getting hold of Linux is to pop over to your local computer store (or online retailer) and buy a boxed copy. You can choose from Red Hat, Mandrake, Libra Net, TurboLinux, Conectiva (if you want foreign language support, although nearly all commercial distributions do a good job of supporting mainstream languages), and many others. Many distributions come on more than a single CD—up to four is the average number at the moment. There are also versions of Linux that come on DVD.

■**Caution** Bearing in mind what I've said about the sharing nature of Linux, you might think it possible to buy a boxed copy of Linux and run off copies for friends, or even sell them for a profit. However, you shouldn't assume this is the case. A minority of distribution companies, such as Xandros and Linspire, incorporate copyrighted corporate logos into their distributions that place restrictions on redistribution. Sometimes they include proprietary software along with the Linux tools, which you cannot copy without prior permission. However, in many cases, reproducing the CDs in small volumes for friends or for use on workstations in a company environment is permitted.

Many of the Linux distributions are also available to download free of charge. In fact, there are also many community-run distributions that are *only* available this way, such as Slackware, Debian, Fedora, or Gentoo (although you can often buy "homemade" CDs from smaller retailers, who effectively burn the CDs for you and produce makeshift packaging). If your PC has a CD-R/RW drive and you have some CD-burning software under Windows (such as Ahead's Nero), you can download an ISO image and make your own installation CD from it.

■**Note** An *ISO image* is a very large file (typically 700MB), which you can burn to CD. This CD is then used to install Linux.

Using SUSE Linux

SUSE Linux is one of the oldest distributions of Linux available, and it was the first version to come out shortly after Linus Torvalds had completed his initial versions of the Linux kernel. SUSE was originally a German company, but nowadays it is owned by Novell, although a large percentage of its staff remains within Europe. In addition, SUSE is a distribution partner of many large computer manufacturers, such as Sun Microsystems and IBM.

SUSE is an acronym for Software und System-Entwicklung, which translates as software and system development. This refers to the days, long passed, when the SUSE company was also a Unix consultancy.

Like many Linux distributions, SUSE Linux formed its formidable reputation as a server operating system. Its unique YaST and SaX system configuration tools made configuring and updating servers easy for those new to Linux and Unix. Recent years have seen the company make a strong push for the desktop market, with the result that SUSE Linux is considered one of the best desktop Linux distributions available, again thanks to its YaST configuration software.

SUSE's engineers have invested time not only in polishing the user interface, but also in improving hardware compatibility, to the extent that SUSE Linux is frequently considered cutting-edge in terms of the sheer number of items of hardware supported. Considering that a major criticism of Linux has been its poor showing in this area, SUSE is to be applauded in this regard.

Unlike some desktop distributions that abandon fundamental Linux concepts in order to mirror the Windows experience, SUSE Linux retains the robust feel and power of Linux. Technical thoroughness isn't sacrificed yet, somehow, SUSE Linux is very easy to use, even for those who are new to computing. It's certainly an ideal distribution for Windows users who are looking for a way into Linux.

Learning how to use SUSE Linux has an added advantage in the corporate workspace. Novell is releasing its own distribution of Linux, which is largely based on SUSE Linux technology. In addition, Sun Microsystems offers its Java Desktop product, which is again based on SUSE Linux.

Make no mistake—SUSE Linux is ideal for both the corporate and home desktop.

Summary

This chapter explained what you can realistically expect when using Linux every day. It also discussed the kind of company you'll be keeping in terms of fellow users.

You learned how people usually get hold of Linux. Of course, with this book, you already have a version of Linux, SUSE Linux, which was introduced in this chapter.

This completes the general overview of the world of Linux. In the next part of the book, you'll move on to actually installing Linux on your hard disk. This sounds more daunting than it actually is. The next chapter gets you started by explaining a few basic preinstallation steps.

## PART TWO

Installing SUSE Linux

CHAPTER 4

■ ■ ■

Preinstallation Steps

The first part of this book discussed the pros and cons of using Linux as part of your day-to-day life. It was intended to help you evaluate Linux and understand what you're buying into should you decide to make it your operating system of choice. Now, we move on to actually installing Linux and, specifically, SUSE Linux, which is included with this book on a DVD.

Installing any kind of operating system is a big move and can come as something of a shock to your PC. However, SUSE Linux makes this complicated maneuver as easy as it's possible to be. Its installation routines are very advanced compared to previous versions of Linux, and even compared to other current distributions. It even puts the Windows installation routine to shame.

What does saying that you're going to install SUSE Linux actually mean? This effectively implies three things:

- Somehow all the files necessary to run SUSE Linux are going to be put onto your hard disk.

- The PC will be configured so that it knows where to find these files when it first boots up.

- The entire system will be set up so that you, the user, can work on it.

However, in order to do all this and get SUSE Linux onto your PC, you must undertake some preparatory work, which is the focus of this chapter.

Understanding Partitioning

Chances are, if you're reading this book, your PC already has Windows installed on it. This won't present a problem. In most cases, SUSE Linux can live happily alongside Windows in what's called a *dual-boot setup*, where you can choose at startup which operating system to run. However, installing SUSE Linux means that Windows must make certain compromises. It needs to cohabit your hard disk with another operating system—something it isn't designed to do.

The main issue with such a situation is that Windows needs to shrink and make some space available for SUSE Linux (unless you install a second hard disk, which we discuss later). SUSE Linux isn't able to use the same file system as Windows, and it needs its own separately defined part of the disk, which is referred to as a *partition*. All of this is handled automatically by the SUSE Linux installation routine, but it's important that you know what happens.

All hard disks are split into partitions, which are large chunks of the disk created to hold operating systems (just like a large farm is partitioned into separate fields). A partition is usually multiple gigabytes, although it can be smaller. You can view your disk's partitions using the Disk Management tool in Windows XP and Windows 2000, as shown in Figure 4-1. You can access this tool by opening Control Panel, clicking the Administrative Tools icon, selecting Computer Management, and then choosing Disk Management.

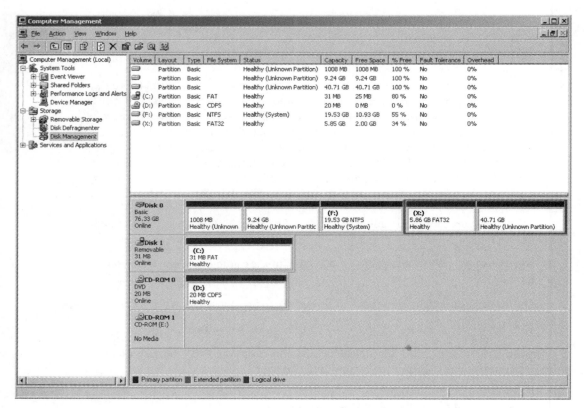

Figure 4-1. *You can view your disk's partitions using Windows XP's Disk Management tool.*

On most desktop PC systems, there's just one partition, unless the user has specifically created new partitions. As I mentioned, SUSE Linux needs a partition of its own. During installation, SUSE Linux needs to shrink the main Windows partition and create a fresh partition alongside it (actually, it creates two partitions; the extra one is used to hold the swap file).

In addition, the SUSE Linux installation routine writes a new *boot sector* (also known as a *boot loader*). This is a small program at the very front of the disk that runs a separate program that lets you choose between operating systems (and therefore partitions) when you first boot up.

Note Not all Linux distributions have the ability to repartition the hard disk. In fact, at the time of writing, it's pretty rare. Most expect to simply take over the entire hard disk, wiping Windows in the process (although they'll always ask the user the confirm this beforehand). The ability to repartition a disk is just one of the reasons that SUSE Linux is among the best Linux distributions currently available.

Of course, SUSE Linux can't shrink a Windows partition that is packed full of data, because there will be no space left for it to reclaim.

SUSE LINUX AND WINDOWS FILE SYSTEMS

One of the benefits of dual-booting Linux and Windows is that SUSE Linux automatically lets you access the files on the Windows partition. This is quite handy and facilitates the easy exchange of data. If the Windows partition is FAT32—used on Windows 95, 98, Me, and (sometimes) XP—then SUSE Linux can both read and write files to the partition. However, if the file system is NTFS—used with Windows NT, 2000, and (sometimes) XP—then SUSE Linux will make the file system available as read-only. Because of this, you might consider converting your NTFS Windows partition to FAT32 before you install SUSE Linux. Doing so means you lose some of the security and performance features of NTFS, however.

Microsoft doesn't include a tool that lets you do this automatically, but third-party disk partitioning programs like Symantec's Partition Magic (www.symantec.com) are able to do so.

Freeing Up Space

The first step before installing SUSE Linux alongside Windows is to check how much free space you have in your Windows partition and possibly free up some space. To see the amount of free space you have, double-click My Computer, right-click your boot drive, and select Properties. The free space is usually indicated in purple on a pie-chart diagram, as shown in Figure 4-2.

You need to have at least 2GB of free space in your Windows partition for SUSE Linux to use. You'll need more space if you wish to install a lot of programs. If you don't have enough free space, you have several options.

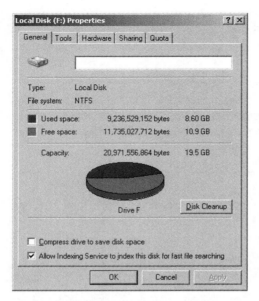

Figure 4-2. *SUSE Linux needs free disk space in which to install, so you might need to clean up your Windows partition.*

Reclaiming Space

On Windows XP, you can run the Disk Cleanup tool to free some space on your hard disk. Click the Disk Cleanup button beneath the pie-chart diagram showing the free disk space (see Figure 4-2). Disk Cleanup is also accessible by choosing Start ➤ All Programs ➤ Accessories ➤ System Tools ➤ Disk Cleanup.

You might also consider turning off System Restore. This takes up a lot of disk space, which you can therefore reclaim. However, deactivating System Restore will mean that you lose the possibility of returning your system to a previous state should anything go wrong. To access the System Restore control, right-click My Computer, click Properties, and then click the System Restore tab.

If you still can't free up enough disk space, consider uninstalling unused software via the Add/Remove Programs applet within Control Panel. If you have any 3D games installed, consider removing them first, because they usually take up large amounts of hard disk space.

In addition, you might consider deleting movie and MP3 music files. Once again, these are renowned for eating up hard disk space. The average MP3 is around 4MB, for example, and one minute of video typically takes up 1MB of disk space!

Removing Windows

Some users might prefer a second, more radical option: getting rid of Windows completely and letting SUSE Linux take over the entire hard disk. If you feel confident that SUSE Linux will fulfill your needs, this is undoubtedly the most straightforward solution. You'll be able to do this during installation. However, this will also mean that any personal data you have will be lost, so you should first back up your data (as described shortly).

■**Caution** You should be aware that installing Windows back onto a hard disk that has SUSE Linux on it is troublesome. Windows has a Darwinian desire to wipe out the competition. If you attempt to install Windows on a SUSE Linux hard disk, it will simply overwrite Linux.

Using Another Hard Disk

There's a third option that is attractive and somewhat safer in terms of avoiding the potential for data loss, but also potentially expensive: fitting a second hard disk to your PC. You can then install SUSE Linux on this disk, letting it take up the entirety of the disk. Unlike with Windows, SUSE Linux doesn't need to be installed on the primary hard disk and is happy on a slave drive.

A second hard disk is perhaps the best solution if you're low on disk space and want to retain Windows on your system. However, you'll need to know how to fit the new drive or find someone to do it for you. In addition, if your PC is less than 12 months old, there is a possibility that you'll invalidate your guarantee by opening up your PC.

If you have an old PC lying around, you might also consider installing SUSE Linux on it, at least until you're sure that you want to run it on your main PC. As noted in Chapter 1, one of the best features of SUSE Linux is that it runs relatively well on older hardware. For example, a Pentium II with 196MB should allow for very good performance.

NO-INSTALL LINUX

If you want to use the Linux operating system but leave your hard disk untouched, there are a number of additional options you might consider. Perhaps the most popular is to use a "live" version of Linux. These are versions of Linux that boot and run entirely from a CD (or DVD); they don't touch the user's hard disk. The most popular is Knoppix (www.knoppix.org). The distribution we discuss throughout this book, SUSE Linux, also has a live CD version, which you can download from www.suse.com/us/private/download/suse_linux/. Using Linux in this way involves downloading an ISO image (a single large file of around 650MB), which then must be burned to CD using a Windows program like Ahead's Nero. Once the CD has been created, you simply boot from it in order to run Linux (after you ensure that your PC's BIOS is set to boot from CD).

Alternatively, you might consider using virtual PC software. This runs under Windows and re-creates an entire PC hardware system within software—effectively a PC within a PC. The hard disk is contained within one or two Windows files. Linux can then be installed on these virtual PC systems. When the program is switched to full-screen mode, it's impossible to tell you're running inside a computer system created in software. There are two commercially sold examples considered worthwhile by many: VMware (www.vmware.com) and Microsoft's Virtual PC (www.microsoft.com/windowsxp/virtualpc/). You should be aware that both are designed to be professional-level tools, so both are quite expensive.

Another option in its infancy at the time of writing is Cooperative Linux, or coLinux for short (www.colinux.org). This is a set of Windows programs that aims to let Linux run under Windows using emulation. Unfortunately, setting up and using coLinux requires some expert knowledge, so you might want to wait until you have more experience with Linux.

Backing Up Your Data

Whichever route you decide to take when installing SUSE Linux, you should back up the data currently on your computer beforehand. Possibly the easiest way of doing this is to burn the data to CD-R/RW discs using a program like Ahead's Nero and a CD-R/RW drive.

If you take the coexistence route, installing SUSE Linux alongside Windows, backing up your data should be done for insurance purposes. Although SUSE tests all its software thoroughly and relies on community reporting of bugs, there's always the chance that something might go wrong. Repartitioning a hard disk is a major operation and carries with it the potential of data loss.

If you intend to erase the hard disk when installing SUSE Linux (thereby removing Windows), you can back up your data, and then import it into SUSE Linux. Table 4-1 shows a list of common personal data file types, their file extensions, where they can be typically found on a Windows XP system, and notes on importing the data into SUSE Linux. Note that earlier versions of Windows may differ when it comes to data storage locations, particularly Windows 95, 98, and Me.

Table 4-1. *Data That Should Be Backed Up*

Type of File	File Extensions	Typical Location	Notes
Office files	DOC, XLS, PPT, PDF, etc.	My Documents	Microsoft Office files can be opened, edited, and saved under SUSE Linux using the OpenOffice.org suite. PDF documents can be viewed with Adobe Acrobat under SUSE Linux.
E-mail files	DBX	\Documents and Settings\ *<username>*\Local Settings\ Application Data\ Identities*<user ID string>*\ Microsoft\Outlook Express	Outlook Express mailboxes can be imported into Kmail under SUSE Linux. Outlook mailbox files *cannot* be imported into SUSE Linux. However, you can import Outlook messages into Outlook Express (select File ➤ Import ➤ Messages), and then back up the DBX file for importing into KDE later. Kmail is also able to import mail from the popular Pegasus e-mail client.
Digital images	JPG, BMP, TIF, PNG, GIF, etc.	My Pictures (within My Documents)	SUSE Linux includes a variety of programs to both view and edit image files.

Table 4-1. *Data That Should Be Backed Up (Continued)*

Type of File	File Extensions	Typical Location	Notes
Multimedia files	MP3, MPG, AVI	Various	SUSE Linux programs can play MP3 music files and some movie file formats. The Kaffeine Media Player under SUSE Linux is able to read a handful of video file formats by default, and more video file formats can be read after some additional downloads are installed.
Internet Explorer Favorites	None	\Documents and Settings\ *<username>*\Favorites	Your Favorites list cannot be imported into SUSE Linux, but the individual files can be opened in a text editor in order to view their URLs, which can then be opened in a SUSE Linux web browser.
Miscellaneous Internet files	Various	Various	You might also want to back up web site archives or instant messenger chat logs, although hidden data such as cookies cannot be imported.

Making Notes

When you're backing up data, a pencil and paper come in handy, too. You should write down any important usernames and passwords, such as those for your e-mail account and other online services. You might want to write down the phone number of your dial-up ISP connection, for example, or your DSL technical settings. Figure 4-3 shows an example of some information you might want to record. In addition, don't forget to jot down essential technical details, such as your IP address if you are part of a network of computers using static addresses (this will usually be relevant only if you work in an office environment).

■**Tip** If you've forgotten any passwords, there are several freeware/shareware applications that are able to "decode" the asterisks that obscure Windows passwords and show what's beneath. You can download these utilities from sites like www.download.com.

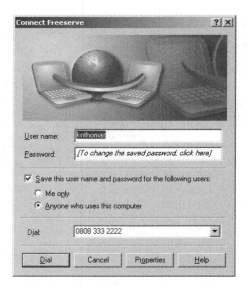

Figure 4-3. *Don't forget to back up "hidden" data, such as Internet passwords.*

Note that there's no need to write down information such as hardware interrupt (IRQ) or memory addresses, because hardware is configured automatically by SUSE Linux. However, it might be worth making a note of the make and model of some items of internal hardware, such as your graphics card, modem (dial-up or DSL), and sound card. This will help if SUSE Linux is unable to automatically detect your hardware, although such a situation is fairly unlikely to arise. You can garner this information by right-clicking My Computer on your desktop, selecting Properties, and then clicking the Device Manager tab. Instead of writing everything down, you might consider taking a screenshot by pressing the Print Scr button and then using your favorite image editor to print it.

■**Tip** SUSE Linux works with a wide variety of hardware, and in most cases, it will automatically detect your system components. If you're in any doubt, you can check your hardware against the SUSE Hardware Database (http://hardwaredb.suse.de/?LANG=en_UK).

Once you're certain that all your data is backed up, you can move on to the next chapter, which provides a step-by-step guide to installing the operating system.

Summary

The aim of this chapter has been to prepare both you and your computer for the installation of SUSE Linux. We've looked at how your hard disk will be partitioned prior to installation and the preparations you should make to ensure your hard disk has sufficient free space. You also learned about the types of files you might choose to back up, in addition to vital details you should record, such as usernames and passwords for your online accounts.

In the next chapter, we move on to a full description of the SUSE Linux installation procedure. The chapter guides you through getting SUSE Linux onto your computer, taking into account any and all issues that might arise.

Summary

CHAPTER 5

■ ■ ■

Installing SUSE Linux

It's now time to install Linux. This chapter details how to install SUSE Linux, as supplied with this book. SUSE uses its own YaST2 program for this purpose.

Installing Linux is a surprisingly quick task to complete and shouldn't take more than 30 minutes on a modern PC. It's also fairly simple, with very few decisions to make throughout. The YaST2 program automates the task to a high degree.

However, you should examine all of the options you're offered to make sure they're correct. Installing an operating system involves a couple of serious maneuvers that, via an incorrect click of the mouse or accidental keystroke, bring with them the possibility of data loss. Be sure to keep your wits about you, and make a backup of your data!

An Overview of the Installation Process

Installing SUSE Linux requires little of the user beyond the ability to use a mouse. The installation program attempts to choose safe default choices in most cases and, if it intends to do something that involves deleting data, it will ensure that you're aware of this by highlighting the option in red on the main menu. In nearly all cases, you should be able to accept the default choices.

You can proceed through the installation by clicking the Next button at the bottom right of each page of choices. Wherever a series of options needs to be confirmed, you should click the Accept button if you're happy with the selections. If not, make your changes, and then click Accept.

No changes will be made to your system until you confirm your choices later on, just prior to starting to copy the files onto your hard disk. This means that you can experiment with different partition combinations, for example, without worrying about damaging or otherwise irreversibly affecting your system. It also means that you can abort installation at any time prior to the file-copying phase.

The installation procedure works through a handful of stages in order to install Linux. First, just after it starts, it will probe your system to discover the nature of your current PC setup, such as whether you already have Windows installed.

At this stage, you will be shown the hard disk partitioning choices and also the selection of software packages that are to be installed. After this, you'll be asked to confirm that you're satisfied with the installation options, and then the installation program will actually partition the disk and copy the Linux files from the DVD.

At the end of this procedure, your PC will reboot, and the postinstallation phase will begin, whereby your hardware will be probed and configured (usually automatically, with negligible user input). This is the stage at which you'll be invited to create users and enter various passwords. After this, setup is complete, and your new system will then be booted, ready for use.

In most cases, the installation of SUSE Linux will run smoothly. If you run into any problems, see Chapter 6, which addresses many of the most common issues and provides solutions.

■**Note** Other Linux installation programs differ from the SUSE Linux routines. However, most involve the same basic steps.

Step-by-Step Guide

As outlined in Chapter 4, you shouldn't start the installation process until you've made sure there is enough space for SUSE Linux on your hard disk and you have backed up your data. With those preparations, you're ready to install SUSE Linux. The remainder of this chapter takes you through the process.

Step 1: Boot from the DVD

With your computer booted up, insert the SUSE Linux disc into the DVD-ROM drive. Close the tray, and then reboot your computer.

SUSE Linux is installed by booting the installation program from DVD. Therefore, the first step is to ensure your computer's BIOS is set to boot from the DVD-ROM drive. How this is achieved varies from computer to computer. However, most PCs let you enter the BIOS setup program by pressing the Delete key just after the computer is first activated, although some use another key or key combination.

When the BIOS menu appears, look for an option such as "Boot" and select it (you can usually navigate around the screen of the BIOS menu using the cursor keys and select options by pressing Enter). On the new menu, look for a separate entry such as "Boot Device Priority" or perhaps "Boot Sequence." Ensure that the entry for the CD/DVD-ROM is at the top of the list, as shown in the example in Figure 5-1. Arrange the list so that it's followed by the floppy drive and then your main hard disk (which will probably be identified as "IDE-0" or "First hard disk"). You can usually press the F1 key for help on how the menu selection system works.

Once you've made the changes, be sure to select the "Exit saving changes" option. Your PC will then reset and boot from the SUSE Linux DVD-ROM, and you'll be greeted by the blue SUSE welcome screen.

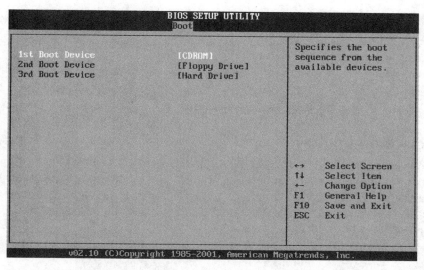

Figure 5-1. *Before starting, you should make sure your computer can boot the DVD-ROM.*

Step 2: Select to Install

After the welcome screen, you should see the DVD-ROM boot menu. From here, you can select to install SUSE Linux (use the cursor keys to move the selection up and down), so do so, as shown in Figure 5-2.

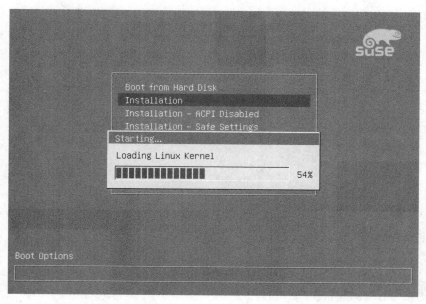

Figure 5-2. *Select to install SUSE Linux from the DVD-ROM boot menu.*

Note that you can also choose to boot from the hard disk, avoiding installing Linux, or you can boot to a rescue system, which will help you fix problems that might arise in the future (in other words, you can also use the SUSE Linux installation DVD as a rescue disc). There's also the option to install Linux using "Safe settings," which will use a text-based installer with many potentially troublesome options deactivated (such as certain power-saving options and performance tweaks, which can cause incompatibilities). This is useful if you run into installation problems, although it isn't necessary in the majority of cases.

Step 3: Select Your Language

SUSE Linux is a fully internationalized operating system, and one of the first steps is to select the language you wish to use during installation, as shown in Figure 5-3. Many European and Asian languages are offered. The default is English (US), although there are other variations of English available for other countries, such as the United Kingdom. After you've selected your language, click the Accept button at the bottom right.

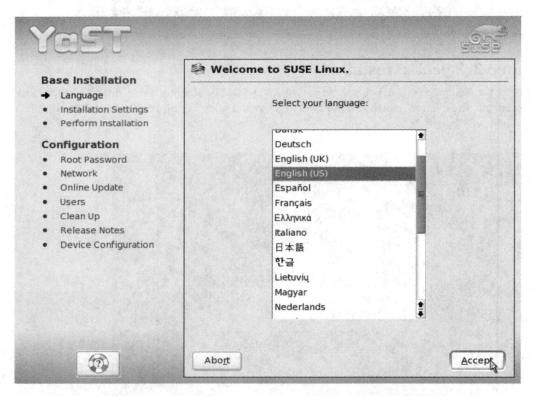

Figure 5-3. *The installation program speaks many languages; select which is best for you.*

Step 4: Choose Installation Settings

After you select the language, the system will work away for a few seconds, examining your system. If you're using an older PC, this might take up to a minute or two. An Installation

Settings screen will then appear, as shown in Figure 5-4. This screen lays out the default installation choices, such as which software will be installed, how the hard disk will be partitioned,
and much more. You can move through these settings using the scroll bar on the right side of
the screen. On the left side of the screen, an installation progress display shows where you're
up to in the procedure. This will stay on your screen throughout the installation process.

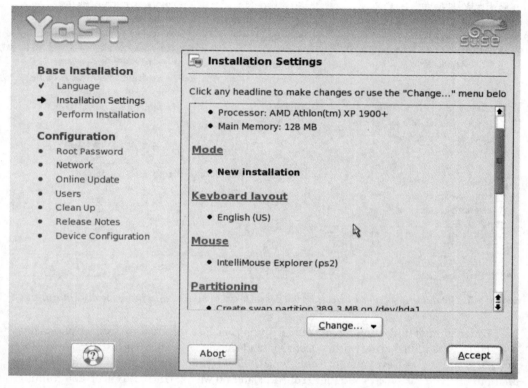

Figure 5-4. *SUSE Linux makes default installation choices, which you can edit if you wish.*

The default installation choices are usually correct, and the user in a hurry can simply click
the Accept button at this stage. However, it's a good idea to check through the selections, to be
sure that you're happy with the changes that will be made to your system and avoid the possibility of overwriting existing data.

Rather like a web browser, each heading in the list can be clicked to reveal a fresh page full
of details and configurable options. For example, you might choose to edit the selection of software that will be installed. By default, SUSE Linux installs a fully functional system, which
includes the KDE desktop, OpenOffice.org office suite, help and support documents, and a
handful of other essential programs. This makes for a system that offers everything you need
but isn't too overwhelming. However, it's possible to select more software by clicking the Software heading, and then clicking the Detailed Selection button. Once you do this, you'll see the
screen shown in Figure 5-5. The software is arranged into groups on the left side of the screen,
and the right side shows a list of the individual software packages, which will be installed as
part of the larger group.

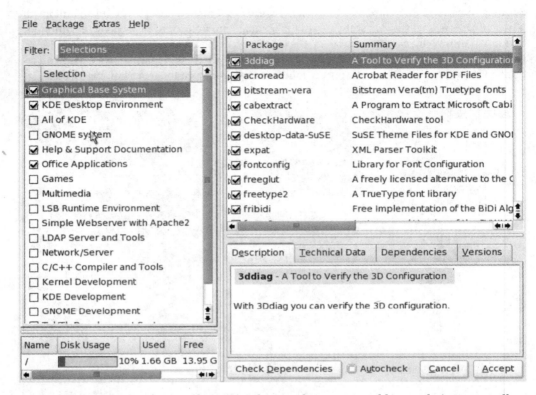

Figure 5-5. *The default software selection is adequate, but you can add more choices manually.*

You might not understand many of the options because they require some experience with Linux. A handful that are worth selecting include All of KDE, which will install useful desktop software, and C/C++ Development Tools, which will let you compile your own software. Keep in mind that you can always add more software later on when SUSE Linux is up and running, so there's no need to make a definitive choice at this stage.

When you're satisfied with your selection, click the Accept button.

Step 5: Partition the Disk

Partitioning the disk is one of the most important steps during installation although, unfortunately, it's one that's also couched in difficult terminology. However, SUSE Linux does a good job of making it easy to understand.

As noted in Chapter 4, you have three main options related to disk partitioning: install on a hard disk that also has Windows, install on a second hard disk, or delete the Windows partition.

Sharing a Hard Disk with Windows

If you're installing SUSE Linux on a hard disk that has Windows on it, by default, SUSE Linux will shrink the Windows partition to make space (provided you have enough free space; see Chapter 4). In the free space, it will automatically create two new partitions: one for data such as programs, known as the *root partition*, and one for the swap file. (By default, on Linux systems, the swap data is held in its own partition, rather than sharing the main hard disk, as with Windows.)

SUSE Linux will make as much space as possible for the main Linux partition when it resizes Windows. On my test PC, it shrunk the partition down to a quarter of its original size! If you don't want this to happen, you can change the default partitioning choices by clicking the Partitioning menu heading. Then select the "Base partition setup on this proposal"option. The next screen will show a list of the partitions. Select your Windows partition—it will be marked either FAT32 or HPFS/NTFS—and click the Edit button. You'll see a graphical display along with a slider, which you can click and drag to alter the sizes of the two partitions, as shown in Figure 5-6. There's no hard-and-fast rule for the partition sizes, apart from the fact that the SUSE Linux root partition should be at least 2GB in size (if you intend to install a lot of software, you should consider a partition of 5GB or more).

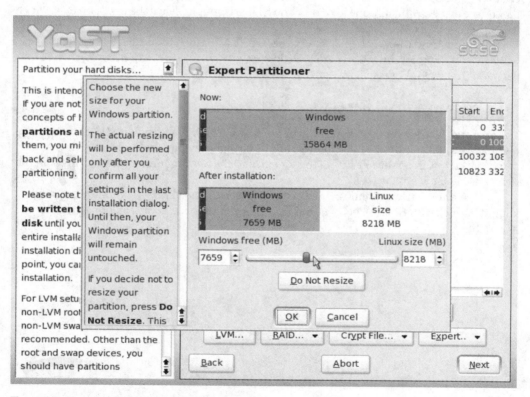

Figure 5-6. *You can resize the Windows partition to make space for SUSE Linux.*

When you're satisfied with the partition setup, click OK, and then click Next on the following screen. Click Finish to complete your changes.

Installing on a Separate Hard Disk

If you intend to install SUSE Linux on a second hard disk installed specifically for the purpose, you must tell SUSE Linux to use it in preference to the first disk. Click the Partitioning heading, and then click Create Custom Partition Setup. You'll then be asked to choose a hard disk on which to install. Click the second hard disk. This will be referred to as number 2 in the list, and you should also see that Linux refers to it as /dev/hdb. After this, you should find that SUSE Linux automatically creates a set of partitions, which you can accept and use to install Linux.

Deleting the Windows Partition

If you intend to delete the Windows partition on your main disk—to remove the Windows operating system from your hard disk in favor of Linux—you must override SUSE Linux's choices and create your own partitions. Click the Partitioning menu heading, and then click Create Custom Partition Setup. You'll then need to choose the disk on which you wish to install Linux. In the case of a PC with only one hard disk, the choice is simple: select the first hard disk, which will be described as /dev/hda.

Click Next, and then click the Use Entire Hard Disk button. Then click Next. Partitioning will be automatic after this. SUSE Linux will delete everything on the hard disk and create Linux partitions, ready for Linux installation.

Step 6: Set the Time Zone

The next step is to set the time zone for where you are. This will mean that SUSE Linux can automatically take into account schemes such as daylight saving time. A list of countries and continents appears on the left side of the screen, and the relevant time zones are listed on the right side, as shown in Figure 5-7.

UTC is another way of referring to Greenwich Mean Time (GMT). If you want to match your PC's clock with GMT, select this option. When you've made your selection, click the Accept button.

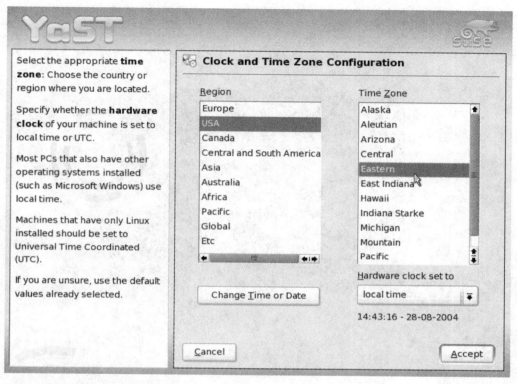

Figure 5-7. *Setting the time zone means that SUSE Linux can adjust to daylight saving time.*

Step 7: Start the Installation

The next step is to click the Yes, Install button, as shown in Figure 5-8. This will start the full installation, and the program will copy SUSE Linux files onto your hard disk. Before doing so, be sure to check all the installation options to make sure they're correct, particularly with regard to hard disk partitioning. Installation will take between 30 and 60 minutes, depending on the speed of your PC. However, there are some additional steps to take at the end of the installation, so you should check on the installation progress periodically.

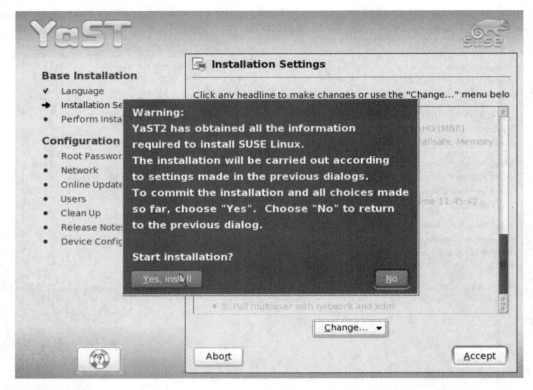

Figure 5-8. *When you're happy with the installation choices, click the Yes, Install button to start copying files.*

Step 8: Monitor the Installation

Although there's no real need to, you can monitor the installation progress and read the on-screen messages that point out some of SUSE Linux's main features, as shown in Figure 5-9. By clicking the Details button, you can see which packages are being copied across. Don't worry if some of the software packages sound complicated, or even unnecessary. The way Linux works means that some software packages rely on other software packages, so often software that will never directly be used is installed.

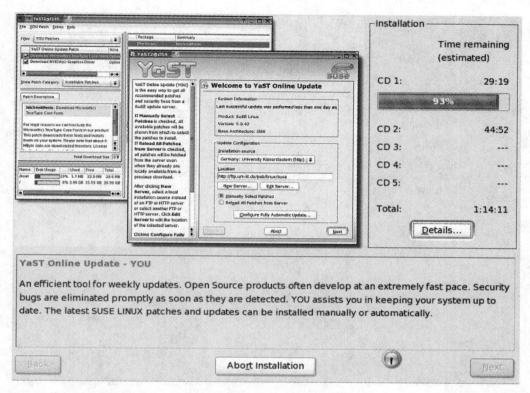

Figure 5-9. *You can monitor the installation and read messages about the features of SUSE Linux.*

Step 9: Reboot After Installation

When the installation program has finished copying files, it will perform some updating and configuration tasks, as shown in Figure 5-10. Next, it will reboot the system. Your PC will most likely boot from the DVD-ROM again. However, this time, you should select to boot from the hard disk. You'll then see a second boot menu, which is read from your hard disk. Choose to boot Linux. This will move you to the next phase of the installation: configuration.

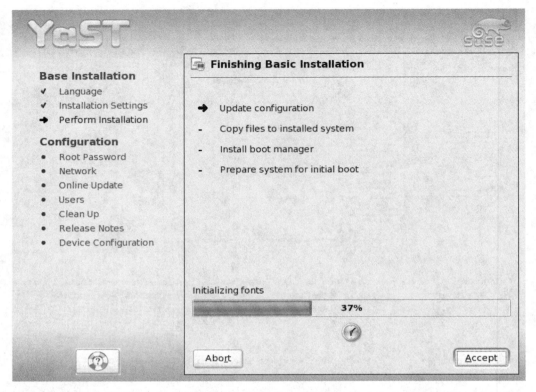

Figure 5-10. *After the files have finished copying across, the installation program will perform some updating and configuration tasks.*

Step 10: Set the Root Password

The first postinstallation step is to set a password for the root user. The root user is like the Administrator user on a Windows PC—the user who has complete control over the system. Although we talk of root as being a "user," in reality, you should rarely, if ever, log in to your computer as root. Instead you should only switch into root when necessary, on a temporary basis. I'll explain how this is done via the GUI and via the command-line prompt, in Chapter 9 and Chapter 15, respectively. For day-to-day use, you should create an ordinary user account, which you'll be invited to do later in the configuration process.

By default, SUSE Linux won't accept passwords with more than eight characters. If this limitation doesn't bother you, type a password into the box and click the Next button. If you would like to use a longer password, click the Expert Options button and select a different Encryption Type. I recommend Blowfish, as shown in Figure 5-11. Then click OK and enter your password.

Tip The best passwords are those that involve letters, numbers, and even symbols, because they're much harder to crack or guess.

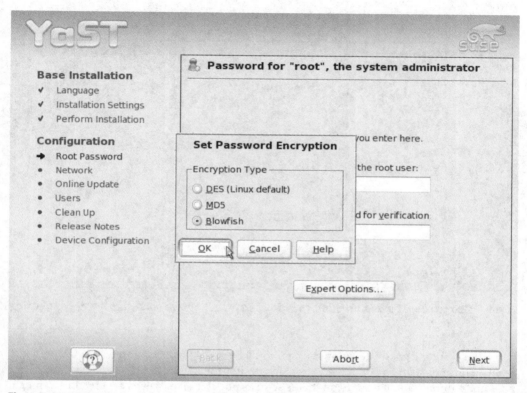

Figure 5-11. *SUSE Linux defaults to eight-character passwords, but you can change this by selecting a different encryption method.*

Step 11: Configure Your Network

The next step is to configure your network devices, as shown in Figure 5-12. The best policy is to configure these devices when SUSE Linux is actually up and running, rather than during installation. That way, you'll be able to alter other vital settings to match, which is impossible to do at this stage. Configuring network devices is covered in Chapter 8. Simply select the default options, and then click Next.

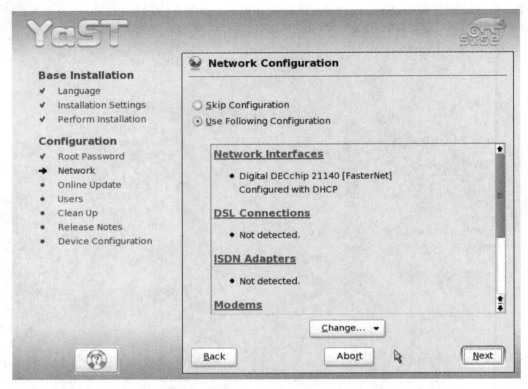

Figure 5-12. *You should wait until Linux has finished installing and booted up before configuring network devices.*

Later on in the postinstallation routine, you'll be asked if you want to test your Internet connection and download updates. You should decline the invitation for now. When everything is up and running, you'll want to do this as soon as possible. This will be covered in Chapter 9.

Step 12: Select the User Authentication Method

You'll next be asked what kind of user authentication you require, as shown in Figure 5-13. In nearly all cases, you can select the Stand-Alone Machine option. If your computer is part of a large corporate network that uses NIS/LDAP authentication, you should choose the Network Client option. You'll then need to speak to your system administrator to find out the address of the authentication server, as well as your username and password.

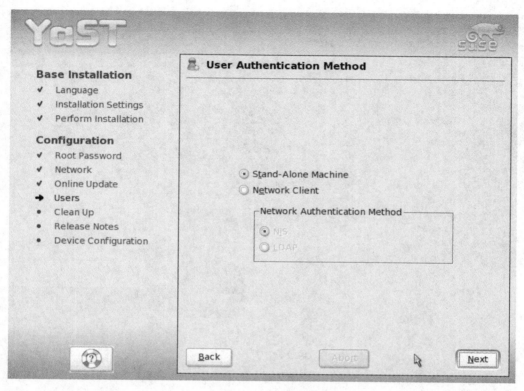

Figure 5-13. *Selecting the correct user authentication mode is easy; most users should select Stand-Alone Machine.*

Step 13: Create Users

Assuming that you selected the Stand-Alone Machine option in the previous step, you'll now be invited to create new user accounts, as shown in Figure 5-14. As mentioned earlier, you should create a simple user account for yourself to use every day, rather than using the root account. You'll be invited to enter various details. Most important are the user login, which will be your username, and the password, which must be entered twice to ensure accuracy. The username cannot have spaces in it. It can be a mixture of capital and lowercase letters. You should avoid using symbols in the username, because this can create problems later on. The password can include numbers, letters, and symbols, but no spaces.

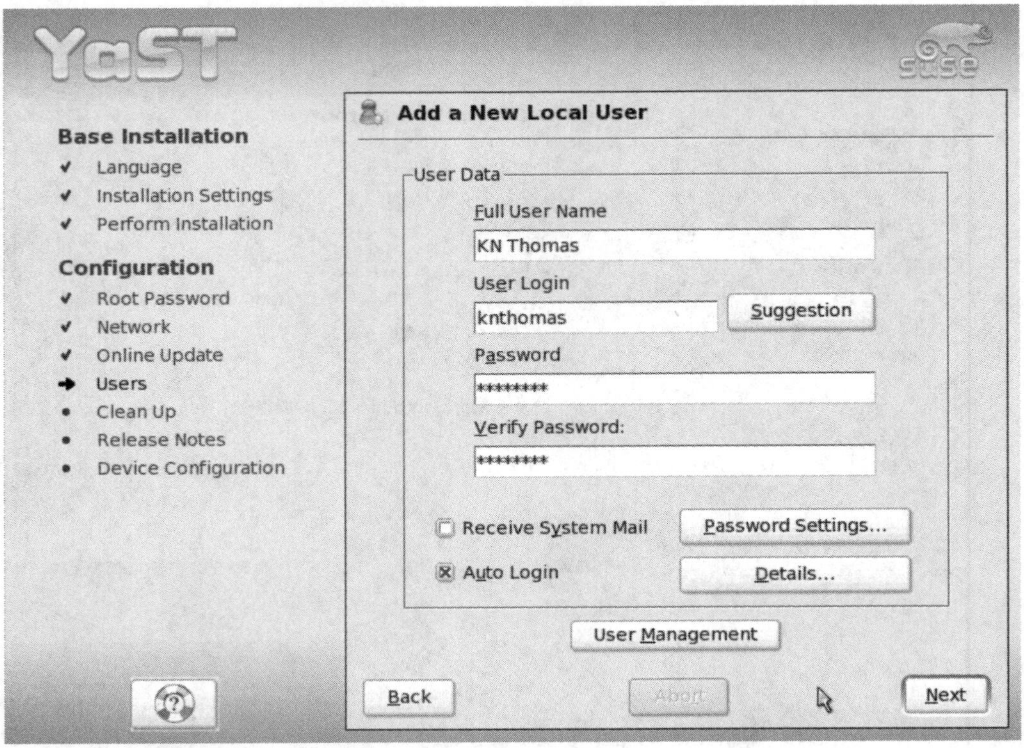

Figure 5-14. *You should create a user account for day-to-day use.*

Note that the Auto Login option is selected by default. This means that Linux will *not* ask for your username and password when it boots up; it will simply boot straight into the default user account. If you require more security (in other words, your PC is located where strangers can access it), you can deselect the Auto Login option. In that case, a username and password prompt will appear after SUSE Linux boots, and no one will be able to access the PC without the correct username and corresponding password.

You can create additional users here, too, but this is best done when Linux is up and running. Adding users is discussed in Chapter 30.

Step 14: Configure Your Hardware

After creating users, the installation routine will clean up some old files and attempt to test the network connection. Following this, you'll be invited to configure your hardware, as shown in Figure 5-15.

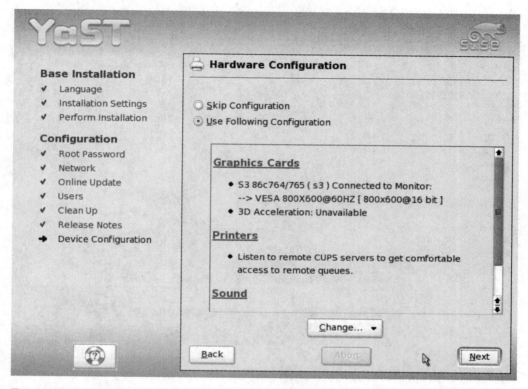

Figure 5-15. *SUSE Linux will automatically probe and configure most of your PC hardware.*

In reality, this is largely a summary of SUSE's autoprobing of your hardware. Generally speaking, if SUSE Linux isn't able to detect your hardware by probing, then it probably won't support it. In other words, if your hardware doesn't appear in the list under the various headings, it's probably not possible to use it under SUSE Linux at this time. However, the chances of this happening are slim. You'll learn about configuring hardware, such as printers, in Chapter 8. You should choose the Skip Configuration option at this stage.

Step 15: Finish Installation

At this point, the installation has finished. The installation routine will quit, and your system will be booted. Note that this doesn't mean your system will reboot. Linux isn't as reliant on rebooting as Windows is. Instead, the system's kernel will load. After a few seconds, if you selected the Auto Login option when creating user accounts, the desktop should appear, as shown in Figure 5-16. If you deselected this option, you'll be greeted with a prompt to enter your username and password.

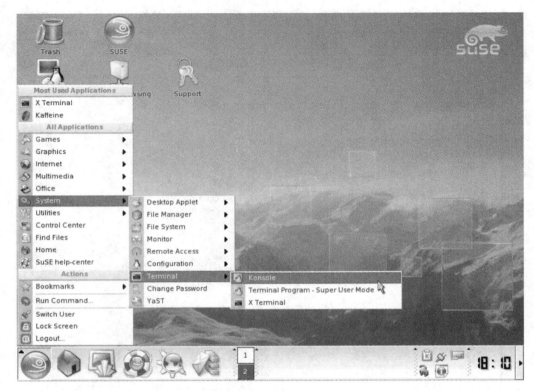

Figure 5-16. *Once installation has finished, your system will boot, and you should be greeted by the desktop!*

Summary

By following the steps outlined in this chapter, you should now have SUSE Linux installed on your computer. I've tried to provide you with enough information to get around any problems, as well as to explain exactly what's happening every step of the way.

Alas, it's still possible that you encountered hurdles that weren't addressed here. In the next chapter, you'll find solutions to common problems associated with SUSE Linux installation.

## CHAPTER 6

Solving Installation Problems

Chances are that your installation of SUSE Linux will complete without a hitch, and you'll find yourself with a new operating system up and running immediately. However, if a problem rears its ugly head, you should be able to find the solution in this chapter, which addresses the most common installation problems. These problems are organized by when they occur: before you begin the installation, during the installation, and after the installation. The final section of this chapter describes how to configure your GUI with the SaX2 configuration utility provided by SUSE, which can be useful if any graphical glitches arise.

Preinstallation Problems

Some problems might arise before you even begin the installation process. These typically involve the DVD. This section addresses four typical problems.

> **Problem:** My PC is unable to boot from a DVD, so I cannot install Linux from the DVD.
> **Solution:** Some older PCs are unable to boot from CD or DVD-ROM drives. However, this doesn't mean that you cannot install SUSE Linux on these PCs. The DVD includes utilities to create a series of three boot floppies, which can be used to trigger the installation routine from the DVD. Here are the steps for creating the installation floppies:

1. Boot into Windows and insert the SUSE Linux DVD into the drive. Insert a blank, 1.44MB floppy disk into the floppy drive.

2. Use My Computer to browse to `\dosutils\rawwritewin\rawwritewin.exe` on the SUSE Linux DVD-ROM. Double-click the program to start it.

3. Locate the Image File box and click the button to the right of it in order to browse to the `\boot` folder on the DVD-ROM.

4. Select the file named `bootdsk1` (you will need to alter the Files of Type drop-down list so that All files (*.*) is selected). Then click the Write button.

5. Watch the percentage progress indicator at the bottom left of the program window. When it reaches 100%, the creation of the boot disk has finished. Label the disk **SUSE Linux install disk 1**.

6. Insert a fresh floppy disk and repeat steps 2 through 5, this time selecting the file named `bootdsk2` and labeling the disk **SUSE Linux install disk 2**.

7. Repeat the process once more, writing the file named `bootdsk3` and labeling the disk **SUSE Linux install disk 3**.

8. When all three floppies have been created, click the Exit button, and then reboot your PC, ensuring the DVD-ROM is inserted and the first boot floppy is in the floppy disk drive. Then follow the instructions on your screen. See the notes in the previous chapter regarding actual installation.

Problem: My PC doesn't have a DVD-ROM drive. It has only a CD-ROM drive.

Solution: In this case, you obviously won't be able to install SUSE Linux from the DVD-ROM supplied with this book. However, DVD-ROM drives are relatively inexpensive and you might consider upgrading your hardware. Alternatively, you can visit `www.suse.com/us/private/ download/suse_linux/`, where you can download a CD-ROM ISO image of SUSE Linux. Once downloaded, this ISO image can be burned to a blank CD-R disc using a Windows utility such as Ahead's Nero (check the program's manual or help file to learn how to burn ISO images).

Problem: When I boot from the DVD, everything appears to run smoothly for a few seconds, but then the system freezes before installation starts.

Solution: Your system cannot boot into SUSE Linux's YaST2 graphical installer. This happens for a variety of reasons with a minority of computers. However, it should still be possible to install Linux using an older version of YaST, which has a text-mode installation routine. To access this version of YaST, hold down the Shift key just before the SUSE Linux DVD starts to boot (just after your PC has finished its boot-time memory testing).

Using the text-mode installation routine is similar to using YaST2's graphical installer, as described in the previous chapter, except that you don't use your mouse. Instead, you must use the keyboard's cursor keys to highlight various options, and the Tab key to move from field to field (rather like using an application within MS-DOS). Press Enter or the spacebar to select options.

The main installation options are virtually identical to those offered within the graphical installation. See Chapter 5 for guidance.

Problem: When I attempt to install, I choose the Installation option from the DVD boot menu, but the progress bar freezes before the actual installation program starts.

Solution: See the previous solution.

Installation Problems

During installation, you may get error messages or experience other difficulties. This section offers some solutions to common problems.

Problem: When I try to install, the partitioning section of the installation program talks about `/dev/sda`, `/dev/sdb`, `/dev/sdc`, and so on, rather than `/dev/hda`.

Solution: If your system uses SCSI hard disks, then this is correct. SCSI disks are mostly used on servers and very rarely on desktop computers.

If you see this message and you use an ordinary computer, it's likely you have a flash memory card inserted into your card reader, or another form of external memory. Unfortunately, SUSE Linux sometimes attempts to install Linux to such devices, which are identified internally by Linux as SCSI devices. The solution is to disconnect or remove the removable memory device during installation.

Problem: When it's time to choose the packages for installation, I see the message: "No base selection available. ERROR: No proposal."

Solution: Restart the installation and, at the DVD-ROM boot menu (prior to starting the installation program), select the Installation option, and then type the following:

```
linux cdromdevice=hdc
```

This is assuming that you have only one CD/DVD-ROM device; if you are installing from a second DVD-ROM device on your system, you might need to enter the following command:

```
linux cdromdevice=hdd
```

If, after this, you find that the same error message appears, restart the installation, and then enter the following:

```
linux cdromdevice=hdd pci=acpi
```

Problem: When it's time to choose the packages for installation, I see the message: "No base selection available. ERROR: No proposal." I have a combination CD-R/RW and DVD-ROM drive, and have tried the previous solution, but it doesn't work.

Solution: Combined CD-R/RW and DVD-ROM drives can cause problems in some cases. The solution is relatively simple. Here are the steps:

1. Boot from the DVD-ROM and highlight the Installation option using the cursor keys.

2. Type the following:

   ```
   hdc=ide-scsi
   ```

   Alternatively, if you have two CD/DVD-ROM drives in your computer, and the drive you're trying to install from is the second of the two, type this:

   ```
   hdd=ide-scsi
   ```

3. Press Enter to start installation.

4. The installation program will report that no installation source can be found. Click OK to clear the box.

5. The text-mode linuxrc rescue program will start. Using the cursor keys, highlight the Kernel Modules – Hardware Drivers entry on the menu and press Enter to select the option. Then select the Load IDE/RAID/SCSI Modules option in the same way.

6. Scroll down the list in the following menu until you find ide-scsi : SCSI emulation for IDE ATAPI devices. Press Enter to select that entry.

7. Clear the dialog boxes confirming that the module has been loaded. Use the Tab key to move focus to the Back button, and then highlight and select Start Installation/System in the following menu.

8. Choose the options to start the installation. Select the CD-ROM when asked (don't worry about the fact you're actually installing from a DVD-ROM).

Problem: The installation program seems to run smoothly, but then crashes/freezes at a random point before completing.

Solution: In the case of freezes, make sure the computer has actually frozen and isn't simply busy with a task. Check the hard disk light for activity on the computer's case and also look at the DVD-ROM drive light to see if it's flashing. Press Ctrl+Alt+F2. If the screen changes to a command prompt, your system is still running but is simply busy (press Ctrl+Alt+F3 to return to the installation GUI). If the computer genuinely has become unresponsive, reboot, and when the boot menu appears, select Installation – Safe Settings. This will start the text-mode installation program. See the previous solution on page 54 for information about how to use the installation program without a mouse.

Problem: The installation fails with the following error message: "Usb.3: read info."

Solution: This problem is caused by an incorrectly configured BIOS. Reboot the computer and, before installation starts, enter the BIOS setup program by pressing the specified key (usually the Delete key). In the PNP/PCI Configuration section, make sure the Assign IRQ for USB option is set to Enabled. (You can use the cursor keys to move around the menus in the BIOS program and use the Enter key to change various values.)

Problem: When I try to install, I receive the following error message: "The password for root could not be set. You won't be able to login."

Solution: This problem is caused by an incorrect or faulty hard disk partition table. Unfortunately, solving this problem is very complicated and can have a variety of causes. One potential solution is to choose the Installation – Safe Settings option during installation, and then ignore the automatic partitioning choices. Instead, choose to create the root and swap partitions manually. However, to truly overcome the problem, the hard disk should be erased and Linux (and Windows if necessary) installed afresh.

Problem: During installation, I see the error message: "Disk doesn't contain a valid partition table." Yet installation seems to continue normally and, afterwards, the system appears to work fine.

Solution: This is simply a glitch in the installation procedure. The error is effectively meaningless and can be ignored.

Postinstallation Problems

Problems might also occur after installing SUSE Linux. This section addresses several possible postinstallation problems.

Problem: I have a PC with onboard VIA graphics. However, when installation has finished, I cannot boot up into a GUI. Instead, the screen briefly flashes and I see a text login prompt.

Solution: The solution to this problem, as well as for many similar problems regardless of which graphics card is in use, is to run the SaX2 graphical configuration program. In the case of a VIA chipset, you must log in as the root user (that is, type **root** as the username, and then enter the root password), and then type the following command:

```
sax2 -m l=via -c 1
```

See the guide to using SaX2 provided at the end of this chapter.

Problem: When I boot up after installation, the system doesn't boot into a GUI. Instead, I see a text login prompt.

Solution: For some reason, YaST2 was unable to correctly configure your graphics card. The solution is to manually configure the graphics card and input devices. You can do this by running the SaX2 program. To do this, log in as root user (that is, type **root** as the username, and then enter the root password). Then find out the make and model of your graphics card by typing the following:

```
sax2 -p
```

Make a note of these details, and then start SaX2 itself in order to configure your system:

```
sax2 --vesa 800x600
```

This will start SaX2. See the guide at the end of this chapter to learn how to use SaX2.

Problem: After installation, SUSE Linux boots and works fine, but I'm no longer able to boot Windows. When I select the option from the boot menu, I see a few lines of text (including "Filesystem type unknown, partition type 0x7"), and then the system hangs.

Solution: This is caused by incompatibilities between the way Linux and Windows access the hard disk's partition table. The easiest solution is to access the BIOS setup program during bootup (by pressing the Delete key, or another key or key combination, to enter setup mode), and then select an option so that the hard disk is manually detected rather than automatically detected. You should also ensure the hard disk access mode is set to LBA or to Large mode (this ensures the hard disk information can be read properly by Windows).

Alternatively, you can use a patch designed to fix the problem, supplied by SUSE Linux. This solution is more complicated, requiring the following steps:

1. Boot Linux normally.

2. Visit the following FTP site using Konqueror: `ftp://ftp.suse.com/pub/suse/i386/update/9.1/misc/parted/`.

3. Download the file named parted.img.gz (right-click and select Copy To). Save it to your home directory.

4. Insert a blank floppy disk. Open a Konsole window and type the following to write the patch to the floppy disk (replace *<username>* with your own username or the name of your home directory):

   ```
   gunzip c /home/<username>/parted.img.gz >/dev/fd0
   ```

5. Eject the floppy disk.

6. Boot the computer using the installation DVD-ROM. At the DVD boot menu, press F6.

7. Use the arrow keys to select Installation from the boot menu. Type the following *before* pressing Enter to select the Installation option:

   ```
   fixpart=1
   ```

8. A message will appear, asking you to choose the drive update medium. Insert the floppy disk and select OK. In the menu following this, select Floppy, and then select OK. Once the driver update has completed, click the Back button.

9. You will see a dialog box showing the status of the partition table. Select the hard disk entry in the menu, and then click OK. This will repair the partition table. Once this has completed, click Back.

10. Reboot your computer by pressing Ctrl+Alt+Delete.

You should now be able to boot into both Linux and Windows.

GUI Configuration with SaX2

SaX2 is a powerful configuration utility provided by SUSE. It's designed to configure XFree86, the software that provides the basis for the GUI under SUSE Linux. It aids in setting up the graphics card, monitor, keyboard, and mouse, and it uses autodetection to make the process easier. However, the default choices can be overridden if necessary.

Usually, you don't need to use SaX2 because, during setup, the YaST2 program automatically installs the graphics card, keyboard, mouse, and monitor based on the results of probing your hardware. However, in a minority of cases, YaST2 gets it wrong, nearly always with regard to the monitor. An incorrect monitor configuration results in a system that boots up but is unable to start the GUI. The screen will usually go blank or flash at the end of the boot procedure, and the user will be taken to a text login prompt.

Note Although the boot procedure features a blue picture background with the SUSE gecko, Linux isn't actually running in GUI mode (run level 5) at that time. This is simply a trick to make the screen look prettier. Effectively, the machine is still in a text mode (run level 3). GUI mode starts when the bootup has finished and is usually indicated by the appearance of the mouse cursor.

Running SaX2

SaX2 needs to be run with administrative powers, because it involves configuring the entire Linux system. Follow these steps to run SaX2:

1. Log in as root. Enter **root** as the username and type the password you entered during setup when prompted.

2. SaX2 cannot operate if your system is in run level 5. It needs to be activated in run level 3. The concepts behind run levels are explained in Chapter 31, but for the moment, you should type the following command:

```
init 3
```

3. You might need to wait a few seconds while a few commands are processed in the background. Press Enter to return to the command prompt, and then type the following:

```
sax2 --vesa 800x600
```

This will run the SaX2 program in Vesa-compatibility mode, with a safe resolution of 800×600. This ensures it will work correctly on nearly all systems.

4. When SaX2 starts, it may show a dialog box claiming that it has worked out the best graphics configuration for your system, as shown in Figure 6-1. You can click OK to exit SaX2 if you wish to try the new configuration.

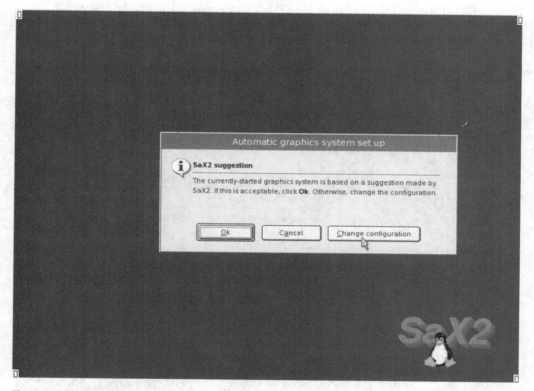

Figure 6-1. *SaX2 will try to autodetect the best settings, and most of the time, it's correct.*

5. Once the program has disappeared, type the following at the command prompt to switch back to GUI mode:

```
init 5
```

If SaX2 has guessed the correct configuration, you should see the desktop or the GUI login prompt appear, complete with a mouse cursor. You can then proceed to use Linux, and no further work with SaX2 is necessary. However, if you return once again to the command prompt, then clearly SaX2 has failed, and some manual configuration is necessary, as described in the next section.

Changing Your Configuration

If you need to manually configure your GUI, repeat the preceding steps to start SaX2, first switching to run level 3 as described. When the dialog box appears asking if you want to accept the default configuration, decline the offer and instead click Change Configuration. This will open a dialog box that lists the various elements you can manually configure. The first step is to configure the monitor because, in the majority of cases, this is what will be causing the problem. Often, SUSE guesses incorrect vertical and horizontal scan rates.

Select the Monitor link, and then click the Change Configuration button. Then click Properties to see a list of monitor models. If you're lucky, your monitor will be included, and you can select it from the list. However, your monitor might not appear, because there are simply too many different types for SUSE to list them all. Therefore, the best solution is often to select from the VESA section, as shown in Figure 6-2. This is a list of generic monitors based on industry standards, which work with most monitors.

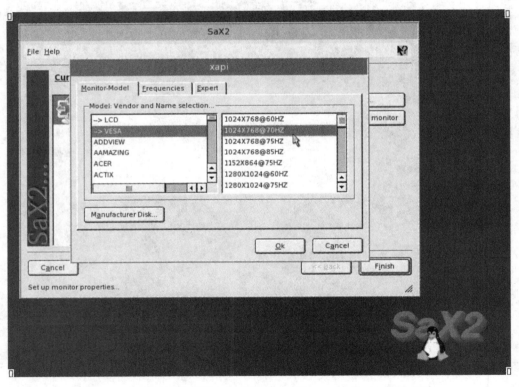

Figure 6-2. *VESA monitor settings will work with virtually any make and model.*

At this point, you'll need to know a little about your monitor's technical settings, such as the resolution at which it normally runs, as well as its horizontal refresh rate. See Table 6-1 for a list of standard monitor sizes and settings. You can choose one of these if you don't know your monitor's exact details. Note that most monitors sold at the present time are 17-inch models. Also note that the table lists refresh rates that should work on the majority of standard cathode ray tube (CRT) monitors, as well as newer thin film transistor (TFT) models.

Table 6-1. *Typical Monitor Settings*

Monitor Size	Typical Resolution (CRT)	Typical Resolution (TFT)	Horizontal Refresh Rate
14 inches	800×600	1024×768	70Hz
15 inches	800×600	1024×768	70Hz
17 inches	1024×768	1280×1024	70Hz
19 inches	1280×1024	1600×1200	70Hz
20 inches	1600×1200	1600×1200	70Hz

After setting up the monitor, you can also change the settings for your graphics card, keyboard, and mouse. However, in the vast majority of cases, these will have been correctly autodetected and configured. Therefore, there's little need to undertake extra configuration.

Note If you're using a Synaptics Touchpad (on a notebook or specialized keyboard), you might want to select this in the mouse configuration screen. See Chapter 10 for more information about configuring a Synaptics Touchpad.

After clicking the Finalize button, you'll be given a chance to test your new configuration. This is highly recommended. If your new configuration is correct, a test screen should appear, as shown in Figure 6-3. The test screen will let you change the screen size and positioning, but this is better done using the controls on your monitor. Therefore, if the picture is too small, too big, or off center, don't worry too much about it. The most important thing is that you are seeing a picture, which means your configuration has worked. Don't forget to test your mouse, too, to ensure it's working.

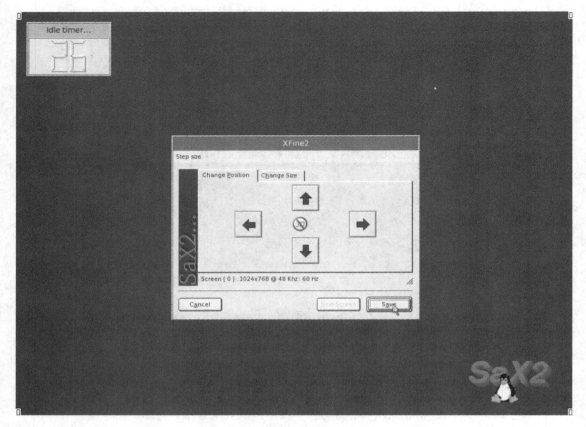

Figure 6-3. *Don't forget to test your new settings before saving them!*

If you're happy with the new configuration, click the Save button, and then quit SaX2. Switch back to graphical mode by typing:

```
init 5
```

If the new settings are incorrect, the screen will go black for a long period. Pressing Escape should return you to SaX2, where you can try an alternative configuration. If you find that SaX2 has crashed your computer, press the reset button on the computer case, and then start SaX2 again, as you did before.

If you're sure your monitor is correctly configured, the next troubleshooting option is to change your graphics card configuration. In SaX2, click the Graphics Card link and select your make and model of card from the list. If you find that, for unknown reasons, the seemingly correct configuration doesn't work on your system, try selecting the VESA Framebuffer model. This is guaranteed to work on any PC. Then repeat the steps to test the setup.

WHAT IF YOU WANT TO REMOVE LINUX FROM YOUR COMPUTER?

Linux isn't for everybody, and you might find that, after trying it out, it's not for you. In that case, you might wish to return to having a Windows-only PC and reclaim the disk space taken up by the Linux partitions. This is easily done using the Windows installation CD.

Before you do this, please think long and hard about your reasons for deciding to give up on Linux. If you found it too difficult to use compared to Windows, consider giving Linux just a bit longer to prove itself. If you find that Linux doesn't support a particular piece of hardware on your PC, try updating the system to see if support has been added. If you find that a piece of software you need isn't supplied with SUSE Linux, search the Internet to see if you can track down that software. Linux has software for just about every need, but, unfortunately, a particular program might sometimes be difficult to find.

If you're certain you want to remove Linux, you'll be pleased to hear it's relatively easy. Assuming you're using Windows XP, insert your installation CD and boot from it. When you are asked whether you want to install Windows, choose to run the Rescue program. After prompting you for your Administrator password (if you have one), and asking you to choose your keyboard and which Windows partition you wish to work on, you'll be returned to a DOS command prompt. At this point you should type:

```
bootcfg /rebuild
```

Then simply issue the following two commands in sequence. These will rewrite the boot sector with Windows code, making Linux no longer accessible:

```
fixboot
fixmbr
```

These commands will likely ask questions for which the answers are obvious, but this depends on your system. After running the commands, boot into Windows and use the Disk Management tools to remove the Linux partitions. Open Control Panel, click Administrative Tools, click Computer Management, click Storage, and finally click Disk Management. Your Windows partitions will be identified with drive letters, and the Linux partitions will be referred to as Unknown Partitions. You can safely delete these, which will eradicate Linux entirely from your system.

Summary

This chapter's goal was to address problems that might occur during the installation of SUSE Linux. It addressed preinstallation, installation, and postinstallation issues. It also covered how to use the SaX2 utility to configure the graphics subsystem, which may be necessary if, for some reason, the installation program failed to properly recognize your graphics card, monitor, keyboard, or mouse.

You should now have SUSE Linux installed. The next part of the book focuses on helping you to get everything up and running. You'll learn essential skills and become a confident Linux user.

The No-Nonsense Getting Started Guide

■ ■ ■

## CHAPTER 7

Booting Linux for the First Time

Now that you have SUSE Linux on your PC, you'll no doubt want to get started immediately, and that's what Part Three of this book is all about. In later chapters, we'll examine specific details of using SUSE Linux and getting essential hardware up and running. We'll also look at personalizing SUSE Linux so that it works in a way that's best for you on a day-to-day basis. But right now, the goal of this chapter is to get you doing the same things you did under Windows as quickly as possible

This chapter looks at starting up SUSE Linux for the first time and working with the desktop. It also looks at how some familiar aspects of your computer, such as using the mouse, are slightly enhanced under SUSE Linux.

Starting Up

The first SUSE Linux screen you will see is the boot loader, which appears shortly after you switch on your PC, as shown in Figure 7-1. This is actually a separate program called GRUB, but you don't need to know that right now. Suffice it to say, this program kicks everything off and starts SUSE Linux.

There are usually three or four choices on the menu, but the default (Linux) is what you need. You might find that you have an entry for Windows if you've chosen to dual-boot. There's usually an entry called Failsafe, which is a little like Safe Mode within Windows, in that only conservative system settings are used (however, unlike Safe Mode, it's entirely possible to fully utilize SUSE Linux when the Failsafe option is selected, which is to say you can start the GUI in standard resolution, and networking devices should still work).

The Linux option will be selected automatically within eight seconds, but you can press Enter to start immediately. (To select any option other than Linux from the boot menu, simply use the arrow keys to move the selection down the list, and then press Enter.)

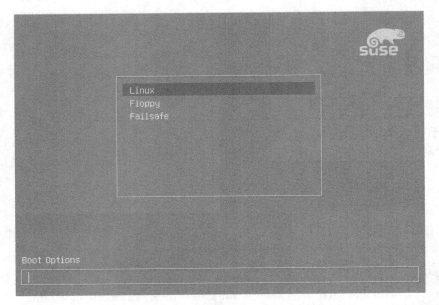

Figure 7-1. *The default choice is fine on the boot menu, so press Enter to start SUSE Linux.*

▪**Note** All operating systems need a boot loader—even Windows. However, the Windows boot loader is hidden and simply starts the operating system. Under SUSE Linux, the boot loader usually has a menu, so you can select Linux or perhaps an option that lets you access your PC for troubleshooting problems. When you gain some experience with SUSE Linux, you might choose to install two or more versions of Linux on the same hard disk, and you'll be able to select among them using the boot menu.

Depending on which options you selected during installation, you'll either boot directly to the desktop or you'll see a login screen first. If you boot to the desktop, you can skip the following section and go directly to "Exploring the Desktop."

Logging In

On the login screen, you can enter the username and password you created toward the end of the installation process. On the left side of the login screen, you should see a list of people who have accounts on your machine, as in Windows XP. You can click the user to have the username filled in automatically, as shown in Figure 7-2.

▪**Note** By clicking the Menu button at the bottom of the login screen dialog box, you can choose to reboot or shut down the machine without logging in.

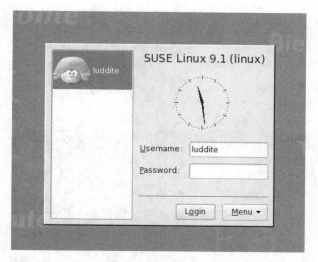

Figure 7-2. *Select your username from the left side of the screen, type in your password, and click Login.*

A common mistake among those who are new to Linux is to use the root account to log in on a daily basis, and therefore avoid using the standard user account created during setup. This is certainly possible, but it's not recommended. One of the reasons why Windows is so fundamentally insecure is that it allows all users to run with Administrator permissions by default. It is possible to run Windows with a limited account, but this must be specially configured by someone who knows what he or she is doing (you've got to love Microsoft's lackluster approach to security). This means that any Windows user can change the entire software and hardware settings of the PC.

In contrast, SUSE Linux prefers people to run as ordinary users. This is restrictive in the sense that it lets you run only particular programs and access certain pieces of hardware, but you shouldn't consider it a limitation. Consider it a security feature. In practice, this will not affect your day-to-day work with Linux.

If a situation arises where you need root powers—to run a program that configures hardware, for example—you'll be given the opportunity to switch temporarily to the root user account. You should find that an Administrator Password box appears, into which you can type the root password. Your root powers will apply to only that program, however, and in all other regards, you'll still be running Linux as an ordinary user. In many ways, this practice of borrowing root powers for certain tasks gives you the best of all worlds, but with minimal hassle.

Exploring the Desktop

The very first time you boot SUSE Linux, a welcome screen will appear. This provides shortcuts to various web sites that offer further help and various getting started guides. Click the Close link at the bottom right to get rid of the welcome screen. If you want to see it again later, you can click the green SUSE desktop icon.

Once the desktop appears, as shown in Figure 7-3, there's nothing stopping you from getting started immediately, so feel free to click around and see what you can discover. Remember that because you're running as a standard user, you can't do any irreversible damage to the system setup. So let yourself go wild!

■Tip Although you can't damage the system by messing around, you might find that you delete essential icons or somehow cause programs to work incorrectly. Don't worry if this happens. You can always create a new account for yourself following the instructions in Chapter 30. When using this new account, you should find all the settings are returned to normal, and you'll be back to square one!

Figure 7-3. *Feel free to experiment with the SUSE Linux desktop and see what you can discover.*

The mouse works largely as it does in Windows, in that you can move it around and click on things. You can also right-click virtually everything and everywhere to bring up context menus, which usually let you alter settings. And you should find that the mouse wheel in between the mouse buttons lets you scroll windows.

Whenever SUSE Linux is busy, an animated clock will appear (you might be used to the hourglass icon in Windows). Whenever a program is launched, you should also find that the cursor bounces, providing a little entertainment while you wait!

Caution Bear in mind that SUSE Linux isn't a clone of Windows and doesn't try to be. Although it works in a similar way—by providing icons and containing programs within windows—there are various potholes in the road that can trip up the unwary.

WRONG RESOLUTION!

You might find when you boot up that SUSE Linux has defaulted to the wrong resolution. In other words, everything might be a little too large or too small. You might have trouble reading text, for example, or you might find that program windows fill the screen to the extent that their contents partially disappear off the edges. Changing the resolution is simple, and the technique is very similar to that in Windows. Just move the mouse to a blank area of the desktop away from any icons and right-click. Select Configure Desktop, and then click the Size and Orientation icon.

In the Screensize drop-down list, select the appropriate resolution for your monitor. For a 17-inch monitor, the standard resolution is 1024×768 (although some people prefer 800×600). If you have a 15-inch monitor (common on PCs made before 2000), you'll probably find 800×600 a maximum setting, with others preferring 640×480.

The SUSE desktop is similar to that of Windows. It has the following elements:

- **Icons:** There are icons that you can click on to activate them, including the usual suspects of My Computer and Trash. You can also click and drag icons to move them around, if you want to alter their position on screen. The actual icon graphic can be changed easily: just right-click the icon, select Properties, and click the icon you want to use in the window that appears.

Note By default, you click only once on the desktop icons to start programs. Don't worry if you find this annoying. In Chapter 10, you learn how to change the settings so you double-click instead, as with Windows.

- **Panel:** The bar at the bottom of the screen, called the Panel, holds the program menu icon and shortcuts to commonly used programs. Just click an icon in the Panel to start that program.

- **Taskbar:** To the right of the Panel, you'll find the Taskbar area, which shows the programs that are currently running. As with Windows, you can simply click each entry to bring that program window "to the top." Alternatively, you can right-click each entry to instantly minimize or maximize that particular window.

- **System tray:** On the right side of the Panel, there's a system tray area, where various handy applet programs are located. These appear and disappear during everyday use, depending on what you're doing on your PC, as with Windows. For example, when you're playing an audio CD,, you'll see an extra icon that offers quick access to your CD player's controls. Generally speaking, you can access each icon's menu by right-clicking it, although some also respond to a single-click or double-click with the left mouse button. Some even respond to both left-clicking and right-clicking!

- **Clock:** Next to the system tray is a clock. Clicking it brings up a handy calendar showing the month at a glance. Clicking the clock again gets rid of this. You can alter the date and time by right-clicking the clock and selecting Adjust Date and Time. You'll need to enter your root password to do this. You can also right-click to change the settings and get rid of the slightly ugly digital clock-style interface. Select Configure Clock from the menu, and in the Clock Type drop-down list, choose whichever option you prefer.

Tip A particular favorite of many is Fuzzy Clock, which tells the time colloquially. Instead of displaying 12:35 PM, for example, it will say "Twenty five to one." The level of fuzziness can be set so that it gets *extremely* colloquial; it might display "lunchtime" or "mid-afternoon," for example. This is nice for those lazy weekends when you don't want to be hounded by timekeeping!

It will take some time to get used to the look and feel of SUSE Linux; everything will initially seem odd. You'll find that the on-screen fonts look a little different from those in Windows, for example. The icons also won't be the same as you're used to in Windows. This can be a little disconcerting, but that feeling will quickly pass, and everything will become second nature. We'll look at how you can personalize the desktop in Chapter 10.

BEHIND THE DESKTOP: KDE

Although I refer to the SUSE Linux desktop, the actual programs behind it are created by the K Desktop Environment (KDE) project. Its home page is www.kde.org. This is one of the most well-established organizations currently producing desktop interfaces for Linux, as well as for other versions of Unix.

Although it's based on KDE, SUSE Linux's desktop has its own set of individual features and programs, as well as a unique look and feel. That said, it works in an otherwise identical way to versions of KDE that are used in other Linux distributions.

The nature of open-source software—whereby anyone can take the source code and create his or her own version of a program—makes SUSE's reinvention of the KDE desktop possible. Unlike with Windows software, there can be more than one current version of a particular program or software suite, and each is usually tailored to the particular needs of one of the various Linux distributions.

Running Programs

Starting a new program is easy. Just click the program menu icon (the green gecko), and then choose a program from the list, as you would in Windows. The program menu, shown in Figure 7-4, is also called the K menu, and this is how I'll refer to it from now on.

Figure 7-4. *The K menu is accessed by clicking the green gecko icon. It is very similar to the Windows Start menu.*

Alternatively, you can click a desktop icon or a program shortcut at the bottom of the screen. Refer to Figure 7-5 for the names of these items on the desktop and to Table 7-1 for a description of what each one does.

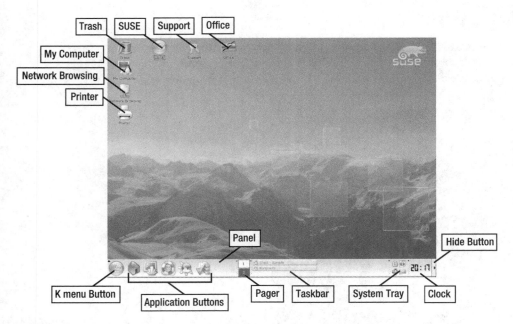

Figure 7-5. *You can run programs by clicking the appropriate desktop icon or shortcut.*

Table 7-1. *Desktop Icons and Program Shortcuts*

Name	Description
My Computer	As in Windows, this lets you access your computer's drives, such as the CD-ROM. If you are dual-booting Windows alongside SUSE Linux, you'll be able to access your Windows partition here.
Trash	This is SUSE's version of the Recycle Bin used in Windows. Any files you delete are stored here for a period of time. You can empty the Trash by right-clicking it and selecting the relevant option. You can drag-and-drop files or desktop icons here if you want to delete them.
SUSE	Clicking this icon brings up the welcome screen you saw when you first booted. Feel free to follow some of its links at your leisure.
Printer	This icon will open the print dialog box, showing which jobs are currently in the queue. You can also delete print jobs if you change your mind after sending them, as well as change various settings on your printer.
Support	This is a web link that takes you to the SUSE Linux Portal (you'll need to be connected to the Internet first, of course). Here, you can register to create a support account (you need to provide only a handful of personal details, such as your name and e-mail address) and browse the support documentation offered by SUSE, such as FAQs and up-to-date answers to common problems.

Table 7-1. *Desktop Icons and Program Shortcuts (Continued)*

Name	Description
Office	This will start the OpenOffice.org office suite. However, this is better done via the K menu.
Network Browsing	Click here to access other computers on your network (provided they're configured to share resources). This lets you tap into any Windows file or printer shares that are set up. Scanning is automatic, although it might take a minute or two, as is often the case with Windows networks.
Panel	This provides a home for the K menu button, application shortcut buttons, and much more. It can be temporarily hidden by clicking the Hide button at the far right.
K menu button	Clicking this button will make the K menu appear, just like clicking the Start button under Windows. Simply click a program in the list to start it. You can hover your mouse cursor over each menu item to expand the list.
Application buttons	These are shortcuts to the most popular programs, such as the web browser and e-mail client. Hover your mouse cursor over each to see a tooltip explaining what that program does. A single mouse click is enough to launch the program.
Pager	This lets you switch between virtual desktops, which are discussed in the next section.
Taskbar	This is where the icons for programs you have open appear. By clicking each entry, as with Windows, you can make each program window come to the front.
System tray	This is where various handy applet programs reside. Once again, hovering the mouse cursor over each will give you a clue as to what they do. There's a volume control, for example, and a tool that helps you learn more about your PC's hardware.
Clock	This shows the current time and can be set to show the date as well. It can also show the time in various cities around the world.
Hide button	This will cause the Panel to disappear off the right of the screen, creating more screen space. It will leave a small button in place which, when clicked, will cause the Panel to return.

At the top right of every program window, you'll see the familiar Close, Minimize, and Maximize buttons, albeit with a slightly different look and feel than you're used to. Clicking Close will end each program, as in Windows. Note the question mark icon. Clicking this and then clicking any part of the program window will bring up context-sensitive help messages. This is a good way to explore the functions of many programs.

You can shut down or reboot your PC by clicking the K menu icon, and then clicking Logout.

Working with Virtual Desktops

Windows works on the premise of everything taking place on top of a "desktop." When you start a new program, it is run on top of the desktop, effectively covering up the desktop. In fact, all programs are run on this desktop, so it can get a bit confusing when you have more than a couple of programs running at the same time. Which Microsoft Word window contains the document you're working on, rather than the one you've opened to take notes from? Where is that My Computer window you were using to copy files?

SUSE Linux overcomes this problem by having more than one desktop area. By using the Pager tool, you can switch between two virtual desktops. This is best explained by a demonstration.

1. Make sure that you're currently on the first virtual desktop (ensure that the 1 square is highlighted on the Pager) and start up the web browser by clicking its icon in the Panel.

2. Click 2 in the Pager. This will switch you to a clean desktop, where no programs are running—desktop number two.

3. Start up the file browser (by clicking the icon just to the right of the K menu icon), and you should see that the browser fills the screen.

4. Click the 1 in the Pager again. You should switch back to the desktop that is running the web browser.

5. Click the 2 square, and you'll switch back to the other desktop, which is running the file browser.

See how it works? In addition to running its own set of programs, each desktop can also have its own icons and wallpaper (although, by default, they just copy the main desktop).

Tip Right-clicking any of the program entries in the Taskbar will bring up a menu where you can move a program from one virtual desktop to another.

You can create more than two virtual desktops—as many as 16—if you want to organize your work this way. Right-click the Pager icon and select Configure Virtual Desktops. In the Configure - Multiple Desktops window, drag the slider until you have the number of desktops you want, as shown in Figure 7-6.

You can also rename each virtual desktop. This allows you to be even more organized. For example, you might reserve desktop 1 for running Internet programs and give it a name that indicates this, such as Net Programs. You might then use desktop 2 to run office programs, giving it an appropriate title; use desktop 3 for file browsing; and so on. If you then hover your mouse over the buttons on the Pager, you should see what each desktop does. Additionally, these titles will appear whenever you right-click and choose to send each program window to a different desktop.

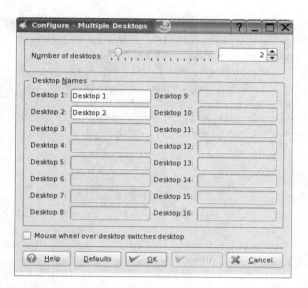

Figure 7-6. *Two virtual desktops are set up by default, but you can have as many as 16.*

Tip Putting your mouse over the Pager tool and scrolling the mouse wheel switches between the various virtual desktops instantly.

The Pager provides a way of organizing your programs and also reducing the clutter. Some people swear by it. Experienced SUSE Linux users may have in excess of ten virtual desktops, although clearly this will appeal only to organizational geniuses! Other users think it's a waste of time. It's certainly worth trying out to see if it suits the way you work.

Using the Mouse

As noted earlier, the mouse works mostly the same under SUSE Linux as it does under Windows: a left-click selects things, and a right-click usually brings up a context menu. Try right-clicking various items, such as icons on the desktop or even the desktop itself.

Tip Right-clicking a blank spot on the desktop and selecting the entry marked New on the menu lets you create shortcuts to applications, as well as create new folders and even new files.

You can use the mouse to drag icons on top of other icons. For example, you can drag a file onto a program icon in order to run it. You can also click and drag in certain areas to create an elastic band and, as in Windows, this lets you select more than one icon at once.

SUSE Linux also makes use of the third mouse button for *middle-clicking*. You might not think your mouse has one of these but, actually, if it's relatively modern, it probably does. Such mice have a scroll wheel between the buttons, and this can act as a third button when pressed. Try using it to click on the desktop. You'll see a second type of context menu appear, this time offering a shortcut to your virtual desktops and the programs running on them, as shown in Figure 7-7.

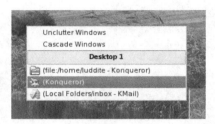

Figure 7-7. *If your mouse has a scroll wheel, you can use it as a third button in SUSE Linux to bring up an extra context menu.*

Middle-clicking has a number of other functions. Middle-click one of the shortcut icons on the Panel, for example, and you'll be able to move the icon, thereby repositioning it on the Panel.

Tip If your mouse doesn't have a scroll wheel, or if it has one that doesn't click, you can still middle-click. Simply press the left and right mouse buttons at the same time. This emulates a middle-click, although it takes a little skill to get right. Generally speaking, you need to press one button a fraction of a second before you press the other button.

You can resize windows using the mouse in much the same way as in Windows. Just click and drag the edges and corner of the windows. There is one difference, however. When a Window is maximized in SUSE Linux, it can subsequently be resized by clicking and dragging the handles at the edges. In other words, it isn't locked into position, as with Windows. Most maximized windows can also be subsequently moved by clicking and dragging the title bar, unlike with Windows. If you try this, you might also notice that the window you're dragging "snaps" back into place. Once a window nears the edge of the screen or, in some cases, another program window, it will jump the few pixels to fit flush against the edge. This makes lining up windows and organizing your desktop much easier.

CUTTING AND PASTING TEXT WITH THE MOUSE

SUSE Linux offers two separate methods of cutting and pasting text. The first method is identical to that under Windows. In a word processor or another application that deals with text, you can click and drag the mouse to highlight text, right-click anywhere on it, and then select to copy or cut the text. In many programs, you can also use the keyboard shortcuts of Ctrl+X to cut, Ctrl+C to copy, and Ctrl+V to paste.

However, there's a quicker method of copying and pasting. Simply click and drag to highlight some text, and then immediately use the middle mouse button to click where you want the text to appear. This will copy and paste the highlighted text automatically.

This special method of cutting and pasting bypasses the usual clipboard, so you should find that any text you've copied or cut previously should still be there. The downside is that it doesn't work across all applications within SUSE Linux, although it does work with the majority of them.

Using the System Tray

A number of handy programs are located in the system tray at the bottom-right side of the screen, as shown in Figure 7-8. They are designed to allow quick access to common functions, such as controlling the printer or altering the volume of your speakers. Table 7-2 describes each of the default programs in the system tray.

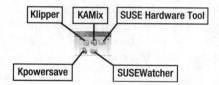

Figure 7-8. *The system tray provides quick access to common functions.*

Table 7-2. *Default System Tray Programs*

Name	Description
Klipper	Every time something is copied to the clipboard, Klipper remembers it. Clicking the icon presents a list of these remembered clipboard contents. Selecting one then puts it into the actual clipboard memory, and you can paste it wherever you like, such as in word processor documents. By right-clicking and selecting Configure Klipper, you can vary the number of items Klipper remembers by dragging the Clipboard History Size slider.
KAMix	This alters the master volume of the computer, providing a quick way of adjusting the sound level if you're watching videos or listening to MP3 music. Right-clicking the icon and selecting Show Mixer Window will present individual volume controls for all elements of the audio system, such as wave output and audio input.

Table 7-2. *Default System Tray Programs (Continued)*

Name	Description
Kpowersave	If you're running a notebook, Kpowersave shows whether you're plugged into the main supply. If you're running on a battery, when you hover the mouse over the icon, it shows the amount of juice left in your battery. Note that this icon should not appear if SUSE Linux is installed on a desktop PC, although it may show up on some computers (and can be safely ignored).
SUSEWatcher	This applet regularly checks when you're online to see if there are any updates available for SUSE Linux. A green gecko icon indicates that your system is up-to-date. If there are updates, it turns into a red exclamation mark. Clicking the exclamation mark launches the SUSE online update service, which is discussed in Chapter 9. To activate SUSEWatcher for the first time, ensure you're online, and then double-click it and choose the relevant option.
SUSE Hardware Tool	This lets you see at a glance your hardware configuration, and helps when it comes to installing new hardware such as USB devices. However, it's designed only to provide information and won't allow you to configure any hardware. This must be done via the YaST2 program, which is discussed in Chapter 8.

On the system tray, some programs will come and go at will, depending on what you're doing on your computer. For example, when you print, you'll find the printer icon appears when the page is being sent, but then disappears after the page has been printed.

Some programs on the K menu will also add their own entry to the system tray when they start up, to give you quick access to their functions. Some of these will be persistent and will stay around even after a reboot. Most of them can be removed by right-clicking their icon and selecting Exit. However, some won't offer this option. In that case, to get rid of them, you might need to start the program that placed the icon there, and then look through the configuration settings to find the relevant option.

Summary

This chapter covered booting into Linux for the first time and discovering the desktop. We've looked at starting programs, working with virtual desktops, using the mouse on the SUSE Linux desktop, and much more. You should have become confident in some basic SUSE Linux skills and ready to learn more!

In the next chapter, we'll look at getting your system up and running, focusing in particular on items of hardware that experience day-to-day use.

■ ■ ■

## CHAPTER 8

Getting Hardware Up and Running

SUSE Linux is extremely good at setting up PC hardware. In fact, it's considered by many to be among the best Linux distributions in this regard. Usually, SUSE Linux automatically recognizes the hardware and makes it available. You just need to activate the hardware, which is usually a simple process involving setting up various configuration details.

In this chapter, we'll look at all popular forms of hardware, and I'll describe how they can be made to work under SUSE Linux.

SUSE Linux Hardware Support

The age-old criticism that the Linux operating system lags behind Windows in terms of hardware support is long dead. The majority of add-ins—such as scanners, digital cameras, and modems—will work with SUSE Linux right away, with little if any configuration.

In fact, most underlying PC hardware is preconfigured during installation without your knowledge, and no further work is required. In addition, nearly all USB and FireWire devices you plug in after initial installation will be supported. In many cases, you can simply attach a device, configure a handful of options, and it will be ready to use.

There are a few hardware items that SUSE Linux doesn't support. Generally, it's a black or white situation: SUSE Linux either works with a piece of hardware or it doesn't. The types of hardware that SUSE Linux doesn't support tend to be esoteric devices that rely on specially written software provided by the hardware manufacturer. It's also sometimes the case that extremely cutting-edge hardware won't work with SUSE Linux.

■**Tip** Before you buy a new piece of hardware, why not ask the salesperson if it runs under Linux? You can only hope that the salesperson knows or can find out for you. Also, compatibility with Linux is often listed on the hardware box or at the manufacturer's web site (even if you sometimes need to search through the FAQ section of the site).

As soon as a new piece of hardware comes out, work is usually undertaken to ensure that Linux is made compatible with it. This can happen in the space of months, weeks, or even days. This is just one reason why you should regularly update your system online (as described in Chapter 9).

Unlike with Windows, where a driver can be installed for new pieces of hardware, support for various pieces of hardware is made available via the core SUSE Linux kernel files. It is possible to use specially written Linux drivers supplied by some hardware manufacturers, but these are a rarity (at least at the time of writing this book). For people using desktop Linux, these drivers are usually limited to hardware such as graphics cards, wireless network cards, and some DSL broadband modems. Generally speaking, you should avoid using such drivers unless you have no other choice.

■Note SUSE Linux usually identifies hardware in a technical way, rather than in the way humans do, which is by manufacturer and model. In other words, if you attach something like a USB CD-R/RW drive, it will recognize the drive hardware and attempt to make it work, rather than trying to find a driver for that specific model of hardware. The end result is that SUSE Linux can work with a lot of hardware it doesn't even know about, including many new products that come on the market.

WHAT HARDWARE WORKS?

SUSE Linux has a web site that contains a database detailing which pieces of hardware are guaranteed to work under its distribution of Linux. You can find this at http://hardwaredb.suse.de/?LANG=en_UK. This is a conservative list and should not be considered comprehensive. One reason for this is that, despite SUSE's best efforts, it cannot test every single piece of hardware.

Experience shows that many pieces of hardware not on the list work very well under SUSE Linux. This happens because modern hardware is very generic in nature. For example, if you purchase a new graphics card, it will most likely be based on one of only three or four hardware reference designs. These designs vary very little between manufacturers, despite what their marketing departments claim! The end result is that the task facing the programmers behind Linux is to make the operating system work with the three or four basic designs. Once this is achieved, Linux will probably be compatible with every graphics card make and model that uses those designs.

The same is true of many types of hardware, such as wireless network cards. Of the two or three types of technologies typically used in wireless cards, SUSE can work with at least one or two. Therefore, SUSE Linux has a good chance of working with a lot of wireless cards that aren't listed within the SUSE Linux hardware database.

In SUSE Linux, you configure hardware using YaST2. You might remember this software from when you installed SUSE Linux (in Part Two of this book). YaST2 is very powerful and lets you configure just about any aspect of your hardware and software setup. To start YaST2, select K menu ➤ Control Center, and then click the YaST2 Modules icon on the left side of the program window. Whenever you attempt to make a change to your hardware settings, you'll be asked to enter your administrator password. This is the root password you entered during installation.

■**Caution** When working as administrator (root) within YaST2, you should be very careful, because there are no safeguards built in and the potential for accidental damage is high. Bear in mind, however, that entering the administrator password in YaST2 doesn't mean that you have root privileges when undertaking any tasks elsewhere on your system. Your superpowers are limited to YaST2.

Getting Online

Getting online is vital in our modern Internet age, and SUSE Linux caters to all the standard ways of doing so. Linux was built from the ground up to be an online operating system and is based on Unix, which pioneered the concept of networking computers together to share data back in the 1970s. However, none of this is to say that getting online with SUSE Linux is difficult! In fact, it's very easy.

If you use a modem to dial up to the Internet over a phone line, you can use KInternet. It's possible to get online using DSL and cable modems, and if you connect to a local or wide area network, you'll find support for most Ethernet cards is built in. There's also good support for wireless LAN cards, so you can connect to Wi-Fi networks.

■**Note** Linux actually runs around 60% of the computers that make the Internet work! Whenever you visit a web site, there's a strong chance that it'll be run using Linux. As your Linux skills increase, you'll eventually get to a stage where you, too, can run your own Internet servers. It sounds difficult, but can be quite easy.

SUSE Linux is very good at autodetecting hardware and configuring the best settings for you. Before attempting to configure your hardware settings to get online, you should check to make sure you aren't already up and running. Open the web browser and attempt to browse to your favorite web site. If that doesn't work, try another just to be absolutely sure. If you have no luck, then you'll need to do some manual configuration.

Using an Ethernet Card

There are a variety of situations where you might go online via an Ethernet card. If you have DSL or cable broadband at your home or workplace, for example, you might use a DSL modem with a router built in. Your Ethernet card will then connect to this, and all you need to worry about on your PC is getting your Ethernet card up and running under SUSE Linux, which is usually a simple task.

■**Note** Using a DSL or cable modem router is the preferred way of going online via broadband. Many routers nowadays offer Wi-Fi network connections, too. However, some people use USB-based DSL modems, which connect to and are operated by your PC. We'll discuss these in the "Setting Up a DSL Modem" section later in this chapter.

If you're running SUSE Linux on a PC in an office environment, it's highly likely that you will connect to the local area network using an Ethernet card. This lets your computer communicate with other computers, as well as printers. In some offices in which an Internet connection is provided, you'll also be able to go online.

Configuring a Network Card

SUSE Linux recognizes and supports very nearly every type of network card. To configure yours, follow these steps:

1. Select K menu ➤ Control Center, click the YaST2 Modules icon on the left, click Network Devices, and then click Network Card.

2. You'll be told you cannot proceed any further without entering Administrator mode, so click the button at the bottom and type in your root password when prompted, as shown in Figure 8-1.

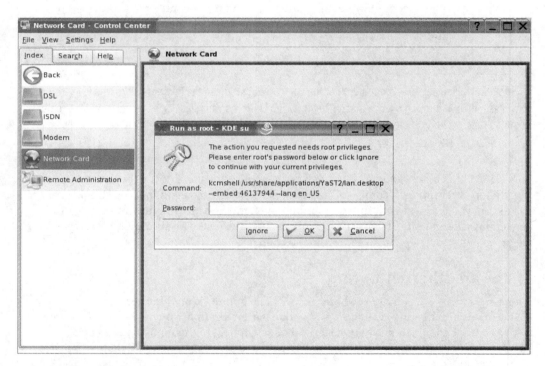

Figure 8-1. *To configure your system using YaST2, you'll need to click the Administrator Mode button and type in your root password.*

3. The program window will be split into two halves. At the top, you should see your network card. It might be identified by its make and model, or alternatively it might just be called eth0. The bottom half of the window should report that no card is currently set up. Click the Configure button.

4. The path you take from here depends on the settings needed for your particular network. In the case of a DSL or cable broadband router, the default settings of DHCP should work fine, so simply click the Next button to move through the configuration screens without changing any settings. The majority of office networks will work in a similar way, so the same applies: further configuration shouldn't be necessary and the default choices should work fine.

5. Click the Finish button when it appears.

You should find yourself online. If not, you may need to configure your static IP address, as described in the next section.

Configuring a Static IP Address

On some networks, you might have been assigned an IP address that you must enter manually, along with the gateway address and your DNS addresses. This is referred to as using a static IP address. You should speak to your system administrator or technical support person to find out these settings.

Note The settings you will get from your system administrator will usually be in the form of a series of four numbers separated by dots, something like 192.168.10.233. You should ask the administrator for your IP address, DNS server addresses (there are usually two or three of these), your subnet mask, and the router address (sometimes referred to as the *gateway address*).

Once you know your settings, after completing the first three steps outlined in the previous section, proceed as follows:

1. Click the Static Address Setup button, and then type your IP address into the relevant field. Enter your subnet mask into the relevant field, too.

2. Click the Host Name and Name Server button. Don't worry about entering a host name and domain name in the fields, unless you were specifically told to do so by your administrator. The defaults should be fine. (These will identify you to other machines on the Internet, so you could type something in that specifically identifies your PC, although this isn't mandatory.) Enter the two DNS numbers you were given into the Name Server 1 and Name Server 2 fields, respectively, as shown in Figure 8-2. Then click the Next button.

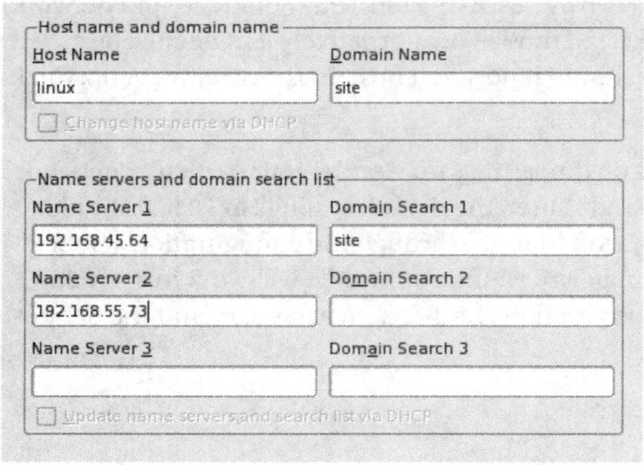

Figure 8-2. *Enter your DNS server addresses into the relevant fields. They should take the form of two IP addresses (numbers separated by dots).*

3. Click Routing. Enter the router address (this is sometimes referred to as the *gateway address*). Then click the Next button.

4. Assuming that your network is otherwise standard, click Next again, and then click Finish.

You should now be online. However, if your system administrator mentioned that a proxy must also be configured, follow the instructions in the "Working with a Proxy Server" section later in this chapter.

Joining a Wireless Network

It's more common for notebooks and handheld computers to use wireless networking, but some desktop computers also do, even though these usually stay in one place. You can probably tell if your computer has wireless capabilities because there will be a small, black antenna somewhere (usually on the back of desktop PCs), a little like the aerials found on very old mobile phones.

Notebooks and PDAs typically use wireless network PCMCIA cards that will have a square antenna, as shown in Figure 8-3, although improving technology means that antennas are starting to disappear.

Figure 8-3. *Most wireless cards rely on an aerial of some kind.*

Configuring a Wi-Fi Card

Configuring a wireless network card is pretty much identical to configuring a standard Ethernet card, and you can follow the instructions for configuring a network card in the previous section, Be aware that if your computer also has a standard Ethernet adapter in addition to Wi-Fi capabilities, you'll need to ensure you select the Wi-Fi card when initially choosing an adapter to configure.

You should set up the wireless network card to use either DHCP (the default SUSE Linux settings) or a static IP address (which means you need to enter the details manually). As explained in the previous section, you'll need to speak to your network administrator to find out which settings you should use.

Note In most instances, wireless network cards are configured with the Dynamic Host Control Protocol (DHCP), so that they grab a network address automatically. The nature of a wireless network, where many people might join or leave the network at will, means that using static IP addresses is a bad idea.

Configuring a Network to Use Wireless Encryption Protocol (WEP)

Some wireless networks use the Wireless Encryption Protocol (WEP). This protects the data being transmitted on the network so it cannot be stolen by hackers with special equipment. It also means that no one can join the network unless they know the encryption key, which is basically an access code.

Your encryption key normally takes the form of a string of letters and numbers, which you should get from your system administrator. Alternatively, you administrator may give you a *passphrase*, which might be a sentence in English; you enter that as a kind of long password.

You might also ask the administrator to give you the name of the access point you should connect to, although SUSE Linux is capable of detecting any nearby access points and connecting automatically.

To configure WEP, follow the procedure to configure the Wi-Fi card. However, before clicking the final Finish button, follow these steps:

1. Click the Advanced button, click Hardware Settings, and then click the Wireless Settings button.

2. In most cases, the only field you'll need to fill in here is the Encryption Key, which is the access code you got from your administrator, as shown in Figure 8-4. The other fields on the same screen can be left blank.

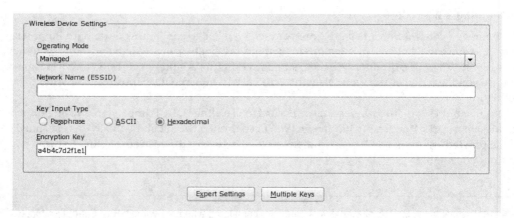

Figure 8-4. *Ask your system administrator for an encryption key if your Wi-Fi network uses WEP protection.*

3. If your system administrator gave you the name of a specific access point (or *hub*) that you should connect to, click the Expert Settings button, and then type it into the Access Point field. Don't worry about filling in the other fields. The default settings should work fine.

4. Click Next, and then click Finish. You should find your network card is configured.

■**Tip** On my test notebook, I found that the wireless connection wouldn't work after initial configuration unless the computer was rebooted. On a different occasion, I found that simply ejecting and then reinserting the wireless PCMCIA card was enough to make it work after it stalled.

WHICH WI-FI CARD?

As this book was being written, SUSE Linux support for particular types of Wi-Fi network cards was very strong. Those based on the following types of wireless chipsets will probably be supported:

- PRISM2/2.5/3

- Lucent Wavelan/Orinoco

- Aironet PC4500/4800

- Cisco 340

So how do you know if a wireless card you're about to buy is based on any of these chipsets and is therefore supported under SUSE Linux? The best way to find out is to phone the manufacturer and ask, or you might find it mentioned in the manual or on the manufacturer's web site as part of the technical specifications. You can also try visiting http://www.hpl.hp.com/personal/Jean_Tourrilhes/Linux/Wireless.html, although this site is primarily designed for those with a high degree of knowledge of how Linux works. Alternatively, you might try searching online. If you type the make and model of your card into a search engine and add *linux* to the search string, you should find you get a lot of results showing the success (or otherwise) that people have had trying to get that particular card to work under Linux. Often, these tips can prove invaluable.

Setting Up Dial-Up Internet Access Using a Modem

You might have heard rumors that Linux cannot work with certain types of PCI cards and PCMCIA-based modems, so called Winmodems. This is partially true. Currently, some Winmodems simply won't work under SUSE Linux, or they will work only with significant extra configuration. However, the majority of other types of non-Winmodem internal modems should work fine, and all external modems will function without any problems.

Configuring Your Dial-Up Modem

To configure your modem, follow these steps:

1. Select K menu ➤ Control Center, click the YaST2 Modules icon on the left, click Network Devices, and then click Modem.

2. Enter your root password when prompted.

3. Select your modem from the list, and then click the Configure button.

Note If you have an external modem that connects via a serial cable to your PC, your might find it isn't automatically detected. In this case, click the Configure button, and then, in the Modem Device drop-down list, select /dev/ttyS0. If you find your modem isn't working after following the configuration steps outlined here, return to this stage and choose /dev/ttyS1 from the list.

---

4. Once you click Configure, there isn't actually much information to be entered on the following screens; in most cases, you can simply click Next. However, in the Dial Prefix field, you can enter any number combination your phone company might use to temporarily turn off features like call waiting, which can throw you offline while you're connected to the Internet. You should also remove the tick from the Detect Dial Tone box if your line uses a pulsed dialing tone to inform you of answering machine messages or call diversion.

5. After this, you'll be asked to set the country in which you're based. This will bring up a list of Internet service providers (ISPs) on the right side of the screen. The list is very comprehensive, especially for the USA, as you can see in Figure 8-5.

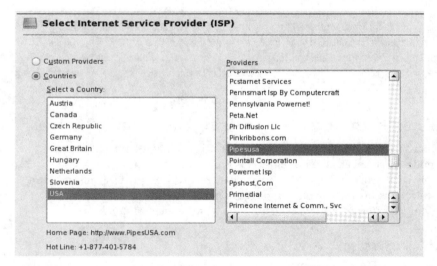

Figure 8-5. *SUSE Linux contains details of many ISPs around the world.*

6. Once you select an ISP, the phone number details will be filled in automatically on the following configuration screens. Many ISPs change their dial-up numbers on a regular basis. Alternatively, you might be using an unmetered ISP deal that means you need to dial a special, toll-free phone number. Because of these factors, I advise you not to use the suggested ISP settings offered by SUSE, but to click the Custom Providers button instead. This will let you enter a phone number of your choice.

7. Click Next, and you'll be prompted to enter your dial-up details. These are what usually appear in the dial-up networking dialog box under Windows. You'll need to type in the access phone number, your username, and your password. The last two are the username and password given to you by your ISP when you signed up, *not* your SUSE Linux username and password. Additionally you should enter the name of the ISP into the Provider Name field (this is merely so you can identify it later; it isn't used by SUSE Linux for any particular purpose).

■**Tip** If you don't know what the dial-up number is, or have forgotten your username and password, you can call your ISP's tech support line to find out. Be careful *not* to mention that you're setting up a SUSE Linux system, however. If you do, you'll probably receive a stony response, because most ISPs support only Windows and Mac operating systems! Just pretend that you're setting up a Windows system and say that you want the details for future reference.

---

8. The next screen can be largely ignored, although you might choose to put a tick in the Active Firewall box if you want to be totally secure (setting up the firewall is covered in Chapter 9).

9. Click Finish to save all your settings. You'll be asked if you want to configure your e-mail. I'll explain how to do this in the "Setting Up E-Mail and Instant Messaging" section later in this chapter, so click No for now.

Going Online with KInternet

After finishing configuration, you might notice a new icon in the bottom-right area of your system tray. It looks like a telephone plug. This is the KInternet applet that lets you go online. From now on, it will always appear in the system tray, even after you reboot.

To go online, all you need to do is click the KInternet icon. Alternatively, you can right-click it and select Dial-in, as shown in Figure 8-6. This will start the dial-up process automatically (the icon will change accordingly to show it's busy, and you should hear your modem dialing, as with Windows). To go offline, right-click the icon and select Hang Up.

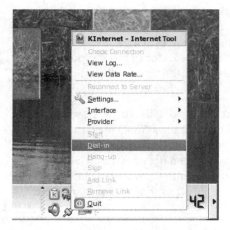

Figure 8-6. *To go online, simply click the KInternet icon or right-click it and select Dial-in.*

Tip If you like to monitor the speed at which you're connected, right-click the KInternet icon and select View Data Rate. This will show a graph of incoming and outgoing connection speeds.

THE PROBLEMS WITH WINMODEMS

In the late 1990s, a new type of modem was introduced to consumers. This was designed to be very inexpensive. Cost savings were made by reducing the hardware on the modem's circuit board and transferring the majority of the calculations necessary to decode data onto the PC's processor. This required a special type of hardware driver and, because much of the modem's work was effectively shifted to Windows, these modems were informally dubbed *Winmodems*.

Support for Winmodems under SUSE Linux is patchy, with some models working and some not. Some work partially, which is to say they're unreliable.

Part of the trouble stems from the fact that SUSE Linux uses version 2.6 of the Linux kernel, for which Winmodem support is not as strong as it was in the older 2.4 version (as this book went to press). This has the rather odd result that older versions of SUSE Linux have *better* support for Winmodems than the latest version.

If you find your dial-up modem isn't supported under SUSE Linux, the simplest solution is to buy an external model that plugs into your PC's serial port (make sure you buy a serial port model, rather than one that works over USB). These can be bought very cheaply from most computer hardware stores. Virtually every modem that connects to your PC via the serial port will work fine under SUSE Linux.

If you have a notebook with a Winmodem PCMCIA card, the same applies, and an external modem will work fine. If this proves too bulky, you might consider buying a non-Winmodem PCMCIA card. You can check the SUSE hardware compatibility database (hardwaredb.suse.de/?LANG=en_UK) to see which PCMCIA cards are supported.

Setting Up a DSL Modem

DSL is one of the most popular ways of getting broadband Internet in a home or small office environment. It usually works over phone lines and gets the most out of standard phone wires. The broadband signal is sent at a very high frequency compared to standard voice calls and is therefore largely inaudible to the human ear.

You need a special modem to use DSL broadband. These special modems usually connect via USB to your PC, and then plug directly into the phone socket.

■Tip If you access broadband using a DSL modem that connects to your PC via USB, I strongly advise you to consider upgrading to a dedicated DSL router. This will take care of the DSL connection for you, and all you need to do is connect to it via an Ethernet network. In fact, an increasing number of DSL routers offer Wi-Fi connections, making cables unnecessary. Another advantage of a DSL router is that the connection can be effortlessly shared among two or more PCs, and the router also lets these PCs create a small network among themselves, allowing file and printer sharing.

SUSE Linux is just starting to support DSL modems. As this book was being written, a quick browse of the supported hardware list (http://hardwaredb.suse.de/?LANG=en_UK) showed that only one modem is guaranteed to work by default: Telekom AG's Teledat 300 LAN.

Support for other DSL modems is on the brink of becoming mainstream, but it is still undergoing testing. By the time you read this, however, the project will almost certainly be much more advanced. You can find more information and download the driver files by visiting the following site: http://eciadsl.flashtux.org/index.php?lang=en.

■Tip Support for virtually all DSL modems will undoubtedly be added to SUSE Linux in the future by SUSE itself. To take advantage of this, ensure that you regularly perform online updates. You'll find instructions on how to do this in Chapter 9.

Downloading a DSL Modem Driver

It's possible to get other DSL modems to work by following a few steps. In most cases, you need to download a driver file and install it on your PC. Note that to get the driver for your DSL modem, you'll need to go online, so you might need to use a standard dial-up modem to get this file.

Possibly the most popular type of DSL modem is the Alcatel SpeedTouch. Here are the steps for installing the driver for a SpeedTouch modem:

1. Open the Konqueror web browser by selecting K menu ➤ Internet ➤ Web Browser ➤ Konqueror. Then type the following into the address bar:

   http://download.ethomson.com/download/speedmgmt.tar.gz

2. Once this file has downloaded, you'll see a list of files. Right-click the top entry, mgmt, and select Extract. Next to the Extract To box will be an icon. Clicking this will let you browse your hard disk. The default choice will be /home/*yourusername*/Documents. This is a good place to save the file, so click OK. Then click OK in the Extract dialog box.

3. Insert your SUSE Linux installation DVD in your DVD drive.

4. Open a command-line console by selecting K menu ➤ System ➤ Terminal ➤ Konsole. (Konsole, which is discussed in Chapter 14, lets you run a command-line shell on the desktop; in other words, it opens a shell window, where you can issue commands directly to SUSE Linux.)

5. Click to put the cursor in the Konsole window and type the following series of commands in turn, making sure to use uppercase and lowercase letters exactly as shown. These instructions will install a few system tools that help install and configure software. Note that these commands will cause output to appear within the Konsole window, which you can ignore. Figure 8-7 shows the process.

```
su
[enter your root password]
mount /media/dvd
rpm -U /media/dvd/i586/make-3* /media/dvd/i586/gcc-3*  /media/dvd/glibc-
devel*
cd Documents/mgmt/
make
make install
exit
exit
```

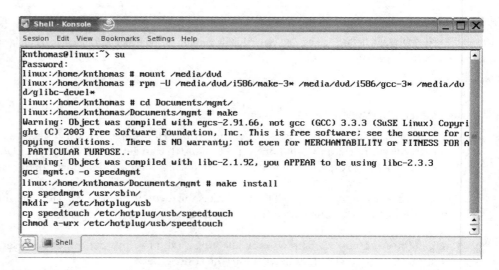

Figure 8-7. *Getting SpeedTouch DSL modems to work under SUSE Linux requires some additional configuration.*

Configuring Your DSL Modem

After you've installed the driver, you must use YaST2 to configure the modem, as follows:

1. Select K menu ➤ Control Center, click the YaST2 Modules icon on the left, click Network Devices, and then click DSL.

2. You might be asked if T-Online is your ISP. If it isn't, click No.

3. Follow the wizard, entering your username, password (if you were given one), and VPI/ VCI numbers. All this information should be provided in documentation given to you by your ISP. If not, phone its technical support line. Once again, the username and password are those supplied by your ISP, *not* your SUSE Linux username and password.

4. Select PPP over ATM in the relevant box.

5. Finish the wizard, and your modem should be set up.

Working with a Proxy Server

Some networks in offices require that you use a proxy server. A *proxy* is a server computer that does two things. First, it provides additional security by providing a single portal to all web pages and certain other types of Internet data. Second, it helps speed up Internet access by storing frequently accessed pages. This means that if ten people request the same web page, there's no need to get the same ten pieces of data from the Internet. The proxy computer can send them its own copies. For various reasons, proxies are becoming less popular nowadays, but larger organizations might still use them.

You'll need to speak to your system administrator to see if your office uses a proxy. If it does, your administrator will most likely give you an address, which may take the form of a web address or an IP address. Once you have this information, follow these steps to configure the proxy:

1. Select K menu ➤ Control Center, click the YaST2 Modules icon on the left, click Network Services, and then click Proxy.

2. Click the Administrator Mode button and enter your root password.

3. Make sure there's a tick in the Enable Proxy box. Then type the address your system administrator gave you into the HTTP Proxy field. Unless you were specifically given an FTP proxy address, that field can be left in its default state, as can the other fields.

4. Click Next, and the settings will be saved. Note that some programs use their own proxy server settings. However, most of the SUSE Linux built-in applications should work fine.

■**Tip** Some ISPs run proxy servers, too. However, unlike proxies in offices, it's up to you whether you choose to use them or not. You might find using a proxy speeds up your connection, especially when you access popular sites, so it's worth trying out. To find out if your ISP offers a proxy, visit its technical support web pages or phone its technical support line.

Setting Up E-Mail and Instant Messaging

Being online is all about staying in touch, and SUSE Linux is no slouch in this regard. SUSE Linux offers a full-featured e-mail program, called Kmail, as well as an instant messaging client called Kopete. Unlike similar instant messaging clients, Kopete supports the variety of Internet chat protocols, such as ICQ, MSN, Yahoo, AIM, and IRC. This means you can chat with all your friends using this one program. Kmail is able to work with both IMAP and the popular POP3 mail servers offered by ISPs or used within corporate environments, and it can send mail using SMTP or even from your own machine using your own SMTP server.

Note It's very likely that your e-mail will come via a POP3 server. This is the preferred way of receiving e-mail across the Internet for most ISPs and companies. However, if you work in an office, you might use Microsoft Exchange mail or Lotus Notes mail. Lotus Notes isn't supported in Kmail, but you can ask your system administrator to alter your account so you have POP3 access. Microsoft Exchange Server isn't supported in Kmail. Consider using the Ximian Evolution e-mail client instead, which is also supplied on the SUSE Linux installation DVD. For more details, see `www.novell.com/linux/ximian.html`. For details on how to install additional software, see Chapter 29.

Configuring Your E-Mail

Before starting your e-mail set up, you'll need your e-mail username and password, and the address of your sending and receiving e-mail server (a URL or an IP address). You can get these from your ISP or system administrator.

To set up your e-mail in SUSE Linux, follow these steps:

1. Start Kmail by clicking its icon (the orange E with an envelope leaning against it) on the system tray. Once the program has started, select Settings ➤ Configure Kmail.

2. Make sure the Identities icon is highlighted on the left side of the screen. There's no need to set up a new account, because Kmail attempts to do so automatically based on your login settings, so click Modify instead.

3. On the General tab, type your name in the Your Name field, as shown in Figure 8-8. This is what will appear on the e-mail you send to others. You can leave the Organization field blank, but you must fill in the Email Address field with the address from which you send and receive mail.

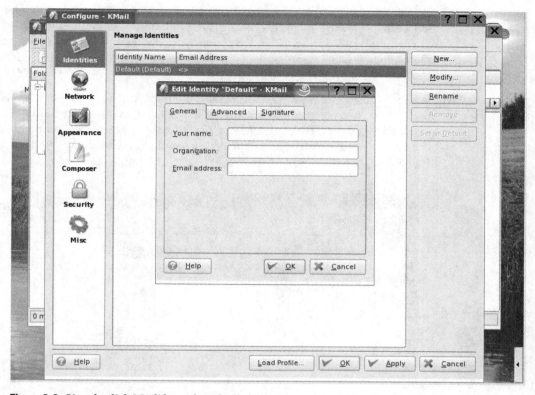

Figure 8-8. *Simply click Modify to alter the default account that Kmail sets up for you.*

4. You can ignore the Advanced and Signature tabs if you wish, but you might want to take a look at them. There's no need to fill in the Reply To Address field on that tab. However, you might want to change the Dictionary setting so that it reflects your locality (if you're in the UK you might want to choose English [British], for example). The Signature tab lets you add an e-mail signature (or *sig*) to the bottom of each message automatically.

5. Click OK, and then click the Network icon on the left side of the Configure - Kmail window.

6. Select the Sending tab, and then click Add. You'll be asked to choose a transport. If you're in an office or using an ISP, click SMTP.

■**Note** It's possible to choose Sendmail as your transport. This will send mail using the Mail Transport Agent (MTA) that is built into SUSE Linux. This has the advantage that you would still be able to send mail if your ISP or company's mail server stopped working temporarily. The problem is that many mail servers around the world refuse to accept mail from anything other than "genuine" mail servers (those registered via the DNS system). This is to prevent spam. All things considered, it's better to use the SMTP address supplied by your ISP or system administrator.

---

7. Select the General tab, and then enter a name for the server. This is just for your reference later, so it can be anything you wish. Beneath this, enter the address of the SMTP server in the Host field. (You'll need to contact your ISP or system administrator for this information.) Usually, it's something like `smtp.myisp.com`, or it may be an IP address in the format of four numbers separated by dots.

8. Click the Security tab. Here, you can set the authentication that your SMTP server supports, as shown in Figure 8-9. Not many SMTP servers offer this feature, but you can quickly check by clicking the Check What the Server Supports button. Authentication brings added security, and if you're choosing a new e-mail service, you should look into this feature. Click OK.

Figure 8-9. *You can check what authentication types (if any) your SMTP server supports.*

9. Click the Receiving tab. Click the Add button and select the type of mail account you want to add. This will very likely be POP3, especially if you go online using an ISP. I assume this to be the case in the following instructions. Click OK.

10. Once again, you'll need to enter a name for future reference. This can be anything you choose. The Login and Password fields are usually the same as your login username and password that you use to go online if you're using an ISP, although they might vary depending on the nature of your service package. In the Host field, type in the address of the server, which will most likely take the format of `mail.myisp.com`. If you're unsure about any of this information, call the technical support line of your e-mail provider or ISP. If you're in an office, you should speak to your system administrator.

11. Put a tick in the Store POP Password in Configuration File check box. This is insecure in that your e-mail password might be accessible to anyone who has access to the PC (although not to other users of your system, aside from the root user account, which has access to all files on the system). The benefit of storing the password in the configuration file is that you won't be asked for it each time you check your mail. If you consider storing the password on the hard disk to be a security risk, remove the tick. However, you will be pestered for the password each time your mail is checked. The other fields can be left blank unless you have particular requirements.

Note Anyone with physical access to a SUSE Linux-based PC can steal data very easily. All they need to do is use a rescue disk, identical to those made during installation. Booting with this disk will then give the user root access to every file on the system, even those root doesn't own. This is why some people opt to type in the password each time, rather than store it in a configuration file.

---

12. Click the Extras tab to see a host of security settings. These are not commonly used, but you might want to speak to your ISP's tech support line or your system administrator to see if you should set them.

13. Click OK after this, and you should find yourself able to send and receive mail!

In most regards, Kmail works like every Windows-based e-mail client. To create a new e-mail message, click the New icon on the Kmail toolbar. To read new e-mail messages, simply double-click them in the list.

Setting Up Instant Messaging

Instant messaging is a way of chatting with other people in real-time. It's as if you were having a phone conversation, but you're typing instead of speaking. You can talk to one other person or a whole group of people, and sometimes share files with them. Instant messaging is one of the technologies that has fostered the idea of online communities.

The instant messaging program under SUSE Linux, Kopete, is a little different from those you might have used under Windows. It offers the same functions and works in an almost identical way, but also supports virtually all the popular chat standards, such as ICQ, MSN (Hotmail/Passport), and AOL Instant Messenger (AIM). One negative aspect is that it doesn't let you register for a new account, unlike the Windows equivalents, although it does provide links to web sites where you can do so. If you've ever used instant messaging programs under Windows, you'll most likely already have an account.

You can have as many accounts as you wish. Each will be based around a login or username for whichever chat service you choose from a list. In most cases, if you're familiar with the Windows equivalents, everything should be self-explanatory. Usually, all you need to do to set up an account in Kopete is enter your username and your password.

Configuring the Chat Protocol

As an example of how to set up a chat protocol in Kopete, we'll walk through the steps for using the popular ICQ network. This will give you a good idea of how the program works.

1. Select K menu ➤ Internet ➤ Chat to start Kopete.

2. As soon as it starts, you'll be taken to the Configure - Kopete screen, as shown in Figure 8-10. Click New to set up a new account. Then click Next.

Figure 8-10. *Kopete supports the majority of instant messaging protocols.*

3. You should see a list of chat services. Click ICQ, and then click Next.

4. In the ICQ UIN field, enter your ICQ number (not your username). Enter your password in the field below.

5. If you click the Connection tab, you can have Kopete connect automatically to this account when SUSE Linux starts up. If you're a chat addict, you may want to enable this option.

6. When you're finished, click Next, and then click Finish.

7. Click OK to close the Configuration window and return to the main program window.

Adding Contacts

The next task is to add contact details of your chat buddies. However, you must first tell the program to go online so that these can be checked against the ICQ databases. We'll step through adding an ICQ contact.

1. Select File ➤ Connection ➤ Connect All.

2. Select File ➤ Add Contact. This will start another wizard.

3. You'll notice there's a tick in the box marked Use KDE Address Book for This Contact. This is an attempt to keep all the details of your contacts in one place, and you will be able to add ICQ numbers to addresses created and stored automatically by programs like Kmail. It's up to you whether you use this function, but there's no harm in giving it a try. Click Next.

4. You'll see a list of e-mail addresses you might have sent mail to in Kmail. If you're just setting up your system after a fresh installation of SUSE Linux, this will be empty.

5. Click Create New Entry. You'll be asked to give the entry a name. This is for your benefit, so make it something you'll understand later on (such as Dad, or Tim in New York). Keep in mind that this will be the entry used in the KDE address book, so it will be how the contact is referred to in Kmail, too.

6. Select the entry you've just made from the list of contacts by clicking it and selecting Next.

7. Search for your contact. You can do this by using his name or address, or by using his ICQ number. Type in part of his name, address, or nickname, and then click the Search button. Alternatively, you can click the UIN tab and enter his ICQ number.

Chatting is then a matter of going online and waiting for your contacts to come online, too.

Adding a Printer

Most people have a printer nowadays, and SUSE Linux supports a wide variety of models—everything from laser printers to color inkjet models, and even some of the very old dot-matrix printers.

If you work in an office environment, you'll probably be expected to share a printer with others. Sharing a printer is usually achieved by connecting a printer directly to the network. The printer itself has special built-in hardware to allow this to happen. Alternatively, the printer might be plugged into a Windows computer, such as a Windows NT, 2000, or XP server (or even simply someone's desktop PC), and shared so that other users can access it. SUSE Linux will work with network printers of both types.

SUSE Linux also provides several very powerful tools for managing print queues, both on your own machine and those on a network printer. In most cases, this software will start automatically when you print from an application, and you'll see a printer icon appear in the system tray. Double-clicking this should give you access to the various configuration options.

Configuring a Printer

As with other hardware configuration tasks, the first thing to do in setting up a printer is to start YaST2.

1. Select K menu ➤ Control Center, the YaST2 Modules icon on the left, click the icon marked Hardware, and then click the Printer icon.

2. You'll need to switch to Administrator mode to set up the printer, so click the button at the bottom and type in your root password.

3. Your printer should be identified at the top of the screen. Simply click it, and then click the Configure button. If your printer isn't shown, click the Restart Detection button.

4. Unless you have any special requirements (which is unlikely), you can breeze through the ensuing screens by clicking the Next button. SUSE Linux will guess the correct make and model of your printer, as shown in Figure 8-11, although you should check to make sure it detected this correctly.

5. When you arrive at the Edit Configuration screen, you can test your settings by clicking the Test button. This will give you a choice of test pages to print. To give your printer a thorough test, click the one that will print both text and a photo (although obviously, this will consume more ink than simply printing a page of text).

6. When the page has finished printing, click the Printout Finished button in the dialog box that appears.

7. Click OK, and then click Finish in the main program window to complete the installation of the printer.

Printing from any application is now exactly the same as it is under Windows. You can either click the Printer icon on the program's toolbar, if it has one, or select File ➤ Print.

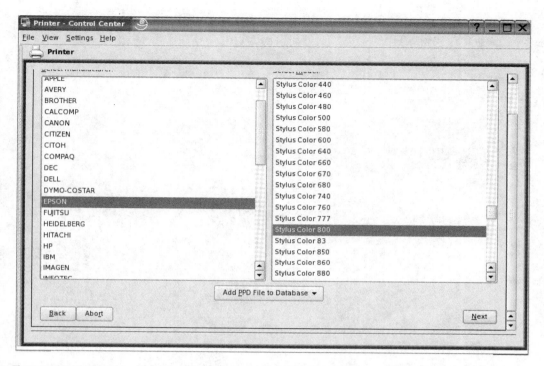

Figure 8-11. *YaST2 should select your printer model automatically, but check to make sure.*

■**Tip** When you print something, a printer icon will appear in the system tray at the bottom-right side of the screen. Double-clicking the icon will open the printer control program, where you can see the progress of your print jobs and even cancel them if you wish.

Adding a Network Printer

The network printer is easiest to set up under SUSE Linux and is the most common method of sharing a printer over a network. As usual, a step-by-step interface will guide you through adding the printer.

To set up a dedicated network printer, follow these steps:

1. Select K menu ➤ Control Center, click the Peripherals icon, and then click Printers. (You don't use YaST2 for this setup.) You'll see that a number of printer-like devices are seemingly already set up, but you can ignore these; they're there for technical reasons and help the overall printing system operate.

2. Click the Add button on the topmost toolbar. Then click Add Printer/Class in the menu that appears, as shown in Figure 8-12.

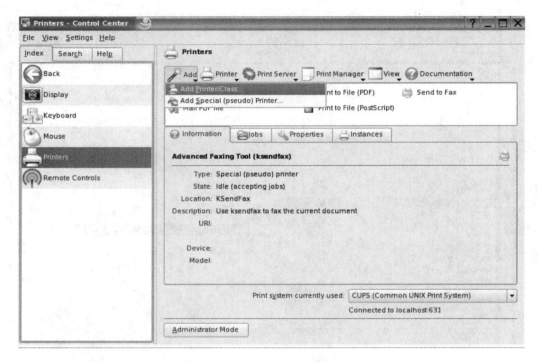

Figure 8-12. *Adding a network printer is easy: just click Add Printer/Class.*

3. You'll need to know what type of network technology is in use to provide the printer service. To find out, simply take a look at it. If a network cable connects straight to it and it's not directly attached to a PC, you can probably use the Network Printer (TCP) option. If the printer is plugged into a computer via a parallel or USB cable, you should skip to the next section of this chapter, Printing to a Windows Share. Otherwise, click Next.

4. Enter the IP address of the printer (get this information from your system administrator) in the Printer Address field. Then click Scan. This will probe the printer to find out its technical details, such as its printer port. If the scan produces no results, try entering 9100 in the Port field; this is a common setting, which will probably work.

5. If you don't know the IP address of the printer, you can scan the local network to discover any in your locality. Just leave the Printer Address field empty and click the Scan button. The software will then use your own IP address as a starting point and attempt to find printers on your subnet. When the scan has finished, select your printer from the list (you might find others turn up on the list, which might be quite long), and then click Next.

6. Enter the make and model of the printer. Again, this information is easily discovered— just take a look at the printer. If the printer is in an inaccessible location, open your web browser and type its IP address into address bar. Network printers frequently have web interfaces that let you administer them. This will no doubt be password-protected, but with any luck, the printer make and model should be identified on the opening screen, as shown in the example in Figure 8-13. Back in YaST2, click Next.

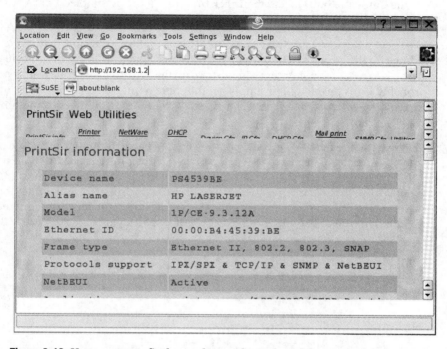

Figure 8-13. *You can try to find out what make and model a network printer is by connecting to it using your web browser.*

7. Finish the wizard, and your network printer should be set up.

Printing to a Windows Share

Connecting to a Windows-connected printer is a little more involved than other configuration tasks. In fact, it has been known to drive grown men to tears, because it's clouded in obtuse terminology and frequently doesn't work.

If at all possible, you should ask your system administrator to set up a true network printer, with a dedicated print server, rather than using a Windows share. Print server hardware is very inexpensive and usually takes the form of a small box that attaches to the USB or parallel port of the printer, allowing it to connect directly to the network. Alternatively, you might be able to buy a dedicated add-on for your printer to give it print server functionality.

If you have no other choice than to use a Windows share, you can try the following:

1. Select K menu ➤ Control Center, click the YaST2 Modules icon, click the Hardware icon, and then click the Printer icon.

2. Click the Administrator Mode button and enter your root password.

3. Click the Configure button, and then click the entry in the list marked Print Via SMB Network Server.

4. On the next screen, you can leave Workgroup blank. In the Host Name field, type in the IP address of the Windows PC to which the printer is attached. To get this information, you'll need to speak to your system administrator or the person who operates that machine. It probably won't be enough to simply get the share name, which is how Windows identifies network computers; you'll need their full numeric IP address (something like 192.168.34.105).

5. In the Name of the Remote Queue field, you shouldn't actually enter the remote print queue name. Instead, you need to enter the name of the printer as it is identified by Windows on the network when it's shared, as shown in Figure 8-14. The best way to find this out is to go to the Windows machine, right-click the printer's entry (under Start ➤ Printers), select Properties, and then click the Sharing tab. Look for what's entered in the Share Name field. The string will usually be less than eight characters and will have no spaces or punctuation.

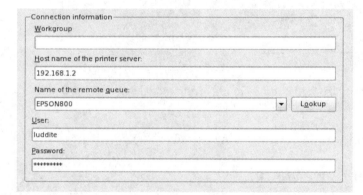

Figure 8-14. *Enter the name of the shared printer as it appears on the network.*

6. Now you need to enter a username and password. Here's where things get a little complicated. The best policy is to have the user of the Windows machine create a special account for you to use for printing. Make sure the username doesn't have any spaces in it, and keep it short. The Windows user should also give you a password, because attempting to access a shared printer which doesn't have a password doesn't seem to work very well under SUSE Linux.

7. Click the Test Remote SMB Access button. With luck, everything will work fine.

8. Click Next and accept the defaults. Click Next again (don't attempt to test the printer at this time), and then select the printer's make and model from the list.

9. Click Next, and then feel free to test the printer. Then click OK.

Getting Pictures onto Your PC

One of the ironies of computers is that they're ruthlessly logical yet allow people to pursue their creative hobbies. Photography is just one example, and there are usually two ways of getting pictures onto your PC: using a digital camera or using a scanner. We'll look at both methods here, starting with digital cameras.

Transferring Photos from a Digital Camera

Digital cameras have been around for a while now and offer a genuine alternative to traditional film photography. They store pictures on computer memory cards rather than on film, meaning their images can quickly and easily be downloaded to a PC. This means you don't need to have prints made, and then scan them in to your PC.

There are usually two ways of getting the pictures off digital cameras: via a direct cable connection to the camera into your USB or serial port, or by using a card reader. The latter requires buying an extra piece of hardware into which you insert the memory card from the camera so you can download images from it, but this is the method preferred by professional digital photographers and serious hobbyists. SUSE Linux supports both ways of working.

Using a Card Reader

When you use a card reader, SUSE Linux simply *mounts* the contents of the memory card into a folder on your hard drive. I'll describe how mounting works in Chapter 15, but basically it makes a virtual folder on your hard disk, from which you can access the contents of the memory card. In most cases, you can read, delete, and even write new contents to the card in this way. No extra software is necessary, and you can simply use Konqueror, the standard hard disk file browser under SUSE Linux, to access the folder's contents.

Note If there's no card in the reader, it probably won't be identified by SUSE Linux when you plug it in. Only when there's a card present will the reader hardware actually be installed and made ready for use.

With a card reader, the setup procedure is simple: attach it to your PC and insert the memory card. You'll see a message on the screen telling you in which folder the contents have been made available, and this should open in a Konqueror window so you can access the files. You'll need to remember this folder name, because you won't be told next time you insert the card; the card reader will simply be mounted in the background without any feedback. However, if necessary, you can usually track down the folder by clicking My Computer on the desktop and browsing to the removable storage devices on your computer, as shown in Figure 8-15.

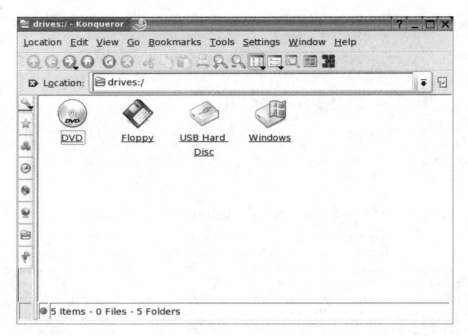

Figure 8-15. *When the card reader or camera has been mounted, it will be available under My Computer on the desktop as USB Hard Disc.*

When you're finished, close the file browser window, and then remove the card.

■**Caution** Be very careful not to remove a memory card from a card reader while you're writing or reading from it on your PC. This will most likely damage the card irreparably. At the very least, it will wipe the contents of the card, so you'll lose your photographs.

Using a Cable Connection

Setting up a digital camera cable connection is usually easy. In most cases, you can simply plug it in to your USB port, turn it on, and SUSE Linux will recognize it and make its contents available in a folder (in a virtually identical way to that described above for a card reader).

SUSE Linux comes complete with the Digikam software, which includes support for the vast majority of digital cameras, including many older cameras (those a few years old that connect to your PC by its serial port). Because of the way these cameras work, they are not usually automatically configured by SUSE Linux, hence the need for a separate software package. To configure your camera through Digikam, follow these steps:

1. Select K menu ➤ Graphics ➤ Photograph to start Digikam.

2. Select Settings ➤ Configure Digikam and click the Cameras tab. This is where you let Digikam know the make and model of your camera, as well as how you connect it to your PC.

3. If your camera connects via USB, as most modern models will, simply click the Auto-Detect button (assuming you've plugged your camera in). With any luck, your PC should automatically find the camera and set it up for you. You can then click the OK button.

4. If your camera isn't detected, click the Add button, and then select it from the list. You should find most of the other settings are selected automatically for you once you make the selection, as shown in Figure 8-16. Click OK.

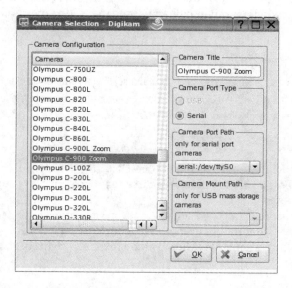

Figure 8-16. *Select your camera from the list, and you should find that the technical settings are chosen automatically.*

■**Tip** If your camera isn't listed but similar models are, try selecting the nearest available match. For example, I used an Olympus C920 Zoom to test this feature. This wasn't in the list, but the C900 Zoom was. Using this setting worked fine with my camera.

---

5. From the main program window, click Camera on the menu and then select your model from the list.

Once you select your camera in Digikam, it will attempt to connect to and read the images on your camera. After a few seconds (possibly longer if you're connecting via a serial cable rather than USB), you should see thumbnails of the images.

Viewing Photos with Digikam

Digikam likes to work with what it calls Albums, which are effectively ordinary folders on your hard disk that you can fill with photos from particular occasions—a wedding, birthday party, and so on. These folders can be browsed using the Konqueror file manager (which we'll discuss in depth in Chapter 12).

After you've loaded some pictures from your camera, as described in the previous section, click the New Album button to create an album into which to store your pictures, giving it a memorable name. To download your pictures into the album, simply click and drag the thumbnail onto the main Digikam program window, and into the right side that shows the contents of the album.

■**Tip** When naming albums, try to be as descriptive as possible. Rather than calling an album Birthday Party, for example, why not call it Jack's 8th Birthday Party – 10 June 04? But remember that, as with Windows, some punctuation marks (such as slashes) are not allowed in file and folder names.

You can then close the camera window. In Digikam, double-click any picture you would like to see full size. If you look at the bottom of the window, you'll see a progress display showing how much of the picture has been downloaded.

Additionally, by clicking various icons on the Digikam toolbar, you can correct minor errors such as brightness and contrast (hover your mouse over each icon to see what it does).

When you're happy with the picture, simply click the Save icon in the top-right corner, and then close the window.

Setting Up a Scanner

Although scanners have fallen out of favor recently with the advent of digital photography, there's little doubt that they're vital for getting photographs and old documents onto your PC.

SUSE Linux scanner support can be a little hit and miss. However, the list of supported models grows bigger by the day, and this is just one reason why regular online updating is a good idea (we'll cover how to update your system online in Chapter 9).

Note Agfa scanners are particularly bad in terms of support. It is possible to get them working, but a firmware upgrade is necessary. To see how it's done and to download the necessary files, see `http://snapscan.sourceforge.net`.

Configuring a Scanner

As with most hardware configuration, YaST2 is used to get the scanner up and running initially. Select K menu ➤ Control Center, click the YaST2 Modules, click the Hardware icon, and then click the Scanner icon. With luck, your scanner will be automatically identified. If not, YaST2 will let you know that it must be manually configured, as shown in Figure 8-17.

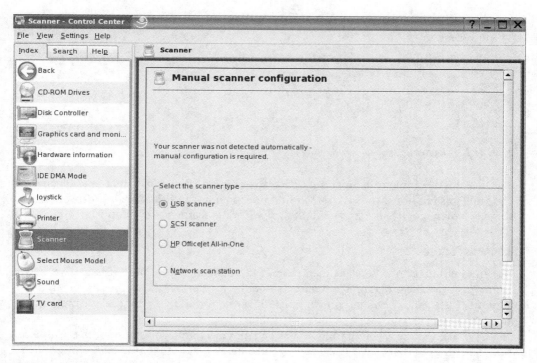

Figure 8-17. *YaST2 will let you know if it cannot automatically detect your scanner.*

To manually configure your scanner, just select your scanner's make and model from the list, as shown in Figure 8-18.

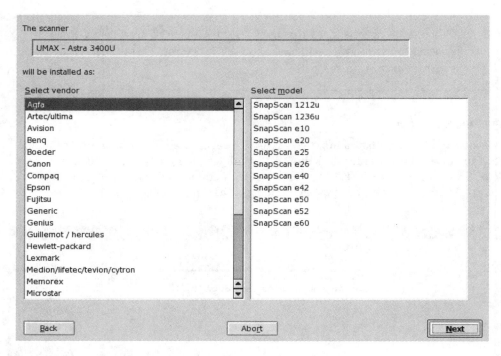

Figure 8-18. *Select your scanner from the list.*

Once this is complete, there's nothing else to set up, and it's simply a matter of clicking the Next and Finish buttons. You can opt to test the scanner if you wish to ensure it's working correctly (you might need to wait a minute or two for the scanner to start up).

Scanning Pictures

You can scan your pictures and documents using the Xsane program. Select K menu ➤ Graphics ➤ Scanning to start the program. It operates in a similar way to TWAIN scanner drivers under Windows, with similar configuration options. However, it works as a stand-alone program, rather than tying in with your favorite image editor.

In the main Xsane program window, you can set the scanning resolution with the topmost slider. A setting of 100 to 300 DPI is usually good enough for photographs; any setting above this will result in a massive file.

Beneath the DPI slider, you can set the gamma and contrast/brightness of the scanned picture. To help judge this, you can click Acquire Preview in the preview window. This will prescan the picture and give you an idea of how it will look when the actual scan takes place, as shown in Figure 8-19.

Figure 8-19. *Once you've previewed the image with Xsane, you can adjust the brightness and contrast to get a better scan.*

When you're happy with the results, return to the main Xsane program window and click the Scan button. This will scan the picture at the resolution you selected and, when it's finished, present the image in another preview window, which will fill the screen. If you're satisfied with what you see, select File ➤ Save the Image to the Hard Disk.

Using 3D Graphic Cards

Virtually all graphics cards are automatically supported and configured within SUSE Linux. However, if you want to use their 3D functionality—usually to play 3D shoot-'em-up games—then some extra steps are necessary. Only recent graphics cards are supported in this way. At the time of writing, these include NVIDIA models of a few years old up to the latest models, such as the GeForce range.

Adding 3D graphics supports simply involves downloading and installing special driver software. This is usually provided by the manufacturer of the graphics card and is normally closed source. There are various drawbacks to a closed-source approach. The chief one is that the drivers are frequently buggy. While open-source drivers can be fixed easily, with closed-source drivers, you must wait patiently for the next release, which can be months, if not years, apart.

Note There really isn't any reason to install 3D graphics drivers unless you want to play 3D games or use 3D modeling software. In most cases, sticking with the default XFree86 drivers installed by SUSE is the best choice. If you experience seemingly random systemwide crashes or freezing after installing a 3D graphics driver, consider reverting to your old setup.

To install a 3D graphics driver, follow these steps:

1. Select K menu ➤ Control Center, click YaST2 Modules, click Software, and then click Online Update (you should go online if you're not already).

2. Changes made here apply to the whole system, so you'll need to click the Administrator Mode button and enter your root password.

3. Click the Next button on the following screen (don't worry about the settings), and you should find yourself presented with a list of system updates. If you haven't already updated your system, now is as good a time as any, although we'll go through this procedure in the next chapter.

4. Look in the list of updates headed YaST Online Update Patch for something like "Download Nvidia Graphics Driver," and click it so that a tick appears in the box next to it, as shown in Figure 8-20. Then click the Accept button in the bottom right of the screen.

Figure 8-20. *NVIDIA 3D graphics can be installed using the SUSE Linux update service.*

5. You'll probably be shown a license agreement for the driver, which you should read. Then click Install Patch.

6. The download should take place, after which you should manually log out and then back in again (click the K menu and select the relevant option). Nothing will appear to have changed, although you might need to adjust your monitor's settings to make the picture fit properly.

To test the 3D function of the graphics card, try selecting an OpenGL screensaver: right-click a blank spot on the desktop, click Configure Desktop, and then click the Screensaver icon on the left. Select the OpenGL heading in the list of screensavers. Click the Test button to see it in action. Note that these screensavers are visually very impressive. This is a good chance to show off your new SUSE Linux setup to friends and colleagues!

Summary

In this chapter, we explored the possibilities offered by the YaST2 program when it comes to configuring hardware. Additionally, we looked at setting up some common software packages.

We stepped through getting online with SUSE Linux (including joining a Wi-Fi network), configuring e-mail and instant messaging, adding and configuring a printer, setting up a digital camera and/or scanner, and configuring a 3D graphics card.

In Chapter 9, we move on to look at how you can ensure the security of your system.

Securing Your System

Linux is widely considered to be one of the most secure operating systems around. SUSE Linux enhances this reputation by making some of the built-in Linux security tools easy to use.

SUSE Linux provides protection by working on the basis of access permissions. In addition, the Linux kernel includes various clever security features, which make the life of a virus writer much more difficult.

So, if SUSE Linux is so secure, should you stop reading at this point and skip to the next chapter? Unfortunately, that's not a good idea. There are still plenty of ways that malicious interests can break into your SUSE Linux computer. As with Windows, using common sense is essential.

Security should be looked into by everyone, regardless of how or where the computer in question is used. It isn't just a matter of online security either. Data theft can take place if someone simply has access to your PC, such as in a working environment.

In this chapter, you'll discover what you should watch out for in terms of security and how SUSE Linux's built-in tools can help protect your system.

Windows Security vs. Linux Security

If you've switched to SUSE Linux from Windows, there's a very good chance that the security failings of Windows featured in your decision. By any measure, Microsoft's record on security within its products is appalling. There's a new and serious security warning seemingly on a daily basis, and a new and devastating virus makes news headlines with similar frequency (usually described as "a PC virus" rather than what it actually is: a Windows virus).

There's an argument that Windows is the target of so many viruses merely because it's so popular. Although it's true that most of the underground crackers who write viruses dislike Microsoft immensely, there's also little doubt that Windows is fundamentally insecure and always has been. The task facing a cracker when creating a virus or worm is trivial in many cases.

Microsoft's latest operating system, Windows XP, provides many good examples of why it's an easy target. Upon installation, the default user is given root powers. True, there are a handful of tasks that only the genuine Administrator user can do, but the default user can configure hardware, remove system software, and even wipe every file from the hard disk, if he or she pleases. Of course, you would never intentionally damage your own system, but hackers use various techniques to get you to run malicious software (by pretending it's a different file, for example) or by simply infecting your computer across the Internet without your knowledge, which is how most worms work.

Viruses and worms also usually take advantage of security holes within Windows software. As just one example, there was a famous security hole within Outlook Express that meant that a program attached to an e-mail message was run when the user simply clicked a particular message to view it. In other words, infecting a Windows machine was as easy as simply sending someone an e-mail message!

I would love to say security holes are not found on Linux, but the sad truth is that they're a fact of life for users of every operating system. Yet Linux is considered nowhere near as insecure as Windows. Why?

Once again, there is a school of thought that Linux isn't attacked by crackers because it's not as popular as Windows, and once again there's a grain of truth to this allegation. The Internet underground that generates viruses and worms holds Linux in high regard. However, there are many so-called *rootkits* available, generated by these same individuals, which aim to exploit holes within the Linux operating system and its software. So this theory clearly isn't true.

The bottom line is that writing a virus or worm for Linux is much harder than doing the same thing on Windows.

No Windows system is complete with an antivirus program. Antivirus programs for Linux are rare, although some are available (see www.centralcommand.com/linux_workstation.html).

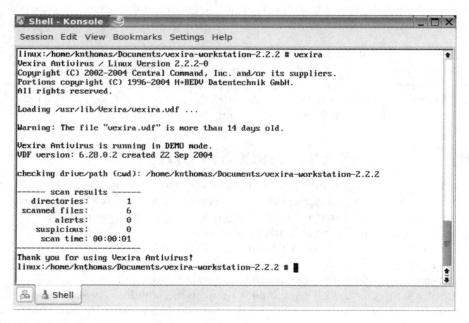

Figure 9-1. *An antivirus program for Linux*

▪**Note** A few companies offer antivirus programs that run under Linux for server computers, such as file servers or e-mail servers. However, these programs don't watch for viruses that run under Linux. Instead, they check files stored on that particular server for viruses that run under Windows. This adds an extra level of protection for Windows machines that use the server.

CRACKER VS. HACKER

Linux users are often described as *hackers*. This doesn't mean they maliciously break into computers or write viruses. It's simply using the word *hacker* in its original sense from the 1970s, when it described a computer enthusiast who was interested in exploring the capabilities of computers. Many of the people behind multinational computing corporations started out as hackers. Examples are Steve Wozniak, a co-founder of Apple Computer, and Bill Joy, cofounder of Sun Microsystems.

The word *hacker* is believed to derive from model train enthusiasts who "hacked" train tracks together as part of their hobby. When computing became popular in the early 1970s, several of these enthusiasts also became interested in computing, and the term was carried across with them.

However, in recent years, the media has subverted the term *hacker* to apply to an individual who breaks into computer systems. This was based on ignorance, and many true hackers find the comparison extremely offensive. Because of this, the term *cracker* was invented to clearly define an individual who maliciously attacks computers.

So, don't worry if an acquaintance describes herself as a Linux hacker, or tells you that she has spent the night "hacking." Many Linux types use the term as a badge of honor.

SUSE Linux Access Permissions

As I've mentioned in earlier chapters, SUSE Linux has the root user and ordinary user types of accounts. By using the ordinary user account for your day-to-day work, you help keep your system secure.

Root and Ordinary Users

The *root user* account has power over the entire system, which is to say that it can read, write, or delete any file. This user is akin to the Administrator account under Windows XP, and you should be very careful when deploying this account because the potential for damage is high.

Then there is the ordinary user account, which is limited in what it can do. This type of user is limited to saving files in his or her own directory within the /home/ directory (although the system is usually configured so that an ordinary user can read files outside the /home/ directory, too). A day-to-day user of SUSE Linux cannot delete files other than those that he created or for which he has explicitly been given permission to modify by someone else, as shown in the example in Figure 9-2. This is the type of user account that you should have set up during installation (as described in Chapter 5) and that you should use every day.

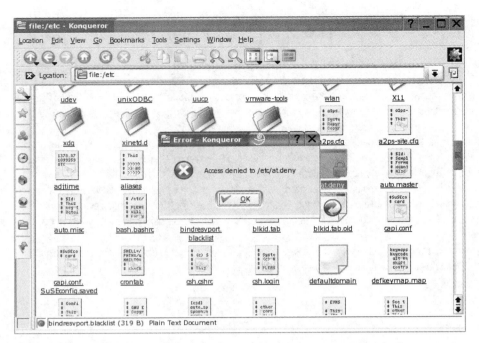

Figure 9-2. *As a limited user, you cannot delete files outside your personal area.*

Within SUSE Linux, only the root user has permission to access all the hardware or the entire file system, for instance. As an ordinary user, you're also limited in what hardware you can use and which settings you can alter. Again, only the root user has complete control over the system. It's practically impossible for ordinary users to do much damage, even if they (or a virus they accidentally download) try their hardest to do so.

Note Along with the root and ordinary user accounts, there is a third type of SUSE Linux account, which is similar to a limited user account, except that it's used by the system for various tasks. These user accounts are usually invisible to ordinary users and work in the background. For example, the audio subsystem has its own user account that SUSE Linux uses to access the audio hardware. The concept of users and files is discussed in more depth in Chapter 15.

This means that you, as an ordinary user, have very few permissions within the system. This isn't much of an issue during day-to-day use. You can run programs and save your files in your private area on the hard disk, but that's about the limit of your powers.

Temporary Root User Access

To install most software, you need to be able to write files to areas outside your private area, so you need to temporarily become the root user. With SUSE Linux, this is easy to do by clicking the Administrator Mode button within YaST2. Also, usually when you attempt to perform an action that requires root privileges, a dialog box will pop up automatically, as shown in Figure 9-3.

Figure 9-3. *Usually, if you attempt an action that needs root privileges, you will automatically be prompted for the root user password.*

You should be careful where and how you use the root password. Once it has been entered, such as to allow a particular program to run, that program then has effective control over your system. If you enter the root password to allow a program to install, for example, that program has access to your entire system and can do what it wants. If it is malicious, there is a clear possibility for damage.

Note You will usually be asked for the root password when you're making changes that affect the entire system and all the users on it. Configuring hardware will always require a root password, because it affects the entire system. Installing software requires a root password because, in many cases, it will be made available to all users on the system. On the other hand, changing your desktop wallpaper will affect only your user account, so no root password is required.

Common-Sense Security

As you start to understand how SUSE Linux works, you'll become more and more aware of common-sense methods that will protect your system. However, I'll outline a couple of these now to get you started:

Be very wary if you're asked to enter your root password. You'll be asked to do so when following many of the configuration steps within this book, for example, and this is acceptable and safe. But if you're asked to do so out of the blue, then you should be suspicious. If the root password prompt dialog box appears when you run a file that shouldn't really need root permissions, such as an MP3 or OpenOffice.org file, you should treat the situation with caution.

Be careful in choosing programs to download and install. Because Linux works on the basis of open-source code, anyone can theoretically tamper with a program, and then offer it for download by the unwary. This very rarely happens in real life. Even so, it's wise to avoid downloading programs from unofficial sources, such as web sites you find online via a Google search and whose authenticity you cannot vouch for. Instead, get software from the web site of the people who made it in the first place or from SUSE's own web site.

Tip SUSE Linux uses the RPM format for program installation, and these files can be "signed" with a secure digital code that can be applied only by SUSE itself or one of its trusted partners. This allows you to check if an installation file you download is secure. I'll explain how this works in Chapter 29, which covers program installation.

Always ensure your system software is completely up-to-date. As with Windows, many SUSE Linux programs have bugs that lead to security holes. Crackers target such vulnerabilities. Downloading the latest versions of SUSE Linux software ensures that you not only get the latest features, but also that any critical security holes are patched. As with most versions of Linux, updating SUSE Linux is easy and, of course, it's also free of charge. You'll learn how to get online updates in the next section.

Limit who has physical access to your PC. Any SUSE Linux system can be compromised by a simple floppy boot disk, such as the rescue disk you created when you installed SUSE Linux. Booting a PC using such a disk gives anyone with sufficient know-how complete root access to your system's files, with no limitations. This is for obvious reasons; the idea of a boot disk is to let you fix your PC should something go wrong, and you cannot do this if you're blocked from accessing certain files. When Linux is used on servers that hold confidential data, it's not uncommon for the floppy and CD-ROM drives to be removed, thus avoiding booting via a boot disk. Such computers are also usually locked away in a room or even in a cupboard, denying physical access to the machine.

Online Updates

The SUSE Linux system tray has an icon for a program that automatically monitors the update sites and tells you when updates are available. This is the SUSEWatcher program. If you're already online and haven't yet updated your system, this icon will have probably turned into a red circle with an exclamation mark in it. This is informing you that updates are available. When your system is completely up-to-date, the icon will turn into the green SUSE gecko.

Clicking the SUSEWatcher icon opens the SUSEWatcher configuration panel, as shown in Figure 9-4. The default settings are fine. To go online and perform an update, click the Start Online Update button. This will start YaST2, and you'll be asked to enter your root password.

YaST2 will automatically find a local update site near you, as shown in Figure 9-5. Usually, all you need to do is click the Next button to agree to its choice. After this, you'll be presented with a list of available updates. You can select or deselect each update by putting a tick in its box.

Figure 9-4. *Use SUSEWatcher to ensure your system is always up-to-date and therefore secure.*

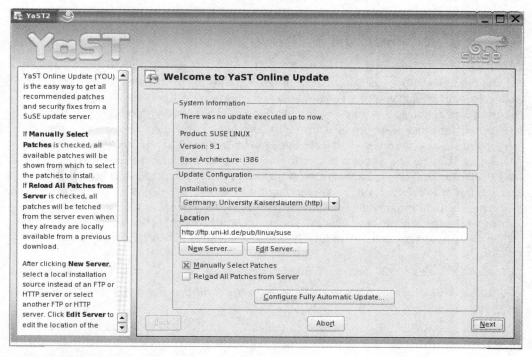

Figure 9-5. *SUSE Linux will find an update site near you automatically.*

Updates take two forms:

- Essential updates are highlighted in red and automatically selected for download. Essential updates are those you cannot do without; ignoring them will put your system at peril.

- Optional updates will be highlighted in blue, and you can choose them yourself. Optional updates merely add new functions to programs and can be skipped if you wish. In the patch description box, you'll find a description of why each update is necessary and what it fixes. If you find there is an unacceptably large list of updates, you might use this information to prune the list to avoid long download times. However, it is fairly essential that you follow the recommendations and download all of the updates.

After this, clicking Accept in the bottom-right corner of the screen will start the process. SUSE Linux will download the updates and automatically install them.

If you're doing this for the first time after installing SUSE Linux, you might find there are hundreds of megabytes of updates. It might even be necessary to leave your PC running overnight to grab the downloads, depending on the speed of your connection. Such huge updates can be avoided in the future by keeping an eye on the SUSEWatcher icon in the system tray and periodically updating your system whenever necessary. This should be considered part of your day-to-day chores when running SUSE Linux.

The SUSE Linux Firewall

A *firewall* is a set of programs that protects your PC when it's online. It does this by watching what data comes into your PC from the Internet and allowing in only what it is sure is secure (which usually is what you've asked for). It also attempts to close off various aspects of your Internet connection so that crackers don't have a way in should they target your system.

SUSE Linux includes a powerful firewall, which can protect everything from a complex server setup to a simple home PC. It really does provide industrial-level protection and, uniquely, steps in early in the boot process to ensure your PC is protected at all times.

Unlike desktop firewall software for Windows, the SUSE Linux firewall keeps itself out of the way and won't bother you once it's configured.

The benefit of running the firewall is that even if your system has security vulnerabilities because of buggy software, crackers will find it a lot harder to exploit them across the Internet. When someone attempts to probe your system, it will appear to be virtually invisible.

▓**Caution** You should never allow yourself to become complacent. Even firewalled systems have been known to be hacked!

You can activate the firewall via the YaST2 configuration tool. Follow these steps to configure your firewall:

1. Select K menu ➤Control Center, and then click the YaST2 Modules icon on the left.

2. Click the Security and Users icon, and then click Firewall. You'll see the first screen in the step-by-step wizard, as shown in Figure 9-6.

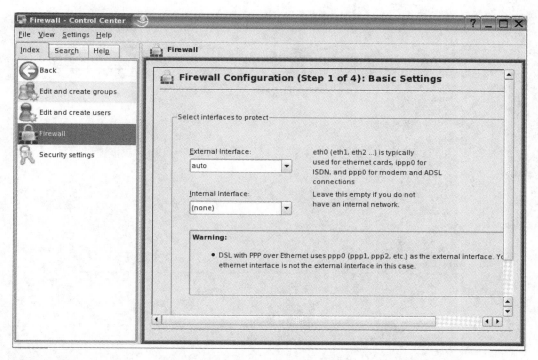

Figure 9-6. *Configuring the firewall is simply a matter of following a step-by-step wizard.*

3. Changes made here apply to the entire system, so you'll need to click the Administrator Mode button on the bottom-left side of the screen, and then enter your root password.

4. Provided your Internet connection is already up and running (follow the steps in Chapter 8 if it isn't), the first step is to choose the network connection you want to protect. You can select the connection from the External Interface drop-down list. In the case of an Ethernet connection (a LAN or DSL/cable modem router connection), you should select Ethernet. In the case of a modem connection—whether it's dial-up or via a directly connected DSL modem—you should select the PPP entry. In any case, unless you've set up more than one network connection on your computer, there will most likely be only one choice in the list. You can leave the Internal Interface box set to (none). This is designed to be used when your computer is operating as a gateway or router for a network. Click Next to move to the next wizard step.

5. The next screen lists services you can enable, as shown in Figure 9-7. Select any services you want to make available to other computers, such as other machines on the Internet. This is vital if your computer is acting as a server. In the case of a desktop computer, this screen can be largely ignored and the check boxes left blank. Click Next to continue.

■Tip In Chapter 34, you'll learn about using Secure Shell (SSH) to connect to your computer remotely across the Internet. You will need to return to the second firewall configuration screen and select SSH here, because you'll need to allow SSH to work through the firewall.

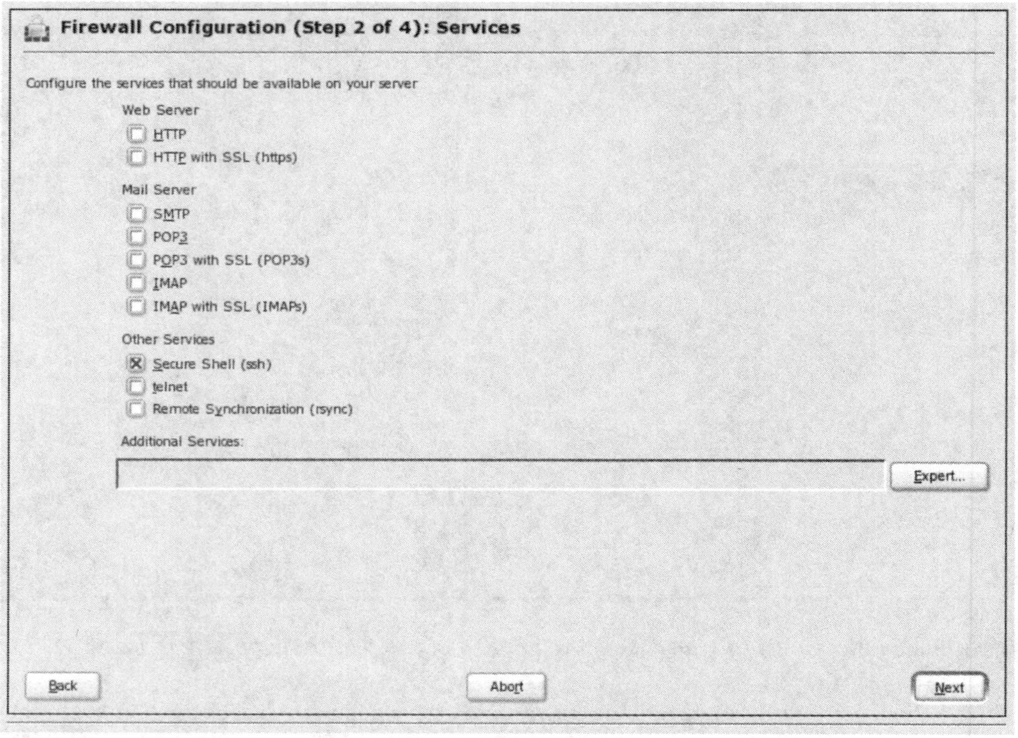

Figure 9-7. *For a desktop PC, you can leave all of these services unchecked, although you might want to enable SSH later on.*

6. Next, you are offered the chance to activate various firewall features, as follows. Click Next after making your selections.

- The Forward Traffic and Do Masquerading option allows your computer to act as a firewall gateway and thereby create a subnet for other computers. This is useful if your computer is acting as a firewall for other computers, but it is not something that most desktop SUSE Linux installations will need to use. You can leave the box unchecked.

- You can select to protect your computer from the internal network, which means computers on the same subnet as your own. Unless you're offering services to computers on your local network (such as file or printer shares), it's a good idea to put a check in this box. This will add an extra layer of security to your system.

- The Protect All Running Services option is a definite necessity, and should be checked. This effectively activates the firewall and ensures it protects your computer (although any services you selected to be accessible on the previous screen won't be affected by this option).

- The Allow Traceroute option lets other computers use the `traceroute` command to discover the network route to your computer (which is to say that your computer will respond to the traceroute command). This is useful in diagnostic situations, especially on local area networks, but removing the check will add an extra degree of security by making it harder for outsiders to detect your computer's presence.

- The Treat IPsec Traffic as Internal option is a system setting within SUSE Linux used to configure virtual private networks. The default setting of disabled is fine for most desktop PC configurations.

7. The final step of the firewall configuration process lets you control the logging function of the firewall. This gives you the option of writing to file a detailed log of any unusual firewall events, such as dropped packets (data that is turned away). This can be useful, and the default options of logging critical accepted and dropped packets is fine. The log file is located at `/var/log/firewall` and can be read using a text editor.

■**Caution** Don't be tempted to click the Log All options on the firewall logging configuration screen. Depending on the nature of your system, your log files could fill up with data very rapidly. This would make tracing problems very difficult. If the files were to become very large, this could even start to affect the performance of your system.

After you've enabled the SUSE Linux firewall, you can test it. A variety of online web sites, such as `www.dslreports.com/scan`, are able to probe your system and pretend to be crackers trying to gain entrance. These are perfectly safe to use. Once you've run this test, you should see that your computer is running in stealth mode and is invisible to the outside world.

Linux offers so much potential when it comes to providing firewall services that, in some instances, it's used for nothing else. This usually involves installing Linux on an old PC (perhaps one that's been abandoned because it's underpowered by modern standards), which is then used to protect a network by filtering all incoming and outgoing Internet data. There are a variety of specialized Linux distributions that offer solely firewall functions and, as your knowledge of Linux increases, you might like to investigate them. Examples include Smoothwall (`www.smoothwall.org`) and LEAF (`http://leaf.sourceforge.net`).

PARANOIA AND SECURITY

There's a fine line between security and paranoia. SUSE Linux gives you the opportunity to ensure your system is secure, without needing to constantly reassess your system for threats and live in fear.

When considering your system security, it's necessary to remember that most burglars don't enter a house through the front door. Most take advantage of an open window or poor security elsewhere in the house. In other words, when configuring your system's security, you should always select every option and extra layer of security, even if it might not appear to be useful. You should lock every door and close every window, even if you don't think an attacker would ever use them.

Provided a security setting doesn't impact your ordinary use of the computer, you should select it. For example, deactivating the `traceroute` response of your computer might sound like a paranoid action, but it's useful on several levels. First, it means your computer is less easy to detect when it's online. Second, and equally important, it means that if there's ever a security flaw in the `traceroute` tool (or any software connected with it), you'll be automatically protected. The `traceroute` and `ping` tools have frequently been misused in past attacks on various systems.

This illustrates how you must think when configuring your system's security: try to imagine every situation that might arise. Remember that you can never take too many precautions!

Summary

In this chapter, we've looked at what threats your system faces and how security holes can be exploited by malicious interests. You learned about measures you can take to protect your system, such as updating it online and configuring the system's firewall. We also discussed some common-sense rules you can follow to keep your system safe.

In the next chapter, we move on to looking at how your SUSE Linux system can be personalized and how to set up everything to suit your own preferences.

CHAPTER 10

■ ■ ■

Personalizing SUSE Linux: Getting Everything Just Right

If you've read this book from Chapter 1, by this stage, you'll no doubt have become comfortable with SUSE Linux. You'll have started to realize its advantages and be on the way to forgetting some of the horrors contained within Windows.

But things might still not be quite right. You might be irritated by the fact that a single-click is enough to launch programs under SUSE Linux, for example, rather than the more familiar double-click under Windows. You might find the color scheme not to your tastes.

In this chapter, we will look at personalizing SUSE Linux so that you're completely happy with your user experience.

Changing the Look and Feel

SUSE Linux is similar to Windows in many ways, but stops short of completely mirroring the experience. This is for various reasons, but perhaps the most prominent is that few people believe Microsoft developers got everything perfect with Windows. There are user-interface tricks they missed and tweaks that they didn't adopt.

SUSE includes many of what it thinks are improvements in the interface of SUSE Linux. For example, it offers multiple virtual desktops—long considered a very useful user-interface feature. And, by default, you need to click desktop icons only once to launch a particular program or user service.

SUSE Linux can match Windows in most regards, including its user interface. But you're not alone if you feel you've run into a few of its annoyances. These are usually related to how SUSE Linux doesn't work quite like Windows, something that can catch newcomers off guard. For example, if you're used to double-clicking desktop icons, you might end up starting the same program twice, as shown in Figure 10-1.

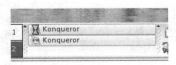

Figure 10-1. *If you're used to double-clicking, SUSE's single-click program launching often means you start the same program twice.*

The good news is that SUSE Linux lets you tweak the way it works so you can get things just right for your tastes. It's even possible to create a faithful reproduction of the way Windows works, if you wish. This might be a good idea if you find the culture shock of the way SUSE Linux works a bit too much. After all, you can always change things back later on.

Tip You might choose to stick with the way SUSE Linux works by default. You'll almost certainly find that, after a few weeks, you'll get used to things so much that you'll wonder how you ever had initial worries. You might even find single-clicking an icon to launch a program much more useful than double-clicking, for example. Think about all the times when you double-clicked but not fast enough, and had nothing happen (or, worse, Windows interpreted your slow double-click as an attempt to rename the file or icon). With a single-click, you really can't go wrong!

Altering the Theme

Tweaking the user interface is done using the KDE Control Center, which you can access from the K menu. The Control Center is a little like the Control Panel within Windows—virtually every setting you could ever need is found there.

The appearance of SUSE Linux is designed to mimic that of Windows XP while introducing a measure of individuality. *Appearance* refers to the borders of the program windows, such as the scroll bars and the Close, Minimize, and Maximize buttons at the top right of each window. Figure 10-2 shows an example of the default appearance of a SUSE Linux window. Together with other items you interact with on the screen, such as buttons and check boxes, these are grouped together under the heading of "themes."

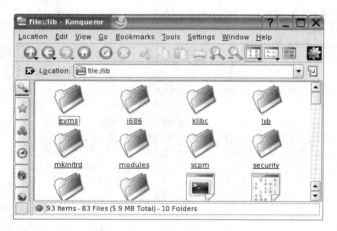

Figure 10-2. *The styling applied to aspects of a program window, such as scroll bars and title bars, is referred to as the "theme."*

SUSE Linux lets you alter the theme and choose from a variety of alternatives, some of which are smaller and perhaps more refined than the default choice. In addition to changing themes, you can also alter the color scheme and tweak miscellaneous items such as the desktop wallpaper. The default fonts used throughout for elements like icons and menus can also be changed, much as they can in Windows.

All in all, you can radically personalize SUSE Linux to your tastes. To show how this is done, we'll work through re-creating the Windows 98/Me look and feel (the so-called "Classic" visual appearance, according to Windows XP's Display Manager applet). This should make any Windows convert feel right at home.

1. Open the Control Center from the K menu, and then click on the Appearance and Themes icon.

2. The first thing we'll do is change the way the windows look, so click the Windows Decorations icon (the last in the list on the left).

3. At the top of the screen is a drop-down list from which you can select a variety of themes. Take a look through them. You'll see a preview of each in the area below.

4. The theme we're interested in is Redmond, so select that. You'll see that it's a pretty passable imitation of Windows 98/Me, as shown in Figure 10-3. If you want to try it out immediately, click the Apply button at the bottom right. This will apply the theme to all the program windows you have open.

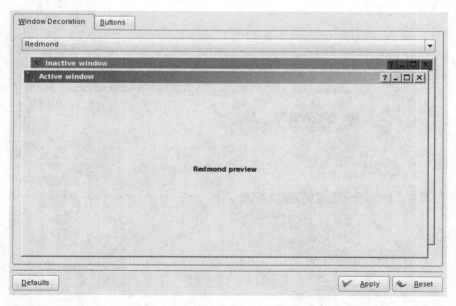

Figure 10-3. *SUSE Linux can do a passable imitation of the Windows look and feel.*

5. Click the Style icon on the left. At the top of the screen is another drop-down list of various themes. Here, your choices apply to visual items such as buttons, sliders, progress bars, and so on (called *widgets*).

6. Try clicking a few entries in the list. Once again, you'll see a preview of what it will look like in practice. The themes range from svelte and neat, all the way to fairly ugly. We're interested in one called MS Windows 9x, so click that.

Tip Later on, you might want to take a look at the Effects tab on the Style configuration screen. Here, you can set various special effects, such as menus fading into view. Unfortunately, some of the features offered here work on a handful of the visual themes and not on the Windows-like theme we've selected (although it is possible to make the menus slide into view, as with Windows 98). Older PCs can be hit quite hard if you use special effects. If you find your PC slowing down or becoming slow and jerky after activating them, consider scaling them back or even turning them off.

7. Click the Splash Screen icon on the left. This lets you change the screen that appears when SUSE Linux's desktop boots up. A variety of designs are offered, but for the complete Windows look and feel, you can again select the Redmond option. This mimics the Windows XP Welcome screen that appears just after bootup.

8. Click the Colors icon on the left. This is where you can change the colors used throughout SUSE Linux, as shown in Figure 10-4. As you might expect by now, a variety of choices are available, including several that imitate the subtle color differences among various versions of Windows. You can choose Redmond 2000, Redmond 98, or Redmond XP. Redmond 2000 is most like that of an actual Windows machine, but the choice is up to you.

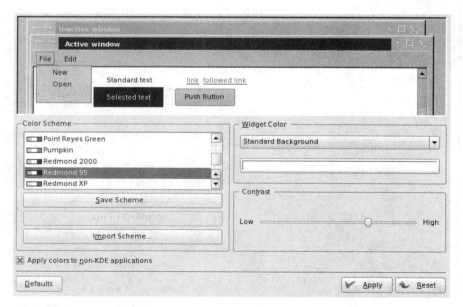

Figure 10-4. *You can choose from various Windows-style color schemes or pick something more colorful.*

9. Click the Background tab. This is where you can choose to change the wallpaper. The default already looks a lot like Windows XP's Bliss wallpaper, but you might want to go with a plain color, just like Windows 95, 98, and Me. To do this, click No Picture, and in the Single Color drop-down list, click the color bar to choose a suitable Windows-inspired shade of teal. This will bring up a color spectrum that you might be familiar with from Windows. Just click and drag the mouse around within the color box until you find a shade you like.

    At this point, you should have a pretty faithful Windows clone (don't forget to click the Apply button to put your changes into practice).

10. There's just one last screen area to tweak: the Panel (the toolbar at the bottom of the screen that contains the icon shortcuts and list of running programs). This still looks a little too flashy and not boring enough to be something you might see in Windows.

    Right-click a blank spot (away from icons) of the Panel and select Configure Panel, as shown in Figure 10-5. This will open up the Configure - Panel screen.

Figure 10-5. *Right-click a blank spot on the Panel and then select Configure.*

    There are various functions here you can play with (you can reposition the Panel so it runs down the side of the screen, for example), but we want to change its appearance, so click the Appearance tab at the top of the window, as shown in Figure 10-6. At the bottom, remove the tick from the Enable Background Image option. Then click Apply. Presto—everything should look fairly dull and uninteresting, just like your favorite version of Windows!

■**Note** Some of the changes to the look and feel won't take effect until you've logged out and logged back in again. You can do this by selecting K menu ➤ Logout ➤ End Session Only.

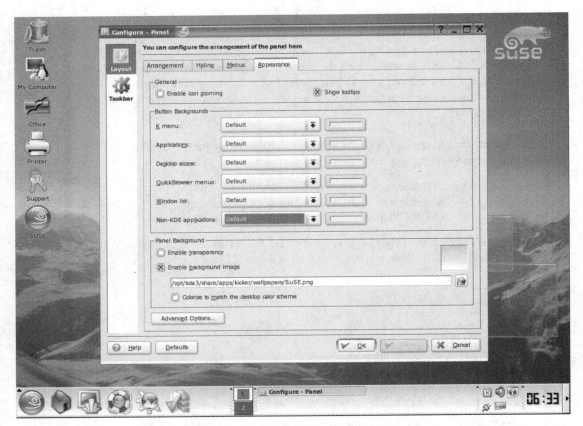

Figure 10-6. *The Configure - Panel screen contains a wealth of options related to customizing your system's appearence just the way you want it.*

Taming the Mouse

The mouse is a little odd in SUSE Linux in that only one click is required for most activities. Some people have Windows set similarly and may want to stick with this way of working, but the rest of us quickly get fed up with starting two instances of the same program via an accidental double-click.

Many of the people I spoke to during my testing while writing this book also felt that the default mouse speed in SUSE Linux is too fast. The cursor seems to fly from one end of the screen to the other with even the lightest push, particularly with the popular Logitech range of mice.

Fortunately, both these settings can be altered quite easily. Once again, you access the settings through the Control Center (listed on the K menu beneath the majority of the program entries). Click the Peripherals icon, and then click the Mouse icon. You'll see the mouse settings shown in Figure 10-7.

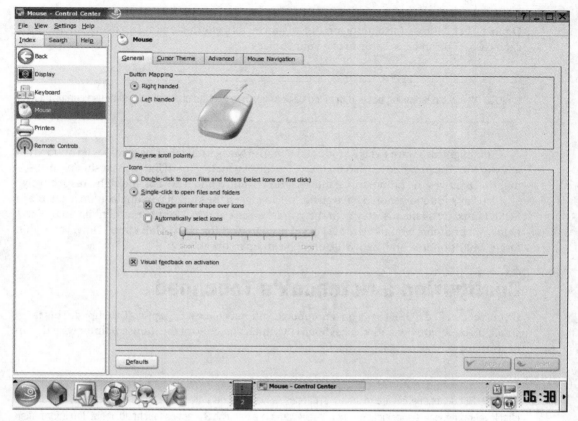

Figure 10-7. *Want to get rid of single-click program activation? Tweak the mouse settings.*

Note YaST2 also has an entry for mouse configuration, but this is to alter the mouse's hardware driver, rather than tweak its day-to-day settings.

To double-click rather than single-click throughout SUSE Linux, select the relevant option under the Icons heading. If you find the small animation that follows a single/double-click annoying, remove the tick from the Visual Feedback on Activation option.

On the Cursor Theme tab, you can also select a different color cursor. The best choice for those who want a plainer format is Crystal White Non-animated. This will remove the perhaps annoying animated clock cursor that appears when the computer is busy.

On the Advanced tab, you can click and drag the slider to alter the mouse acceleration. There's a setting beneath this that you might not be familiar with: Pointer Threshold. This is the amount of pixels the cursor must move before acceleration kicks in (before it starts to move more quickly). Most people will find a larger value works best here, to allow for accurate clicking in confined areas. However, you should experiment to see which is best for you. All the other settings should be fine as they are, although if you have a physical disability that prevents you from double-clicking quickly (or you are just a little slow when clicking), you might find the Double Click Interval (also found on the Advanced tab) worth cranking up a few notches. In each case, you can click Apply to test your choices.

■**Note** You will need to log out and then log back in again to see the changes to the mouse cursor themes.

You might also want to take a look at the Mouse Navigation tab. This includes an option that lets you turn the numeric keypad on the right side of your keyboard into a makeshift mouse—pressing 8 moves the pointer up, 2 moves it down, and 3 and 6 are left and right, respectively.

This introduction should have given you an idea of the kind of personalization available in SUSE Linux. By all means, stay with the Windows look and feel for the moment if you find it helps you or others who use your PC to get used to working with SUSE Linux. However, don't forget what's offered and, above all, don't be afraid to tweak!

Configuring a Notebook's Touchpad

If you've installed SUSE Linux on a notebook, you may have a Synaptics Touchpad. This is a small, black square beneath the keyboard by which you control the mouse pointer with the tip of your finger.

■**Note** Not all touchpads are made by Synaptics. Several models are made by its competitors. You should check your notebook's specification list to see if yours is a genuine Synaptics touchpad. If not, the information presented here does not apply.

Your touchpad should work fine with the default SUSE Linux settings, but you can configure some additional functionality. Synaptics supplies a special utility under Windows that turns the right and bottom edges of the pad into scroll bars. Dragging your finger in these areas causes the window you're working in to scroll either up and down or from side to side (it's usually the former that is most useful). In this way, it emulates the scroll wheel in a regular mouse, saving you a lot of work clicking and dragging the scroll bars on the screen.

The good news is that SUSE Linux emulates this functionality. The bad news is that you need to change your mouse driver to use this emulation, but that isn't difficult to do. Here are the steps:

1. Select K menu ➤ System ➤ Configuration ➤ SaX2. (Note that YaST2 and Control Center are *not* used to configure this aspect of your setup.)

2. The changes you make here affect the entire system, so you'll need to enter the root password when prompted, to enter Administrator mode.

3. When SaX2 appears, click the small plus symbol to the left of the Input Devices icon, and then click Mouse.

4. Click the Change Configuration button, and then click Add New Mouse. You should see Synaptics in the list on the left, so select it, as shown in Figure 10-8. Don't worry about any of the other settings at this stage; just click OK.

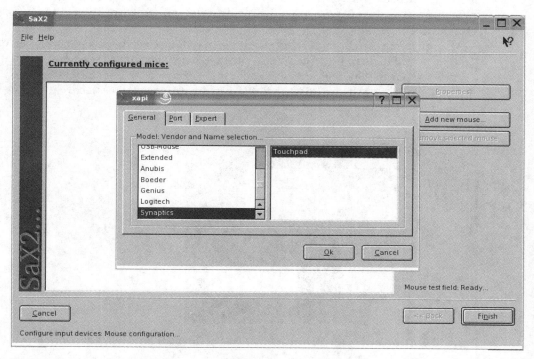

Figure 10-8. *If you have a Synaptics touchpad, choose Synaptics from the list within SaX2.*

5. Select your old mouse in the list and click Remove Selected Mouse. Click Finish, and then click the Finalize button.

6. A dialog box will appear, letting you test your new mouse driver. I strongly advise that you do so. When the test screen appears, be *very* careful not to change any of the settings, such as the screen size, but try moving the mouse around. It might be a little slow or a little quick, but this is okay for the moment—at least it's working.

  • If the mouse cursor stays resolutely still and won't budge, it's probably because you do not have a genuine Synaptics touchpad (there are several look-alike clones) or because your particular version of the touchpad isn't compatible with the driver. In this case, press the Tab key several times until the dotted highlight outline appears on the Cancel button, and then press the spacebar. When you're back in SaX2, click the Cancel button, and quit the program without saving your changes.

  • If the touchpad works fine, save your changes in SaX2. Note that you'll need to log out and then back in again before the new driver will work.

If the mouse is too quick or too slow, simply follow the instructions in the previous "Taming the Mouse" section to alter its acceleration.

Adding and Removing Shortcuts

Like any modern desktop operating system, SUSE Linux works on the principle of icons and shortcuts. There are icons on the desktop that provide quick access to frequently used programs and functions, and shortcut icons on the Panel that let you access your e-mail and browse the Web quickly.

Creating your own icons in either location is easy. Just select the program you want on the K menu, but rather than single-clicking it, click and hold. Then drag it to where you want the shortcut to appear. When you release the mouse button, you'll be asked if you want to Copy Here or Link Here, as shown in Figure 10-9. Select Copy Here (you're effectively copying the program shortcut from the K menu).

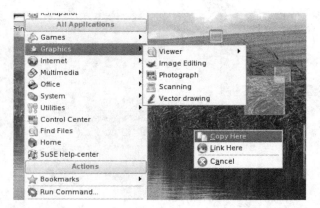

Figure 10-9. *Creating a new desktop shortcut is easy: just click and drag from the K menu.*

■**Tip** Icons can move between the desktop and the Panel, too. Just click and drag them. This makes it easy to duplicate on the desktop the icons you have on the Panel, and vice versa.

Deleting icons is just as easy. To remove desktop icons, you can just click and drag them to the Trash icon. For both Panel and desktop icons, you can right-click them and select Delete.

To move icons around on the Panel, simply right-click the icon you want to move and select the relevant option from the menu. You'll see a live preview as you move the cursor. When the icon is positioned as you want it, click the mouse.

Note that, unlike with Windows, the K menu button itself can also be moved to a different position. It can even be deleted if you wish! This isn't too ridiculous an idea. Once you have your system set up with the shortcuts to your favorite programs, removing the K menu can save space on the Panel and help you avoid annoying misclicks.

The Pager, Taskbar, system tray, and clock can be moved, too. Just click and drag the small handles to the left of each (you might need to hover your mouse over the left side of each to make the handle appear; sometimes it's set to be invisible). Additionally, you can change the order of these elements, so that the clock is at the left of the Panel, for example, as shown in Figure 10-10.

Figure 10-10. *You can move any item on the Panel to any location.*

Adding and Removing Applets

If you find that you don't use the Pager (the virtual desktop selection tool), you can remove it to save space. Simply right-click a blank space on the Panel and click Remove, and then Applet, and then Pager. Alternatively, you can bring it back by right-clicking the Panel, selecting Add, then Applet, and then Pager.

There are many more applets available than those set up to appear by default. Just right-click a blank area of the Panel, select Add, then Applet, and take your pick. Those that are grayed out are already in use on the Panel. There are even more applets available on the K menu. Just select K menu ➤ System ➤ Desktop. Click the icon for the applet you want to add to activate it and put it on the Panel. Table 10-1 lists the available applets, along with brief descriptions.

Table 10-1. *SUSE Linux Desktop Applets*

Applet	Description
Application Launcher	This applet adds a small box into which you can type commands or program names in order to launch them (akin to Start ➤ Run under Windows).
Clock	This shows the current time and provides a means by which the time and date can be altered. It is set up by default.
Color Picker	This lets you click anywhere on screen and immediately view the RGB decimal and hex values of the color under the cursor. This can be useful when creating web sites or editing images.
Devices	This provides quick access via icons to any removable media devices you may have installed on your system, such as the CD-ROM and floppy drives. It also lets you mount and unmount drives quickly.
KBinaryClock	This is like the Clock applet, except it displays the time as a graphical display showing binary values! It can be quite fun to learn how to tell the time using binary.
Klipper	This applet gives you more control over your clipboard history, allowing you to recall items that were cut or copied some time ago.
KNewsTicker	This displays scrolling headlines from various web sites, such as the popular Slashdot.org geek news site and the KDE home page. It can be configured to work with any site that offers Resource Description Framework (RDF) feeds.
KSysGuard	Despite what its name might imply by way of security, this applet actually displays system resource usage figures, such as how much memory is in use or how busy the CPU is.

Table 10-1. *SUSE Linux Desktop Applets (Continued)*

Applet	Description
Lock/Logout Applet	As its name suggests, this applet provides two small icons which, when clicked, either log out the user or lock the computer so that the user's password must be entered to restore functionality.
Media Control	This applet gives quick control over the SUSE media player (although it can be configured to work with other compatible software, too). It provides controls for pausing the media player or skipping tracks, for example.
Pager	This provides control over the virtual desktop system. It is set up by default.
Public File Server	This effectively lets you create a temporary web server on your machine by which you can make files available to other computers on your network or (firewall permitting) across the Internet. All the user of the remote computer needs to do is enter your IP address into his web browser together with the port number you specify during setup (this can be done by clicking the applet icon).
Quick Launcher	This adds a miniature icon bar to the Taskbar, which you can use to start various programs or services. Its main benefit is that it takes up very little space.
Runaway Process Catcher	This applet is a legacy from the older age of SUSE Linux when some software was buggy and would consume system resources at a runaway rate. It effectively watches for runaway processes and automatically kills them. Nowadays, it's useful only if you're deliberately using beta (testing) software. It can cause problems such as false alarms if used incorrectly.
System Monitor	Like KSysGuard, this provides graphed information about system resources. However, it's much smaller than KSysGuard.
XMMS-KDE	This puts a miniature version of the XMMS media player program on the Taskbar. It includes some of the controls of the media player, but right-clicking allows access to more options.

Setting Power-Saving Features

Power saving is a handy feature designed to save electricity as well as wear and tear on your PC's components. It periodically turns off various bits of PC hardware without actually shutting down the entire PC, which still runs in the background. Usually "waking up" a PC in this state causes everything to power back up, and you can resume where you left off.

Adjusting the Screen Power Settings

In most instances, the best form of power saving is to turn off the screen, because it consumes a lot of electricity. SUSE Linux can be set so that the screen powers down after a certain period of inactivity—perhaps if you leave your desk to attend to another matter.

Note A standard CRT monitor (not a TFT flat-panel screen) consumes around 40 to 60 watts of electricity. This is the same amount as a household light bulb. You wouldn't leave a light switched on unnecessarily, so why leave your monitor switched on when your PC is not in use?

The power-saving features are once again accessed through the Control Center. Start the Control Center from the K menu, click the Power Control, and then click the Display Control icon on the left side of the screen. Here, you can alter various settings for powering down your monitor, as shown in Figure 10-11. Not all the modes are supported on all monitors but the most useful is the Power Off After setting. Try dragging this to around 15 minutes.

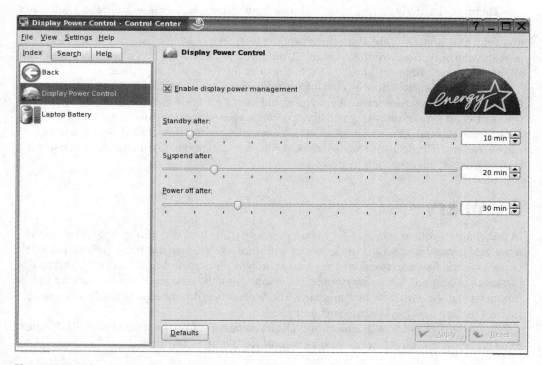

Figure 10-11. *Altering power-saving features avoids wear and tear on your PC components and saves electricity.*

Adjusting the Computer Power Settings

In addition to the screen setting, you can set the power-saving mode for the entire machine. Mostly, this means the hard disk is temporarily spun down but, depending on the age of your PC, you can also set to throttle (slow down) the CPU during periods of inactivity. These options are intended to reduce the wear on your PC's components, as well as to save electricity.

This feature is also found in the Control Center. If you're on the Display Control screen, click the Back button to return to the initial Control Center screen, and then select YaST2 Modules. Click Misc, and then click Power Management. The changes you make here will apply to the entire system, not just your user account, so you'll need to click the Administrator Mode button and enter your root password.

Many of the settings here apply to only relatively modern PCs that have Advanced Configuration and Power Interface (ACPI) support.

Note Even if you happen to know that your PC has ACPI support, there's no guarantee SUSE Linux will support it. ACPI is a relatively new feature in the Linux kernel. At the moment, support for all types of hardware is a little shaky.

There are effectively three settings to choose from for both AC-powered and battery computer use (you can ignore the battery choices on a desktop PC): Acoustic, Powersave, and Performance. Unfortunately there's not much explanation given of what each does. Powersave is probably the best choice for the average PC, but if you must have your PC running at full speed all the time, even when you're not using it, consider the Performance setting.

You can edit each setting by clicking the Edit Schemes button. Here, you can select which kinds of overall power-saving features you would like to enable. For example, you can select to run your PC at a quiet setting, which limits performance so that less heat is generated, and therefore the system fans won't spin too fast, generating noise. If your CPU is compatible, you can also select to throttle the speed of the CPU during quiet periods, or alternatively, ensure it's kept running at full speed all the time.

Summary

In this chapter, you've learned how to take control of the Linux desktop, getting rid of annoyances and generally making it work the way you want. We've looked at personalizing the SUSE Linux look and feel, and tweaking the mouse configuration (including setting up a notebook's Synaptics touchpad). We've also looked at personalizing the desktop by adding new applet programs and shortcuts to other programs. The final section discussed how to tailor the power-saving function of SUSE Linux to suit your needs.

In the next chapter, we'll look at the various pieces of software supplied with SUSE Linux that can be used as direct swap-in replacements for Windows favorites.

CHAPTER 11

■ ■ ■

Using Linux Replacements for Windows Programs

SUSE Linux aims to be similar to Windows in order to ease the transition for Microsoft migrators. As such, it supplies a core collection of software that borrows more than a few ideas from Microsoft products, as well as from the third-party companies that create software for Windows. For example, OpenOffice.org looks and operates in a similar fashion to Microsoft Office. K3b borrows the look and feel of Ahead's Nero CD-burning software. Some people might have trouble telling the Kontact application apart from Outlook.

In this chapter, we will take a tour of some of the Linux replacements for Windows programs and tell you where you can find the vital features you'll use often.

Linux Has It All

Modern Linux is a professional operating system, and its archives contain a mind-boggling amount of software to meet just about every need. For example, it can be used for office tasks, to make music, to play games, to design circuit boards, to edit digital photographs, and much, much more. If you can think of it, Linux has a program that can do it!

It isn't so much a case of Linux chasing Windows's tail and cloning what's available under Microsoft's operating system. It's more the case that Linux has a selection of software that is larger and far more esoteric than that of Windows, but that also includes several programs that provide powerful alternatives to Windows favorites.

Not only that, but diversity is vitally important within Linux. For example, rather than offering just one e-mail program, you'll find there are many available. They compete against each other in a gentle way, and it's up to you which one you settle down with and use.

■**Note** The diversity in Linux programs means that no two Linux users are alike. You might use Konqueror for your web browsing, for example, while your friend might use Mozilla (an alternative browser program). You might use OpenOffice.org for your word processing, while your colleague at work might use Koffice. Compare this to the world of Windows, where virtually everyone uses Outlook Express for e-mail, Microsoft Office for office tasks, and Internet Explorer for browsing.

There's a lot of choice out there, and part of the fun of using Linux is exploring what's available. Of course, the added bonus is that virtually all this software is free of charge, so you can simply download, install, and play around. If you don't like it, just remove the program from your system. However, don't forget to revisit the program's home page after a few months; chances are the program will have been expanded and improved in that short period, and it might be better at meeting your needs.

Table 11-1 lists various popular Windows programs alongside their counterparts for SUSE Linux. Remember that the SUSE Linux versions come installed by default and are included free of charge. You'll find the programs listed on the K menu. You certainly don't need to purchase any additional software, as with Windows!

Table 11-1 also includes a number of other mainstream alternatives, which aren't installed by default under SUSE Linux. You might wish to try some of these after you've read later chapters in this book covering program installation. Most are on the SUSE Linux DVD-ROM that comes free with this book or, in a minority of cases, just a quick download away.

Note Table 11-1 lists only a fraction of the programs available under Linux. There are quite literally hundreds, if not thousands, of others. The programs listed here are those that work like their Windows equivalents and therefore provide an easy transition.

Table 11-1. *Comparisons of Windows and Linux Software*

Type of Program	Windows	SUSE Linux	Alternative Choices
Word processor	Microsoft Word	OpenOffice.org Writer	Abiword (www.abisource.com), Koffice Kword (www.koffice.org/kword)
Spreadsheet	Microsoft Excel	OpenOffice.org Calc	Gnumeric (www.gnome.org/projects/gnumeric/), Koffice Kspread (www.koffice.org/kspread)
Presentations	Microsoft PowerPoint	OpenOffice.org Impress	Koffice Kpresenter (www.koffice.org/kpresenter)
Drawing (vector art)	Adobe Illustrator	OpenOffice.org Draw	Sodipodi (www.sodipodi.com), Koffice Karbon14 (www.koffice.org/karbon)
Web page creation	Microsoft FrontPage	OpenOffice.org Writer	Mozilla Composer (www.mozilla.org), Amaya (www.w3.org/Amaya/)
E-mail	Outlook	Kmail	Evolution (www.ximian.com/products/evolution/)
Contacts manager/ calendar	Outlook	Kontact	Evolution (www.ximian.com)

Table 11-1. *Comparisons of Windows and Linux Software (Continued)*

Type of Program	Windows	SUSE Linux	Alternative Choices
Web browser	Internet Explorer	Konqueror	Mozilla (www.mozilla.org), Firefox (www.mozilla.org), Opera (www.opera.com)*
CD/DVD burning	Ahead Nero	K3b	X-CD-Roast (www.xcdroast.org)
MP3 player	Winamp	XMMS	AlsaPlayer (www.alsaplayer.org)
CD player	Windows Media Player	KsCD	AlsaPlayer (www.alsaplayer.org)
Movie/DVD player	Windows Media Player	Kaffeine (or Xine)	Mplayer (www.mplayerhq.hu/homepage/)
Image editor	Adobe Photoshop	The Gimp	Koffice Krita (www.kofffice.org/krita)
Zip files	WinZip	Ark	File Roller (http://fileroller.sourceforge.net/)
MS-DOS prompt	cmd.exe/command.exe	Konsole	Xterm (installed by default in SUSE Linux)
Calculator	Calc	KCalc	Too many to mention!
Text editor/viewer	Notepad	Kate	Kwrite (www.kde-apps.org/content/show.php?content=9901)
Desktop games	Minesweeper/Solitaire	Kmines/Kpatience	Too many to mention!

* A free version of Opera is available, but it is proprietary software, rather than open source.

A Quick Start with Common Linux Programs

The remainder of this chapter outlines a handful of the programs listed in Table 11-1. My goal is to give you a head start in using each program, pointing out where most of the main functions can be found.

In some cases, I'll cover the programs in much more depth in later chapters (particularly the office and multimedia programs), but you should find enough information here to get you started.

Keep in mind that Linux doesn't aim to be an exact clone of Windows. Some of the programs will work in a similar way to Windows software, but that's not true of all of them. Because of this, it's very easy to get frustrated early on when programs don't seem to work quite how you want, or respond in strange ways. Some programs might hide functions in what seem like illogical places compared with their Windows counterparts. Some patience is required. This will eventually pay off as you get used to Linux.

Word Processing: OpenOffice.org Writer

OpenOffice.org is an entire office suite for Linux that was built from the ground up to compete with Microsoft Office. Because of this, you'll find much of the functionality of Microsoft Office is replicated in OpenOffice.org, and the look and feel are also similar. The major difference is that OpenOffice.org is open source and therefore free of charge. The entire OpenOffice.org suite is covered in much more detail in Part Six of this book.

OpenOffice.org Writer (K menu ➤ Office ➤ Wordprocessor), shown in Figure 11-1, is the word processor component. As with Microsoft Word, it's fully WYSIWYG (What You See Is What You Get), so you can quickly format text and paragraphs. This means the program can be used for elementary desktop publishing, and pictures can be easily inserted (using the Insert menu).

Writer features a number of toolbars running across the top of the screen that provide quick access to the formatting tools, as well as to other common functions. The vast majority of menu options match those found in Word. Right-clicking the text itself offers quick access to text-formatting tools. Table 11-2 provides an overview of Writer's user interface components.

A number of higher-level functions are provided, such as Mail Merge, spell-checking, and a thesaurus (all found on the Tools menu). As with Microsoft Word, spell-checking can be performed on the fly, with incorrect words underlined in red as you type.

As with all OpenOffice.org packages, Writer is fully compatible with Microsoft Office files, so you can both save and open DOC files. Just select the file type in the Save As dialog box. The only exception is password-protected Word files, which cannot be opened. You can also export documents as PDF files (using File ➤ Export As PDF), so they can be read on any computer that has Adobe Acrobat Reader installed.

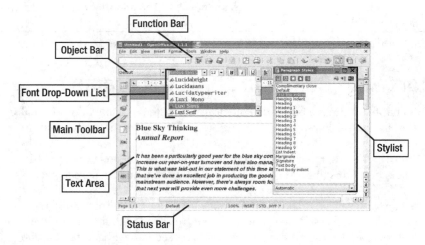

Figure 11-1. *OpenOffice.org Writer*

Table 11-2. *OpenOffice.org Writer Interface Elements*

Element	Description
Function bar	This toolbar provides quick access to file and print operations, and lets you control on-screen elements such as floating palettes.
Object bar	This toolbar provides quick access to text-formatting tools, such as applying bold or italic and centering text.
Font drop-down list	This list provides previews of the fonts available for use in the document. Simply select the one you wish to use.
Stylist	This floating palette lets you quickly apply text styles to the document, as well as create new text styles from scratch.
Main toolbar	This toolbar provides access to various functions within Writer, such as spell-checking and the table-creation tool.
Text area	This is where you compose your document.
Status bar	This lets you see at a glance which page you're editing, as well as other vital information regarding your editing mode.

Spreadsheet: OpenOffice.org Calc

As with most of the packages that form the OpenOffice.org suite, Calc (K menu ➤ Office ➤ Spreadsheet) does a good impersonation of Excel, both in terms of powerful features and also the look and feel, as you can see in Figure 11-2. In fact, it goes beyond what Excel can offer in some areas, although it doesn't run Excel VBA macros. Table 11-3 provides brief descriptions of the main parts of Calc's interface.

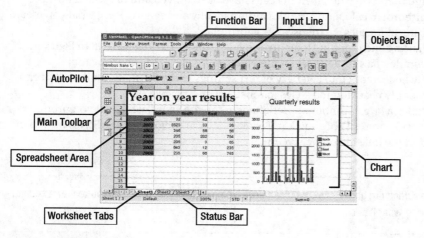

Figure 11-2. *OpenOffice.org Calc*

Table 11-3. *OpenOffice.org Calc Interface Elements*

Element	Description
Function bar	As with all OpenOffice.org components, this allows quick access to file and print functions, and lets you activate the palettes.
Object bar	This toolbar allows the quick formatting of cells, including text, currency, and other styles.
Main toolbar	This provides access to Calc functions, such as the automatic graphing tool.
AutoPilot	Clicking this icon opens a helper dialog box, which makes it easier to select and use formulas.
Input line	This is where you can construct formulas or simply type data for entry into the highlighted cell.
Spreadsheet area	This is the main spreadsheet area, consisting of cells in which data can be entered.
Worksheet tabs	These tabs let you move between the separate spreadsheets that make up the worksheet document.
Status bar	This lets you see at a glance vital information, such as the zoom level and which sheet you're currently editing.

Calc has a vast number of mathematical functions. To see a list, choose Insert ➤ Functions. The list includes a brief explanation of what each function does to help you get started. Just as with Excel, these functions can also be accessed via the toolbar by clicking the AutoPilot button, or entered directly into cells by typing an equal sign and then the formula code. The program is intelligent enough to realize when formula cells have been moved and to recalculate accordingly. It can even attempt to calculate formulas automatically and can work out what you mean if you type something like "sales + expenses" as a formula.

Automated charting and graphing tools are provided (under Insert ➤ Chart). In Figure 11-2, you can see an example of a simple chart created automatically by the charting tool.

Cells can easily be formatted to a variety of text settings using the main toolbar. You can also automatically apply user-defined styles (choose Format ➤ Stylist).

Calc also includes a large number of predefined template styles, which let you produce very professional results remarkably quickly. To take a look at them, click the Styles button on the main toolbar (on the left side of the screen).

▓Tip In all the OpenOffice.org applications, you can hover the mouse cursor over each button for a second to see a tooltip showing what it does.

If you're a business user, you'll be pleased to hear that you can import databases to perform serious number-crunching. Use Insert ➤ Data to get the data, and then the tools on the Data and Tools menu to manipulate it.

As with all OpenOffice.org programs, compatibility with its Microsoft counterpart—Excel files in this case—is guaranteed. You can also open other common data file formats such as comma-separated values (CSV) and Lotus 1-2-3 files.

Presentations: OpenOffice.org Impress

Anyone who has used PowerPoint will immediately feel at home with OpenOffice.org's Presentation package (K menu ➤ Office ➤ Presentation), shown in Figure 11-3. Once again most of the common features found in PowerPoint are duplicated, with a helping of OpenOffice.org-specific extras. Table 11-4 describes the user interface elements.

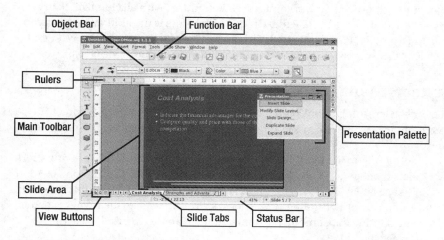

Figure 11-3. *OpenOffice.org Impress*

Table 11-4. *OpenOffice.org Impress Interface Elements*

Element	Description
Function bar	This provides quick access to file and print operations, and lets you activate or deactivate on-screen palettes.
Object bar	This offers quick access to formatting tools for both text and objects drawn on screen.
Main toolbar	The toolbar offers quick access to core functions, such as tools that let you draw shapes, lines, and text boxes.
Rulers	These help with the precise positioning of objects, as well as the measurement of objects.
Slide area	This is the document area, where you can edit your slides.
Presentation palette	This provides a shortcut for inserting and otherwise manipulating slides.
View buttons	These small buttons let you quickly switch between slide, master, and layer views of your document.
Slide tabs	Here you can select between the various slides within the current presentation, as well as insert new ones by clicking in a blank space.
Status bar	This shows important information such as the x and y coordinates of the cursor, as well as the current slide number.

The program works via templates into which you enter you data. Starting the program causes the AutoPilot to appear. The AutoPilot guides you through selecting a style of presentation fitting the job you have in mind. At this point, you can even select the type of transition effects you want between the various slides.

Once you're actually entering data, you can choose from the usual master and outline modes (look under the View menu and the small icons at the bottom left of the program window), until you find the best way of working. Along with slide presentations, Impress also lets you produce handouts to support your work.

Pictures, other graphics, and sound effects can be inserted easily. The Fontwork tool (under the Format menu) makes it easy to create and manipulate 3D-effect text.

You can open and edit existing PowerPoint (PPT) files and, as with all OpenOffice.org packages, save your presentation as a PDF file. Unique to Impress is the ability to export your presentation as a Macromedia Flash file (SWF). This means that anyone with a browser and Macromedia's Flash plug-in can view the file, either after it's put online or via e-mail.

E-mail/Contacts Manager: Kontact

If you're familiar with Microsoft Outlook, you'll feel immediately at home with Kontact (K menu ➤ Office ➤ Kontact), which mirrors Outlook's look and feel, as well as providing identical functionality.

As shown in Figure 11-4, on the left side of the screen are various icons that provide shortcuts to e-mail, contacts management, a calendar, and a to do list. In fact, the functions within Kontact are available separately. Its e-mail function is provided by Kmail, for example, which has its own K menu entry. However, running everything within Kontact is an ideal way of keeping yourself organized and sharing data among the applications. Table 11-5 briefly describes Kontact's main interface elements.

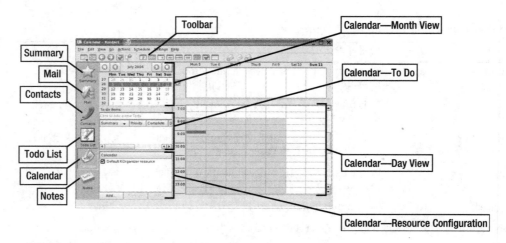

Figure 11-4. *Kontact, Calendar view*

When you click each icon on the left side of the screen, the toolbar and menu change accordingly, to offer features appropriate to whatever you're doing.

Table 11-5. *Kontact Interface Elements*

Element	Description
Summary	This presents a summary of today's information, such as appointments and anniversaries, and if you have any new mail.
Mail	This effectively opens the Kmail e-mail client within the Kontact window.
Contacts	This opens the KDE address book, which lets you search and edit your contacts list.
Todo List	This lets you create and edit a sophisticated to do list, which you can use to plan for the coming time period.
Calendar	This lets you organize events according to a day-by-day calendar.
Notes	This lets you create sticky notes, which are "stuck" on-screen as impromptu reminders.
Toolbar	This changes depending on which component of Kontact is active and offers quick access to the key functions of each tool.
Calendar, month view	With the Calendar component active, the left corner of the screen shows the month's appointments at a glance.
Calendar, to do items	In Calendar view, you also see a small preview of your to do list, and you can edit it from here, too.
Calendar, resource configuration	This area of the Calendar view lets you choose your data source. Most of the time, it can be ignored.
Calendar, day view	In this Calendar view, the day is split into hours and you can see at a glance what appointments are due, as well as edit them.

In the contact manager, you can either create new contacts from scratch or edit those that have been added by programs like Kmail (contacts are generated automatically when you reply to e-mail). Simply double-click the entry you want to edit, or click the New icon on the main toolbar. In most cases, the only contact information that is absolutely necessary is the name and e-mail address of the person, but you might want to fill in the other fields.

The Todo List is fairly advanced. To create a new task, right-click in some empty space and select New Todo. As well as simply letting you create a list of tasks, it allows you to mark each as completed to a certain percentage. So, if you get only half a job done despite your best intentions, you can simply mark the task as 50% complete! Just double-click the task to alter its settings. Each task can have attendees attached to it, and you can even attach files to each task (which could be a spreadsheet that you're working on, for example).

The calendar ties into the Todo List tool, in that it will remind you when tasks are due. However, it also adds a variety of other organizational functions. Events can be added for every half hour of every day. Alarms can be set for each event, and you can set recurrences, so that you might remind yourself every day to do a certain task, for example.

The e-mail program, provided by Kmail, is extremely powerful in itself. The program can understand HTML e-mail and includes powerful filtering tools by which you can sort new mail. To create a new filter, simply right-click the e-mail message you want to base the filter on and select the relevant option from the menu. You can also search e-mail messages—according to their message body, sender, or a variety of other options—by clicking the button on the toolbar. Kmail can import e-mail from other programs (via Tools ➤ Import Messages), such as from Microsoft's Outlook Express.

Web Browsing and File Management: Konqueror

Konqueror (K menu ➤ Internet ➤ Web Browser ➤ Konqueror) uses the same browsing concept as Windows, in that the same program is used to manage local files as well as to browse the Internet. This means that you can quickly jump from seeing what's in a folder on your hard disk to browsing your favorite web site, without needing to start up a new program. FTP and SFTP sites are handled natively within Konqueror, too, providing a graphic way to upload and download files.

As shown in Figure 11-5, Konqueror features everything you might find in Internet Explorer, such as a bookmarks list and a packed toolbar that lets you navigate even the most complicated site. Table 11-6 provides an overview of the Konquerer interface components.

■**Note** Konqueror offers two similar-looking buttons. The left arrow provides the Back function, and the up arrow lets you move backward in the web server's file system (for example, clicking it will move you from `www.mysite.com/folder1/` to `www.mysite.com`).

Figure 11-5. *Konquerer*

Table 11-6. *Konquerer Interface Elements*

Element	Description
Toolbar	Here, you'll find the usual complement of browser buttons, such as Back, Forward, Stop, Home, and so on.
Address bar	This is where the address of the site or location you're current browsing is both displayed and entered.
Animated logo	This graphic revolves when Konqueror is busy fetching data. Clicking it opens a duplicate program window, showing the current site.

Table 11-6. *Konquerer Interface Elements (Continued)*

Element	Description
Go button	This can be clicked to make Konqueror visit the location in the address bar.
Browser window	This is where the contents of the site or location you're currently browsing appear.

SUSE Linux includes several plug-ins with Konqueror, such as Macromedia Flash and RealPlayer, which let you take advantage of multimedia aspects of web sites. These are automatically configured and ready to go; just visit your favorite site, and they should kick in automatically.

Like many non-Internet Explorer-based browsers, Konqueror also includes tabbed browsing, which lets you access more than one site at any one time. To start a new tab, press Ctrl+T.

■**Tip** Middle-clicking a link causes it to appear in a new Konqueror browser program window.

If you find the default size of text too large or too small, you can select View ➤ Increase/ Decrease Text Size. Note also that you can remove a sidebar that appears, such as the bookmark list, by clicking its right edge and dragging it to the left of the window.

Audio Playback: KsCD and XMMS

Audio playback under SUSE Linux is very strong, although the tasks of playing back music files and playing back CDs are handled by separate programs. XMMS (K menu ➤ Multimedia ➤ Audio Player) is ordinarily used for playback of MP3 or Ogg files (these are the open-source equivalent of MP3 files; see Chapter 19 for more details.) KsCD (K menu ➤ Multimedia ➤ CD Player) is used for the playback of CDs.

Inserting an audio CD should cause KsCD to start, as shown in Figure 11-6. Playback should occur automatically. KsCD keeps things very simple. It lets you move backward and forward through tracks, as well as click and drag a slider to skip through the song to your favorite section. Adjust the volume by clicking the icon just to the left of this.

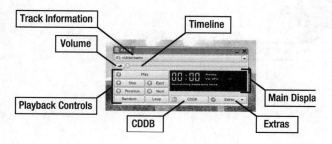

Figure 11-6. *KsCD*

Additionally, KsCD will attempt to download track and artist information in the background via the online CD Database (CDDB) service, so you no longer need to deal with just track numbers. You can even edit the track information if you find it wrong or unacceptable; just click the CDDB button to make changes. Table 11-7 summarizes KsCD functions.

Table 11-7. *KsCD Interface Elements*

Element	Description
Track information	Here, you'll see the track name and artist information, provided KsCD was able to look up your CD online.
Volume	Click the button, and then drag the slider to alter the volume of the CD playback.
Timeline	This shows at a glance your progress through the current track. Click and drag to move backward and forward.
Playback controls	These are similar to the controls on most multimedia equipment, and they control the playback of the CD tracks.
CDDB	This lets you add your own artist and track information and, optionally, upload it to the central online CD database server.
Extras	This lets you access the configuration options for KsCD, and it also contains shortcuts to popular music-related web sites.
Main display	This displays the time a track has been playing.

XMMS, shown in Figure 11-7, should start up automatically if you double-click an MP3 track. XMMS borrows a lot from Winamp, the popular Windows application, and operates virtually identically. You can control the track using the player buttons at the bottom of the program. To create a playlist, click the PL button. Graphic equalization can be applied to the sound by clicking the EQ button. The menu that appears when you right-click the program window lets you change various options, including adding various visualizations, if you like to have something to watch while the music plays. Table 11-8 provides a rundown of XMMS functions.

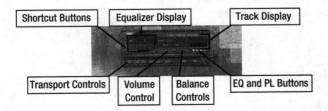

Figure 11-7. *XMMS*

Table 11-8. *XMMS Interface Elements*

Element	Description
Equalizer display	This shows a graphical equalizer-style display of the frequencies in the current track.
Track display	Here, you'll see details of the artist and track information (provided that data is contained in the file you're playing).
Transport controls	On this part of the interface are the Play, Pause, Stop, and other buttons that control playback.
Shortcut buttons	Several very small letters, which let you control functions of the XMMS interface. Hold down the mouse button and drag it over each letter to see a description in the main window.
Volume control	Click and drag this slider to alter the volume of the currently playing track.
Balance control	Click and drag this slider to move the sound from left to right in the stereo field.
EQ button	Clicking the EQ button will bring up the graphical equalizer screen, where you can alter the quality of the sound.
PL button	Clicking the PL button opens the playlist, where you can cue tracks for later playback.

Movie Playback: Kaffeine Media Player

Kaffeine (K menu ➤ Multimedia ➤ Video Player), shown in Figure 11-8, can be used to play back the majority of video file types, with a couple of notable exceptions. Because of issues surrounding copyright, Kaffeine cannot play DVD movies, and it also doesn't support the Windows Media Player WMV format. However, it will happily play AVI and MPG files, which are among the most popular file types on the Internet. (You can use RealPlayer to play RAM and RM files, which are usually found online.)

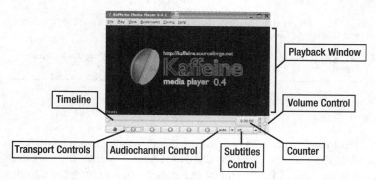

Figure 11-8. *Kaffeine Media Player*

▪Note Although Kaffeine cannot play DVD movies and WMV/ASF files, it can be configured to do so with some add-on software (see www.xinehq.de, or read Chapter 20, in which Kaffeine is discussed in more depth). However, installing these programs can be a complicated procedure, and the software itself lies in a legally gray area. DVD movies are copy-protected to the extent that they cannot be played on certain software. To overcome this restriction and let Linux users play DVD movies, the software bypasses this protection. To use such software is a criminal offense in some countries, including the United States, and this is why it isn't supplied by default with SUSE Linux, and its use is not advocated in this book.

Kaffeine integrates with the Konqueror web browser, and it will immediately start up when you click any video links on web sites (if you want to avoid this and save the video file to disk, right-click the link and select Save Link As). Kaffeine will also start automatically when you click video files on your hard disk. It can play videos full screen (an option on the View menu) and apply audio equalization to the sound. You can attempt to improve the picture quality by adjusting the brightness, contrast, and other aspects; select Config ➤ Video Settings to access these options. Table 11-9 provides an overview of Kaffeine's interface.

Table 11-9. *Kaffeine Media Player Interface Elements*

Element	Description
Playback window	This is where the video file you're playing will appear. The window resizes itself automatically to fit various movie aspect ratios.
Timeline	Click and drag this slider to move backward and forward within the movie file.
Transport controls	Clicking these buttons lets you stop, pause, play, and move between chapters within the movie.
Counter	This display shows the time elapsed since the movie started playing.
Audio channel control	On movie files that have such an option, this control lets you select which audio channels are used during playback.
Subtitles control	This button lets you activate or deactivate subtitling, if such a feature is provided with the movie file you're playing.
Volume control	Clicking and dragging this slider will alter the overall playback volume of the movie.

CD/DVD Burning: K3b

Once again, users of popular Windows CD-burning programs will feel utterly at home with K3b (K menu ➤ CD/DVD Burning ➤ K3b). You can use it to create data, audio, and DVDs. K3b lets you create audio CDs from MP3s and copy CDs. As shown in Figure 11-9, K3b provides a fully graphic interface that employs click and drag for most of its functions.

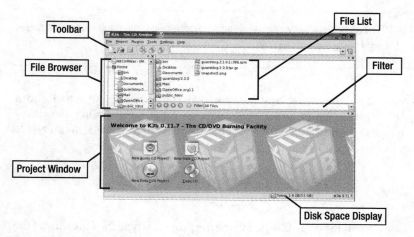

Figure 11-9. *K3b*

To create a disc, simply click the icon representing the project type at the bottom of the program window. After this, compiling a disc is simply a matter of clicking and dragging files from the top of the window to the bottom. This applies to both data and music CDs. Watch the green line at the bottom to see how full your CD is. Table 11-10 summarizes the K3b user interface components.

Table 11-10. *K3b Interface Elements*

Element	Description
Toolbar	This provides access to key functions within K3b, such as starting the CD-burning process.
File browser	This tree view lets you select the folder that contains the files you want to burn.
File list	This list shows the files contained in the folder selected in the file browser. Just drag-and-drop them onto the window below.
Project window	When a project type is selected, this window shows details of the files chosen to be burned to CD.
Filter	This lets you filter by filename. The filter box accepts simple wildcards and isn't case-sensitive.
Disk space display	This displays the hard disk space available as a temporary store for your project. It must exceed the size of your project.

When you're ready to create your disc, click the Burn button at the bottom right of the program window (or the button on the toolbar). In the dialog box that appears, you can choose the writing speed and also whether you want to do a test burn first.

■Tip To create a CD-ROM that can be read by Windows systems, click the Filesystem tab in the burn dialog box and put a tick in the Generate Joliet Extensions box.

Depending on your system's hardware configuration, K3b sometimes won't actually burn a CD unless the program is run as the root user. You'll see an error message saying that you don't have permission to access the CD-R/RW drive. To run K3b as root, select K menu ➤ System ➤ Terminal ➤ Konsole. At the command line, type the following:

```
xhost +
su -
nohup /opt/kde3/bin/k3b
```

As a security precaution, when you're finished using the program, type the following at the command line:

```
exit
xhost -
```

Photo Editing: The GIMP

While most of the other programs we've introduced so far mirror the Windows look and feel in some way, The GIMP (K menu ➤ Graphics ➤ Image Editing ➤ The GIMP) walks a different path. It has its own unique way of working, which takes a little getting used to. But it's very much worth the effort, because The GIMP offers photo-editing tools on par with professional products like Adobe Photoshop. It's certainly more than powerful enough for tweaking digital camera snapshots.

When you initially run The GIMP, it will install itself to your hard disk. Some of the questions it asks look complicated, but you can stick with the default choices throughout.

Once the program is running, you'll notice that it's actually little more than a large toolbar on the left side of the screen, as shown in Figure 11-10. Everything else that runs within The GIMP—whether it's a window containing the image you're editing or an additional configuration dialog box—uses its own program window. This also means that each program item that you activate gets its own button on the Taskbar at the bottom of the screen.

To open a picture, select File ➤ Open and select your image from the hard disk. Once an image file is opened, you can manipulate it using the tools on the toolbar (which are similar to those found in other image editors). On the bottom half of the main program window, you'll find the settings for each tool, which can be altered, usually via click-and-drag sliders. For more details of the user interface, see Table 11-11.

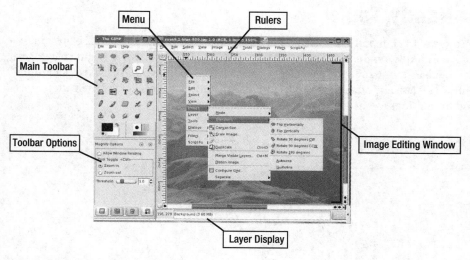

Figure 11-10. *The GIMP*

Table 11-11. *The GIMP Interface Elements*

Element	Description
Main toolbar	This offers quick access to all mouse-driven image-editing tools.
Toolbar options	Here, you can set the individual options for the various image-editing tools selected in the main toolbar.
Menu	This appears when you right-click the image and allows access to various functions within The GIMP.
Image editing window	This is a separate program window where the image is actually edited.
Rulers	You can use the rulers for accurate measurement and guidance when editing.
Layer display	This area of the screen shows the layer currently being edited.

To apply filters or other corrective changes, right-click anywhere on the image to bring up a context menu with a variety of options. Simple tools to improve brightness and contrast can be found on the Layer ➤ Colors submenu.

Like all image editors, The GIMP is a complex piece of software with its own terminology and toolset. This means it can be daunting at first. However, persistence really does pay off. For an in-depth look at this package, see Chapter 21.

Other Handy Tools

A quick browse of the K menu will reveal other pieces of software that you can use on a day-to-day basis. For example, on the Utilities menu, you'll find a calculator, which is shown in Figure 11-11. This appears to mirror a simple calculator on startup, but if you wish to use scientific functionality, you can add statistical and trigonometric functions by clicking the various options on the Settings menu.

Figure 11-11. *If you ever need a calculator, you'll find one on the K menu, under the Utilities heading.*

Under Graphics ➤ Viewer ➤ Kuickshow, you'll find a tool you can use to view images quickly and easily, without needing to fire up The GIMP. By right-clicking most image files in Konqueror when browsing your hard disk files, you should be able to select Kuickshow from the menu, too.

Adobe Acrobat is located under Office ➤ Document Viewer. This will let you view any PDF files, just as in Windows, although it should automatically start when you double-click any PDF files within Konqueror.

If you're a fan of Internet newsgroups (Usenet), you'll find Knode under the Internet ➤ Usenet News Reader menu entry. This lets you subscribe to virtually any newsgroup and post messages. It allows you to track newsgroups and score messages, so that you know which discussion threads to watch.

If you have a microphone plugged into your PC, you can record sounds from it using Krecord, which is virtually identical to Microsoft's Sound Recorder. It is located on the K menu under Multimedia ➤ Recording.

Last but not least, you'll find some valuable relaxation tools on the Games menu. There are clones of Windows favorites Minesweeper and Solitaire, called Kmines and Kpatience, respectively.

Summary

In this chapter, we've taken a look at some SUSE Linux programs that provide vital functions that you might have used daily under Windows. The aim was to get you started with this software as quickly as possible by pointing out key features. You've seen how some programs mirror the look and feel of their Windows counterparts almost to the letter, while others resolutely strike out on their own path. In both instances, it takes just a little time to become familiar with SUSE Linux software, and then using these programs will become second nature.

In the next chapter, we'll move on to more fundamental SUSE Linux task: manipulating files. However, once again, this is not too dissimilar from the Windows experience, which makes getting used to the system very easy.

CHAPTER 12

■ ■ ■

Managing Your Files

Files are what make the world of SUSE Linux go round. They're the currency of any kind of operating system, because every time you use your computer, you generate new files, even if they're only temporary.

How SUSE Linux views files, as well as the disks and partitions that contain them, varies somewhat from how Windows handles files. In many ways, the Linux system of file management is far simpler than that in Windows (which, ironically, was created as an attempt to make everything easy!). The Linux system is also much more established.

In this chapter, I will explain how you can manage your files under SUSE Linux. This isn't a definitive guide; you'll need to wait until Chapter 15 to learn the technical ins and outs of the file system. However, it provides enough information for you to understand how the system works, and where and how you should store your data.

File System Concepts

Just like Windows, SUSE Linux has a file system that is shared among components and your own personal data, which you generate within various applications, or perhaps download from the Internet. However, SUSE Linux differs from Windows in a couple of important ways.

Drive References

Perhaps the most important differences in Linux are that it doesn't use drive letters and it uses a forward slash (/) instead of a backslash (\) in filename paths. In other words, something like /home/john/myfile is typical under SUSE Linux, as opposed to C:\Documents and Settings\John\myfile under Windows. The root of the hard disk partition is usually referred to as C:\ under Windows. In SUSE Linux, it's referred to simply with a forward slash (/).

If you have more than one drive, the drives are usually combined together into the one file system under Linux. This is done by *mounting*, so that the drives appear as virtual folders under the file system. We'll discuss mounting in Chapter 15.

Case Sensitivity

There's another important difference between SUSE Linux and Windows: filenames in SUSE Linux are case-sensitive. This means that MyFile is distinctly different from myfile. Uppercase letters are vitally important. In Windows, filenames might appear to have uppercase letters in them but, actually, these are ignored when you rename or otherwise manipulate files.

The importance of uppercase and lowercase in SUSE Linux means that you could have two separate files existing in the same place, one called MyFile and another called myfile. In fact, you could also have myFile, Myfile, MYFILE, and so on, as shown in Figure 12-1.

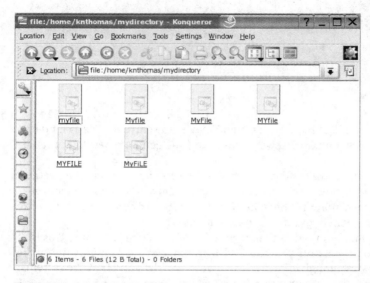

Figure 12-1. *SUSE Linux filenames are case-sensitive, so many similar filenames can exist, differing only in which letters are capitalized.*

File Access and Storage

Under Windows on a desktop computer, you have access to the entire hard disk. You can write, read, or delete files anywhere (unless the system has specifically been configured otherwise). You can save your personal files in C:\Windows, for example. Under SUSE Linux, you can browse most of the hard disk, but you won't be able to write files to the majority of folders (in some cases, won't even be able to access files).

Although we'll cover the file system in much more depth in Chapter 15, for the moment, it's enough to know that you've been given your own part of the hard disk in which to store your stuff. This is a directory located within the /home directory, and its name is taken from your username. If your login name is louisesmith, your private place for storing files will be /home/louisesmith. Figure 12-2 shows an example of a user's home directory.

■**Note** SUSE Linux generally uses the terms *directory* and *subdirectory* for the places you put files, whereas Windows XP refers to them as *folders*. It's merely a matter of semantics. However, within the Konqueror file browser, directories are pictured as folders and are referred to as such, thus furthering the confusion!

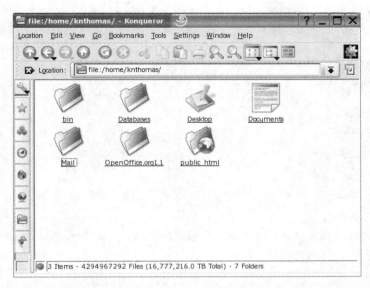

Figure 12-2. *Your personal area on the hard disk is in the /home directory and is named after your username (/home/knthomas, in this case).*

SUSE Linux also creates a Documents folder that you can use in the same way as My Documents under Windows. Several other programs aim to create similar folders. For example, the digital camera software Digikam will create a Pictures folder within your /home folder. It's up to you whether you use these folders. The standard practice within the Linux community is to simply save everything into your /home subdirectory (for example, /home/knthomas) and sort it out later!

Files within SUSE Linux remember who owns them. If user johnsmith creates a file, he can make it so that only he can read or write the file (the default setting is that other users will be able to read the file but not write any new data to it). Directories, too, are owned by people, and by default, only johnsmith will be able to access his folder in /home/johnsmith. In other words, his folder within /home is genuinely his private area.

■**Note** The root user (referred to as Administrator in Windows) has access to all of the system, regardless of who the user is. This is so he or she can perform essential system maintenance. In most instances, you will also be the root user, because you installed SUSE Linux and created the account during installation. But if you share a PC that you did not set up, it means the owner of that PC potentially has access to your personal files.

Using Konqueror

In the previous chapter, Konqueror was introduced as a web browser. However, it's also the principle GUI-based method for handling files on your hard disk.

You can click the Web Browser button on the Panel and start Konqueror that way, but it's also possible to click the link on the K menu, which is located at the bottom of the K menu and is marked Home, as shown in Figure 12-3. This starts it in file-browsing mode, which is what you want in this case.

Figure 12-3. *You can browse to your own personal file storage area by clicking the Home link on the K menu.*

Tip There's also a shortcut to start Konqueror in file browsing mode on the shortcut bar, just to the left of the SUSE icon (the icon in question looks like a small house). You can add a shortcut to run Konqueror from the desktop by dragging this icon onto the desktop, and choosing Copy Here from the menu you are presented with when you release the mouse button.

Clicking Home on the K menu should open Konqueror and present a list of files in your /home directory (your private area on the disk). This directory actually contains more than it appears to, because, along with your personal data, all your program settings are stored in your /home folder. They're just hidden. (To view hidden files and folders in Konqueror, select View ➤ Show Hidden Files.)

Caution You should never delete your /home folder. Doing so will most likely destroy your personal SUSE Linux setup.

Konqueror is virtually identical to Windows Explorer/My Computer within Windows, at least in terms of functionality. You double-click folders to open them, and then click the Back button to return to where you were. When you right-click a file, you see a context menu with options for copying, pasting, renaming, and more, as shown in Figure 12-4. You can drag-and-drop files from one location to another. If you open another Konqueror window, you can drag-and-drop files between the two windows.

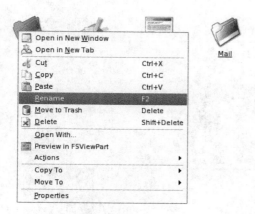

Figure 12-4. *You can perform most file operations by right-clicking, as in Windows.*

▌Note You might be used to dragging-and-dropping files onto program windows or taskbar buttons within Windows in order to cause the file to open. This works with only some programs within SUSE Linux. Generally, the best policy is to try it and see what happens. If the cursor turns into a 'No Entry' icon, then it's not allowed with that particular program.

SUSE Linux defaults to an icon view of files within Konqueror. This has various advantages. If you open a folder full of pictures, for example, it will automatically create thumbnail previews of each one, as shown in Figure 12-5. However, such large, chunky icons are not particularly useful when you're navigating a folder full of hundreds of files. Selecting View ➤ View Mode lets you choose from a variety of ways of presenting your files. The one most like the list setting in Windows, which presents all the details you need alongside small icons, is Detailed List View.

You can also create bookmarks for various locations on your hard disk. This is more useful to advanced SUSE Linux users, but it's easy to do. Just select Bookmarks ➤ Add Bookmark.

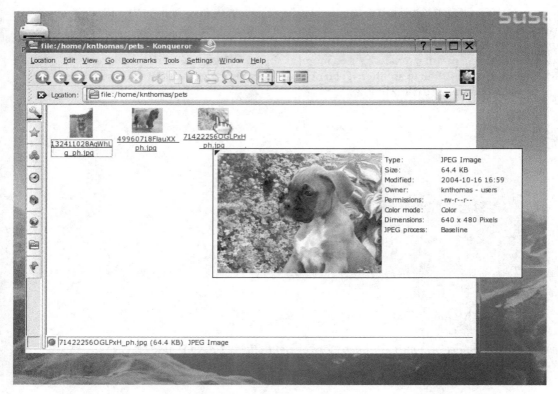

Figure 12-5. *Konqueror will automatically provide thumbnail previews of your digital images.*

Launching Files and Running Programs

As with Windows, most of the programs on your SUSE Linux system automatically associate themselves with various file types that they understand. For example, double-clicking an MP3 track will automatically start the XMMS player application, and double-clicking a .doc file will start OpenOffice.org Writer.

You should find that SUSE Linux is automatically set up to view common file types. However, you might find Table 12-1 useful. It shows which programs are required for viewing certain types of documents.

Table 12-1. *Common File Types*

File Type	File Extension	Viewer	Location on K Menu
Word processor document	DOC, RTF	OpenOffice.org Writer	Office ➤ Wordprocessor
Spreadsheet	XLS	OpenOffice.org Calc	Office ➤ Spreadsheet
Presentation	PPT	OpenOffice.org Impress	Office ➤ Presentation

Table 12-1. *Common File Types (Continued)*

File Type	File Extension	Viewer	Location on K Menu
PDF file	PDF	Adobe Acrobat	Office ➤ Document Viewer ➤ Adobe Acrobat
Compressed file	ZIP, TAR, GZ, BZ2, etc.	Ark	Utilities ➤ Archiving ➤ Ark
Image file	JPG, GIF, TIF, BMP, etc.	Kuickshow	Graphics ➤ Viewer ➤ Kuickshow
HTML file	HTM, HTML	Konqueror	Internet ➤ Web Browser
Text file	TXT, LOG	Kate	Utilities ➤ Editor ➤ Kate
Audio file	WAV, MP3	XMMS	Multimedia ➤ Audio Player
Video file	MPG, MPEG, AVI	Kaffeine	Multimedia ➤ Video Player
RealPlayer movies/audio	RAM, RM, RPM	RealPlayer	Multimedia ➤ RealPlayer

If you want to change the choice of program associated with a file type, either temporarily or permanently, right-click the file and select Open With from the menu, as shown in Figure 12-6. You might see a few choices of other programs in the list, but to make a permanent change, click the Other button. You'll see a K menu-like list of programs. Make your selection and, if you want it to be the application that opens files of this type from now on, click Remember Application Association for This Type of File.

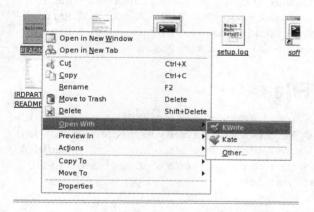

Figure 12-6. *You can select which program to use to open a file by right-clicking and selecting Open With.*

Under Windows, you can use Windows Explorer to launch program executables by just browsing to their location within Program Files and double-clicking their .exe file. It's technically possible to run programs by browsing to their location using Konqueror, but this is discouraged. One reason is that SUSE Linux doesn't store most of its programs in one central folder, as does Windows.

You can launch programs under SUSE Linux by using the K menu. Virtually everything that is installed by default will have an entry here. If there's a program you've added yourself, or that isn't on the menu for some reason, you can run it by clicking Run Command. Just type the program's name in the Run Command dialog box, as shown in Figure 12-7, and then click the Run button. This component is fairly clever, because it will attempt to guess the name of the program as you type it; you'll see the rest of the program name appear in gray. The icon will also change to match the program, giving you a clue that you have the correct filename.

Figure 12-7. *You can run programs you've installed yourself by using the Run Command option on the K menu.*

Generally, typing the program name in lowercase in the Run Command dialog box runs the majority of programs. Unlike with Windows, executable files within SUSE Linux don't have an .exe extension, and the system is able to recognize the file as being runnable by less obvious means (as explained in Chapter 15). To give an example, if you wish to run the Kmines game, simply type kmines in the Run Command dialog box. This rule isn't universally applicable, however, and sometimes abbreviations are used. You can start OpenOffice.org's Writer application by typing OOo-writer, for example. To start OpenOffice.org Writer with a particular file, type the program name and then the filename: OOo-writer myfile.doc.

Accessing Windows Files

Running SUSE Linux on your PC makes you a relative stranger in a world of Windows users. It's likely that you'll need to access Windows files on a regular basis. If you've chosen to dual-boot with Windows, you might want to grab files from the Windows partition on your own hard disk. If your PC is part of a network, you might want to access files on a Windows-based server or workstation on which a shared folder has been created.

Working with Files in Windows Partitions

SUSE Linux automatically makes available any Windows partitions when you dual-boot. They're made available in a virtual way as a folder on your hard disk (this is a process called *mounting* and will be described in Chapter 15). All you need to do is look under /Windows, and you should find the entire contents of your Windows partitions ready and waiting, as shown in Figure 12-8.

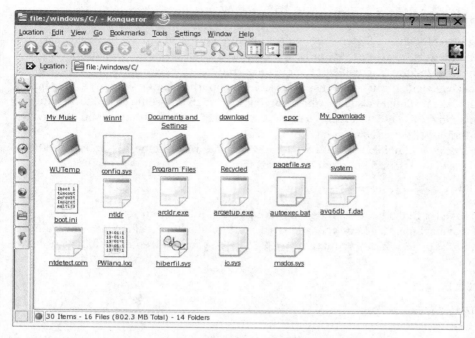

Figure 12-8. *If you've chosen to dual-boot, you should find the contents of your C: drive available in the /Windows/C/ folder. If you have multiple Windows partitions, the next one would be under /Windows/D/, and so on.*

If your Windows partition is formatted with the FAT32 file system, you should be able to copy files from the Windows folder and also save files into it. If you're running Windows 95, 98, or Me, you're almost certainly using FAT32.

If you're running Windows NT, 2000, or XP, it's likely you're using NTFS. In this case, you'll be able to view and copy files in the Windows folder but not write to the disk. In other words, the Windows folder will be read-only.

It is actually feasible to write files to an NTFS partition from within SUSE Linux, but it's not recommended, and it cannot be achieved without heavy-duty additional configuration. It will also very probably result in data loss. This is because NTFS is more than simply a file system, and it relies on a secret file to keep track of where things are. It's simply impossible for SUSE Linux to be able to safely write to this file.

■**Tip** Windows 2000 and XP are compatible with both the FAT32 and NTFS file system. If you have a desperate need to write files to your Windows partition from within SUSE Linux, you might consider converting NTFS to FAT32. This can be done using a variety of commercial partitioning programs, such as PartitionMagic (www.symantec.com).

Accessing Networked Files

Accessing servers or shared folders on Windows machines over a network is relatively easy, and there are a variety of ways to do this. The easiest method is to double-click the Network Browsing icon on the KDE desktop. This will start Konqueror and attempt to search for Windows machines on your local network. If you've ever used Network Neighborhood under Windows, this should be very familiar. You might also know how unreliable this can be—some computers simply don't appear in the list, others appear eventually after a wait, and others appear but then prove to be mysteriously inaccessible.

A far quicker and reliable method of accessing a Windows machine is to enter something similar to the following into Konqueror's address bar:

```
smb://Windows computer's IP address/
```

You'll need to find out the IP address by asking your system administrator or the person in charge of that machine. Make sure your address bar entry ends with a trailing slash. For example, if the IP address of the Windows computer is 192.168.1.24, you would enter the following in the address bar:

```
smb://192.168.1.24/
```

See Figure 12-9 for an example.

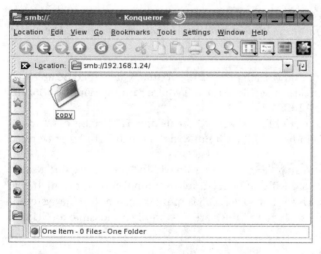

Figure 12-9. *You can browse Windows network shares by typing smb://, followed by the IP address of the share, into Konqueror.*

■**Note** You might be able to browse network computers in Windows using their network names (which is to say their plain English names, such as "John_computer"). You can try this in Konqueror, but it's not guaranteed to work. Using the IP address is much quicker.

If the Windows machine has a username and password for the shared folder, you'll be prompted to enter them. If you're accessing a Windows 95, 98, or Me shared folder, then only password protection will have been set (these versions of Windows are unable to specify a username). When prompted by Konqueror, you will still need to type something into the user-name box to gain access—anything will do, as long as the password is correct. Note that you *cannot* leave the username box blank.

Accessing Floppies, CDs, and DVDs

SUSE Linux automatically makes available any floppy disks, CDs, or DVDs you use on your computer. Accessing them is simple: double-click My Computer on the desktop (as with Windows), and you should find all your drives available in one place, as shown in Figure 12-10.

Note In days of old, special tools were used to access MS-DOS floppies under SUSE Linux. Nowadays, you can simply use My Computer or Konqueror without needing to take any special steps.

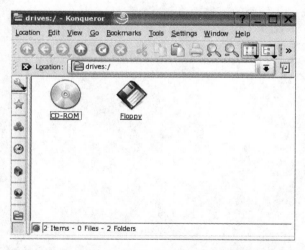

Figure 12-10. *Under My Computer on the desktop, you'll find all your removable storage drives.*

Because My Computer is effectively another rendition of the Konqueror file manager, the tricks and tips discussed in the previous sections apply. You can copy files by clicking and drag-ging, and right-clicking files offers virtually all the options you could need.

Tip You don't need to use My Computer each time to access your floppy, CD, or DVD drive. These drives are available in the following virtual folders on your hard disk: /media/floppy, /media/cd, and media/ dvd. Just type these addresses into Konqueror's address bar. You can copy files to and from each folder as if it were a genuine folder on your hard disk. Note that inserting a CD-ROM into a DVD-ROM drive will cause its contents to appear under /media/DVD, even though it isn't a DVD-ROM disc.

Ejecting Media from Drives

Because of the way SUSE Linux operates, you won't be able to eject a CD or DVD if you're still browsing it. You must either close the Konqueror window or use the Back button to return to the main My Computer screen. If you try to eject a CD or DVD before you stop browsing it, you'll find the eject button on the drive won't respond.

The same applies to the floppy drive. Although you're able to eject the floppy at any time, you should *never* do so unless the access light has gone out on the drive itself, and you're no longer browsing it via Konqueror. If you do eject a floppy under these conditions, it will probably result in data loss.

Formatting Floppies

Formatting floppy disks isn't done in Konqueror. Instead, you must use a special program called Kfloppy. To start Kfloppy, select K menu ➤ System ➤ File System ➤ Kfloppy. You'll see the program window shown in Figure 12-11.

Figure 12-11. *Formatting floppy disks is done using the Kfloppy tool.*

Kfloppy is similar to the disk-formatting tool in Windows, and most of the options are self-explanatory. If you intend to share the disk with Windows users, make sure DOS is selected in the File System box (it's possible to format a floppy using SUSE Linux's own ReiserFS file system format, but there's little to be gained by doing so).

Summary

This chapter has led you on your first steps in exploring the SUSE Linux file system. The file system is vitally important to how Linux works, and we'll go into it in much depth in upcoming chapters.

Here, you were introduced to elementary concepts, such as where personal files are stored and the basic rules that govern what you can and cannot do with files. We also looked at the principle method of accessing files via the GUI: the Konqueror file manager. Additionally, you learned how to run programs manually, as well as how to access any Windows partition or files that may exist on your hard disk or across a network.

In Chapter 13, we'll move on to look at typical problems that can arise with SUSE Linux, and see how they can be fixed.

■ ■ ■

Dealing with Problems

No doubt, you've heard wide-ranging claims about Linux being stable and secure, implying that it won't give you any problems. This is certainly true to an extent, but the reality is that any kind of computer operating system can go wrong. While SUSE Linux is infinitely more stable than its Windows counterpart, problems will occasionally arise.

In this chapter, we look at problems you might encounter and look at ways you can fix things to get back to normal as quickly as possible.

SUSE Linux Stability

It's widely agreed that Linux is very stable and Windows is unstable. Although the situation is improving with each new version, it's rare for Windows users to see a month, week, or even day without a crash or a forced reboot. Yet Linux has been known to quite literally keep running for years. Why this is so comes down to differences in approaches to producing software.

Windows is closed source, which is to say that only Microsoft employees and a select group of individuals around the world can see its source code (the original listing created by the programmers). This means that when a serious bug arises and causes the operating system to become unstable, only Microsoft engineers can diagnose the cause of the problem, and only they can fix it. The world is at their mercy. If they don't consider the bug serious enough to be fixed immediately, you're out of luck and will need to wait until the next major update is released.

Linux is completely the opposite. The source code is always open and available for anyone to see. The end result of this is that if a bug is identified, many people around the world attempt to diagnose the cause. What they discover is then fed back to the original programmer, who is able to fix the bug very quickly. A new version of the program is then made available immediately, and everyone can download and use it (although many people wait for the release of a full update—a so-called *point release*).

However, none of this is to say that Linux is perfect. It rains even in paradise, and from time to time, you might run into problems with your Linux setup. Programs will occasionally crash, and you might need to do a little problem solving. Fortunately, the creators of Linux realized that things go wrong and built in a variety of tools to help.

CRASHING DRIVERS

Windows works on the basis of hardware manufacturers producing drivers for the hardware you use on your system. While this means that most new hardware is instantly able to work with Windows, it also creates many problems. Few drivers are bug-free, and if the hardware in question is a fundamental part of the system (such as the graphics card or a RAID controller), its driver can crash the entire system. If this happens, you must wait for the manufacturer to release a new version of the driver, which can take weeks or months.

It is possible to use third-party driver software with SUSE Linux, but it's not very common. Instead, support for most hardware is built into the SUSE Linux kernel. Sometimes, this is provided by the manufacturers of the hardware, although most of the time it's written by one of the core kernel team who reverse-engineers the hardware. This means that the Linux developer attempts to find out how the hardware works and produces software based on these discoveries.

If the manufacturer does provide driver software, the open-source nature of Linux means that the code can be inspected before it's allowed to be a part of the kernel program. This means that bugs have a much greater chance of being unearthed.

Crash Recovery

Crashes in SUSE Linux are not like crashes in Windows. A typical crash within Windows will usually take the rest of the system with it, or certainly damage the system so that it malfunctions until you reboot. You might be able to recover to some degree, and perhaps even keep on working, but in a lot of cases, you'll need to reboot.

In SUSE Linux, programs are far more independent and "clean." If a program crashes, it will usually leave the rest of the system intact. Even if the system appears to have completely locked up, there's a strong chance that you'll be able to recover and carry on as if nothing had gone wrong.

■**Note** Ctrl+Alt+Delete is familiar to all Windows users. It's the magical key combination that either restarts the system or brings up the Task Manager, which you can use to restart the system or terminate wayward programs. Under SUSE Linux, Ctrl+Alt+Delete has a different effect: it brings up the shutdown dialog box, which you can use to log out, restart, or shut down your system.

If an individual program crashes, it will usually do so in a fuss-free manner. The first thing you'll notice is that the program simply disappears. If it's a KDE application, it may crash, and then a window might appear asking you to file a bug report, as shown in Figure 13-1. This usually just sends an e-mail message to the developers, telling them what happened. It's a good idea to send these, because relaying this information will inevitably lead to better software in the future.

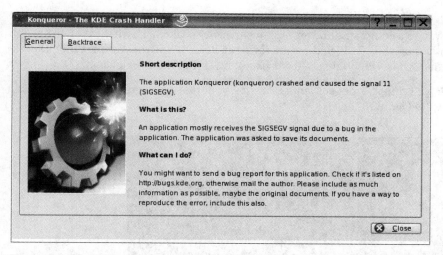

Figure 13-1. *If a KDE program crashes, it will ask you to file a bug report. This will help produce better software in the future.*

If a program crashes but its window lingers on screen, and the mouse cursor is still responsive, select K menu ➤ Run Command, and then type xkill in the box. The cursor should change into a skull and crossbones to indicate that the program is active. Then click on the program window that has crashed. You should find it disappears, and you can keep on working. Be very careful with this approach, because xkill can also destroy perfectly healthy programs. Make sure you click on the right program window!

■**Tip** To cancel xkill after it has started (if the crashed program disappears on its own accord before you can get to it, for example), simply right-click anywhere.

Salvaging Lock-Ups

If a program crashes completely and seems to jam everything else, including the mouse (which may freeze on the spot or just stop being able to click anything), there's still no need to reach for your PC's reboot button yet.

The first potential cure is to try to terminate the graphical display completely. Doing so will cause it to instantly restart. It will also result in the loss of the data in any programs you have open, which might not be ideal. But it's a quick and efficient way of regaining control of your machine. You can kill the graphical display by pressing Ctrl+Alt+Backspace (not the Delete key!).

However, if you do find your system has apparently locked up just as you were editing a vital file that you haven't saved, there's another less drastic trick you can try:

1. Press Ctrl+Alt+F2 (the function keys run along the top of most keyboards). This will switch you to a command-line prompt (technically speaking, it switches you to an alternative console, of which there are six available to be used at any one time). Don't worry, the GUI is still running in the background and you haven't killed it.

2. At the login prompt, type root, and then enter your root password when it's requested, as shown in Figure 13-2.

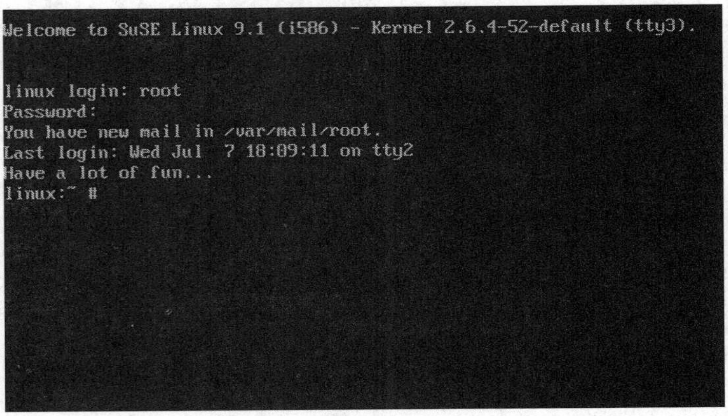

Figure 13-2. *Type* root *as your username and then enter your root password.*

3. At the command-line prompt, type top. This will start a program in which you'll be shown all the running programs (the top program is covered in Chapter 17).

4. Look down the list and try to find the program that has crashed. Once you find it, look at the very left of its entry in the list. You should see a four- or five-digit number, which is the program's process ID (PID).

5. Type k (lowercase) and type in the PID number. Then press Enter. See Figure 13-3 for an example.

6. Now switch back to the GUI by pressing Ctrl+Alt+F7. With any luck, you should find the crashed program has disappeared, and you now have control of your computer again.

```
top - 17:42:20 up  1:12,  3 users,  load average: 0.11, 0.15, 0.18
Tasks:  66 total,   1 running,  65 sleeping,   0 stopped,   0 zombie
Cpu(s):  4.6% us,  7.7% sy,  0.0% ni, 85.7% id,  0.6% wa,  0.1% hi,  1.3% si
Mem:    256608k total,    248120k used,     8488k free,    46760k buffers
Swap:   514040k total,        4k used,   514036k free,    99120k cached
PID to kill: 1944
  PID USER      PR  NI  VIRT  RES  SHR S %CPU %MEM   TIME+  COMMAND
 4558 root      17   0  1756  820 1540 R  1.9  0.3  0:00.04 top
    1 root      16   0   588  240  444 S  0.0  0.1  0:04.97 init
    2 root      34  19     0    0    0 S  0.0  0.0  0:00.01 ksoftirqd/0
    3 root       5 -10     0    0    0 S  0.0  0.0  0:00.99 events/0
   16 root       5 -10     0    0    0 S  0.0  0.0  0:01.22 kblockd/0
   26 root      15 -10     0    0    0 S  0.0  0.0  0:00.00 pdflush
   27 root       5 -10     0    0    0 S  0.0  0.0  0:02.78 pdflush
   29 root      15 -10     0    0    0 S  0.0  0.0  0:00.00 aio/0
   28 root      15   0     0    0    0 S  0.0  0.0  0:00.03 kswapd0
  177 root      25   0     0    0    0 S  0.0  0.0  0:00.00 kseriod
  218 root      19   0     0    0    0 S  0.0  0.0  0:00.00 scsi_eh_0
  235 root       5 -10     0    0    0 S  0.0  0.0  0:02.36 reiserfs/0
  634 root       6 -10     0    0    0 S  0.0  0.0  0:00.00 kcopyd/0
 1002 root       9 -10  2500 1256 2288 S  0.0  0.5  0:00.00 hotplug
 1003 root      10 -10  1360  380 1200 S  0.0  0.1  0:00.01 logger
 1010 root       8 -10  2500 1248 2288 S  0.0  0.5  0:00.00 block.agent
 1011 root       6 -10  1360  480 1200 S  0.0  0.2  0:00.02 logger
 1015 root       6 -10  1412  428 1200 S  0.0  0.2  0:00.02 hwscand
 1046 root      15   0  1504  580 1316 S  0.0  0.2  0:04.00 vmware-guestd
 1670 root      15   0     0    0    0 S  0.0  0.0  0:00.00 khubd
 2016 root      16   0  1436  608 1260 S  0.0  0.2  0:00.12 syslogd
 2019 root      16   0  2360 1528 1212 S  0.0  0.6  0:00.17 klogd
 2082 bin       17   0  1420  560 1248 S  0.0  0.2  0:00.04 portmap
 2084 root      16   0  1588  660 1416 S  0.0  0.3  0:01.52 resmgrd
 2220 root      22   0  4708 1800 4320 S  0.0  0.7  0:00.11 sshd
 2594 lp        16   0  6364 3100 3340 S  0.0  1.2  0:02.47 cupsd
 2738 root      16   0  4176 1448 3960 S  0.0  0.6  0:00.18 master
 2748 postfix   17   0  4220 1420 4004 S  0.0  0.6  0:00.09 pickup
 2749 postfix   17   0  4252 1456 4036 S  0.0  0.6  0:00.08 qmgr
 2896 root      16   0 42624  780 1468 S  0.0  0.3  0:00.74 nscd
```

Figure 13-3. *Find the misbehaving program in the list, press* k, *then type its PID number.*

Unfreezing by Connecting over a Network

But what if your entire system has completely locked up and none of the previous tricks work? To be honest, this is highly improbable and quite literally a once-in-a-lifetime event for most SUSE Linux users, unless they're using highly experimental software. But in this situation, there's one last trick you can attempt.

If the crashed machine is connected to a network, you can try connecting to it from another Linux machine. This is done via a program called Secure Shell (SSH). Effectively, this program lets you log in to the machine as if you were sitting in front of it. It's a very useful program that we'll discuss in Chapter 34. For the moment, however, we're only concerned with using SSH to try to salvage a crashed machine.

■ **Note** SSH will work only if it's activated (running) on the machine you want to connect to, and the remote machine's firewall has been previously opened to allow connections from outside.

On another Linux machine elsewhere on your network, open a command-line prompt (if the other machine is also running SUSE Linux, select K menu ➤ System ➤ Terminal ➤ Konsole). Then type the following:

```
ssh root@[IP address of crashed machine]
```

This will attempt to connect to the crashed computer. If it's not completely crashed, you should get a response asking if you want to save the computer's cryptographic key (a code by which you can authenticate the computer in future). Agree to do so, and then type in the root password for the crashed machine. Figure 13-4 shows an example of this procedure.

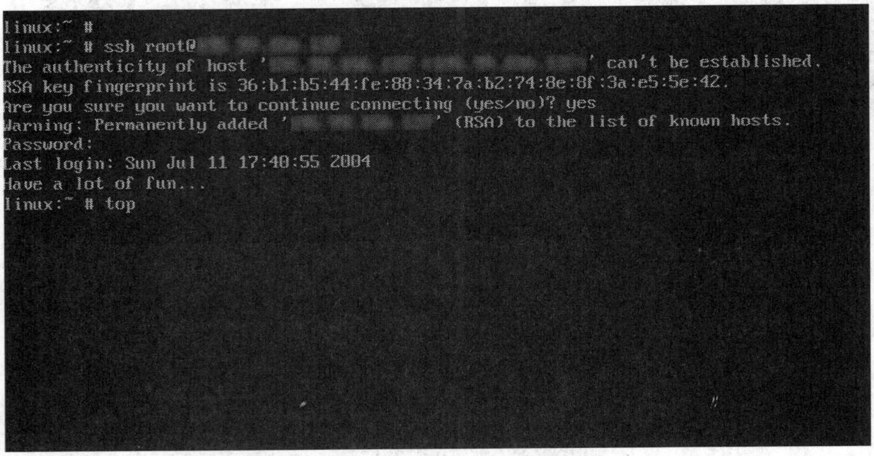

Figure 13-4. *You can attempt to unfreeze a crashed machine by connecting to it over the network.*

With any luck, you should find yourself with a command prompt. From there, follow the instructions in the previous section to terminate the crashed program using the top program.

If SSH simply hangs and doesn't appear to be doing much, chances are the crashed machine is beyond salvaging. At this point, it's time to hit its reset button. You gave it your best shot!

FILE SYSTEM MAINTENANCE

Under Windows, you might be used to regularly defragmenting your disk and also running the Scandisk program to check the file system for errors.

SUSE Linux includes a Scandisk-like program, called `fsck`, but the system is configured so that this runs automatically if your system shuts down unexpectedly. Running it manually is possible but requires the use of a rescue disk, because a file system that is currently in use (booted into) cannot be scanned.

If you feel that your partition needs to be scanned manually, insert your SUSE Linux installation DVD-ROM and boot from it. At the boot menu, select Rescue System. Select your keyboard layout when prompted. When the username prompt appears, type `root`. You won't be prompted for a password. Then type the following:

```
fsck -p /dev/hda3
```

This assumes SUSE Linux is installed on the third partition of your hard disk, which is usually the case if you're dual-booting with Windows. You can check to see which partition number your SUSE Linux partition is by typing this:

```
fdisk -l /dev/hda
```

Alternatively, if you installed SUSE Linux on a second hard disk installed specifically for the purpose, it's likely SUSE Linux will be installed on the `/dev/hdb2` partition, so you should type that with the `fsck` command. As for defragmenting the hard disk, this is unnecessary under SUSE Linux because a different methodology is used to store data compared to Windows. On a well-used system, fragmentation might still occur, but not in the extreme levels found on Microsoft file systems and certainly not enough to cause performance issues.

General Problem-Solving Tips

There are a number of tips for solving various problems on your computer—from freezes to incorrect software operation. In most cases, these tricks are noninvasive, and they shouldn't cause you to lose data or adversely affect your system. Therefore, they're certainly worth a try.

Emptying the /tmp Folder

The first trick is to empty the /tmp folder. This clears away all temporary application data, which can lead to software not working correctly or even systemwide freezes or crashes. Most applications store temporary data as part of their day-to-day working (including the KDE desktop environment) and, theoretically at least, this data should be deleted or discarded after use. But this doesn't always happen.

To clear the /tmp folder, start the machine in Failsafe mode by choosing that option at startup. This will boot the machine to the command prompt. Enter root as the username and type the password when prompted. Then type the following:

```
rm -rf /tmp/* /tmp/.*
```

Be sure to type this line *exactly* as it's written, because there's the very strong possibility of damage if you get even one character incorrect! Don't worry if you receive an error message stating that . and .. cannot be removed (these refer to the current directory and the current directory's parent directory, respectively).

When you're finished, reboot the machine by typing reboot.

Disabling Power-Saving Functions

Many problems with computer operating systems are caused by incorrect operation of the power-saving functions: Advanced Power Management (APM) and the more recent Advanced Configuration and Power Interface (ACPI) standard. Disabling power saving can often clear up many problems, including system crashes and freezes. The downside is that your system will not be able to power down its components during periods of inactivity, such as when you're away from it for short periods.

■**Note** Problems with power saving might not be the fault of SUSE Linux. The implementations of APM and ACPI vary widely from computer to computer, and few companies follow the standards laid down by the industry bodies behind APM and ACPI. In fact, Linux generally follows the standards to the letter. It's just a shame that PC manufacturers can't!

Disabling power saving is achieved at the GRUB boot menu that appears when you first start your system. Make sure Linux is highlighted, and then type the following:

```
apm=off acpi=off
```

If you find this tip is successful at clearing up the problems, you can add it to the boot menu automatically to avoid typing it at startup each time, as follows:

1. Start YaST2 by selecting K menu ➤ Control Center and clicking the YaST2 Modules icon on the left. Click System, and then click Boot Loader Configuration.

2. Click the Administrator Mode button and enter your root password.

3. Click the Available Selections line, and then click the Edit button.

4. On the next screen, select the entry marked Linux, and then click Edit again.

5. On the following screen, select the line marked kernel and click Edit.

6. In the dialog box that appears, use the cursor keys to move the end of the line and, after inserting a space, type the following:

   `apm=off acpi=off`

7. Click OK to save the change.

8. Click OK, OK, and Finish on the ensuing screens.

Running SuSEconfig

Some problems can be cleared up by running the SuSEconfig program. SUSE Linux is slightly different from other distributions of Linux because it holds copies of most of the systemwide configuration files in one location, rather than in various application-chosen locations on the hard disk (although most tend to be stored in the `/etc` directory). The SuSEconfig program ensures that all configuration files across the system are up-to-date.

Running the program is easy. Simply open a Konsole window (K menu ➤ System ➤ Terminal ➤ Konsole), switch to root user (i.e. type `su`), and type `SuSEconfig`.

You might find it useful to log out and then back in after this has finished in order to reload various configuration files, particularly if the problem appears to be affecting the running of the desktop.

Getting Help Online

If you run into any kind of problem within SUSE Linux on virtually any level, chances are you won't be alone. At least one other person will have had the same problem, and it's likely that someone has come up with a solution. Frequently, that person will have written about the solution online, usually on a web site forum, perhaps in response to someone else with the same problem.

The Internet is the biggest and best form of support for Linux, and it's also usually free of charge. There are hundreds of web sites dedicated to technical help. SUSE itself runs a handful of forums on its web site dedicated to its distribution, but there are many others. Here is a sampling:

- Linuxhelp (`www.linuxhelp.net`) is a busy site with many forums offering help on all aspects of Linux use, from installation through to distro-specific guides.

- LinuxQuestions.org (`www.linuxquestions.org`) is a newbie-friendly site covering hardware, software, installation, distros, and much more.

- Computing.Net (`www.computing.net`) is one of the best and busiest forum sites, covering not just Linux, but all types of computing. Figure 13-5 shows an example of what you'll find there.

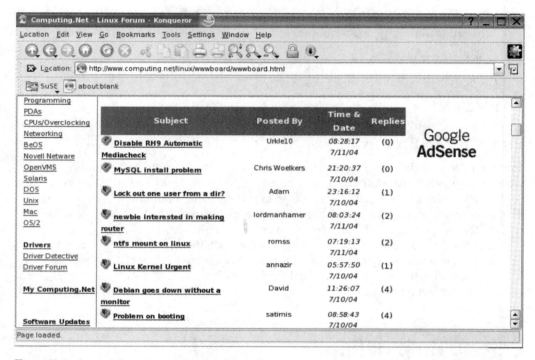

Figure 13-5. *Computing.Net is just one of a great many web sites that aim to help Linux users of all levels.*

- JustLinux (www.justlinux.com) is another popular site aimed at newbies, offering help with all aspects of Linux use.

In addition, if you're a fan of newsgroups (Usenet), you'll find there are many Linux-related groups. You can both post messages and search to find the answers to problems. Newsgroups starting with comp.os.linux (news://comp.os.linux.*) offer help on Linux, and there are groups for just about every type of Linux use. A great program available on SUSE Linux for viewing newsgroups is KNode, as shown in Figure 13-6. You can access this program by typing in the knode command from a shell. Alternatively, select K menu ➤ Run Command, and then type knode in the box. Adding new newsgroups is as simple as clicking the New Groups button and selecting the groups you want from the list that appears.

Another way of finding help is to subscribe to a mailing list. After you sign up with a mailing list, you will receive mail from others on the list, usually asking for help, but sometimes just discussing various matters. You can respond if you wish, or you can simply read what people have to say. The problem with mailing lists is that you receive an enormous amount of mail, particularly on popular lists. However, the messages are usually archived online, and you can browse through them at your leisure without needing to sign up. If you're interested, at http://lists.suse.com/archive/, you can sign up for the mailing list covering SUSE Linux or just read past postings.

All of these online information sources serve an important role. In addition to problem solving, they encourage you to learn about how Linux works. By reading how various problems were overcome, you learn more about how everything functions.

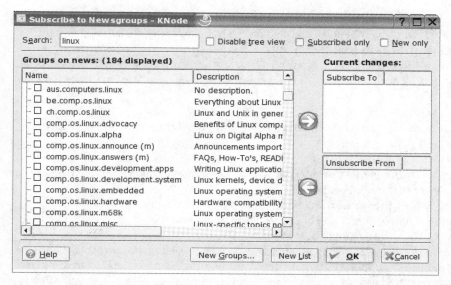

Figure 13-6. *You can use KNode to connect to newsgroups that provide help for Linux newbies.*

■**Tip** Don't worry too much about seeming naïve when you ask for help online. Just be polite and don't be afraid to mention that you're a beginner, although you're advised to do your research first. You should read any manuals and documentation you have to try to find a solution. It also helps if you provide as much information as possible, such as any error messages and configuration details of your system.

Solving Common Problems

This section addresses some common issues, in problem/solution format.

Problem: My computer has frozen. The mouse still moves, but I can't click anywhere.

Solution: You can fix the situation by pressing Ctrl+Alt+Backspace. This will kill the X server and instantly restart it (assuming you're in run level 5).

However, finding the cause of the underlying problem is difficult. If the mouse cursor still moves, this is likely to be a software issue, so you might consider updating your software online if you haven't already. Select K menu ➤ Control Center, click on the YaST2 Modules icon, click Software, and then click Online Updates.

If the freeze always happens when you use a particular application, the problem may be linked to that piece of software. Try keeping a list of when the crash occurs, and write down what you were doing at the time. Then try to see if you can spot a pattern.

Problem: My computer has frozen completely. I can't even move the mouse!

Solution: See the previous answer to learn how to attempt to regain control of your system. If that doesn't work, the quickest solution is to press the reset button on your computer case.

Getting to the bottom of PC lockups is very hard to do, although they tend to be linked to hardware issues. If you have Windows installed on the same machine, try running that for some time and see if the lockup problem persists. If it does, it's unlikely to be linked to SUSE Linux. For example, freezes can often be caused by faulty or overheating system components. However, it's a good idea to also follow the previous instructions to update your system online.

Problem: I can't get any sound!

Solution: Click the Volume icon in the system tray. If the Mute button is checked, you know what's causing the problem!

Problem: The keyboard mostly works fine, but some of the symbols are on the wrong keys. The @ sign isn't where it should be, for example.

Solution: It's likely that your keyboard has been set for the wrong country layout. Start YaST2 (K menu ➤ Control Center and click YaST2 Modules), and then click System ➤ Select Keyboard Layout. Click the Administrator Mode button, enter your root password, and select your country from the list. This suggestion assumes that you're using the correct keyboard for your country. Some PCs supplied in English-speaking countries such as the United Kingdom come with United States keyboards. You can tell if this is the case because the @ sign will be above the numeral 2 key.

Problem: When I click to run a certain program, nothing happens! (Alternatively, the program becomes prone to bugs or crashes, but it worked correctly previously.)

Solution: It's possible that the program has become corrupted. YaST2 includes a function by which a program can be "refreshed," which means effectively reinstalled but without losing any configuration data. Start YaST2 (K menu ➤ Control Center and click YaST2 Modules), click Software, and then click Install and Remove Software. Search for the program in question using the text box and click its check box in the list a few times until the Update symbol appears (a small lightning flash). Then click the Accept button. Note that you will need to insert your SUSE Linux installation DVD.

Problem: I've forgotten my password!

Solution: If you've forgotten your user password, you can log in as root and change it. Log in as root when prompted by typing root as the username and entering your root password. Then open a Konsole window (K menu ➤ System ➤ Terminal ➤ Konsole). Then type this:

```
passwd <username>
```

where *<username>* is your username.

Problem: When SUSE Linux is starting, it gets to the stage where KDE is starting, but then it freezes. The splash screen simply stays on the screen and pauses at a particular stage.

Solution: Sometimes, the KDE desktop environment used by SUSE Linux freezes during startup. This can be for any number of reasons, including a misconfigured X server setup or the power-management system not working correctly. However, if you found that you were able to boot into the desktop in the past but cannot do so any longer, it's possible that one of your KDE configuration files has become corrupted. First, follow the instructions in the "Emptying the /tmp Folder" section earlier in this chapter to clear the /tmp folder.

If this doesn't solve the problem, there's a more drastic course of action you can take. This involves losing all your KDE configuration files, however, which will mean settings for many of your desktop applications will be lost (for example, your Kmail account details will need to be reentered, although your mail won't be lost). It will effectively return you to a pristine state. Open a Konsole window (K menu ➤ System ➤ Terminal ➤ Konsole) and type the following:

```
su
[Enter root password]
init 3
```

This will switch you to run level 3, which will shut down the GUI. Log in under your username and then, making sure you're in your home directory, type this:

```
mv .kde .kde_old
```

This will rename the hidden KDE settings folder. Then restart the GUI by typing this:

```
su
[Enter root password]
init 5
```

When the GUI restarts, the KDE folder will be re-created from scratch, and with any luck, you will be able to boot into the desktop without hindrance.

Summary

Although problems under SUSE Linux are few and far between, in this chapter, we looked at resolving some of the more common issues that can affect users. You saw some ways to clear up crashes, and how SUSE Linux provides functions to help unlock an otherwise doomed session at your computer. You also learned how to get online help from the Linux community. The last part of the chapter suggested cures for a handful of specific Linux problems.

In Part Four of this book, starting in the next chapter, we will look at some of the underlying technology that makes SUSE Linux work and how you can gain more control over your system.

The Shell and Beyond

■ ■ ■

## CHAPTER 14

Introducing the BASH Shell

As you learned in Chapter 1, strictly speaking, the word *Linux* refers to just the kernel, which is the fundamental, invisible program that runs your PC and lets everything happen. On its own, the kernel is completely useless. It needs programs to let users interact with the PC and do cool stuff, and it needs a lot of system files (also referred to as *libraries*) to provide vital functions.

The GNU Project provides many of these low-level pieces of code and programs. This is why many people refer to the Linux operating system as GNU/Linux, giving credit to the fact that, without the GNU components, Linux wouldn't have got off the starting blocks.

The GNU Project provides various shell programs, too. Some of these offer graphical functionality, but most are text only. These text shell programs are also known as *terminal programs*, and they're often colloquially referred to as *command-line prompts*, in reference to the most important component they provide. This kind of shell lets you take control of your system in a quick and efficient way. Like a GUI, it's another way of interfacing with your computer, except that you type commands, rather than use a mouse.

By learning the shell, you'll become the true master of your own system. In this part of the book, you'll learn all you need to know about using the shell. This chapter introduces the BASH shell, which is the default one in SUSE Linux.

What Is the BASH Shell?

The best way of explaining the BASH shell to a Windows user is to compare it to the DOS command prompt. It lets you issue commands directly to the operating system via the keyboard without needing to mess around with the mouse and windows (although it is sometimes possible to use the mouse within a BASH shell to copy and paste text, and sometimes to control simple text-based menus). The big difference is that the BASH shell has commands for just about everything you might do on your system, whereas the DOS command prompt merely offers tools to manipulate files or, on Windows 2000/XP machines, configure certain system settings.

In the old days, the DOS command prompt was also the visible layer of an entire operating system in which DOS programs were designed to be run. However, the shell is merely *one* of the many ways of accessing the Linux kernel and subsystems. It's true that there are many programs designed to run via the BASH shell, but technically speaking, most actually run on the Linux operating system, and simply take input and show their input via the BASH shell.

■Note Linux purists will point out another reason why the shell isn't exactly the same as a DOS command prompt within Windows: it doesn't run in virtual machine mode, a CPU trick by which part of the memory is subdivided to let programs run as if they had the PC all to themselves.

Linux finds itself with the BASH shell largely because Linux is a clone of Unix. In the early days of Unix, the text-based shell was all that was offered as a way of letting users control the computer. Typing commands in directly is one of the most fundamental ways of controlling any type of computer and, in the evolutionary scale, comes straight after needing to set switches and watch blinking lights in order to run programs.

That the BASH shell can trace its history back to the early days of Unix might sound like a tacit indication that the BASH is somehow primitive. Far from it. It's one of the most efficient and immediate ways of working with your computer. Many people consider the command-line shell to be a way of using a computer that has yet to be superseded by a better method.

■Note When you run a shell on a Linux system, the system refers to it as a `tty` device. This stands for teletypewriter, a direct reference to the old system of inputting data on what were effectively electronic type-writers connected to mainframe computers. These, in turn, took their names from the devices used to automate the sending and receiving of telegrams in the early part of the twentieth century.

Most Linux distributions come with a choice of different kinds of shell programs. However, the default shell is BASH, as is the case in SUSE Linux. BASH stands for Bourne Again SHell. This is based on the Bourne shell, a tried-and-tested program that originated in the early days of Unix.

The other shells available include PDKSH (Public Domain Korn SHell, based on Korn Shell, another early Unix shell), and ZSH (Z SHell), a more recent addition. These are usually used by people who want to program Linux in various ways, or by those who simply aren't happy with BASH.

The BASH shell is considered by many to be the best of all worlds in that it's easy enough for beginners to learn, yet is able to grow with them and offer more power as necessary. BASH is capable of scripting, for example, which means you can even create your own simple programs.

■Note Technically speaking, a *shell* refers to any type of user interface. The windowing system offered by Windows and Macintosh operating systems are a type of shell. However, many people in the Linux and Unix worlds use the word *shell* as shorthand for a shell that offers a command line.

Why Bother with the Shell?

You might have followed the instructions in Part Two of this book and consider yourself an expert in Linux. But the real measure of a Linux user comes from his or her abilities at the shell.

In our modern age, the GUI is mistakenly considered "progress." We've been led to believe by companies like Microsoft and Apple that using a mouse and clicking on icons is always the most efficient way of using a computer. While it's handy in certain situations—it would be difficult to imagine image editing without a mouse, for example—in many other situations, such as when manipulating files, directly typing commands is far better.

Most modern Linux distributions prefer you to use the GUI to do nearly everything. This is because they acknowledge the dominance of Windows and realize they need to cater to mouse users who might not even know the shell exists. To this end, they provide GUI tools for just about every task you might wish to undertake. SUSE Linux is particularly strong in this regard, and you can configure virtually everything using the YaST2 program.

However, it's well worth developing at least some command-line shell skills, for a number of reasons:

- **It's simple and fast.** The shell is the simplest and fastest way of working with SUSE Linux. As just one example, consider the task of changing the IP address of your network card. You *could* click on the K menu, and then on Control Center, and then on YaST2 Modules, and then on Network Devices, and then follow the wizard interface through several screens where you can change settings. That will take at least a minute or two if you know what you're doing, and perhaps longer if it's new to you. Alternatively, you could simply open a shell and type `ifconfig eth0 192.168.0.15 up`.

- **It's versatile.** Everything can be done via the shell—from deleting files, to configuring hardware, to creating MP3s. A lot of GUI programs actually make use of programs you can access via the shell.

- **It's consistent among distributions.** All Linux systems have shells and understand the same commands (broadly speaking). However, not all Linux systems will have YaST2. Red Hat Linux uses its own GUI configuration tools, as does Mandrake Linux. Therefore, if you ever need to use another system, or decide to switch distributions, a reliance on GUI tools will mean learning everything from scratch. Knowing a few shell commands will let you get started instantly.

- **It's crucial for troubleshooting.** The shell offers a vital way of fixing your system should it go wrong. Your Linux installation might be damaged to the extent that it cannot boot to the GUI, but you'll almost certainly be able to boot into a shell. A shell doesn't require much of the system other than the ability to display characters on the screen and take input from the keyboard, which most PCs can do, even when they're in a sorry state. This is why most rescue floppies offer shells to let you fix your system.

- **It's useful for remote access.** One handy thing about the shell is that you don't need to be in front of your PC to use it. Programs like ssh let you log in to your PC across the Internet and use the shell to control your PC (as described in Chapter 34). This is invaluable in accessing data on a remote machine, or even fixing it when you're unable to attend the machine's location. This is why Linux is preferred on many server systems when the system administrator isn't always present on the site.

- **It's respected in the community.** Using a shell earns you enormous brownie points when speaking to other Linux users. It separates the wheat from the chaff and the men from the boys (or women from the girls). If you intend to use Linux professionally, you will most certainly need to be a master at the shell.

Seen in this light, learning at least a handful of shell commands is vital to truly mastering your PC.

The drawback when using a command-line shell is that it's not entirely intuitive. Take the command to change the network card's IP address:

```
ifconfig eth0 192.168.0.15 up
```

If you've never used the shell before, it might as well be Sanskrit. What on Earth does ifconfig mean? And why is there the word up at the end?

Learning to use the shell involves learning terms like these. There are hundreds of commands available, but you really need to learn only around 10 or 20 for everyday use. The comparison with a new language is apt because, although you might think it daunting to learn new terminology, with a bit of practice, it will all become second nature. Once you've used a command a few times, you'll know how to use it in the future.

The main thing to realize is that the shell is your friend. It's there to help you get stuff done as quickly as possible. When you become familiar with it, you'll see that it is a beautiful concept. The shell is simple, elegant, and powerful.

When Should You Use the Shell?

The quantity of use the Linux shell sees is highly dependent on the user. Some Linux buffs couldn't manage without it. They use it to read and compose e-mail, and even to browse the Web (usually using the Mutt and Lynx programs, respectively).

However, most people simply use it to manage files, view text files (like program documentation), and run programs. All kinds of programs—including GUI and command-line—can be started from the shell. As you'll learn in Chapter 29, unlike with Windows, installing a program on SUSE Linux doesn't necessarily mean the program will automatically appear on the K menu. In fact, unless the installation routine is specifically made for the version of Linux you're running, this is unlikely. Therefore, using the shell is a necessity for most people.

Note Unlike with DOS programs, SUSE Linux programs that describe themselves as "command-line" are rarely designed to run solely via the command-line shell. All programs are like machines that take input at one end and output objects at the other. Where the input comes from and where the output goes to is by no means limited to the command line. Usually, with a command-line program, the input and output are provided via the shell, and the programmer makes special dispensation for this, but this way of working is why GUI programs often make use of what might be considered shell programs. You'll often find that a GUI program designed to, for example, burn CDs, will also require the installation of a command-line program that will actually do the hard work for it.

There's another reason why the shell is used to run programs: you can specify how a particular program runs before starting it. For example, to launch the Kaffeine video player in full-screen mode playing the `myvideofile.mpg` file, you could type:

```
kaffeine -f myvideofile.mpg
```

This saves the bother of starting the program, loading a clip, and then selecting the full-screen option. Once you've typed the command once or twice, you'll be able to remember it for the next time. No matter how much you love the mouse, you'll have to admit that this method of running programs is simply more efficient.

When you get used to using the shell, it's likely you'll have it open most of the time behind your other program windows.

Getting Started with the Shell

You can start the shell in a number of ways. The most common is to use a terminal emulator program. As its name suggests, this runs a shell inside a program window on your desktop.

You can start Konsole, the built-in KDE shell emulator, by selecting K menu ➤ System ➤ Terminal ➤ Konsole. Alternatively, you can click the shortcut on the Panel, which is the one with the icon of a sea shell set against a monitor, as shown in Figure 14-1.

Figure 14-1. *The Konsole terminal emulator can be quickly started by clicking the icon on the toolbar.*

The first thing you'll see when you start Konsole is a help box offering tips. Your instinct might be to get rid of this and also check the box so that it never reappears, but it actually offers quite a few handy hints.

After you've dismissed the help box, you'll see the terminal window. It will show what's referred to as a *command prompt*: a few words followed by the following symbol: >. On my test system, this is what I see:

```
knthomas@linux:~>
```

The first part is my username—the user account I created during installation and use to log in to the PC. After the @ sign is the name of the PC, which I also chose when installing SUSE Linux. The name of the PC isn't important on most desktop PCs; it's a legacy from the days of Unix. After the colon is indicated the current directory you're browsing. In this example, the ~ symbol appears instead of an actual path or directory name. This is merely SUSE Linux short-hand for the user's home directory. In other words, wherever I see a ~ on my test PC, I read it as /home/knthomas. After this is a cursor, and this is where you can start typing commands!

Note Your PC might be called localhost. This is simply the default name for a computer that Linux uses when it hasn't been told to use anything else.

Running Programs

When we refer to *commands* at the shell, we're actually talking about small programs. When you type a command to list a directory, for example, you're actually starting a small program that will do that job. Seen in this light, the shell's main function is to simply let you run programs— either those that are built into the shell, such as ones that let you manipulate files, or other, more complicated programs that you've installed yourself.

The shell is clever enough to know where your programs are stored. This information was given to it when you first installed SUSE Linux and is stored in a system variable.

Note A variable is the method SUSE Linux uses to remember things like names, directory paths, or other data. There are many system variables that are vital for the running of SUSE Linux.

The information about where your programs are stored, and therefore where SUSE Linux should look for commands you type in, as well as any programs you might want to run, is stored in the PATH variable. You can take a look at what's currently stored there by typing the following:

```
echo $PATH
```

Don't forget that the difference between uppercase and lowercase letters matters to SUSE Linux, unlike with Windows and DOS.

The echo command merely tells the shell to print something on screen. In this case, you're telling it to "echo" the PATH variable onto your screen. On my test PC, this returned the following information:

```
/home/knthomas/bin:/usr/local/bin:/usr/bin:/usr/X11R6/bin:/bin:/usr/games:/opt/
gnome/bin:/opt/kde3/bin:/usr/lib/java/jre/bin
```

There are actually several directories in that list, and each is separated by a slash.

Don't worry too much about the details right now. The important thing to know is that whenever you type a program name, the shell looks in each of the listed directories in sequence. In other words, when you type ls, the command that will give you a directory listing, the shell will look in each of the directories, starting with the first in the list, to see if the ls program can be found. The first instance it finds is the one it will run.

But what if you want to run a program that is not contained in a directory listed in your PATH? In this case, you must tell the shell *exactly* where the program is. Here's an example:

```
/home/knthomas/myprogram
```

This will run a program called myprogram in the /home/knthomas directory. It will do this regardless of the directory you're currently browsing, and regardless of whether there is anything else on your system called myprogram.

If you're already in the directory where the program in question is located, you can type the following:

```
./myprogram
```

So, just enter a dot and a forward slash, followed by the program name.

Getting Help

Of course, there are a lot of tricks you can use to get help at the shell. Each command usually has help built in, which you can query (a little like typing /? after a command when using DOS). This will explain what the command does and how it should be used. For example, you can get some instant help on the ifconfig command by typing this:

```
ifconfig --help
```

You'll see the help screen shown in Figure 14-2.

The --help option is fairly universal, and most programs will respond to it, although sometimes you might need to use a single dash. Just type the command along with --help to see what happens. You'll be told if you're doing anything wrong.

Nearly always when you use the help command option, you'll be shown an example of the command in use, along with the range of command options that can be used with it.

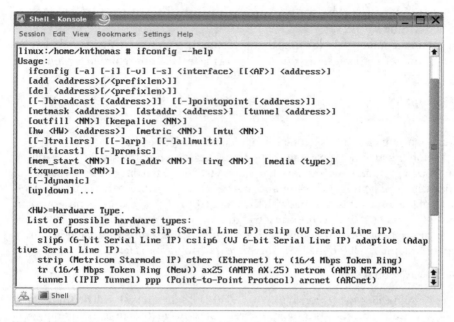

```
linux:/home/knthomas # ifconfig --help
Usage:
  ifconfig [-a] [-i] [-v] [-s] <interface> [[<AF>] <address>]
  [add <address>[/<prefixlen>]]
  [del <address>[/<prefixlen>]]
  [[-]broadcast [<address>]]  [[-]pointopoint [<address>]]
  [netmask <address>]  [dstaddr <address>]  [tunnel <address>]
  [outfill <NN>] [keepalive <NN>]
  [hw <HW> <address>]  [metric <NN>]  [mtu <NN>]
  [[-]trailers]  [[-]arp]  [[-]allmulti]
  [multicast]  [[-]promisc]
  [mem_start <NN>]  [io_addr <NN>]  [irq <NN>]  [media <type>]
  [txqueuelen <NN>]
  [[-]dynamic]
  [up|down] ...

  <HW>=Hardware Type.
  List of possible hardware types:
    loop (Local Loopback) slip (Serial Line IP) cslip (VJ Serial Line IP)
    slip6 (6-bit Serial Line IP) cslip6 (VJ 6-bit Serial Line IP) adaptive (Adap
tive Serial Line IP)
    strip (Metricom Starmode IP) ether (Ethernet) tr (16/4 Mbps Token Ring)
    tr (16/4 Mbps Token Ring (New)) ax25 (AMPR AX.25) netrom (AMPR NET/ROM)
    tunnel (IPIP Tunnel) ppp (Point-to-Point Protocol) arcnet (ARCnet)
```

Figure 14-2. *Most commands contain built-in help to give you a clue as to how they're used.*

In addition, most commands have manuals that you can read to gain a fairly complete understanding of how they work. Virtually every SUSE Linux setup has a set of these *man* pages, which can be accessed by typing this:

man *<command>*

However, man pages are often technical and designed for experienced SUSE Linux users who understand the terminology.

There are also info pages, which offer slightly more down-to-earth guides. You can read these by typing this:

info *<command>*

Some commands aren't covered by the info system, however, in which case you'll be shown the default screen explaining basic facts about how the info command works.

Note that both man and info have their *own* man and info pages, explaining how they work. Just type man man or info info.

Running the Shell via a Virtual Console

As noted earlier, there are a number of ways to start a shell. The most common way among Linux diehards is via a virtual console. To access a virtual console, press Ctrl+Alt, and then press one of the function keys from F2 through F6 (the keys at the top of your keyboard).

Using a virtual console is a little like switching desks to a completely different PC. Pressing Ctrl+Alt+F1 will cause your GUI to disappear, and the screen to be taken over by a command-line prompt (don't worry; your GUI is still there and running in the background). You'll be asked to enter your username and your password.

Any programs you run in a virtual console won't affect the rest of the system, unless they're system commands and you're logged in as the root user. (As discussed in Chapter 13, one way to rescue a crashed GUI program is to switch to a virtual console, become root user, and attempt to terminate the program from there.)

You can switch back to the GUI by pressing Ctrl+Alt+F7. Don't forget to quit your virtual console when you're finished with it, by typing `exit`.

BOOTING INTO THE SHELL

If you're really in love with the shell, you can choose to boot into it, avoiding the GUI completely (although you can later start the GUI by typing `startx` at the command line).

Booting into the shell is done by altering the current run level. A *run level* is how the operating mode that SUSE Linux is currently running in is described. Run level 5 is most widely used on desktop PCs and means that SUSE Linux is running with a graphical interface. Run level 3 will put the system in text-only mode, although it's still possible to start a GUI manually. Run level 1 is the single-user mode. When this mode is in force, the networking aspect of SUSE Linux is deactivated, and several other system processes are stopped, too. This lets you fix things. It's a bit like Safe Mode under Windows.

You can change the run level on the fly by typing the following commands:

```
su -
[enter your root password]
init <run level no>
```

The first command, `su`, makes you temporarily the root user (and ensures you adopt the root user's PATH, so you can run root-only commands). You should be careful what you type when switched to root user, because an error can cause serious damage.

The `init` command is used to switch to a different run level. Typing `init 3` will switch you to run level 3, for example, although beware that this will also mean your GUI is instantly killed, and SUSE Linux won't ask if you want to save your files first!

Working with Files

So let's start actually using the shell. If you've ever used DOS, then you have a head start over most shell beginners, although you'll still need to learn some new commands. Table 14-1 shows various DOS commands alongside their SUSE Linux equivalents. This table also serves as a handy guide to some BASH commands, even if you've never used DOS. In Appendix B, you'll find a comprehensive list of useful shell commands, together with explanations of what they do and examples of typical usage.

Table 13-1. *DOS Commands and Their Shell Equivalents*

Command	DOS Command	Linux Shell Command	Usage
Copy files	COPY	cp	cp <filename> <new location>
Move files	MOVE	mv	mv <filename> <new location>
Rename files	RENAME mv	mv <old filename> <new filename>[1]	
Delete files	DEL	rm	rm <filename>[2]
Create directories	MKDIR	mkdir	mkdir <directory name>
Delete directories	DELTREE/RMDIR	rm	rm -rf <directory name>
Change directory	CD	cd	cd <directory name>
View directories graphically	TREE	tree	tree
Edit text files	EDIT	vi	vi <filename>
View text files	TYPE	less	less <filename>[3]
Print text files	PRINT	lpr	lpr <filename>
Compare files	FC	diff	diff <file1> <file2>
Find files	FIND	find	find -name <name of file>
Check disk integrity	SCANDISK	fsck	fsck[4]
View network settings	IPCONFIG	ifconfig	ifconfig[5]
Check a network connection	PING	ping	ping <address>
View a network route	TRACERT	traceroute	traceroute <address>[5]
Clear screen	CLS	clear	clear
Get help	HELP	man	man <command>[6]
Quit	EXIT	exit	exit

[1] *The SUSE Linux shell offers a rename command, but this is chiefly used to rename many files at once.*

[2] *To avoid being asked to confirm each file deletion, you can add the -f option. Be aware that the rm command deletes data instantly, without the safety net of the Recycle Bin, as with the KDE desktop.*

[3] *Use the cursor keys to move up and down in the document. Press Q to quit.*

[4] *This is a system command and can be run only on a disk that isn't currently in use. To scan the main partition, you'll need to use a rescue floppy (see Chapter 13).*

[5] *This is a system command that can be run only by users with root privileges.*

[6] *The info command can also be used.*

CREATING ALIASES

If you've ever used DOS, you might find yourself inadvertently typing DOS commands at the shell prompt. Some of these will actually work, because most distribution companies create command aliases to ease the transition of newcomers to Linux.

Aliases mean that whenever you type certain words, they will be interpreted as meaning something else. However, an alias won't work with any of the command-line switches used in DOS. In the long-term, you should try to learn the BASH equivalents.

You can create your own command aliases quickly and simply. Just start a BASH shell and type the following:

```
alias <DOS command>='<Linux shell command>'
```

For example, to create an alias that lets you type copy instead of cp, type this:

```
alias copy='cp'
```

Note that the SUSE Linux command must appear in single quotation marks.

Listing Files

Possibly the most fundamentally useful BASH command is ls. This will list the files in the current directory, as shown (with a few other typical commands), in Figure 14-3. If there are a lot of files, they might scroll off the screen. If you're running Konsole, you can use the scroll bar on the right side of the window to view the list.

Figure 14-3. *The ls command lists the files in the current directory.*

Having the files scroll off the screen can be annoying, so you can cram as many as possible onto each line by typing the following:

```
ls -m
```

The dash after the command indicates that you're using a command option. These are also referred to as command-line *flags* or *switches*. Nearly all shell commands have options like this. In fact, some commands won't do anything unless you specify various options. In the case of the ls command, only one dash is necessary, but some commands need two dashes to indicate an option.

You can see a list of all the command options for ls by typing the following (ironically, itself a command option):

```
ls --help
```

Once again, the output will scroll off the screen, and you can use the window's scroll bars to examine it. (In Chapter 18, you'll learn a trick you can use to be able to read this output without needing to fiddle around with the scroll bars, even if there's screen after screen of it.)

Other interesting command options for the ls command include -l, which produces "long" output. This lists file sizes and ownership permissions, among other details (permissions are covered in the next chapter).

With most commands, you can use many command options at once, as long as they don't contradict each other. For example, you could type the following:

```
ls -lh
```

This tells the ls command to produce "long" output (-l) and also to produce "human-readable" output. The human-readable option (-h) means that rather than listing files in terms of bytes (such as 1029725 bytes), it will list them in kilobytes and megabytes. In other words, you can simply list the options after the dash; you don't need to give each option its own dash.

■**Caution** I've said it before, and I'll say it again: don't forget that case sensitivity is vitally important in SUSE Linux! Typing ls -L is *not* the same as typing ls -l. It will produce different results.

Copying Files

So what other useful commands are there for dealing with files? Well, you can copy files with cp. You can use the cp command in the following way:

```
cp myfile /home/knthomas/
```

This will copy the file to the location specified.

One important command-line option for cp is -r. This stands for *recursive* and tells BASH that you want to copy a directory and its contents (as well as any directories within this directory). Most commands that deal with files have a recursive option.

Note Only a handful of BASH commands default to recursive copying. Even though it's extremely common to copy folders, you still need to specify the -r command option most of the time.

One curious trick is that you can copy a file from one place to another but, by specifying a filename in the destination part of the command, change its name. Here's an example:

```
cp myfile /home/knthomas/myfile2
```

This will copy myfile to /home/knthomas, but rename it as myfile2. Be careful not to add a final slash to the command when you do this. In the example here, doing so would cause BASH to think that myfile2 is a directory.

This way of copying files is a handy way of duplicating files. By not specifying a new location in the destination part of the command, but still specifying a different filename, you effectively duplicate the file within the same directory:

```
cp myfile myfile2
```

This will result in two identical files: one called myfile and one called myfile2.

Moving Files

The mv command can be used in a similar way to cp, except that rather than copying the file, the old one is removed. You can move files from one directory to another, for example, like this:

```
mv myfile /home/knthomas/
```

You can also use the mv command to quickly rename files, as shown in Figure 14-4:

```
mv myfile myfile2
```

Note Getting technical for a moment, moving a file in Linux isn't the same as in Windows, where a file is copied and then the original deleted. Under SUSE Linux, the file's absolute path is rewritten, causing it to simply appear in a different place in the file structure. However, the end result is the same.

Figure 14-4. *You can also use the* mv *command to rename files.*

Deleting Files

But how do you get rid of files? Again, this is relatively easy, but first a word of caution: the shell doesn't operate any kind of Recycle Bin. Once a file is deleted, it's gone forever. (There are utilities you can use to recover files, but these are specialized tools and aren't to be relied on for day-to-day use.)

Removing a file is achieved by typing something like this:

```
rm myfile
```

It's as simple as that.

You'll be asked to confirm the deletion after you issue the command. If you want to delete a file without being asked to confirm it, type the following:

```
rm –f myfile
```

The f stands for force (that is, force the deletion).

If you try to use the rm command to remove a directory, you'll see an error message. This is because the command needs an additional option:

```
rm –rf mydirectory
```

As noted in the previous section, the -r stands for recursive and indicates that any folder specified afterwards should be deleted, in addition to any files it contains.

■Tip You might have used wildcards within Windows and DOS. They can be used within SUSE Linux, too. For example, the asterisk (*) can be used to mean any file. So, you can type `rm -f *` to delete all files within a directory, or type `rm -f myfile*` to delete all files that start with the word *myfile*.

Changing and Creating Directories

Another handy command is `cd`, for change directory. This lets you move around the file system, from directory to directory. Say you're in a directory that has another directory in it, named `mydirectory2`. Switching to it is easy:

```
cd mydirectory2
```

But how do you get out of this directory once you're in it? Try the following command:

```
cd ..
```

The `..` refers to the "parent" directory, which is the one containing the directory you're currently browsing. Using two dots to indicate this may seem odd, but it's just the way that SUSE Linux (and Unix before it) does things. It's one of the many conventions that Unix relies on and that you'll pick up as you go along.

You can create directories with the `mkdir` command:

```
mkdir mydirectory
```

Summary

This chapter introduced the command-line shell, considered by many to be the heart of Linux. We've discussed its similarities to MS-DOS, and shown that these are only cursory; knowledge of DOS doesn't equate to skill within BASH. In the long run, you should work to polish your BASH skills.

This chapter also introduced some elementary commands used within BASH, such as those used to provide directory listings and to copy files. We looked at how command-line options can be used to control BASH tools. In many cases, these are mandatory, so you learned how the BASH shell itself can be used to investigate a command and find out vital information about how it works.

At this point, your newfound knowledge will have no doubt caused you to venture into the SUSE Linux file system itself, which can be a confusing, if not terrifying, place for the inexperienced. But don't worry. The next chapter explains everything you need to know about the file system and what you'll find in it.

CHAPTER 15

■ ■ ■

Understanding Linux Files and Users

Most of us are used to dealing with files—the things that live on our hard disks, floppies, and CD-ROMs, and contain data and program code. It should come as no surprise that Linux has its own file structure, which is different from Windows, in terms of where data is stored and also the underlying technology.

Mimicking Unix before it, SUSE Linux takes the concept and use of the file system to extremes when compared to Windows. To SUSE Linux, almost everything is treated as a file: your PC's hardware, network computers connected to your PC, information about the current state of your computer... almost everything finds a home within the Linux file system.

Linux places an equal emphasis on the users of the system. They own the various files and can decide who can and cannot access various files they create.

In this chapter, we'll delve into users, files, and permissions. You'll be introduced to how SUSE Linux handles files and how files are tied into the system of user accounts.

Real Files and Virtual Files

Linux sees virtually everything as a series of files. This might sound absurd and certainly requires further explanation.

Let's start with the example of plugging in a piece of hardware. Whenever you attach something to a USB socket, the Linux kernel finds it, sees if it can make the hardware work, and, if everything checks out okay, it will usually make the hardware available as a file under the /dev directory on your hard disk (dev is short for devices). Figure 15-1 shows an example of a /dev directory.

The file created in the /dev directory is not a *real* file, of course. It's a file system shortcut plumbed through to the input and output components of the hardware you've just attached.

■**Note** As a user, you're not expected to delve into the /dev directory and deal with this hardware directly. Most of the time, you'll use various software packages that will access the hardware for you, or use special BASH commands or GUI programs to make the hardware available in a more accessible way for day-to-day use.

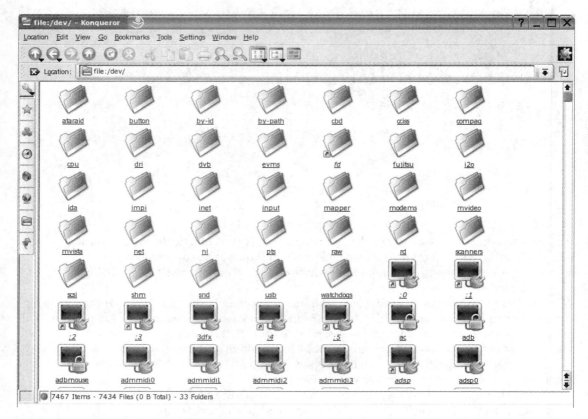

Figure 15-1. *Hardware devices under Linux are accessed as if they were files and can be found in the* /dev *folder.*

Here's another example. Say you're working in an office and you want to connect to a central file server. To do this under Linux, you must "mount" the files that the server offers, making it a part of the SUSE Linux file system. Doing this involves creating an empty directory (or using one that already exists) and using the mount command at the BASH shell to make the server's contents magically appear whenever that directory is accessed. We'll discuss how this is done later in this chapter, in the "Mounting" section (but remember that Konqueror will do this automatically, as discussed in Chapter 12).

Once the network server is mounted, it is treated exactly like a directory on your hard disk. You can copy files to and from it, just as you would normally, using the same tools as you use for dealing with any other files. In fact, less knowledgeable users won't even be aware that they're accessing something that isn't located on their PC's hard disk (or, technically speaking, within their SUSE Linux partition and file system).

By treating everything as a file, Linux makes system administration easier. To probe and test your hardware, for example, you can use the same tools you use to manipulate files.

So how do you know which files are real and which are virtual? One method is to use the following command, which was introduced in the previous chapter:

```
ls -l
```

The -l option tells the ls command to list nearly all the details about the files. If you do this in Konsole, you'll see that the listing is color-coded. Table 15-1 shows what each color indicates. The command returns a lot of additional information, including who owns which file and what you and others can do with it. This requires an understanding of users and file permissions, which we'll discuss next.

■**Tip** The command ls -la will give you even more information—perhaps too much for general use. In most instances, ls -l should show enough information.

Table 15-1. *Color-Coding Within Konsole*

Color	Type of File
Black text	Standard file
Light-blue text	Directory
Black outline with yellow text	Virtual device[1]
Green text	Program or script[2]
Cyan text	Symbolic link to another file[3]
Pink text	Image file
Red text	Archive[4]

[1] *This is found only in the /dev directory.*

[2] *Technically speaking, green text indicates a program or script that has merely been marked as being executable.*

[3] *This is similar to a Windows desktop shortcut.*

[4] *Installation files are also marked red because they're usually contained in archives.*

Users and File Permissions

The concept of users and permissions is as important to SUSE Linux as the idea of a central and all-encompassing file system. In fact, the two are implicitly linked.

When initially installing Linux, you should have created at least one user account. By now, this will have formed the day-to-day login that you use to access Linux and run programs. (Remember that you should use the root account only for essential maintenance work; if you're using it for day-to-day work, stop doing so immediately!)

Although you might not realize it, as a user, you also belong to a group. In fact, every user on the system belongs to a group. Under SUSE Linux, all ordinary users belong to a group called users by default (under other versions of Linux, you might find that you belong to a group based on your username).

■Note Groups are yet another reminder of SUSE Linux's Unix origins. Unix is often used on huge computer systems with hundreds or thousands of users. By putting each user into a group, the system administrator's job is a lot easier. When controlling system resources, the administrator can control groups of users rather than hundreds of individual users. On most home user PCs, the concept of groups is a little redundant, because there's normally a single user, or at most, two or three. However, the concept of groups is central to the way that Linux handles files.

A standard user account under SUSE Linux is normally limited in what it can do. This is set when the account is first set up. As a standard user, you can save files to your own private area of the disk, located in the /home directory, as shown in Figure 15-2, but usually nowhere else. You can move around the file system, but some directories are strictly out of bounds. In a similar way, some files can be opened as read-only, so you cannot save changes to them. All of this is achieved using file permissions.

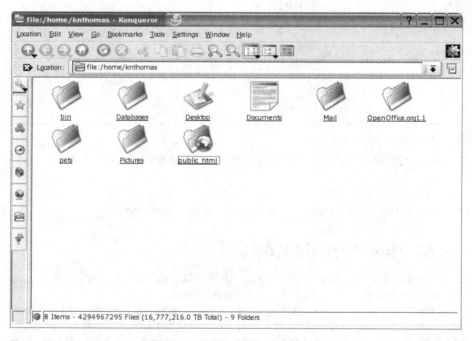

Figure 15-2. *Your personal directory within home is your area on the hard disk. This is enforced via file permissions.*

Every file and directory is owned by a user. In addition, files and directories have three separate settings that indicate who within the Linux system can read them, who can write to them, and, if the file in question is "runnable" (usually a program or a script), who can run it ("execute" it). In the case of directories, it's also possible to set who can browse them, as well as who can write files to them. If you try to access a file or directory for which you don't have permission, you'll be turned away with an "access denied" error message.

Viewing Permissions

When you issue the `ls -l` command, each file is listed on an individual line. Here's an example of one line of a file listing from my test PC:

```
-rw-r--r--  2 knthomas users 673985982 2004-07-07 17:19 myfile
```

The r, w, and – symbols on the very left of the listing indicate the file permissions. The permission list usually consists of the characters r (for read), w (for write), x (for execute), or - (meaning none are applicable).

They're followed by a number indicating the link count, which you can ignore. After this is listed the owner of the file (knthomas in the example) and the group that he belongs to (users). This is followed by the file size (in bytes), then the date and time the file was last accessed, and finally the filename itself appears.

The file permissions part of the listing might look confusing, but it's actually quite simple. To understand what's going on, you need to split it into groups of four, as illustrated in Figure 15-3.

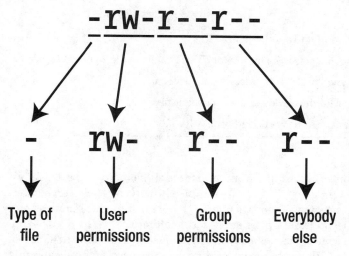

Figure 15-3. *The file permissions part of a file listing can be broken down into four separate parts.*

The four groups are as follows:

- **Type of file:** This character represents the file type. A standard data file is indicated with a dash (-). Most files on your system fall into this category. A d shows that the entry is not a file, but a directory. Table 15-2 lists the file type codes.

- **User permissions:** Next come the permissions of the person who owns the file. The three characters indicate what the person who owns the file can do with it. The owner of a file is usually the user who created it, although it's also possible to change the owner later on. In this example, you see rw-. This means that the owner of the file can read (r) and write (w) the file. In other words, he can look at it and also save changes to it. However, there's a dash afterwards, and this indicates that the user *cannot* execute the file. If this were possible, there would be an x in this spot instead.

- **Group permissions:** After the owner's permissions are the permissions given to members of that user's group. This is indicated by another three characters in the same style as those for user permissions. In our example, the group's permission is r--, which means that the group members can read the file but *don't* have permission to write to it, since there's a dash where the w would normally appear. In other words, as far as they're concerned, the file is read-only.

- **Everyone else's permissions:** The last set of permissions indicates the permissions of everyone else on the system (other users in other groups). In our example, they can only read the file (r); the two dashes afterwards indicate that they cannot write to the file or execute it.

Table 15-2. *File Type Codes*

Code	File Type
-	Standard file
d	Standard directory
l	Symbolic link (a shortcut to another file)
p	Named pipe (a file that acts as a conduit for data between two programs)
s	Socket (a file designed to send and receive data over a network)
c	Character device (a hardware device driver, usually found in /dev)
b	Block device (a hardware device driver, usually found in /dev)

As you might remember from Windows, programs are stored as files on your hard disk, just like standard data files. On Linux, program files need to be explicitly marked as being executable. This is indicated in the permission listing by an x. Therefore, if there's no x in a file's permissions, it's a good bet that the file in question isn't a program or script (although this isn't always true for various technical reasons). To make matters a little more confusing, if the entry in the list of files is a directory (indicated by a d), then the rules are different. In this case, an x indicates that the user can access that directory. If there's no x, then the user's attempts to browse to that directory will be met with an "access denied" message.

Instead of the x in the list of permissions for a directory, you might sometimes see a t. This means that the only people who can delete or alter a file in that directory are the users who created the file in the first place. This is a useful option to have in some circumstances.

You might sometimes see a set of permissions like rws. The s stands for setuid. Like x, it indicates that the file is executable, except, in this case, it means that the file will be run with the permissions of the person who owns it, rather than the user who is executing it. In other words, if user frank tries to run a program owned by knthomas that has the execute permission set as s, that program will be run as if knthomas were running it. This is very useful, because the root user can use this trick to make programs that require root access usable by ordinary users, although this brings with it obvious security risks.

File permissions can be difficult to understand, so let's look at a few real-world examples. We'll assume that we're logged in to Linux as the user knthomas throughout.

Typical Data File Permissions

Here's the first example:

```
-rw-rw----   2 knthomas users 1450 2004-07-07 09:19 myfile2
```

You see immediately that this file is owned by user knthomas because that username appears directly after the permissions. You also see that this user is a member of the group users.

Reading the file permissions from left to right, you see that the initial character is a dash. That indicates that this is an ordinary file and has no special characteristics. It's also not a directory.

After that is the first part of the permissions, rw-. These are the permissions for owner of the file, knthomas. You're logged in as that user, so this file belongs to you, and these permissions apply to you. You can read and write the file, but *not* execute it. Because you cannot execute the file, you can infer that this is a data file rather than a program (there are certain exceptions to this rule, but we'll ignore them for the sake of simplicity).

Following this is the next part of the file permissions, rw-. This tells you what other members of your group can do with the file. It's fairly useless information if you're the only user of your PC but, for the record, you're told that anyone else belonging to the group called users can also read and write the file, but not execute it.

■Note If there *is* more than one user on your computer, then the group permissions are clearly important. SUSE Linux adds all new users to the group users by default. In this example, any user on the PC can read and write to this file, which is not always desirable. The next section describes how file permissions can be changed to prevent this happening.

Finally, the last three characters tell you the permissions of everyone else on the system. The three dashes (---) mean that they have no permissions at all regarding the file. There's a dash where the r normally appears, so they cannot even read it. The dashes afterwards tell you they cannot write to the file or execute it. If they try to do anything with the file, they'll get a "permission denied" error.

Permissions on a User's Directory

Here's example number two:

```
drwxr-xr-x   7 knthomas users 824 2004-07-07 10:01 mydirectory
```

The list of permissions starts with d, which tells you that this isn't a file but a directory. After this is the list of permissions for the owner of the directory (knthomas), who can read files in the directory and also create new ones there. The x indicates that you can access this directory, as opposed to being turned away with an "access denied" message. You might think being able to access the directory is taken for granted if the user can read and write to it, but that's not the case.

Next are the permissions for the group members. They can read files in the directory but not write any new ones there (although they can modify files already in there, provided the permissions of the individual files allow this). Once again, there's an x at the end of their particular permission listing, which indicates that the group members can access the directory.

Following the group's permissions are those of everyone else. They can read the directory and browse it, but not write new files to it, as with the group users' permissions.

Permissions on a Directory Owned by Root

Here's the last example:

```
drwx------   25 root    root    1000 2004-08-06 15:44 root
```

You can see that the file is owned by root. Remember that in this example you're logged in as knthomas and your group is users.

The list of permissions starts with a d, so you can tell that this is actually a directory. After this, you see that the owner of the directory, root, has permission to read, write, and access the directory.

Next are the permissions for the group: three dashes. In other words, members of the group called root have no permission to access this directory in any way. They cannot browse it, create new files in it, or even access it.

Following this are the permissions for the rest of the users. This includes you, because you're not the user root and don't belong to its group. The three dashes means you don't have permission to read, write, or access this directory.

SWITCHING USERS

It's possible to switch users on the fly while you're working at the shell. On my test PC, I have an additional user account called frank. While logged in as any user, I can temporarily switch to this user by typing the following command, which stands for substitute user:

```
su frank
```

I'll then be asked for user frank's password. Once this is typed, I will effectively have logged in as user frank. Any files I create will be saved with frank's ownership.

When the su command is used on its own, the shell will assume I want to become root user. This is a handy way of quickly switching to root in order to undertake system administration tasks. If a dash is added, su -, then I also take on the root user's $PATH, meaning I can access certain essential system tools. In both cases, I can log out of the user I've temporarily switched into by typing exit.

Remember to keep an eye on the command prompt. This will tell you which user you're currently logged in as.

Altering Permissions

Changing permissions of files and directories is easy and can be done using the chmod command. For example, if you want to change a file so that everyone on the system can read and write to it, type the following:

```
chmod a+rw myfile
```

In other words, you're adding add read and write (rw) permissions for all users (a).

Here's another example:

```
chmod a-w myfile
```

This tells Linux that you want to take away (-) the ability of all users (a) to write (w) to the file. However, you want to leave the other permissions as they are. You can substitute a with g to change group permissions instead.

The most useful use of chmod is in making a program file that you've downloaded executable. Due to the way the Internet works, if you download a program to install on your computer, it can lose its executable status while in transit. In this case, issue the following command:

```
chmod +x myprogram
```

Because nothing is specified before the +x, the shell assumes that the changes to be applied to the file are for the current user only.

To change the owner of a file, use the chown command. For example, to set the owner of myfile as frank, type this command:

```
chown frank myfile
```

The chown command is handy if you create or download a file as root and want to make it accessible by your standard user login.

It goes without saying that standard users can change permissions only if they're already the owner of the file. Otherwise, you won't have permission! However, the root user has powers to change file permissions and ownership of all files, regardless of who owns them.

The File System Explained

Now that you understand the principles of files and users, we can take a bird's-eye view of the Linux file system and start to make sense of it.

You might already have ventured beyond the /home directory and wandered through the file system. You no doubt found it thoroughly confusing, largely because it's not like anything you're used to. The good news it that it's not actually very hard to understand. If nothing else, you should be aware that nearly everything can be ignored during everyday use.

■**Note** The SUSE Linux file system is referred to as a *hierarchical* file system. This means that it consists of a lot of directories that contain files. Windows also uses a hierarchical file system. SUSE Linux refers to the very bottom level of the file system as the *root*. This has no connection with the root user.

You can switch to the root of the file system by typing the following shell command:

```
cd /
```

When used on its own, the forward slash is interpreted as a shortcut for root.

If I do this on my PC and then ask for a long file listing (ls -l), I see the following:

```
[knthomas@testpc knthomas]$ cd /
[knthomas@testpc /]$ ls -l
total 223
drwxr-xr-x    2 root     root      2840 2004-06-11 17:14 bin
drwxr-xr-x    3 root     root       544 2004-08-05 09:34 boot
drwxr-xr-x   34 root     root    180096 2004-08-07 07:17 dev
drwxr-xr-x   63 root     root      6064 2004-08-07 07:18 etc
drwxr-xr-x    4 root     root        96 2004-06-14 15:14 home
drwxr-xr-x   12 root     root      3096 2004-06-11 17:13 lib
drwxr-xr-x    6 root     root       176 2004-06-11 16:29 media
drwxr-xr-x    2 root     root        48 2004-04-06 17:04 mnt
drwxr-xr-x   10 root     root       304 2004-06-17 12:40 opt
dr-xr-xr-x  143 root     root         0 2004-08-07 08:16 proc
drwx------   25 root     root      1000 2004-08-06 15:44 root
drwxr-xr-x    3 root     root      7696 2004-08-05 09:34 sbin
drwxr-xr-x    4 root     root        96 2004-06-11 16:11 srv
drwxr-xr-x    8 root     root         0 2004-08-07 08:16 sys
drwxrwxrwt   81 root     root      3488 2004-08-07 12:15 tmp
drwxr-xr-x   12 root     root       344 2004-06-11 16:19 usr
drwxr-xr-x   15 root     root       384 2004-06-14 11:32 var
```

The first thing you'll notice from this is that the root of the file system contains nothing but directories and that they're all owned by root.

Only the root user can write files to the root of the file system. This is to prevent damage from ordinary users, since most of the directories in the root of the file system are vital to the correct running of Linux and contain essential programs or data.

Caution It's incredibly easy to slip up when using the command-line shell and thereby cause lots of damage. For example, simply mistyping a forward slash in a command can mean the difference between deleting the files in a directory and deleting the directory itself. This is just another reason why you should always work as a standard user and log in as root only when it's absolutely necessary. It also explains why, by default, all the system directories are owned by the root user and protected against ordinary users making changes to them.

As you can see from the file permissions of each directory in the root of the file system, most directories allow all users to browse them and access the files within (the last three characters of the permissions read r-x). You just won't be able to create new files there or delete the directories themselves. You might be able to modify or execute programs contained within the directory, but this will depend on the permissions of each individual file.

Table 15-3 provides a brief description of what each directory in the SUSE Linux root file system contains. This is for reference only; there's no need for you to learn this information.

The SUSE Linux file system broadly follows the principles laid down in the Filesystem Hierarchy Standard, as with most versions of Linux, but it does have its own subtleties.

Table 15-3. *Directories in the SUSE Linux Root File System*

Directory	Contents
bin	Vital tools necessary to get the system running or for use when repairing the system and diagnosing problems
boot	Boot loader programs and configuration files (the boot loader is the menu that appears when you first boot Linux)
dev	Virtual files representing hardware installed on your system
etc	Central repository of configuration files for your system
home	Where each user's personal directory is stored
lib	Shared system files used by Linux as well as the software that runs on it
media	Where the directories representing various mounted removable storage devices are made available
mnt	Directory in which external file systems can be temporarily mounted
opt	Software that is theoretically optional and not vital to the running of the system (many software packages you use daily can be found here)
proc	Virtual directory containing data about your system and its current status
root	The root user's personal directory
sbin	Programs essential to administration of the system
srv	Configuration files for any network servers you might have running on your system
sys	Mount point of the sysfs file system, which is used by the kernel to administer your system's hardware
tmp	Temporary files stored by the system
usr	Programs and data that might be shared with other systems (such as in a large networking setup with many users)[1]
var	Used by the system to store data that is constantly updated, such as printer spooling output

[1] *The usr directory contains its own set of directories that are full of programs and data. Many system programs, such as the X11 and KDE GUI software, are located within the /usr director. Note that the /usr directory is used even if your system will never act as a server to other systems.*

TYPES OF FILE SYSTEMS

Linux is all about choice, and this extends to the technology that makes the file system work. Unlike with Windows, where you can choose between just NTFS and FAT32 (with the emphasis being on NTFS), Linux offers many different types of file system technology. Each is designed for varying tasks. Most are scalable, however, which means that they will work just as happily on a desktop PC as on a massive cluster of computers. SUSE Linux uses the `reiserfs` file system. The Red Hat distribution normally offers the `ext3` system. People are constantly arguing about which file system is best. The principal measuring stick is performance. Your computer spends a lot of time writing and reading files, so the faster a file system is, the faster your PC will be overall (although, in reality, the hardware is of equal importance).

It's worth noting that we're talking here about the underlying and invisible technology of the file system. In day-to-day use, the end user won't be aware of any difference between `ext3`, `reiserfs`, or another file system technology (although when things go wrong, different tools are used to attempt repairs; their selection is automated within SUSE Linux).

Here are the various types along with notes about what they offer:

- **ext2:** Fast, stable, and well established, `ext2` was once the most popular type of file system technology used on Linux. It's now been eclipsed by `ext3`.

- **ext3:** An extension of `ext2`, `ext3` allows *journaling*, a way of recording what's been written to disk so that a recovery can be attempted when things go wrong.

- **reiserfs:** This is another journaling file system, which claims to be faster than others and also offers better security features.

- **jfs:** This is a journaling file system created by IBM. It's used on industrial implementations of Unix.

- **xfs:** This is a 64-bit journaling file system created by Silicon Graphics, Inc. (SGI) and used on its own version of Unix, as well as Linux.

Mounting

Described in technical terms, *mounting* is the practice of making a file system available under Linux. This can take the form of a partition on your hard disk, a CD-ROM, a network server, or many other things.

Mounting drives might seem a strange concept, but it actually makes everything much simpler than it might be otherwise. For example, once a drive is mounted, there's no need to use any special commands or software to access its contents. You can use the same programs and tools that you use to access all of your other files. Mounting creates a level playing field on which everything is equal and can therefore be accessed quickly and efficiently.

Using the mount Command

Mounting is usually done via the `mount` command. Under SUSE Linux, you must be the root user to do this, although other versions of Linux are less strict and let ordinary users use the command, too.

With most modern versions of Linux, `mount` can be used in two ways: by specifying all the settings immediately after the command, or by making reference to an entry within the `fstab` file. This is a configuration file stored in the `/etc` directory that contains details of all file systems of the PC that can be mounted.

Note The root file system is itself mounted automatically during bootup, shortly after the kernel has started and has all your hardware up and running. Every file system that Linux uses must be mounted at some point.

Let's say that you insert a CD or DVD into your computer's DVD-ROM drive. To mount it and make it available to Linux, you would type:

```
mount /media/dvd
```

The `mount` command first looks in your `fstab` file in the `etc` directory to find what you're referring to. Figure 15-4 shows an example of the contents of that file. (The example in the figure uses the `cat` command, which is discussed in Chapter 16). Using this information, the mount command attempts to make the contents of the CD available in the `/media/cdrom` directory. Note that this is done in a virtual way; the files are not literally copied into the directory. The directory is merely a magical conduit that allows you to read the CD's contents.

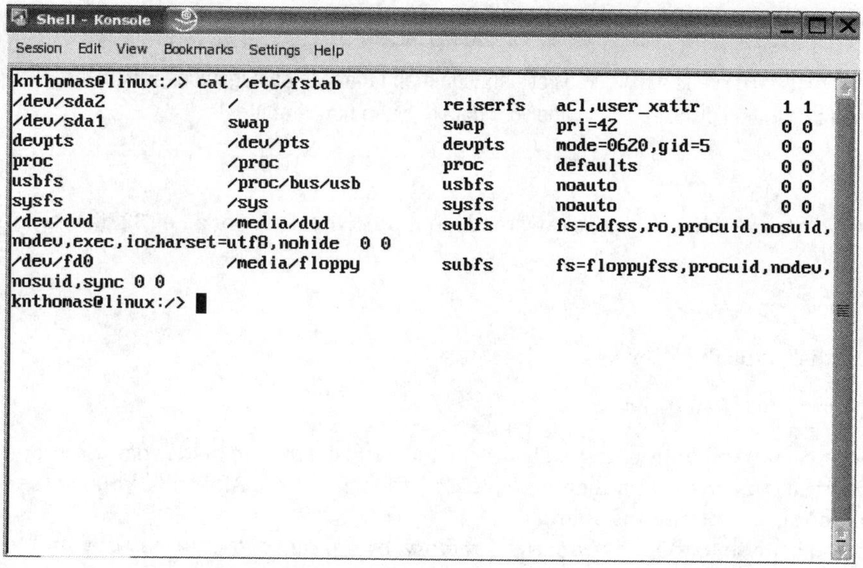
Shell - Konsole
Session Edit View Bookmarks Settings Help
knthomas@linux:/> cat /etc/fstab
/dev/sda2 / reiserfs acl,user_xattr 1 1
/dev/sda1 swap swap pri=42 0 0
devpts /dev/pts devpts mode=0620,gid=5 0 0
proc /proc proc defaults 0 0
usbfs /proc/bus/usb usbfs noauto 0 0
sysfs /sys sysfs noauto 0 0
/dev/dvd /media/dvd subfs fs=cdfss,ro,procuid,nosuid,
nodev,exec,iocharset=utf8,nohide 0 0
/dev/fd0 /media/floppy subfs fs=floppyfss,procuid,nodev,
nosuid,sync 0 0
knthomas@linux:/>

Figure 15-4. *Details of all frequently mounted file systems are held in the `/etc/fstab` file.*

There aren't any special commands used to work with mounted drives. The shell commands discussed in Chapter 14 should do everything you need.

The `mount` command doesn't see widespread usage by most users nowadays, because most removable storage devices like CDs, and even photographic memory card readers, are mounted automatically under SUSE Linux. However, there will be occasions when you need to mount a drive manually.

Mounting a Drive Manually

Let's look at an example of when you might need to mount a drive manually. Suppose that you've just added a second hard disk to your PC that has previously been used on a Windows system. This has been added as the primary slave.

The first thing to do is create a *mount point*, which is an empty directory that will act as a location where you can tell mount to make the disk accessible. You can create this directory anywhere, but under SUSE Linux, the convention is to create it in the /mnt directory. Therefore, the following command should do the trick (assuming you've switched to root user):

```
mkdir /mnt/windows
```

You now need to know what kind of partition type is used on the disk, because you need to specify this when mounting. To find this out, use the fdisk command (you'll have to switch to root first—type su -). Type the following exactly as it appears:

```
fdisk -l /dev/hdb
```

This will list the partitions on the second disk drive (assuming an average PC system). With most hard disks used under Windows, you should find a single partition that will be either NTFS or FAT32.

■Caution Be aware that fdisk is a dangerous system command that can damage your system. The program is designed to partition disks and can wipe your data if you're not careful!

With this information in hand, you're now ready to mount the disk. For a FAT32 disk, type the following:

```
mount -t vfat /dev/hdb1 /mnt/windows
```

For an NTFS disk, type the following:

```
mount -t ntfs /dev/hdb1 /mnt/windows
```

You use the -t command option to specify the file type and list the file in the /dev directory (this file is only virtual, of course, and merely represents the hardware). After this, you list the directory that is acting as your mount point.

Now when you browse to the /mnt/windows directory, by typing cd /mnt/windows, you should find the contents of the hard disk accessible.

For more information about the mount command, read its man page (type man mount).

Removing a Mounted System

What if you want to get rid of a mounted system? You might have noticed that you're unable to eject your CD while it's mounted—the button on the front of the drive just won't work.

There's a special command designed for the purposes of unmounting: umount (notice there's no *n* after the first *u*). It's used in the following simple way:

```
umount /media/cdrom
```

This will unmount the CD-ROM.

Note that if you're currently browsing the mounted directory, you'll need to leave it before you can unmount it. The same is true of all kinds of access to the mounted directory. If you're browsing the mounted drive with Konqueror or if a piece of software is accessing it, you won't be able to unmount it until you've quit the program and closed the Konqueror window (or browsed to a different part of the file system).

File Searches

Files frequently get lost. Well, technically speaking, they don't actually get lost. We just forget where we've put them. But because of this, the shell includes some handy commands to search for files.

Using the find Command

The find command is installed on SUSE Linux by default. Like the Search option on the Windows XP Start menu, this command manually searches through all the files on the hard disk in order to find what you're looking for. It's not a particularly fast way of finding a file, but it is reliable.

Here's an example:

```
find /home/knthomas -name "myfile"
```

This will search for myfile using /home/knthomas as a starting point (which is to say that it will search all directories within /home/knthomas, and any directories within those directories, and so on, because it's *recursive*).

You can search the entire file system by leaving out the initial path. In this case, find will assume you want the search to start from /, the root of the file system.

If the file is found, you'll see it appear in the output of the command. The path will be shown next to the filename.

Period punctuation symbols have interesting meanings within file listings and therefore within the output of the find command. As you learned in Chapter 14, .. refers to the parent directory of the one you're currently browsing. In a similar way, a single . refers to the directory you're in at the moment; it's shorthand for "right here." So, if find returns a result like ./myfile, it means that myfile is right here in the current directory. However, when a single period is used at the beginning of a filename, such as in .bashrc, it has the effect of hiding the file. In other words, that file won't appear when you type ls (although you can type ls -a to see all files, even those that are hidden).

If you give find a try, you'll see that it's not a particularly good way of searching. Apart from being slow, it will also return a lot of error messages about directories it cannot search. This is because, when you run the find command, it takes on your user permissions. Whenever find comes across a directory it cannot access, it will report it to you, as shown in the example in

Figure 15-5. There are frequently so many of these warnings that the output can hide the instances where find actually locates the file in question!

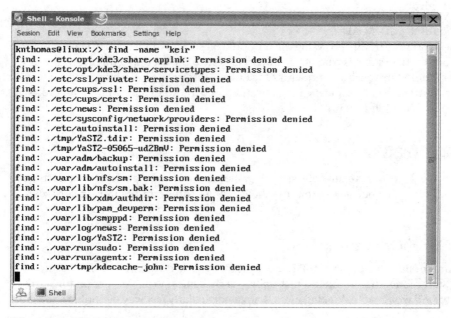

```
knthomas@linux:/> find -name "keir"
find: ./etc/opt/kde3/share/applnk: Permission denied
find: ./etc/opt/kde3/share/servicetypes: Permission denied
find: ./etc/ssl/private: Permission denied
find: ./etc/cups/ssl: Permission denied
find: ./etc/cups/certs: Permission denied
find: ./etc/news: Permission denied
find: ./etc/sysconfig/network/providers: Permission denied
find: ./etc/autoinstall: Permission denied
find: ./tmp/YaST2.tdir: Permission denied
find: ./tmp/YaST2-05065-ud2BmV: Permission denied
find: ./var/adm/backup: Permission denied
find: ./var/adm/autoinstall: Permission denied
find: ./var/lib/nfs/sm: Permission denied
find: ./var/lib/nfs/sm.bak: Permission denied
find: ./var/lib/xdm/authdir: Permission denied
find: ./var/lib/pam_devperm: Permission denied
find: ./var/lib/smpppd: Permission denied
find: ./var/log/news: Permission denied
find: ./var/log/YaST2: Permission denied
find: ./var/run/sudo: Permission denied
find: ./var/run/agentx: Permission denied
find: ./var/tmp/kdecache-john: Permission denied
```

Figure 15-5. *The* find *command is useful for finding files but isn't problem-free.*

There are various ways around avoiding error messages, but perhaps the quickest solution is to use the su command to switch to root user before using the find command. Because the root user has access to every file on the hard disk, the find command will be unrestricted in where it can search, so it won't run into any directories it doesn't have permission to enter.

However, an even better solution for finding files is to use the locate command.

Using the locate Command

Although locate comes as standard on most versions of Linux, it's not installed on SUSE Linux by default. You can easily install it with two steps:

1. Insert your SUSE Linux installation DVD-ROM. To install the software automatically via a command-line version of the YaST2 tool, type the following at the shell:

    yast2 -i /media/dvd/suse/i586/findutils-locate-4.1.7-860.i586.rpm

2. Next, you need to update the locate database. Switch to root user and type the following command:

    updatedb

    This will probably take a minute or two to complete.

After this, you can use the following command to search for a file (you don't need to be logged in as root to do so):

```
locate myfile
```

The benefit of using the `locate` command is that it's instantaneous. Instead of searching the file system, a database is searched instead. When `locate` installs, it adds a daemon to your system, which means that the database is periodically and automatically updated in the background (usually once a day).

Note The downside of using the `locate` command is that it relies on the database being up-to-date. If you save a file, and then an hour later use `locate` to find it, the chances are the database won't have been updated during that period. In such a case, the `find` command is a better bet.

Using the whereis Command

There's one other command worth mentioning in the context of searching: `whereis`. This locates where programs are stored and is an excellent way of exploring your system. Using it is simply a matter of typing something like this:

```
whereis cp
```

This will tell you where the `cp` program is located on your hard disk. It will also tell you were its source code and man page are located (if applicable). However, the first path returned by the search will be the location of the program itself.

File Size and Free Space

Often, it's necessary to understand how large files are and to know how much space they're taking up on the hard disk. In addition, it's often handy to know how much free space is left on a disk.

Viewing File Sizes

Using the `ls -l` command option will tell you how large each file is in terms of bytes. Adding the `-h` option converts these file sizes to kilobytes, megabytes, and even gigabytes, depending on how large they are.

In order to get an idea of which are the largest files and which are the smallest, you can add the `-S` command option. This will order the files in the list in terms of the largest and smallest files.

The following will return a list of all the files in the current directory, in order of size (largest first), detailing the sizes in kilobytes, megabytes, or gigabytes:

```
ls -Slh
```

There's another more powerful way of presenting this information: using the `du` command, which stands for disk usage. When used on its own without command switches, `du` simply presents the size of directories alongside their names (starting in the current directory). It will show any hidden directories (directories whose names start with a period), and will also present a total at the end of the list. This will probably be quite a long list. Once again, you can add the -h command option to force the du command to produce human-readable measurements of kilobytes and megabytes.

If you specify a file or directory when using the du command, along with the –s command option, you can find out its total file size:

```
du -sh mydirectoryname
```

This will show the size taken up on the disk by mydirectoryname, adding to the total any files or subdirectories it contains.

However, du is limited by the same file permission problems as the find tool, as shown in Figure 15-6. If you run du as an ordinary user, it won't be able to calculate the total for any directories you don't have permission to access. Therefore, you might consider running the command as root.

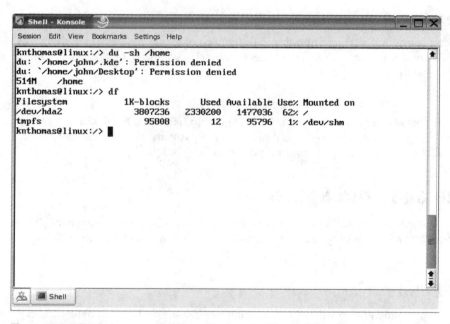

Figure 15-6. *The du command shows the size of a file, and the df command can be used to gauge the amount of free space on the disk.*

Finding Out the Amount of Free Space

What if you want to find out how much free space there is left on the disk? In this case, you can use the df command. This command is also demonstrated in Figure 15-6.

The df command works on a partition-by-partition basis. Typing it at the command prompt will show you how much space is free on the entire disk. Once again, you can add the –h option to the df command to have the file sizes returned in megabytes and gigabytes (and even terabytes if your hard disk is big enough!).

Note There's as much space free in any directory as there is space on the disk, which is why df displays data about the entire partition. If you're using a system managed by a system administrator within a business environment, you might find that quotas have been used to limit how much disk space you can take up. However, if you're using a desktop PC and are the only user, this won't be activated.

Summary

In this chapter, we examined how the SUSE Linux file system lies at the heart of an understanding of how the operating system works. We also discussed how the file system and user accounts go hand-in-hand and are inextricably linked. This involved discussing the concept of file owner-ship and usage permissions, plus how these can be manipulated using command-line shell tools.

We also discussed the overall structure of the SUSE Linux file system and how external file systems can be mounted and made available within SUSE Linux. Finally, we looked at how to find files and how to gauge how much free space there is within the file system.

In the next chapter, we'll look at how the BASH shell can be used to view and otherwise manipulate text files, which are also important to the way SUSE Linux works.

■ ■ ■

## CHAPTER 16

Working with Text Files

Windows views text files as just another file type, but to SUSE Linux, they can be essential system components that make the system work. Configuration files are stored as plain text, and program documentation is also stored as text. This is clearly different from Windows, where it's very likely any information you're supposed to read will be contained in a Windows Help file, a rich text format (RTF) file, or even a Microsoft Word document.

Because of the importance of text files, the shell includes several commands that let you display, edit, and otherwise manipulate text files in various ways. Learning to use the shell, and therefore learning how to administer your SUSE Linux system, involves having a good understanding of these text tools. You'll use text tools for editing configuration files and viewing log files, as just two examples.

Viewing Text Files

You can easily view files using command-line tools, including `cat`, `less`, `head`, and `tail`. The simplest command for dealing with text files is `cat`.

Using the cat Command

When followed with a filename, the `cat` command will display the text file on screen:

```
cat mytextfile
```

`cat` is short for concatenate, and it isn't designed just to display text files. That it can do so is simply a side effect of its real purpose in life, which is to join two or more files together. However, when used with a single file, it simply displays its contents on screen.

If you try to use `cat`, you'll realize that it's only good for short text files; large files scroll off the screen.

Using the less Command

Because `cat` works well only with short files, and to give you more control when viewing text files, the `less` and `more` commands were created. The `more` command came first but was considered too primitive, so someone came up with `less`, which is preferred by many Linux users. However, both are usually available on the average Linux installation.

Let's look at using `less` to read the OpenOffice.Org `README` file, which contains information about the current release of the office suite.

The file is located at /opt/OpenOffice.org/share/readme/README01, so to use less to read it, type the following:

```
less /opt/OpenOffice.org/share/readme/README01
```

You can scroll up and down within the less display by using the cursor keys. If you want to scroll by bigger amounts of text, you can use the Page Up and Page Down keys. Alternatively, you can use the spacebar and B key, both of which are commonly used by Linux experts. In addition, the Home and End keys will take you to the start and end of the document, respectively.

When using less, keep an eye on the bottom part of the screen, where you'll see a brief status bar. Alongside the filename, you'll see how many lines the document has and which line you're currently up to. In addition, you'll see as a percentage the amount of document you've already read through, so you'll know how much is left to go.

less lets you search forward through the file by typing a slash (/), and then entering your search term. Any words that are matched will be highlighted on screen. To repeat the search, type n. To search backward in a file from your current point, type a question mark (?). To quit less, simply type q.

Although it's supposedly a simple program, less is packed with features. You can see what options are available by reading its man page or by typing less --help.

Using the head and tail Commands

There are a couple of other handy commands that you can use to view text files: head and tail. As their names suggest, these let you quickly view the beginning (head) of a file or the end (tail) of it.

Using the commands is simple:

```
tail mytextfile
```

or

```
head mytextfile
```

By default, both commands will display ten lines of the file. You can override this by using the -n command option followed by the number of lines you want to see. For example, the following will show the last five lines of mytextfile:

```
tail -n5 mytextfile
```

These two commands are very useful when viewing log files that might contain hundreds of lines of text. The most recent information is always at the end, so tail can be used to see what's happened last on your system, as shown in the example in Figure 16-1.

Although they're powerful, all of these shell commands don't let you do much more than view text files. If you want to edit files, you'll need to use a text editor such as vi.

Figure 16-1. *tail can be very useful for viewing the last few lines of a log file.*

STANDARD INPUT AND OUTPUT

If you've read any of the SUSE Linux man pages, you might have seen references to *standard input* and *standard output*. Like many things in SUSE Linux, this sounds complicated but is merely a long-winded way of referring to something that is relatively simple.

Standard input is simply the device that SUSE Linux normally takes input from. In other words, on the majority of desktop PCs when you're using the command-line shell, standard input refers to the keyboard. However, it's important to note that it could also feasibly refer to the mouse or any other device on your system capable of providing input; even some software can take the role of providing standard input.

Standard output is similar. It refers to the device to which output from a command is usually sent. In the majority of cases at the command line, this refers to the monitor screen, although it could feasibly be any kind of output device, such as your PC's sound card and speakers.

The man page for the `cat` command says that it will "concatenate files and print on the standard output." In other words, for the majority of desktop SUSE Linux installations, it will combine (concatenate) any number of files together and print the results on screen. If you specify just one file, it will display that single file on your screen. In addition to hardware devices, input can also come from a file containing commands, and output can also be sent to a file instead of the screen, or even sent straight to another command. This is just one reason why the command-line shell is so flexible and powerful.

Using a Command-Line Text Editor

There are a variety of text editors used within the shell, but three stand out as being ubiquitous: ed, vi, and emacs. The first in that list, ed, is by far the simplest. That doesn't necessarily mean that it's simple to use or lacks powerful features, but it simply doesn't match the astonishing power of both vi and emacs. To call vi and emacs simple text editors is to do them a severe disservice, because both are extremely powerful interactive environments. In particular, emacs is considered practically an operating system in itself, and some users of Linux treat it as their shell, executing commands and performing everyday tasks, such as reading and sending e-mail from within it. There are entire books written solely about emacs and vi.

Tip A fourth shell-based text text editor found on many Linux systems is pico. This offers many word processor-like features that can be helpful if you've come to Linux from a Windows background. It isn't installed by default on SUSE Linux. To install it, insert your SUSE Linux installation DVD and type the following command at the command-line prompt: yast -i /media/dvd/suse/i586/pico-4.58-145.i586.rpm. After this, you can view the man page by typing man pico.

The downside of all the power within emacs and vi is that both packages can be difficult to learn to use. They're considered idiosyncratic by even their most ardent fans. Both involve the user learning certain unfamiliar concepts, as well as keyboard shortcuts and commands.

Although there are debates about which text editor is better and which is best, it's generally agreed that vi offers substantial text-editing power but isn't too all-encompassing. It's also installed by default on SUSE Linux. On SUSE Linux, emacs must be installed as an optional extra. Both text editors are normally available on virtually every installation of Linux or Unix. We'll concentrate on using vi here.

It's important to understand that there isn't just one program called vi. There are many versions. The original vi program, supplied with Unix, is rarely used nowadays. The most common version of vi is a clone called vim, for vi improved, and this is the version supplied with SUSE Linux. However, there are other versions, such as Elvis. Most work in a virtually identical way.

Note There's always been a constant flame war between advocates of vi and emacs, as to which is better. This could be quite a vicious and desperate debate, and the text editor you used was often taken as a measure of your character! Nowadays, the battle between the two camps has softened, and the emacs versus vi debate is considered an entertaining cliché of Linux and Unix use. Declaring online which text editor a user prefers is often followed by a smiley symbol to acknowledge the once-fevered emotions.

Understanding vi Modes

The key to understanding how vi works is to understand the difference between the various modes. Three modes are important: Command mode, Insert mode, and Command-Line mode.

Command Mode

Command mode is vi's central mode. When the editor starts up, it's in Command mode, as shown in Figure 16-2. This lets you move around the text and delete words or lines of text. vi returns to Command mode after most operations. In this mode, the status bar at the bottom of the screen shows information such as the percentage progress through the document. Although you cannot insert text in this mode, you can delete and otherwise manipulate words and lines within the file. You can also move through the text using the cursor keys and the Page Up and Page Down keys.

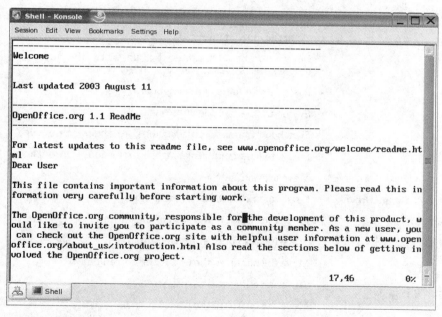

Figure 16-2. *In vi, the central mode is Command mode.*

Table 16-1 shows a list of the commands you can use in Command mode (consider photocopying it and sticking it to the side of your monitor as a handy reference).

Table 16-1. *vi Command Mode Commands*

Action	Command	Description
Delete text	dd	Delete current line
	*n*dd	Delete *n* number of lines (for example, 5dd will delete five lines)[1]
	dw	Delete the current word under the cursor[2]
	db	Delete the word before the cursor[2]
	D	Delete everything from the cursor to the end of the line[1]
Search	/	Search forward (type the search text straight afterwards)
	?	Search backwards
	n	Repeat search in a forward direction
	N	Repeat search in a backward direction
Cut and paste	yy	Copy the current line[2]
	*n*yy	Copy *n* number of lines into the buffer from the cursor downwards (for example, 5yy copies five lines of text)
	p	Paste the contents of the clipboard[3]
Insert text	i	Switch to Insert mode at the cursor
	o	Switch to Insert mode, placing the cursor below current line
	O	Switch to Insert mode, placing the cursor above current line
Navigation	Cursor keys	Move around the file
	Page Up/Page Down	Move up and down a page at a time
	0 (zero)[4]	Move the cursor to the start of the current line
	Shift+0 (zero)[4]	Move forward one sentence (until the next full stop)
	$	Move the cursor to the end of the current line
	w	Move the cursor to the next word
	b	Move the cursor to the previous word
Miscellaneous	.[4]	Repeat the last command
	u	Undo the last command

[1] *A line ends where a line break control character occurs in the file. Because of this, a line of text may actually take up several lines of the on-screen display.*

[2] *This will delete the remainder of current word before/after cursor if the cursor is in the middle of a word.*

[3] *The standard documentation refers to copying as "yanking" and the clipboard as the "buffer."*

[4] *Press the character on the main keyboard, not the numeric keypad.*

Insert Mode

To type your own text or edit text, you need to switch to Insert mode. This is normally done by typing i, but you can also type 0 or o to change to Insert mode, which is indicated by the word *INSERT* appearing at the bottom of the screen, as shown in Figure 16-3. The difference between the commands required to switch into Insert mode is that some let you insert before or after the cursor. Generally, i is most useful, because what you type will appear before the character under the cursor, as with most word processors. See Table 16-1 for a description of how the other insert commands work.

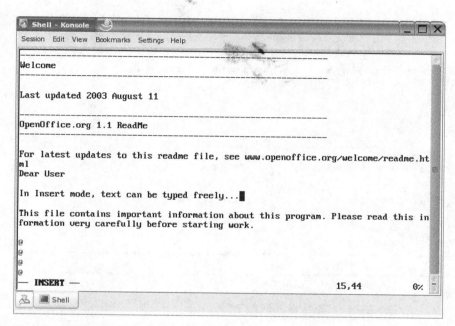

Figure 16-3. *Use* vi*'s Insert mode to add and edit text.*

In Insert mode, you can still move around the text using the cursor keys. Anything you type will appear the point of the cursor. To quit this mode, press the Esc key. This will return you to Command mode.

Command-Line Mode

The third mode you should be aware of is Command-Line mode (note that, irritatingly, this is not the same as the Command mode). As its name suggests, this is the mode in which you can enter commands to save and load files, as well as perform other fundamental tasks to control vi or to quit the program. You can enter Command-Line mode by typing a colon (:), although if you're in Insert mode, you'll first need to leave it by pressing the Esc key. You can identify when vi is in this mode because the cursor will be at the bottom of the screen next to a colon symbol, as shown in Figure 16-4. To quit Command-Line mode, press the Esc key. You'll be returned to Command mode. Note that you'll automatically leave Command-Line mode after each command you issue has completed.

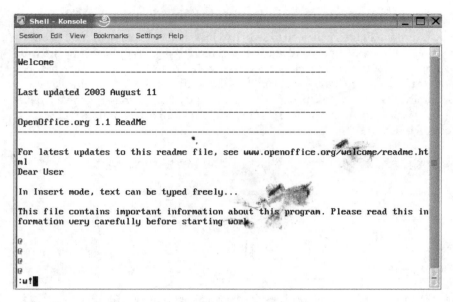

Figure 16-4. *Use* vi*'s Command-Line mode to issue commands.*

For a list of basic Command-Line mode commands, see Table 16-2.

Table 16-2. *Some vi Command-Line Mode Commands*

Command	Description
:w	Save file to disc
:w!	Save file and ignore errors such as an existing file with the same filename
:q	Quit vi
:q!	Quit vi and ignore errors such as an unsaved file
:s/*word*/*replacement*/	Search from the cursor downwards and replace any examples of word with replacement[1]
:help	View help documentation

[1] *The search tool is very powerful and uses a number of command options for additional flexibility. Read the* vi *help file to learn more.*

Using vi to Edit a File

As an example, let's use vi to edit the OpenOffice.org README file. We don't want to actually alter this file, so start by making a copy of it in your home directory:

```
cp /opt/OpenOffice.org/share/readme/README01 .
```

This will copy the file README01 to the current location, which you indicate using a single period.

After this, you need to change the file's permissions, because, by default, this file is read-only for all users (r--r--r--). Use the following command to change the permissions:

```
chmod +w README01
```

Then fire up vi with the file, like this:

```
vi README01
```

■**Note** Windows makes a lot of use of file extensions in order to recognize files and therefore know what program to use to run them. By default, a file with a .doc extension tells Windows that it should use Microsoft Word to open the file, for example. Linux uses a different system based on the first few bytes of each file. Because of this, file extensions are used within Linux simply to let the users know what type of file they're dealing with. Often, they're not used at all. If a file is called README, you can be fairly certain that it's a text file, for example.

Once the file is opened, you'll find yourself automatically in Command mode and will be able to move around the file using the cursor keys. Altering the text is achieved using various commands (see Table 16-1). For example, typing dd will delete the line of text that the cursor is currently within. Typing x will delete the letter under the cursor. Typing dw will delete the current word under the cursor. Try some of these to see how they work.

To actually edit a file and type text, you'll need to switch to Insert mode. Type i to do this. Insert mode is fairly easy to understand. You can move around the text using the cursor keys, and then simply start typing wherever you want. The Backspace key will delete text behind the cursor, and the Delete key will delete text in front of the cursor.

When you're finished, press the Esc key to return to Command mode. Once back in Command mode, you can page through the text. The Page Up and Page Down keys will move a screenful of text at a time. Pressing the up and down cursor keys will cause the screen to scroll when the cursor reaches the top or bottom.

After you're finished editing, you'll need to save the file. This is done in Command-Line mode. You can enter this mode by typing a colon (:). You'll see a colon appear at the bottom of the screen, and this is where you type the commands. Note that after you type a command, you'll immediately exit Command-Line mode, so if you want to issue another command, you'll need to type a colon again.

To save a file, in Command-Line mode, type :w (which stands for "write"). If you want to save the current file with a different name, you'll need to enter a filename after the w command, like this:

```
:w mytextfile
```

To quit vi, type :q. However, if you've edited a file, you won't be able to quit until the file has been saved. If you want to save the file and then quit, you can type :wq. If you don't want to save the file, type :q!. The exclamation point tells vi to override any objections it might have. You can also use it with the save command—:w!—to force the overwriting of a file that already exists.

■**Note** If you don't have the correct permissions to write a file, `vi` might tell you that you can use `:w!` to override. In this case, it's wrong. The only way to write to a file for which you don't have permissions is to change its permissions.

Creating a New Text File Using vi

Creating and editing a new file with `vi` is easy. From any command-line shell, simply type:

`vi myfile`

This will start `vi` and give your new file a name. However, the file won't be saved until you manually issue the save command (`:w`) in `vi`. This means that if your computer crashes before you save, the file will be lost!

■**Note** The version of vi provided with SUSE Linux, `vim`, includes some elementary file-save protection. If, for any reason, `vim` is not shut down properly, there's a chance you'll be able to recover a version of file the next time `vim` starts. However, as with all such protection in any kind of program, you shouldn't rely on this. You should use the `:w` command to save your file periodically.

As always with `vi`, you start out in the default Command mode. To start typing immediately, enter Insert mode by typing `i`. You'll notice when typing that although the text is wrapped on each line, words are not carried over, and they often break across lines in an ugly way. This is because `vi` is primarily a text editor, not a word processor. For people who create text files, like programmers, having line breaks shown in this way can be useful.

When you're finished typing a sentence or paragraph, you can press the Enter key as usual to start a new line. You should then be able to move between lines using the up and down cursor keys. You'll notice an odd thing when you try to do this, however: unlike with a word processor, moving up a line of text that spreads across more than one line on screen will take the cursor to the start of the line, rather than into the middle of it. This again relates to `vi`'s text editor background, where such a feature is useful when editing documents such as program configuration files.

When you're finished, press the Esc key to switch to Command mode. Then type a colon to enter Command-Line mode. Type `:w` to save the file according to the filename you gave it earlier. If you started `vi` without specifying a filename, you'll need to specify a filename with the save command, such as `:w myfile`.

Searching Through Files

You can search for particular words or phrases in text files by loading the file into `less` or `vi` (see Table 16-1). The maneuverability offered by both programs lets you leap from point to point in the text, and their use is generally user-friendly.

However, using vi or less can take precious seconds. There's a quicker command-line option that will search through a file in double-quick speed: grep.

Using grep to Find Text

grep stands for Global Regular Expression Print. grep is an extremely powerful tool that can use pattern-based searching techniques to find text in files. *Pattern-based searching* means that grep offers various options to loosen the search so that more results are returned.

The simplest way of using grep is to specify some brief text, followed by the name of the file you want to search. Here's an example:

```
grep 'helloworld' myfile
```

This will search for the phrase *helloworld* within myfile. If it's found, the entire line that *helloworld* is on will be displayed on screen.

If you specify the * wildcard instead of a filename, grep will search every file in the directory for the text. Adding the -r command option will cause grep to search all the files, and also search through any directories that are present:

```
grep -r 'helloworld' *
```

Another handy command option is -i, which tells grep to ignore uppercase and lowercase letters when it's searching. Figure 16-5 shows an example of using grep.

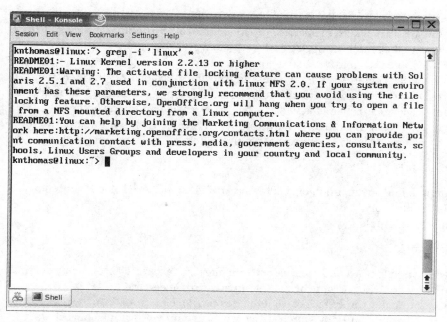

Figure 16-5. *grep is a powerful tool that can search for text within files.*

■Tip You might never choose to use grep for searching for text within files, but it can prove very handy when used to search through the output of other commands. This is done by "piping" the output from one command to another, as explained in Chapter 18.

Using Regular Expressions

The true power of grep is achieved by the use of search patterns known as *regular expressions*, or *regexes* for short. Put simply, regexes allow you to be vague rather than specific when searching, meaning that grep (and many similar tools that use the system of regexes, such as the find tool discussed in Chapter 15) will return more results.

For example, you can specify a selection or series of characters (called a *string* in regex terminology) that might appear in a word or phrase you're searching for. This can be useful if you're looking for a word that might be spelled differently from how you anticipate, for example.

The most basic form of regex is the bracket expansion. This is where additional search terms are enclosed in square brackets within a search string. For example, suppose you want to find a file that refers to several drafts of a document you've been working on. The files are called myfile_1draft.doc, myfile_2draft.doc, and so on. To find any document that mentions these files, you could type:

```
grep 'myfile_[1-9]draft\.doc' *
```

The use of square brackets tells grep to fill in details within the search string based on what's inside the square brackets. In this case, 1-9 means that all the numbers from one to nine should be applied to the search string. It's as if you've told grep to search for myfile_1draft.doc, and then told it to search for myfile_2draft.doc, and so on. Notice that the example has a backslash before the period separating the file extension from the filename. This indicates to grep that it should interpret the period as an element of the string to be searched for, rather than as a wildcard character, which is how grep usually interprets periods.

You don't need to specify a range of characters in this way. You can simply enter whatever selection of characters you want to substitute into the search string. Here's an example:

```
grep 'myfile[12345]\.doc' *
```

This will attempt to find any mention of myfile1.doc, myfile2.doc, myfile3.doc, and so on, in any file within the directory.

Here's another example:

```
grep '[KCkc]onqueror' *
```

This will let you search for the word *Konqueror* within files but takes into account any possible misspelling of the word with a *C*, and any use of uppercase or lowercase.

This is only scratching the surface of what regexes can do. For example, many regexes can be combined together into one long search string, which can provide astonishing accuracy when searching. Table 16-3 contains some simple examples that should give you an idea of the power and flexibility of regexes.

Table 16-3. *Some Examples of Regular Expressions*

Search String	Description
`'document[a-z]'`	Returns any lines containing the string "document" followed by any single letter from the range *a* through *z*.
`'document[A-Za-z]'`	Returns any lines containing the string "document" followed by the letters *A* through *Z* or *a* through *z*. Note that no comma or other character is needed to separate possibilities within square brackets.
`'document.'`	Returns any lines containing the string "document" followed by any other character. The period is used as a wildcard signifying any single character.
`'document[[:digit:]]'`	Returns any lines containing the string "document" followed by any number.
`'document[[:alpha:]]'`	Returns any lines containing the string "document" followed by any character.
`'^document'`	Returns any lines that have the string "document" at the beginning. The caret symbol (^) tells grep to look only at the beginning of each line.
`'document$'`	Returns any line that has the string "document" at the end of the line. The dollar sign symbol ($) tells grep to look for the string only at the end of lines.
`'document[^1-6]'`	Returns lines that have the string "document" in them but not if it's followed by the numbers 1 through 6. When used in square brackets, the caret character (^) produces a nonmatching list—a list of results that don't contain the string.

grep is very powerful. It can be complicated to master, but it offers a lot of scope for performing extremely precise searches that ensure you find only what you're looking for. It's well worth reading through its man pages. You can also refer to books on the subject, of which there are many. A good example is *Regular Expression Recipes: A Problem-Solution Approach*, by Nathan A. Good (Apress, 2004; ISBN: 1-59059-441-X).

Comparing Text Files

If you want to compare the differences between two text files, one way to do this is to use the diff command. This is designed primarily to uncover small changes in otherwise identical documents, such as revisions made by another person. Of course, it can also be used to prove that two files are identical. If you run the files through diff, and it shows no output, it has been unable to spot any differences.

diff is ordinarily used like this:

```
diff mytextfile1 mytextfile2
```

If diff spots any differences between the files, the results are a little more complicated than you might be used to. Any lines that are different within the files will appear on screen. Those lines that are identical won't be displayed. Lines preceded with a left angle bracket (<) are from the first file, while those with a right angle bracket (>) are from the second file.

For a different display, you could type something like this:

```
diff -y mytextfile1 mytextfile2
```

This places the two lists side-by-side and highlights lines that are different with a pipe symbol (|). However, it requires a lot more screen space than using diff without the -y option.

Note When you use the -y command option with diff, it will struggle to fit the output in a standard Konsole window. If it is maximized on a 17-inch screen (1024×768 resolution), it should be just large enough to fit the information in, depending on the complexity of the files being compared.

By specifying the -a command option, you can make diff process binary files, too. This is a handy way of comparing virtually any kind of files, including program files, to see if they're identical. If there's no output from diff, then the two files are identical. If your screen fills with gibberish, then the files are clearly different.

Incidentally, if you want to compare three documents, you can use a very similar command: diff3. Check the command's man page to learn more about how it works.

Summary

In this chapter, we examined how text files can be manipulated. In many ways, the BASH shell is built around manipulating text, and we explored various tools created with this goal in mind. We started with the commands that can display text files (or part of them).

We then looked at how the vi text editor can be used to both edit and create documents. Next, we explored how regexes can be used with the grep command to create sophisticated search strings, which can uncover any text within documents. Finally, you saw how to compare text files.

In the next chapter, we'll look at how you can use various command-line tools to take control of your system.

■■■

Taking Control of the System

By now, you should be starting to realize that the shell offers an enormous amount of power when it comes to administering your PC. The commands it provides gives you quick and efficient control over most aspects of your Linux setup. However, there's one area at which it truly excels: controlling the processes on your system.

Controlling processes is essential for administration of your system. You can tidy up crashed programs, for example, or even alter the priority of a program so that it runs with a little more consideration for other programs. Unlike with Windows, this degree of control is not considered out of bounds. This is just one more example of how Linux provides complete access to its inner workings and puts you in control.

Without further ado, let's take a look at what can be done.

Viewing Processes

A *process* is something that exists entirely behind the scenes. When the user runs a program, one or many processes might be started, but they're usually invisible unless the user specifically chooses to manipulate them. You might say that programs exist in the world of the user, but processes belong in the world of the system.

Processes can be started not only by the user, but also by the system itself to undertake tasks such as system maintenance, or even to provide basic functionality, such as the GUI system. Many processes are started when the computer boots up, and then they sit in the background, waiting until they're needed (such as programs that send mail). Other processes are designed to work periodically to accomplish certain tasks, such as ensuring system files are up-to-date.

You can see what processes are currently running on your computer by running the top program. Running top is simply a matter of typing the command at the shell prompt.

As you can see in Figure 17-1, top is comprehensive in the information it provides and can be a bit overwhelming at first sight. However, the main area of interest is the list of processes (which top refers to as *tasks*).

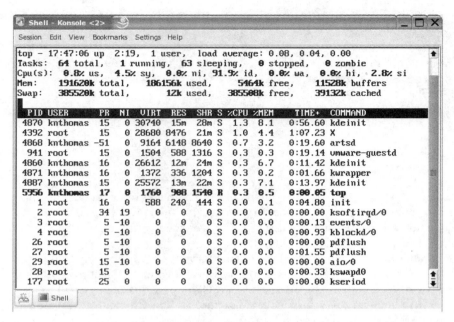

Figure 17-1. *The top program gives you an eagle's eye view of the processes running on your system.*

Here's an example of a line taken from top on my test PC, shown with the column headings from the process list:

```
PID  USER   PR  NI  VIRT   RES  SHR S %CPU %MEM   TIME+  COMMAND
5499 root   15   0  78052  25m  60m S  2.3  5.0  6:11.72 X
```

A lot of information is presented here, as described in Table 17-1.

Table 17-1. *The top Program Process Information*

Column	Description
PID	The first number is the process ID (PID). This is the unique number that the system uses to track the process. This comes in handy if you want to kill (terminate) the process. I'll explain how this is done in the next section of this chapter.
USER	This column lists the owner of the particular process. As with files, all processes must have an owner. A lot of processes will appear to be owned by the root user. Some of them are system processes that need to access the system hardware, which is something only root is allowed to do. Other processes are owned by root for protection; root ownership means that ordinary users cannot tamper with these processes.
PR	This column shows the priority of the process. This is a dynamic number, showing where the particular process is in the CPU queue at the present time.
NI	This column shows the "nice" value of the process. This refers to how charitable a process is in its desire for CPU time. A high figure here (up to 19) indicates that the process is willing to be interrupted for the sake of other processes. A negative value means the opposite: the process is more aggressive than others in its desire for CPU time. Some programs need to operate in this way, and this is not necessarily a bad thing.

Table 17-1. *The top Program Process Information (Continued)*

Column	Description
VIRT	This column shows the amount of virtual memory used by the process.[1]
RES	This column shows the total amount of physical memory used.[1]
SHR	This column shows the amount of shared memory used. This refers to memory that contains code that is relied on by other processes and programs.
S	This column shows the current status of the task. Generally, the status will either be sleeping, in which case an *S* will appear, or running, in which case an *R* will appear. Most processes will be sleeping, even ones that appear to be active. Don't worry about this; it just reflects the way the Linux kernel works. A *Z* in this column indicates a zombie process (a child of a process that has been terminated).
%CPU	This column shows the CPU use, expressed as a percentage.[2]
%MEM	This column shows the memory use, again expressed as a percentage.[2]
TIME+	This column shows a measure of how long the process has been up and running.
COMMAND	This shows the actual name of the process itself.

[1] *Both VIRT and RES are measured in kilobytes unless an* m *appears alongside the number, in which case you should read the figure as megabytes.*

[2] *The %CPU and %MEM entries tell you in easy-to-understand terms how much of the system resources a process is taking up.*

This list will probably be longer than the screen has space to display, so top orders the list of processes by the amount of CPU time the processes are using. Every few seconds, it updates the list. You can test this quite easily. Let your PC rest for a few seconds, without touching the mouse or typing. Then move the mouse around for a few seconds. You'll see that the process called X leaps to the top of the list (or appears very near the top). X is the program that provides the graphical subsystem for Linux, and making the mouse cursor appear to move around the screen requires CPU time. When nothing else is going on, moving the mouse causes X to appear as the number one user of CPU time on your system.

■**Tip** Typing d while top is running lets you alter the update interval, which is the time between screen updates. The default is three seconds, but you can reduce that to one second or even less if you wish. However, a constantly updating top program starts to consume system resources and can therefore skew the diagnostic results you're investigating. Because of this, a longer, rather than shorter, interval is preferable.

It's possible to alter the ordering of the process list according to other criteria. For example, you can list the processes by the quantity of memory they're using, by typing M while top is up and running. You can switch back to CPU ordering by typing P.

RENICING A PROCESS

You can set how much CPU time a process receives while it's actually running. This is done by *renicing* the process. This isn't something you should do on a regular basis, but it can prove very handy if you start a program that then uses a lot of system resources and makes the system unbearably slow.

The first thing to do is to use `top` to spot the process that needs to be restrained and find out its PID number. This will be listed on the left of the program's entry on the list. Once you know this, press `r`, and then type in the PID number. You'll then be asked to specify a `renice` value. The scale goes from –20, which is considered the highest priority, to 19, which is considered the lowest. Therefore, you should type **19**. After this, you should find some responsiveness has returned to the system, although how much (if any) depends on the nature of the programs you're running.

You might be tempted to bump up the priority of a process to make it run faster, but this might not work because of complexities in the Linux kernel. In fact, it might cause serious problems. Therefore, you should renice with care and only when you must.

Controlling Processes

Despite the fact that processes running on your computer are usually hidden away, Linux offers complete, unrestricted, and unapologetic control over them. You can terminate processes, change their properties, and learn every piece of information there is to know about them.

This provides ample scope for damaging the currently running system but, in spite of this, even standard users have complete control over processes that they personally started (there is one exception, so-called *zombie* processes, described a bit later in this section). As you might expect, the root user has control over all processes that were created by ordinary users, as well as those processes started by the system itself.

The user is given this degree of control over processes in order to enact repairs when something goes wrong, such as when a program crashes and won't terminate cleanly. It's impossible for standard users to damage the currently running system by undertaking such work, although they can cause themselves a number of problems.

■**Note** This control over processes is what makes Linux so reliable. Because any user can delve into the workings of the kernel and terminate individual processes, any crashed programs can be cleaned up with negligible impact on the rest of the system.

Killing Processes

Whenever you quit a program or, in some cases, when it completes the task you've asked of it, it will terminate itself. This means ending its own process and also that of any other processes it created in order to run. The main process is called the *parent*, and the ones it creates are referred to as *child* processes.

■Tip You can see a nice graphical display of which parent owns which child process by typing `pstree` at the command-line shell.

While this should mean your system runs smoothly, badly behaved programs sometimes don't go away. They stick around in the process list. Alternatively, you might find that a program crashes and so isn't able to terminate itself. In very rare cases, some programs that appear otherwise healthy might get carried away and start consuming a lot of system resources. You can tell when this happens because your system will start slowing down for no reason, as less and less memory and/or CPU time is available to run actual programs.

In all of these cases, the user usually must *kill* the process in order to terminate it manually. This is easily done using `top`.

The first task is to track down the crashed or otherwise problematic process. This can be done in `top` by looking for a process that matches the name of the program, as shown in Figure 17-2. For example, the Firefox web browser generally runs as a process called `firefox-bin`. The Konqueror web browser uses processes called `konqueror`.

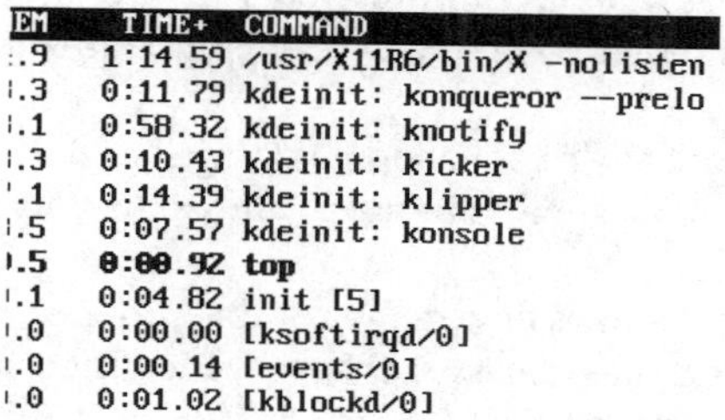

```
EM    TIME+   COMMAND
:.9   1:14.59 /usr/X11R6/bin/X -nolisten
!.3   0:11.79 kdeinit: konqueror --prelo
!.1   0:58.32 kdeinit: knotify
!.3   0:10.43 kdeinit: kicker
'.1   0:14.39 kdeinit: klipper
!.5   0:07.57 kdeinit: konsole
).5   0:00.92 top
!.1   0:04.82 init [5]
!.0   0:00.00 [ksoftirqd/0]
!.0   0:00.14 [events/0]
!.0   0:01.02 [kblockd/0]
```

Figure 17-2. *You can normally identify a program by its name in the process list.*

■Caution You should be absolutely sure that you know the correct process before killing it. If you get it wrong, you could cause other programs to stop running.

Because `top` doesn't show every single process on its screen, tracking down the trouble-causing process can be difficult. A handy tip is to make `top` show only the processes created by the user you're logged in under. This will remove the background processes started by root. You can do this within `top` by typing u, and then entering your username.

Once you've spotted the crashed process, make a note of its PID number, which will be at the very left of its entry in the list. Then type k. You'll be asked to enter the PID number. Enter that number, and then press Enter once again (this will accept the default signal value of 15, which will tell the program to terminate).

With any luck, the process (and the program in question) will disappear. If it doesn't, the process you've killed might be the child of another process that also must be killed.

To track down the parent process, you need to configure top to add the PPID field, for the parent process ID, to its display. To add this field, type f, and then b. Press Enter to return to the process list afterwards. The PPID column will appear next to the process name on the right of the window. It simply shows the PID of the parent process. You can use this information to look for the parent process within the main list of processes.

The trick here is to make sure that the parent process isn't something that's vital to the running of the system. If it isn't, you can safely kill it. This should have the result of killing the child process you uncovered prior to this.

■**Caution** If the PPID field in top displays a value of 1, that means the process doesn't have a parent process. In both the PPID and PID fields, you should always watch out for low numbers, particularly one-, two- or three-digit numbers. These are usually processes that started early on when Linux booted and that are essential to the system.

Controlling Zombie Processes

Zombie processes are those that are children of processes that have terminated. However, for some reason, they failed to take their child processes with them. Zombie processes are rare on most Linux systems.

Despite their name, zombie processes are harmless. They're not actually running and don't take up system resources. However, if you want your system to be spick-and-span, you can attempt to kill them.

In the top-right area of top, you can see a display that shows how many zombie processes are running on your system, as shown in Figure 17-3. Zombie processes are easily identified because they have a Z in the status (S) column within top's process list. To kill a zombie process, type k, and then type its PID. Then type **9**, rather than accept the default signal of 15.

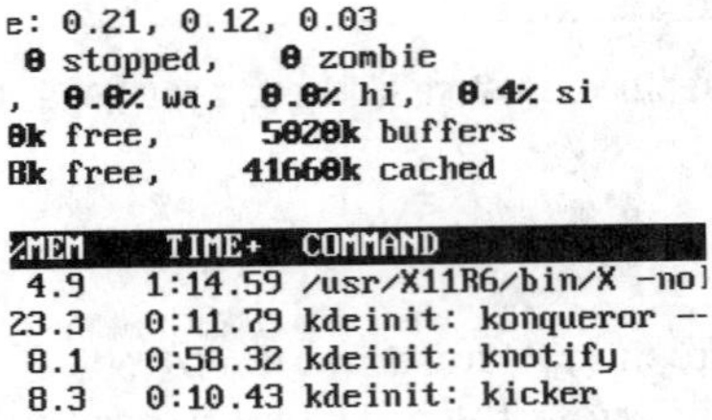

```
e: 0.21, 0.12, 0.03
  0 stopped,    0 zombie
, 0.0% wa,   0.0% hi,  0.4% si
0k free,      5020k buffers
0k free,     41668k cached

%MEM    TIME+  COMMAND
 4.9   1:14.59 /usr/X11R6/bin/X -no]
23.3   0:11.79 kdeinit: konqueror --
 8.1   0:58.32 kdeinit: knotify
 8.3   0:10.43 kdeinit: kicker
```

Figure 17-3. *You can see at a glance how many zombie processes are on your system by looking at the top right of top's display.*

■**Note** There's no magic involved in killing processes. All that happens is that `top` sends them a "terminate" signal. In other words, it contacts them and asks them to terminate. By default, all processes are designed to listen for commands such as this; it's part and parcel of how programs work under Linux. When a program is described as *crashed*, it means that the user is unable to use the program itself to issue the terminate command (such as Quit). A crashed program might not be taking input, but its processes will probably still be running.

In many cases, zombie processes simply won't go away. When this happens, you have two options. The first is to restart the program that is likely to be the zombie's owner, in the hope that it will reattach with the zombie, and then quit the program. With any luck, it will take the zombie child with it this time. Alternatively, you can simply reboot your PC. But it's important to note that zombie processes are harmless and can be left in peace on your system!

Using Other Commands to Control Processes

You don't always need to use `top` to control processes. There are a range of quick and cheerful shell commands that can diagnose and treat process problems.

The first of these is the `ps` command. This stands for Process Status and will report a list of currently running processes on your system. This command is normally used with the `-aux` option:

```
ps -aux
```

This will return a list something like what you seen when you run `top`.

If you can spot the problematic process, look for its PID and issue the following command:

```
kill <PID number>
```

For example, to kill a process with a PID of 5122, you would type this:

```
kill 5122
```

If, after this, you find the process isn't killed, then you should use the `top` program, as described in the previous sections, because it allows for a more in-depth investigation.

There's another handy process-killing command that lets you use the actual process name. The `killall` command is handy if you already know from past experience what a program's process is called. For example, to kill the process called `firefox-bin`, which is the chief process of the Firefox web browser, you would use the following command:

```
killall firefox-bin
```

■**Caution** Make sure you're as specific as possible when using the `killall` command. Issuing a command like `killall bin` will kill all processes that might have the word `bin` in them!

CLEARING UP CRASHES

Sometimes, a crashed process can cause all kinds of problems. The shell you're working at may stop working, or the GUI itself might stop working properly.

In cases like this, it's important to remember that you can have more that one instance of the command-line shell up and running at any one time. For example, if a process crashes and locks up Konsole, simply start a new instance of Konsole using the K menu. Then use `top` within the new Konsole window to kill the process that is causing trouble for the other Konsole window.

If the crashed program affects the entire GUI, you can switch to a virtual console by pressing Ctrl+Alt+F2. Although the GUI disappears, you will not have killed it, and no programs will stop running. Instead, you've simply moved the GUI to the background while a shell console takes over the screen. Then you can use the virtual console to run `top` and attempt to kill the process that is causing all the problems. When you're ready, you can switch back to the GUI by pressing Ctrl+Alt+F8.

Controlling Jobs

Whenever you start a program at the shell, it's assigned a *job* number. Jobs are quite separate from processes and are designed primarily for users to understand what programs are running on the system.

You can see which jobs are running at any one time by typing the following at the shell prompt:

```
jobs
```

When you run a program, it usually takes over the shell in some way and stops you from doing anything until it's finished what it's doing. However, it doesn't have to be this way. Adding an ampersand symbol (&) after the command will cause it to run in the background. This is not much use for commands that require user input, such as `vi` or `top`, but it can be very handy for commands that churn away until they're completed.

For example, consider the `updatedb` command, which updates the database used for the `locate` command (see Chapter 15). Once run, this command could take many minutes to complete, during which time the shell will effectively be unusable. However, you can type the following to retain use of the shell:

```
updatedb &
```

When you do this, you'll see the following:

```
[1] 7483
```

This tells you that `updatedb` is running in the background and has been given job number 1. It also has been given process number 7483 (although bear in mind that when some programs start, they instantly kick off other processes and terminate the one they're currently running, so this won't necessarily be accurate).

Tip If you've ever tried to run a GUI program from the shell, you might have realized that when it's running, the shell is inaccessible. Once you quit the GUI program, the control of the shell will be returned to you. By specifying that the program should run in the background with the & (ampersand symbol), you can run the GUI program and still be able to type away and run other commands.

You can send several jobs to the background, and each one will be given a different job number. In this case, when you wish to switch into a running job, you can type its number. For example, the following command will switch you to the background job assigned the number 3:

```
%3
```

You can exit a job that is currently running by pressing Ctrl+Z. It will still be there in the background, but it won't be running (officially, it's said to be *sleeping*). To restart it, you can switch back to it, as just described. Alternatively, you can restart it but still keep it in the background. For example, to restart job 2 in the background, leaving the shell prompt free for you to enter other commands, type the following:

```
%2 &
```

You can bring the command in the background into the foreground by typing the following:

```
fg
```

When a background job has finished, something like the following will appear at the shell:

```
[1]+  Done            updatedb
```

Using jobs within the shell can be a good way of managing your workload. For example, you can move programs into the background temporarily while you get on with something else. If you're editing a file in vi, you can press Ctrl+Z to stop the program. It will remain in the background, and you'll be returned to the shell, where you can type other commands. You can then resume vi later on by typing fg or typing % followed by its job number.

Summary

This chapter has covered taking complete control of your system. We've looked at what processes are, how they're separate from programs, and how they can be controlled or viewed using programs such as top and ps. In addition, we explored job management under BASH. You saw that you can stop, start, and pause programs at your convenience.

In the next chapter, we'll take a look at several tricks and techniques that you can use with the BASH shell to finely hone your command-line skills.

CHAPTER 18

■ ■ ■

Cool Shell Tricks

The BASH shell is the product of many years of development work by a lot of people. It comes from the old days of Unix and was an important step in computer software evolution. It's a program that retains complete simplicity, yet packs in more features than most users could ever hope to use.

One of the best things about BASH is its sheer power. If you ever wonder if you can do a task differently (and more efficiently), you'll probably find that one of the many BASH developers has implemented a method to do so. Once you learn these techniques, you'll find you can whiz around the shell at blinding speed. It's just a matter of exploring the far reaches of BASH, and that's what you'll do in this chapter. Hold onto your hats because it's an exciting ride!

Using Autocompletion

The Tab key is your best friend when using the shell. It will cause BASH to automatically complete whatever you type. For example, if you want to type konqueror, you can type konq, and then press Tab. You'll then find that BASH fills in the rest for you. It does this by caching the names of the programs you might run according to the directories listed in your $PATH variable (see Chapter 14).

Of course, there are limitations to autocompletion. On my SUSE Linux test system, typing loc didn't autocomplete locate (which I know is installed). Instead, it caused BASH to beep. This is because, on a default SUSE Linux installation, there is more than one possible match. Pressing Tab again shows what they are. Depending on how much you type (how much of an initial clue you give BASH), you might find there are many possible matches.

In this case, the experienced BASH user simply types another letter, which will be enough to distinguish the almost-typed word from the rest, and presses Tab again. With any luck, this should be enough for BASH to fill in the rest.

Autocompletion with Files and Paths

Tab autocompletion also works with files and paths. If you type the first few letters of a folder name, BASH will try to fill in the rest. This also obviously has limitations. There's no point in typing cd myfol and pressing Tab if there's nothing in the current directory that starts with the letters myfol. This particular autocomplete function works by looking at your current directory and seeing what's available.

Alternatively, you can specify an initial path for BASH to use in order to autocomplete. Typing cd /ho and pressing Tab will cause BASH to autocomplete the path by looking in the root directory (/). In other words, it will autocomplete the command with the directory home.

In a similar way, typing cd myfolder/myfo will cause BASH to attempt to autocomplete by looking for a match in myfolder.

If you want to run a program that resides in the current directory, such as one you've just downloaded for example, typing ./, followed by the first part of the program name, and then pressing Tab should be enough to have BASH autocomplete the rest. In this case, the dot slash tells BASH to look in the current directory for any executable programs or scripts (programs with X as part of their permissions) and use them as possible autocomplete options.

BASH is clever enough to spot whether the command you're using is likely to require a file, directory, or executable, and it will autocomplete with only relevant file or directory names.

Viewing Available Options

The autocomplete function has a neat side effect. As I mentioned earlier, if BASH cannot find a match, the dot slash tells BASH to show what all the available options are. For example, typing ba at the shell, and then pressing Tab twice will cause BASH to show all the possible commands starting with the letters *ba*.

On my test PC, doing this produces the following list of commands:

```
basename      bash
bashbug       batch
```

This can be a nice way of exploring what commands are available on your system. You can then use each command with the --help command option to find out what it does, or browse the command's man page.

When this trick is applied to directory and filename autocompletion, it's even more useful. For example, typing cd in a directory, and then pressing the Tab key twice will cause BASH to show the available directories, providing a handy way of getting a brief directory listing. Alternatively, if you've forgotten how a directory name is spelled, you can use this technique to find out prior to switching into it.

Figure 18-1 shows a few examples of using this technique with BASH.

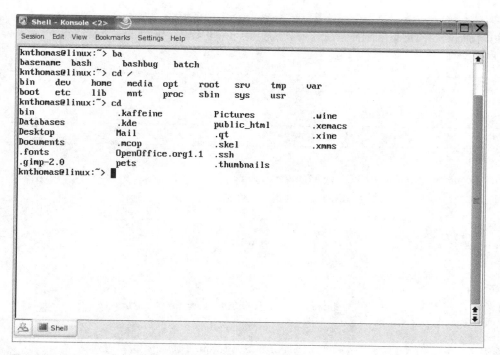

Figure 18-1. *Autocompletion makes using BASH much easier.*

Keyboard Shortcuts

Your other friend when using BASH is the Ctrl key, although you'll also find the Alt key handy. These keys provide shortcuts to vital command-line shell functions. They also let you work more efficiently when typing by providing what most programs call keyboard shortcuts.

Shortcuts for Working in BASH

Table 18-1 lists the most common keyboard shortcuts in BASH (there are many more; see BASH's man page for details). If you've explored the emacs text editor, you might find these shortcuts familiar. Such keyboard shortcuts are largely the same across many of the software packages that originate from the GNU Project. Often, you'll find an option within many SUSE Linux software packages that lets you use emacs-style navigation, in which case, these keyboard shortcuts will most likely work equally well.

■**Tip** It might be useful to photocopy Table 18-1 and stick it on the side of your monitor or keyboard as a reference guide.

Table 18-1. *Keyboard Shortcuts in BASH*

Shortcut	Description
Navigation	
Left/right cursor key	Move left/right in text
Ctrl+A	Move to beginning of line
Ctrl+E	Move to end of line
Alt+F	Move forward one word[1]
Alt+B	Move back one word[1]
Editing	
Ctrl+U	Delete everything behind cursor to start of line
Ctrl+K	Delete from cursor to end of line
Ctrl+W	Delete from cursor to beginning of word
Alt+D	Delete from cursor to end of word
Ctrl+T	Transpose characters on left and right of cursor
Alt+T	Transpose words on left and right of cursor
Miscellaneous	
Ctrl+L	Clear screen (everything above current line)
Ctrl+U	Undo everything since last command[2]
Alt+R	Undo changes made to the line[3]
Ctrl+Y	Undo deletion of word or line caused by using Ctrl+K, Ctrl+W, and so on[4]
Alt+L	Lowercase current word (from the cursor to end of word)

[1]*This is specific to SUSE Linux. Not all Linux distros let you use these shortcuts.*

[2]*In most cases, this has the effect of clearing the line.*

[3]*This is different from Ctrl+U, because it will leave intact any command already on the line, such as one pulled from your command history.*

[4]*This allows primitive cutting and pasting. Delete the text and then immediately undo, after which the text will remain in the buffer and can be pasted with Ctrl+Y.*

Shortcuts for System Control

In terms of the control over your system offered by keyboard commands, as mentioned in Chapter 17, pressing Ctrl+Z has the effect of stopping the current program. It suspends the program until you switch back into it or tell it to resume in another way, or manually kill it.

In the same style, pressing Ctrl+C while a program is running will quit it. This sends the program's process a termination signal, a little like killing it using the top program. Ctrl+C can prove handy if you start a program running by accident and quickly want to end it, or if a command takes longer than you expected to work and you cannot wait for it to complete. It's also a handy way of attempting to end crashed programs. Some complicated programs don't take too kindly to being quit in this way, particularly those that need to save data before they terminate. However, most should be okay.

Ctrl+D is another handy keyboard shortcut. This sends the program an end-of-file (EOF) message. In effect, this tells the program that you've finished your input. This can have a variety of effects, depending on the program you're running. For example, pressing it on its own at the shell prompt when no program is running will cause you to log out (if you're using a GUI terminal emulator like Konsole, the program will quit). This happens because pressing Ctrl+D informs the BASH shell program that you've finished your input. BASH then interprets this as the cue that it should log you out. After all, what else can it do if told there will be no more input?

While it might not seem very useful for day-to-day work, Ctrl+D is vital for programs that expect you to enter data at the command line. You might run into these as you explore BASH. If ever you read in a man page that a program requires an EOF message during input, you'll know what to press.

Command History

The original hackers who invented the tools used under Unix hated waiting around for things to happen. Being a hacker is all about finding the most efficient way of doing any particular task. (For the record, this is why many Unix fans dislike GUIs: messing around with mice and icons seems like a slow way of doing what can be done far more quickly at the command-line shell.)

Because of this, the BASH shell includes many features designed to optimize the user experience. The most important of these is the command history. All this means is that BASH remembers every command you enter (even the ones that don't work!) and stores them as a list on your hard disk.

During any BASH session, you can cycle through this history using the up and down cursor keys. Pressing the up arrow key takes you back into the command history, and pressing the down arrow key takes you forward.

The uses of the command history are enormous. For example, rather than type that long command that runs a program with command options, you can simply use the cursor keys to locate it in the history and press Enter.

On my SUSE Linux test system, BASH remembers 1,000 commands. You can view all of the remembered commands by typing history at the command prompt. This will scroll off the screen because it's so large, but you can use the scroll bars of the Konsole window to read it.

Each command in the history list is assigned a number. You can run any of the history commands by preceding their number with an exclamation mark, referred to as a *bang*, or sometimes a *shriek*. For example, you might type !923. On my test system, command number 923 in the BASH history is cd .., so this has the effect of switching me into the parent directory.

Command numbering remains in place until you log out (close the Konsole window or end a virtual console session). After this, the numbering is reordered. There will still be 1,000 commands, but the last command you entered before logging out will be at the end of the list, and the numbering will work back 1,000 places until the first command in the history list.

Tip One neat trick is to type two bangs: !!. This tells BASH to repeat the last command you entered. There are more tricks you can use. For example, typing !-3 will cause BASH to move three paces back in the history file and run that command. In other words, it will run what you entered three commands ago.

Rather than specifying a command number, you can type something like !cd. This will cause BASH to look in the history file, find the last instance of a command line that started with cd, and then run it.

Pressing Ctrl+R lets you search the command history from the command prompt. This particular tool can be tricky to get used to, however. As soon as you start typing, BASH will autocomplete the command based on matches found in the history file, starting with the last command in the history. What you type appears before the colon, while the autocompletion appears afterwards.

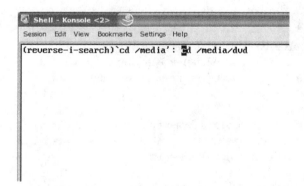

Figure 18-2. *BASH history completion is very useful but can also be confusing.*

Because BASH autocompletes as you type, things can get a little confusing when you're working with the command history, particularly if it initially gets the match wrong. For example, typing cd will show the last instance of the use of cd, as in the example in Figure 18-2. This might not be what you're looking for, so you must keep typing the command you do want until it autocompletes, despite BASH often making several incorrect assumptions.

Piping and Directing Output

It's not uncommon for a directory listing or output from another command to scroll off the screen. When using a GUI program like Konsole, you can use the scroll bars to view the output, but what if you are working at the bare command-line prompt?

By pressing Shift+Page Up and Shift+Page Down, you can "scroll" the window up to take a look at some of the old output, but very little is cached in this way and you won't see more than a few screenfuls. A far better solution is to pipe the output of the directory listing into a text viewer like less. Another useful technique is to redirect output to a file.

Piping the Output of Commands

Piping was one of the original innovations provided by Unix. It simply means that you can pass the output of one command to another, which is to say the output of one command can be used as input for another.

This is possible because shell commands work like machines. They usually take input from the keyboard (referred to technically as *standard input*) and, when they've done their job, usually show their output on the screen (known as *standard output*).

The commands don't need to take input from the keyboard, and they don't need to output to the screen. Piping is the process of diverting the output before it reaches the screen and passing it to another command for further processing.

Let's assume that you have a directory that is packed full of files. You want to do a long directory listing (ls -l) to see what permissions various files have. But doing this causes reams of output that fly off the screen. Typing something like the following provides a solution:

```
ls -l | less
```

The | symbol between the two commands is the pipe. It can be found on most US English-based computer keyboards next to the square bracket keys (above the Enter key; you'll need to hold down the Shift key to get it).

What happens in the example is that ls -l is run by the shell, but rather than sending the output to the screen, the pipe symbol (|) tells BASH to send it to the command that follows, to less. In other words, the listing is displayed within less, where you can read it at leisure. You can use Page Up and Page Down or the arrow keys to scroll through it. Once you quit less, the listing evaporates into thin air; the piped output is never actually stored as a file.

In the previous section, you saw how you can use the history command to view the command history. At around 1,000 entries, its output scrolls off the screen in seconds. However, you can pipe it to less, like so:

```
history | less
```

Figure 18-3 shows the result on my test PC.

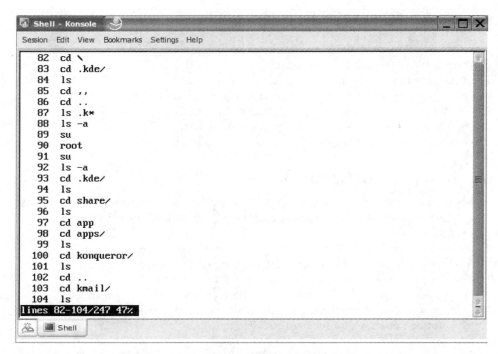

Figure 18-3. *Piping the output of the history command into the* `less` *command lets you read the output fully.*

You can pipe the output of any command. One of the most common uses is when searching for a particular string in the output of a command. For example, let's say you know that, within a crowded directory, there's a file with a picture of some flowers. You know that the word *flower* is in the filename, but can't recall any other details. One solution is to perform a directory listing, and then pipe the results to grep, which is able to search through text for a user-defined string (see Chapter 16):

```
ls -l | grep -i 'flower'
```

In this example, the shell runs the `ls -l` command, and then passes the output to grep. The grep command then searches the output for the word *flower* (the `-i` option tells it to ignore uppercase and lowercase). If grep finds any results, it will show them on your screen.

The key point to remember is that grep is used here as it normally is at the command prompt. The only difference is that it's being passed input from a previous command, rather than being used on its own.

You can pipe more than once on a command line. Suppose you know that the filename of the picture you want involves the words *flower* and *daffodil*, yet you're unsure of where they might fall in the filename. In this case, you could type:

```
ls -l | grep -i flower | grep -i daffodil
```

This will pass the result of the directory listing to the first grep, which will search the output for the word *flower*. The second pipe causes the output from grep to be passed on to the *second* grep command, where it's then searched for the word *daffodil*. Any results are then displayed on your screen.

Redirecting Output

Alongside piping is the concept of *redirecting*. This is like piping, except that the output is passed to a file rather than to another command. Redirecting can also work the other way: the contents of a file can be passed to a command.

If you wanted to create a file that contained a directory listing, you could type:

```
ls -l > directorylisting.txt
```

The angle bracket (>) between the commands tells BASH to direct the output of the ls -l command into a file called directorylisting.txt. If a file with this name exists, it's overwritten with new data. If it doesn't exist, it's created from scratch.

You can add data to an already existing file using two angle brackets:

```
ls -l >> directorylisting.txt
```

This will append the result of the directory listing to the end of the file directorylisting.txt, although, once again, if the file doesn't exist, it will be created from scratch.

Redirecting output can get very sophisticated and useful. Take a look at the following:

```
cat myfile1.txt myfile2.txt > myfile3.txt
```

As you learned in Chapter 16, the cat command joins two or more files together. If the command were used on its own without the redirection, it would cause BASH to print myfile1.txt on the screen, immediately followed by myfile2.txt. As far as BASH is concerned, it has joined myfile1.txt to myfile2.txt, and then sent them to standard output (the screen). By specifying a redirection, you have BASH send the output to a third file. Using cat with redirection is a handy way of combining two files.

It's also possible to direct the contents of a file back into a command. Take a look at the following:

```
sort < textfile.txt > sortedtext.txt
```

The sort command simply sorts words into alphanumeric order (it actually sorts them according to the ASCII table of characters, which places symbols and numbers before alphabetic characters). Directly after the sort command is a left angle bracket, which directs the contents of the file specified immediately after the bracket into the sort command. This is followed by a right angle bracket, which directs the *output* of the command into another file.

■**Tip** To see a table of the ASCII characters, type man 7 ascii at the command-line prompt.

There aren't many instances in day-to-day usage where you'll want to use the left angle bracket. It's mostly used with the text-based mail program (which lets you send e-mail from the shell), and in shell scripting, in which a lot of commands are combined together to form a simple program.

REDIRECTING STANDARD ERROR OUTPUT

Standard input and standard output are what BASH calls your keyboard and screen. These are the default input and output methods that programs use unless you specify something else, such as redirecting or piping output and input.

When a program goes wrong, its error message doesn't usually form part of standard output. Instead, it is output via standard error. Like standard output, this usually appears on screen.

Sometimes, it's very beneficial to capture an error message in a text file. This can be done by redirecting the standard error output. The technique is very similar to redirecting standard output:

```
cdrecord --scanbus 2> errormessage.txt
```

The `cdrecord` command is used to burn CDs, and with the `--scanbus` command option, you tell it to search for CD-R/RW drives on the system, something which frequently results in an error message if your system is not properly configured.

After the initial command, you see the redirection. To redirect standard error, all you need to do is type `2>`, rather than simply `>`. This effectively tells BASH to use the second type of output: standard error.

You can direct both standard output and standard error to the same file. This is done in the following way:

```
cdrecord --scanbus > error.txt 2>&1
```

This is a little more complicated. The standard output from `cdrecord --scanbus` is sent to the file `error.txt`. The second redirect tells BASH to include standard error in the standard output. In other words, it's not a case of standard output being written to a file, and then standard error being added to it. Instead, the standard error is added to standard output by BASH, and then this is written to a file.

Summary

In this chapter, we've looked at some tricks and tips to help you use the BASH shell more effectively. You've seen how BASH can help by autocompleting commands, filenames, and directories. You also learned about keyboard shortcuts that can be used to speed up operations within the shell.

This chapter also covered the history function and how it can be used to reuse old commands, saving valuable typing time. Finally, we looked at two key functions provided by BASH: redirection and piping. This involved the explanation of standard input, output, and error.

In Part Five of the book, starting with the next chapter, we move on to discuss the powerful multimedia functionality within SUSE Linux.

Multimedia

CHAPTER 19

■ ■ ■

MP3s and CDs

SUSE Linux is a thoroughly modern operating system, loaded with tools for working with music, movies, and images. We will discuss all this over the next few chapters. You'll see how your Linux-equipped PC really is ready to become the center of your multimedia world.

As you'll learn in this chapter, support for digital audio is built into SUSE Linux. Playback facilities are offered for MP3 music as well as CDs. It's even possible to record your own audio by plugging a microphone or other source into your sound card. If you have the skills and inclination, you can install additional software to turn your PC into a music-making machine.

Playing MP3 Music

MP3 files are in the process of revolutionizing the recorded music industry. The technology was largely responsible for bringing music to the PC scene, allowing small, but high-quality, audio files to be swapped by people across the Internet. Most of these were taken from commercially available CD tracks, however, and this was illegal (it might have been legal if permission of the copyright holder was sought, but this rarely happened). But, in recent years, the music industry has worked with the likes of Apple to make MP3 music legitimately available, albeit at a price.

The good news is that SUSE Linux supports the playback of MP3 music. The bad news is that it cannot, at the time of writing, work with online schemes like Apple's iTunes or the new Napster. Such schemes rely on special software to protect and restrict use of the music files. For example, it stops the track being played on more than three "unauthorized" computers. This software isn't available under Linux.

Note The companies that release the legal MP3s use digital rights management (DRM) software to severely restrict how and where you can play the music files. For example, most DRM protection schemes mean you cannot play the MP3 files in personal MP3 players unless you buy special models that are officially sanctioned and usually very expensive. Because of this restriction, and also because it goes against the spirit of freedom inherent in Linux, many think that it's a good thing that DRM technology hasn't been ported across from Windows.

However, Linux does support the playback of standard MP3 files and also the "ripping" of music from audio CDs into Ogg format (described in the "Ripping CDs" section later in this chapter). You can then put these files onto a memory card for use in a personal music player, or you can use them in your own music CD compilations. In addition, as with Windows, there are several file-sharing programs you can download and install in order to share music with others.

In terms of MP3 playback, there are two programs that will do the job within SUSE Linux. Kaffeine Media Player will tackle MP3 music given half a chance and appears to be the default for streaming MP3 audio (audio designed to be played across the Internet, usually via your web browser, rather than being downloaded to your hard disk first). However, the X Multimedia System (XMMS) program is a better choice in most cases. If you've ever used Winamp under Windows, you'll feel right at home, because XMMS looks the same and operates in an almost identical way.

To run XMMS, select K menu ➤ Multimedia ➤ Audio Player. The XMMS window appears, as shown in Figure 19-1. Using it is easy. Along the bottom of the program window are tape recorder–like controls allowing you to stop, play, pause, and cue through the music. Above this is a progress bar that shows your progress through the particular track. And above that is a time display showing how much of the track has been played (clicking this will change the display to show how much of the track is left to play). The track and artist name are displayed in the top right of the program window (provided the track has these details embedded within it), and beneath this are volume and balance controls.

Figure 19-1. *XMMS mirrors the look and feel of Winamp under Windows, and operates in a very similar way.*

To the right of the program window is a button that you can use to set the graphical equalization (10 frequency bands are available). There's also a button that lets you create *playlists*—lists of MP3 tunes to be played in sequence. The best way of doing this is to open a Konqueror file-browsing window and simply drag-and-drop your MP3 tunes onto the playlist window. Once your tracks are in the playlist window, you can change their order in the playlist by clicking and dragging the tracks up and down.

As with Winamp under Windows, right-clicking any nonfunctional part of the window will bring up a menu offering further program options, as shown in Figure 19-2. Right-clicking and selecting Options ➤ Preferences lets you change the various plug-ins the program relies on to work. You can add, activate, and play other plug-ins (such as echo), and also add some visualization effects, such as colorful patterns that pulsate to the beat of the music.

■**Caution** You should avoid making any changes on the Audio I/O Plugins tab of XMMS's Preferences dialog box. It's possible to misconfigure XMMS and cause it to stop working.

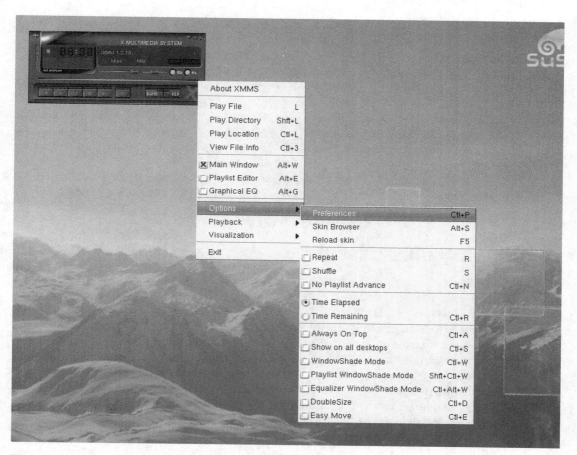

Figure 19-2. *Right-clicking anywhere on the XMMS program window will bring up a wide range of options and preferences.*

You may find that the XMMS's default black look makes it hard to see the various buttons. To change the look and feel of the program, right-click on the program window and select Options ➤ Skin Browser. This option will let you choose different "skins," which are color and graphical schemes that can be applied to the program.

ADJUSTING VOLUME LEVELS

Most PC systems have three volume controls for audio playback, and getting the volume levels right among them can be a trial!

For starters, there's the physical volume control on your speakers. On most models, this should ordinarily be set to around 33% (or a third of the dial) for pleasant playback that isn't too loud. If you have a speaker system with a bass unit that has its own volume control, you should set this to a comfortable level.

After this, you should set the PCM volume on your PC. PCM volume is also called *wave* volume on some systems. This refers to the ability of your sound card to play back sampled digital music such as MP3 tunes. To set the PC volume, you'll need to start the volume control program, KAMix by selecting K menu ➤ Multimedia ➤ Volume Control. Make sure the Playback tab is highlighted in the program window, and click and drag the sliders above the PCM heading until they're between 50% and 75% of the way to the top. Next, start an MP3 track playing, and click and drag the master volume control sliders until you reach an appropriate volume level. If it proves impossible to reach a volume you like, or if the audio sounds distorted, click and drag the PCM sliders to a lower or higher level, and then adjust the main volume again.

Once KAMix has been started, its applet will always appear in the system tray at the bottom of the screen. This provides a quick way to change the master volume in the future: just click it, and then drag the slider.

Ripping Music from CDs

Although it might seem feasible to simply copy audio tracks straight off a CD and onto your hard disk, this isn't possible because of the way audio CDs are designed. The audio data must be extracted using special software.

Although SUSE Linux supports the playback of MP3 music, it doesn't provide any tools that allow you to create your own MP3 tunes from CD tracks. This is because of legal issues surrounding the patenting of MP3 technology. (Most people, companies, and organizations in the Linux and open source community object to the kind of patents applied to software.) However, support for the Ogg format is included.

Ogg format is similar to MP3 in that it shrinks music files, and it also maintains a similar audio quality. The difference is that Ogg is an open and free standard, which is to say that anyone can use it without needing to pay fees to a large corporation. It's developed by the Xiph.org Foundation, which makes the code libraries and software freely available in a similar way to the other software offered under SUSE Linux.

Vorbis and Ogg files are the same thing, and people sometimes refer to Ogg Vorbis files, too. These are all exactly the same type of file. Technically speaking, Vorbis is the name given to the compression technology, and Ogg is the name given to the "container," or the method by which the compressed audio data stream is turned into a file.

SUSE Linux provides two GUI programs to rip music from CDs, transferring the disc's digital data to your PC as Ogg files: KAudioCreator, which is designed to fit in with the KDE desktop offered by SUSE Linux, and Grip. KAudioCreator is rather basic, so I'll describe how to use Grip instead. I'll also explain how to use the command line to rip CDs, because it's a fast and simple method.

Using Grip

Grip doesn't come installed by default under SUSE Linux, so you'll need to take care of that first. Then you'll find it easy to rip CDs with Grip.

Installing Grip

Follow these steps to install Grip:

1. Insert your SUSE Linux installation DVD into your DVD-ROM drive.

2. Start YaST2 by selecting K menu ➤ Control Center ➤ YaST2 Modules.

3. Click the Software icon, and then click Install and Remove Software. Enter your root password when it is requested.

4. In the search box, type **grip** and press Enter.

5. Put a check in the box when Grip appears in the search results, and then click Accept. You'll notice that some additional programs need to be installed, so agree to this by clicking Accept again.

Ripping with Grip

After you've installed Grip, you can rip a CD as follows:

1. Start Grip by clicking K menu ➤ Multimedia ➤ CD/DVD Tools ➤ Grip.

2. Insert an audio CD into your drive to initialize the ripping process. Grip will not only sense the CD, but will also look up its track details on the online CD Database (CDDB) service, as shown in the example in Figure 19-3. This will mean that all the files you save will have the correct track and artist information.

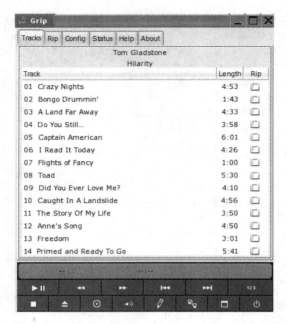

Figure 19-3. *Grip will not only sense the insertion of an audio CD, but will even look up the track names online!*

3. Put a check in the boxes (arranged down the right side under the Rip column) according to which tracks you want to transfer from the CD to your PC's hard disk.

4. Click the Config tab, and then click the Encode tab. Here, you must select the audio encoder you want to use to convert the CD tracks into files. Although Grip offers many encoders, only one is installed under SUSE Linux: oggenc. This will convert the CD tracks into Ogg files, so select this from the list.

5. When you're ready, click the Rip tab, and then click Rip + Encode, as shown in Figure 19-4. This will automatically turn the tracks into Ogg files, which will be saved in your home directory, with the .ogg filename extension.

■**Caution** When ripping tracks, try to avoid using your computer for other tasks. Doing so can cause glitches in the audio files.

You can play your Ogg files by double-clicking them.

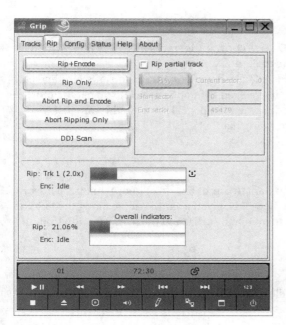

Figure 19-4. *Ripping a CD with Grip*

■**Tip** It is possible to add MP3 encoding support to SUSE Linux by downloading and installing the `bladeenc` or `lame` programs from third-party sources (that is, those not connected with SUSE Linux). The download point for both projects is `www2.arnes.si/~mmilut/`. You'll also find instructions on how to use the program, which, in most cases, is similar to using `oggenc`. However, neither program is supported by SUSE Linux in any way. Once installed, you can use either program within Grip by selecting the relevant encoder under the Config tab.

Command-Line Ripping

Although using command-line tools don't present any difficulties, I advise you to read Part Four of this book if you haven't already familiarized yourself with the basics of the command-line shell.

Why use command-line tools to rip audio tracks? Well, they offer speed, simplicity, and ease of use, provided you take the time to get to know them.

■**Note** Many GUI multimedia programs use what are fundamentally command-line programs such as those discussed here. In each case, the GUI simply adds an additional way of accessing the programs.

Converting to WAV Format

The first step in ripping music from audio CDs is to convert the tracks into WAV files. WAV files are pure digital audio files that are uncompressed.

The oddly titled cdparanoia program is installed by default on SUSE Linux systems and can do this job. Like many Linux shell programs, it's packed with options to let you get the most from your audio CDs, and it's well worth reading the man page. However, the simplest way of using it is to insert the CD and then type something like:

```
cdparanoia 5
```

This will rip track five of the CD to the disk.

There's no need to specify which drive you want to use, or any other information. cdparanoia will either guess or fill in default details. The file will be given a simple name along the lines of track05.cdda.wav. You can then change this to match the artist and track information from the CD inlay card.

Ripping and Playing the CD

Ripping an entire CD is easy. Assuming the file has 12 tracks, you should type:

```
cdparanoia -B [1-12]
```

The -B command option is used to indicate batch mode—another way of saying that the program should rip many tracks at once. After this, in the square brackets, you specify a range of tracks to be ripped. This example specifies [1-12] for 12 tracks. If you wanted to rip just tracks 1 through 5, you would type [1-5] instead.

Note While ripping audio tracks, both cdparanoia and Grip give clues as to how well they're getting on by displaying a smiley icon. This is located toward the end of the status display line. A happy smiley indicates that the ripping procedure is working well. A smiley with a straight face indicates possible problems. An unhappy face indicates that there's considerable "jitter" (problems caused by damaged CDs). For more information, see the cdparanoia man page.

Once the tracks are on the hard disk in WAV format, you can load them into XMMS and listen to them as if they were MP3 tracks. However, if you take a look at their file size, you'll spot a problem: each minute of audio will take up around 10MB, so an average four-minute song takes up around 40MB. This is because they're uncompressed audio. In contrast, MP3 and Ogg use compression methods to shrink the file to around one-tenth of this size.

Converting to Ogg Format

Converting the WAV files to Ogg files is as easy as ripping the tracks. If you have a directory full of WAV files, you can simply type:

```
oggenc *.wav
```

This command uses a wildcard to convert all the files into Ogg files, using the filenames they already have (the converted files will be given an .ogg file extension).

If you don't want to convert all the files into Ogg format, you can specify just one by typing its filename, or specify multiple files by typing their filenames on the same line after the command, separated by a space, like this:

```
oggenc track01.wav
```

or

```
oggenc track01.wav track02.wav
```

As shown in Figure 19-5, an Ogg file takes up a lot less space than its WAV counterpart.

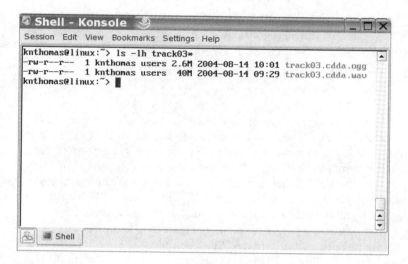

Figure 19-5. *From 40MB to 2.6MB—encoding WAV files to Ogg means smaller file sizes and negligible loss of quality.*

FILE SHARING

The original Napster program single-handedly created the file-sharing craze, whereby people can download MP3s from others and share their own collections of music. Several other file-sharing technologies have since arisen. The most common ones in use today are Gnutella and BitTorrent. Nowadays, the programs are used for far more than simple MP3 sharing. BitTorrent is a common way of distributing ISO images of Linux installation CDs, for example.

There are many Gnutella-style programs for Linux. One example is Qtella, which you can learn about by visiting www.qtella.net. There's also a version of the popular Windows program LimeWire available for Linux - www.limewire.com (although this isn't open source).

The official BitTorrent home page is http://bittorrent.com/. However, that site offers a simple shell program, which some people might find hard to use. A good GUI alternative is Azureus, available from http://azureus.sourceforge.net/.

Playing Audio CDs

SUSE Linux uses the KsCD application to play audio CDs. Once again, if you've ever used practically any CD-playing application under Windows, then you'll know what to expect, because KsCD offers similar functions.

To start KsCD, select K menu ➤ Multimedia ➤ CD Player. When the program has started, it will instantly minimize to the system tray. Once you insert an audio CD, KsCD will go into action and start playing the CD automatically. You can access its controls by double-clicking its icon, although you can also right-click the icon to gain quick access to the most commonly used controls.

■**Note** KsCD plays CDs using the analog link from your CD/DVD-ROM drive to your PC's motherboard. In other words, it doesn't play CDs digitally by grabbing the data using the IDE cable, as Windows sometimes does. On most PCs, this won't be an issue, because the analog link is nearly always set up by the PC manufacturer, but if you've built your own PC, you'll need to make sure this cable is in place.

KsCD is fairly simple to use, and its main buttons are clearly labeled. It's important to note that Linux tends to lock the CD/DVD drive when it's in use, so if you want to eject a disc, you'll need to use the Eject button on KsCD's interface, rather than the button on the front of the drive (it's also possible to unmount the CD from the shell, as described in Chapter 15).

One handy feature of the player is its CDDB support. As noted earlier, CDDB is an online database of CDs, complete with track and artist information. By clicking the CDDB button on the interface, you can automatically search this database and fill in the information in the KsCD playlist (provided you're online, of course), as shown in Figure 19-6. If the CD isn't found, which is rare, you can type in the information yourself. When you click the Submit button, this information will then be added to the main CDDB database for others to use. The track information for any CDs you look up in this way, or for whose details you enter, will then be held on your hard disk for future reference when you play the CD.

Figure 19-6. *KsCD can look up the names of your CD tracks online.*

Altering the volume of CD playback differs from altering the volume of MP3/Ogg playback. Instead of clicking and dragging the PCM slider in KAMix, you must click the Ext Source Playback tab, and then click and drag the CD sliders instead.

Note that once it's activated, KsCD will always appear in the system tray every time you reboot. This can have an unfortunate effect: if your PC boots up and an audio CD is in the drive, it will be played as soon as the desktop appears. You can avoid this by right-clicking the KsCD icon and selecting Quit. This will end the program and also stop it from starting whenever the computer boots.

Recording Audio

If you have a microphone, you can record your own music using your PC. You can e-mail voice messages to relatives overseas, for example, or capture yourself strumming your guitar!

In addition to this, most PC sound cards have line-in inputs to which you can attach a variety of domestic equipment. For example, by attaching your cassette recorder, you can digitize your old pre-CD tape collection. If your record player or audio amplifier has a line-out, you can transfer your old vinyl records.

SUSE Linux includes a quite sophisticated sound-recording program called KRecord, seen in Figure 19-7. To run this program, select K ➤ Multimedia ➤ Sound Recorder. It's a little like Windows' Sound Recorder program, but with a lot more functions.

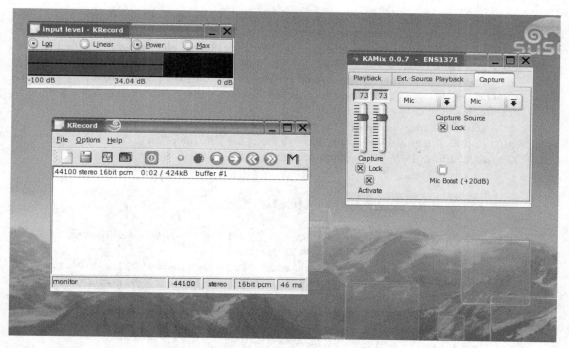

Figure 19-7. *KRecord is a powerful little program that can record audio from a microphone, line-in, or another source. If necessary, you can use KAMix to set input sound levels.*

To record from a microphone, start by plugging the microphone into the relevant socket. (Most PC microphones and sound cards are color-coded; the microphone socket and jack are usually pink.)

Once it's plugged in, start KRecord. The next step is to make sure that the microphone's input level is set correctly, so select Options ➤ Input Level. This will show a VU meter-style graph of the incoming sound levels. Try speaking into the microphone. With any luck, the VU meter should respond, and rise and fall to the sound of your voice.

If nothing appears to be happening, or if the rise and fall is very minor, select Options ➤ Run Mixer. This will bring up KAMix, which in addition to controlling volume levels also lets you set the input sound levels. Click the Capture tab (to the very right of the program window) and ensure that Mic is selected in the drop-down lists, as shown in Figure 19-7. Then click and drag the Capture sliders and speak into the microphone, dragging the sliders until you reach an acceptable level of input. If this seems impossible, try putting a tick in the Mic Boost box.

Once the levels have been set, click the red record icon on the toolbar of KRecord. When you've finished speaking, click the Stop button.

Caution   Any recording you make will be uncompressed audio. This will rapidly fill up your hard disk, since one minute of audio will roughly equate to 10MB of disk space!

KRecord works on the concept of buffers. Every time you make a recording, it's held in a buffer and must be deliberately saved to disk or it will be lost when the program is quit. To save it, simply highlight it in the program window (if it's not already highlighted), and then choose File ➤ Save Buffer As.

Once you've recorded the audio to disk, you can use the instructions provided earlier in this chapter to turn it into an Ogg file. This will make it smaller but without losing any discernable audio quality.

Recording using the line-in of your sound card is virtually identical to recording from a microphone. The only difference is that you select the Line In option in the drop-down list in KAMix and adjust the levels so that they're appropriate.

MAKING MUSIC

As you might expect, powerful audio-editing and music-making programs run under Linux. However, these are specialized tools and not commonly found in most distros.

As usual, there are many programs available for each task, but perhaps one of the best audio editors is Audacity. This can be found at `http://audacity.sourceforge.net/` and is also included on the SUSE Linux installation DVD-ROM (just search for it using the software section of YaST2). Audacity can perform simple tasks, such as recording, playing, importing, and exporting sounds. It also comes with a wide variety of effects (including the ability to use professional-level VST and LADSPA plug-ins). Additionally, it features an amplitude envelope editor, customizable spectrogram mode, and much more.

If you want to make music using MIDI (using your sound card's wave table sounds), many consider MusE to be one of the best programs for the task. It features audio and MIDI sequencing—effectively a complete recording studio running under Linux. For more details, visit `http://lmuse.sourceforge.net/`. This program is also included on the SUSE Linux DVD-ROM.

Creating Audio CDs

If you have a collection of MP3s or Ogg files, you might consider making your own compilation audio CD. To do this, you'll obviously need a CD-R/RW drive, but other than that, all the software you need is built into SUSE Linux and is very easy to use.

The program that will do all this for you is K3b. This generally mirrors the look and feel of the Nero CD burning program under Windows, as you can see in Figure 19-8.

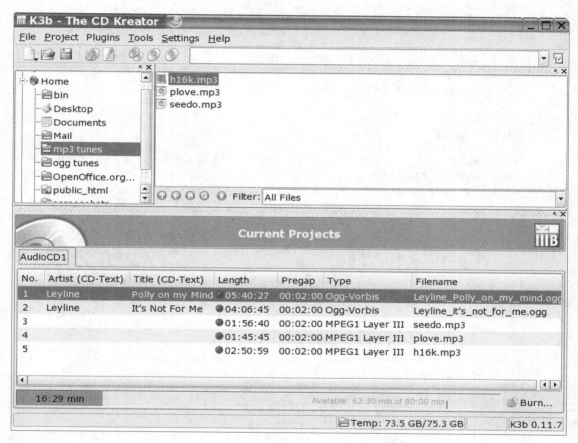

Figure 19-8. *K3b mirrors the look and feel of Windows CD-burning programs, so is very easy to use.*

Start K3b by selecting K ➤ Multimedia ➤ CD/DVD Burning. To burn a CD, click the New Audio CD Project icon. After this, it's simply a matter of using the topmost pane in the window to browse to your MP3 or Ogg collection, and then dragging the files down to the bottom part of the program window. As each track is added, keep an eye on the timeline display at the bottom of the window, which shows how many minutes have been taken up with the tracks on the disc. Remember that most blank CD-Rs can store around 74 minutes of audio, although some high-capacity discs can store 80 minutes. (Some older CD players are unable to read 80-minute discs, so you might consider sticking to 74 minutes.)

Once your compilation is complete, click the Burn icon on the toolbar (the icon that looks like a CD that is on fire). After this, you'll be prompted to set the writing speed as well as various other details; in most cases, the defaults should be fine. When you're ready, ensure there's a suitable blank CD-R disc in the drive, and then click the Burn button.

■**Caution** As with any kind of CD production on a PC, it's not a good idea to use your machine while it's burning a disc. This is because errors can be caused in the CD itself.

K3b can also copy audio CDs. All you need to do is select the option on the program's welcome screen, and then put the original CD in your CD/DVD-ROM drive and a blank CD in your CD-R/RW drive. Then follow the instructions on your screen.

Summary

This chapter covered the audio functions built into SUSE Linux. We started by looking at how you can play back MP3 and CD music, and then moved on to how various programs provided with SUSE Linux can be used to rip CD music to files that can be stored on your hard disk.

Next, you learned how you can record your own audio using a microphone or other sound source. Finally, we examined how all of these audio files can be burned to music CDs.

In Chapter 20, we will look at the video functions built into SUSE Linux.

CHAPTER 20

■■■

Viewing Movies and Video

Playing music files is only a part of SUSE Linux's abilities when it comes to multimedia. It's also a powerful movie player. It's capable of streaming video across the Internet, as well as playing video files stored on your hard disk or video CDs.

If you have a TV card installed in your PC, you can watch TV or grab video from sources such as VHS video cameras. Everything you need for competent multimedia playback is built right into SUSE Linux, as you'll learn in this chapter.

Watching Movies

SUSE Linux provides the Kaffeine Media Player application, shown in Figure 20-1, for watching video files. This works with Konqueror while you're browsing the Web and will automatically start up when it's needed to play a video file. Alternatively, you can start the application from the K menu (Multimedia ➤ Video Player) and browse to a video file already on your hard disk.

Figure 20-1. *Kaffeine Media Player can play back a variety of video files, both online and offline.*

Upgrading Kaffeine

On a default installation of SUSE Linux, a problem arises during playback of some video files, including some types of AVI and MPG movies. This is because there are many different types of technologies available for digital video, and new standards are being created all the time. The end result is that you might find your system is incompatible with certain video file formats.

In order to play video files, your computer needs a *codec*, which is a small, invisible piece of code that takes care of the background work needed to decode a video file. By default, SUSE Linux comes with several codecs, but for full compatibility, your first step should be to download and install a better set of codecs.

Kaffeine is closely based on Xine, which is a long-running project designed to bring video playback to Linux. Therefore, upgrading Kaffeine is simply a matter of installing the latest Xine software.

Unfortunately, the people behind Xine release only the source files for their software. We'll discuss how source files can be compiled into actual programs in Chapter 29. However, for the beginner, compiling programs can be daunting.

As an alternative, you can download an already-compiled version of Xine. Several third parties compile the program and offer it for download as a free service. The only downside of this is that it involves breaking one of the security rules of thumb mentioned earlier in this book: you should download only from official sites and avoid sites whose authenticity you cannot establish. However, sometimes this is simply unavoidable.

For several years, the PackMan site has offered downloads of many packages for SUSE Linux, including the latest release of Xine. Here are the steps for getting Xine from this site:

1. Go to `http://packman.links2linux.org/`. Use the Search facility to look for Xine.

2. Look down the list of results for `xine-lib`. This is the behind-the-scenes system component that provides the playback codecs. Once you've found it, right-click the file and select Save Link As. Then select a destination in which to save the file.

3. When it's finished downloading, open a shell (K menu ➤ System ➤ Terminal ➤ Konsole), switch to root user, and type the following in the same directory where you downloaded the file, replacing *<filename>* with the name of the file:

```
rpm -Uvh <filename>
```

After you've downloaded and installed `xine-lib`, Kaffeine should be compatible with many more video file formats.

On the same download screen where you found `xine-lib`, you might also find a version of `libxine` designed to let you play the popular QuickTime and Microsoft WMA formats. This is also worth downloading and installing, following the same steps as outlined here.

Note Some codec files that you can download are in a gray area legally in terms of copyright. Many of them are Windows DLL files that have been modified to work under Linux. The files in question are usually provided as part of a program that comes with Windows, such as QuickTime or Windows Media Player. Because of this, some people argue that as long as you dual-boot between Windows and Linux, and have the programs that ordinarily use the system files installed on Windows, then using the files under Linux is legal.

Using Kaffeine

Using Kaffeine is fairly straightforward. The playback controls run along the bottom of the screen. Above the controls is a slider for moving backward and forward in movie files (although some movie file formats don't allow you to cue backward and forward in this way).

The Video Settings option on the Config menu offers several controls to adjust the picture quality. You can also alter the sound quality using the Equalizer option on the Config menu.

Using RealPlayer

In addition to Kaffeine, SUSE Linux also includes the RealPlayer application, as shown in Figure 20-2. This is designed primarily to work with online video streams, and it's automatically integrated into the Konqueror web browser. However, you can also use RealPlayer to play RAM or RM video files that you download.

Figure 20-2. *RealPlayer comes with SUSE Linux and can be used to view streaming video online.*

RealPlayer can be found on the K menu under the Multimedia heading. If you're offered a choice of streaming movie formats, it's generally a good idea to choose Real Media.

PLAYING DVD MOVIES

DVD movies are copy-protected using a system called the Content Scrambling System (CSS). This relies on a software key to decrypt the content before playback can happen. These keys are strictly controlled and handed out by an industry body that controls the DVD technical standard. So far, no organization that creates Linux software has been able to license one of these keys.

CyberLink has ported its Windows-based DVD movie player over to Linux, but this is the only example of Linux-compatible DVD-playing software. It is also a commercial product and, at the time of writing, available only as part of specialized distros such as TurboLinux.

Because of this state of affairs, the DeCSS software was created. This cracks the CSS protection so that DVD movies can be played on Linux. The trouble is that it is illegal to do this. In many countries around the world (particularly the United States), such a program is considered a tool designed to overcome copy-protection mechanisms. Even owning this program file is illegal. In several countries, offering it for download is a criminal offense. For this reason, getting the DeCSS software is very difficult, and I won't discuss it any further in this book.

Watching TV

If you have a TV card installed in your PC, SUSE Linux might be able to make use of it. You may want to watch TV courtesy of an aerial plugged into the TV card, or you may want to view video from equipment like VHS video cameras using the card's composite or S-Video inputs. SUSE Linux comes with a TV viewer application you can use for these purposes.

Before you can use the TV viewer application, however, you must set up the hardware using YaST2. Prior to this, you must install some extra system files. Here are the steps for setting up SUSE Linux to use your TV card:

1. Open a Konqueror window and switch to root.

2. Insert your SUSE Linux installation DVD-ROM, and then type the following commands in sequence (ignoring any output):

   ```
   rpm -Uvh /media/dvd/suse/i586/tv-common-3.91-59.i586.rpm
   rpm -Uvh /media/dvd/suse/i586/v4l-conf-3.91-59.i586.rpm
   rpm -Uvh /media/dvd/suse/i586/v4l-tools-3.91-59.i586.rpm
   ```

3. Now you can configure the hardware itself through YAST2. Select K menu ➤ Control Center ➤ YAST2 Modules ➤ Hardware ➤ TV Card.

4. Choose your TV card from the list, and then click Configure. This starts up a wizard that will ask questions about your hardware setup.

5. The first question is whether your TV card has an audio line output to the line-in of your sound card. You can figure this out easily by examining the back of your PC. Look for a lead from the TV card to the sound card. This should be relevant only for older TV cards.

6. After this, you'll be asked if you want to set up IR—an infrared remote control. For the time being, click No. If you have such a device, or get one later, you might want to return to this screen to set it up.

7. Next, you'll be asked to confirm your geographical region and TV format. These should be automatically filled in for you, based on the information you entered when you installed SUSE Linux. North American users should find their country selected in the Frequency Table drop-down list, along with NTSC selected in the TV Norm section. Most European and Australian users should have the relevant geographical region selected in the Frequency Table section and PAL selected in the TV Norm drop-down list.

8. Don't choose to scan for channels. Simply click OK, and then click Finish.

9. Once your configuration has been written to disk, close Control Center.

10. Select K menu ➤ Multimedia ➤ TV to start the TV software, called kdetv.

11. You'll be asked to confirm the device you want to use to grab video. Next, you'll be asked to select the source of the video (which will be television if you want to watch TV or composite/S-Video if you have a camera plugged into either of those sockets). You can also once again confirm your video encoding, although this should be set automatically.

12. Click OK, and the Channel Wizard will start automatically. This will scan through the channels in the same way that most TVs are able to autotune in order to find the local stations. You'll be again asked to select your geographical region, so do so. Once the scan has finished, you'll be presented with a list of channels, which you can then select to save for use later.

Once it's set up, using kdetv is straightforward. Figure 20-3 shows the kdetv screen. You can alter the channels by clicking the plus and minus buttons on the toolbar. On the right side of the program window is a slider you can use to alter the volume level. To switch to full-screen mode, so the TV picture fills your entire screen, press the PageUp key.

Figure 20-3. *The kdetv program lets you watch TV on SUSE Linux, provided you have a TV card installed in your PC.*

MOVIE EDITING

At the time of writing, there are only a few movie-editing titles available for Linux, and the software scene surrounding movie editing is in its infancy. In other words, many of the programs available are still in the testing (beta) stage, so they might contain a few bugs.

One of the better movie-editing packages is Cinelerra, which you will find at `http://heroinewarrior.com`. This software lets you both capture and edit video. However, even its makers point out that it's not for beginners. Using it requires some knowledge of video technology and terminology, as well as some programming skills. It can also be difficult to install.

Users who are new to video editing might want to look at MainConcept's MainActor, which you'll find at `www.mainconcept.com`. This is a port of a Windows product and is proprietary rather than open source, and it isn't free of charge. However, many agree that it's the most comprehensive video editor available for Linux, as well as the easiest to use.

It's always worth remembering that the Linux software scene moves extremely quickly. So, if you try one of the movie-editing programs and don't like it, check it out again later. The software can change beyond all recognition within months or even weeks.

Summary

In this chapter, we've looked at how the Kaffeine Media Player application can play back video files of various types. You also learned how to update Kaffeine to allow the playback of even more video files. Then we explored how you can configure a TV card so that you can use your PC to watch TV broadcasts, using the kdetv application.

In the next chapter, we will look at image editing with Linux. There, you'll learn about one of the software jewels in the SUSE Linux crown: The GIMP.

◼◼◼

## CHAPTER 21

Image Editing

The PC has become increasingly useful in the field of photography. It's hard to imagine a professional photographer who doesn't use a computer in some way, either to download digital camera images or to scan in images taken using traditional film-based cameras.

SUSE Linux includes a sophisticated and professional-level image-editing program called The GIMP. The title stands for GNU Image Manipulation Program. This chapter introduces this jewel in the crown of Linux software.

Getting Pictures onto Your PC

Before you can undertake any image editing or improving, you need to transfer your digital images to your PC. Depending on the source of the pictures, there are a variety of ways of doing this. We have already looked at transferring images to your PC in Chapter 8, but let's briefly recap the procedure here.

Most modern cameras use memory cards to store the pictures. If you have a model like this, when you plug the camera into your PC's USB port, you should find that it's recognized instantly. A message should appear telling you in which folder the memory card contents have been mounted (see Chapter 15 for an explanation of mounting).

If your camera doesn't appear to be recognized by SUSE Linux, then you should consider buying a USB card reader. Usually, these devices are inexpensive and can read a wide variety of card types, making them a useful investment for the future. Some new PCs come with card readers as part of the deal.

You can check the online SUSE hardware database (http://hardwaredb.suse.de/?LANG=en_UK) to see if your camera and/or card reader is compatible with SUSE Linux. If you cannot find your make and model in the list, that does not necessarily mean it won't work; most generic card readers should work fine under Linux, as will most new digital cameras.

If your camera isn't recognized, however, or if it's a few years old and uses the serial port to connect to your PC, you can try using the Digikam software (select K menu ➤ Graphics ➤ Photograph), as explained in Chapter 8.

If you have pictures, negative film, or transparencies, you can use a scanner to scan them in using the Xsane program, also covered in Chapter 8. This works in a virtually identical way to the TWAIN modules supplied with Windows scanners, in that you need to set the dots per inch (DPI) figures, as well as the color depth. Generally speaking, 300 DPI and 24-bit color should lead to a true-to-life representation of most photos (although because of their smaller size, transparencies or negative film will require higher resolutions, on the order of 1,200 or 2,400 DPI).

Bring Out The GIMP

The GIMP is an extremely powerful image editor that offers the kind of functions usually associated with top-end software like Adobe Photoshop. Although it's not aimed at beginners, it is possible for those new to image editing to get the most from of it, provided they put in a little work.

The program relies on a few unusual concepts within its interface, which can catch many people off guard. The first of these is that each of the windows within the program, such as floating dialog boxes or palettes, gets its own taskbar entry. In other words, The GIMP's icon bar, image window, settings window, and so on have their own buttons on the Taskbar alongside your other programs, as if they were separate programs.

■**Note** The GIMP's way of working is referred to as a Single Document Interface, or SDI. It's favored by a handful of programs that run under Linux and seems to be especially popular among programs that let you create things.

Because of the way that The Gimp runs, before you start up the program, it's a wise idea to switch to a different virtual desktop (virtual desktops are discussed in Chapter 7), which you can then dedicate entirely to The GIMP. You should also turn off the Show Windows from All Desktops feature of the Taskbar, which will limit The GIMP's Taskbar buttons to its own desktop. To do this, right-click a blank part of the Taskbar, select Configure Panel, click the Taskbar icon on the left, and remove the tick from the relevant box.

Then you can switch to your separate virtual desktop and select K menu ➤ Graphics ➤ Image Editing to run The Gimp. When the program starts for the first time, it will run through its setup routine. Usually, you can use the default answers to the various questions asked by the wizard.

After program has setup,, you'll be greeted by what appears to be a complex assortment of program windows. Now you need to be aware of a second unusual aspect of the program: its reliance on right-clicking. Whereas right-clicking usually brings up a context menu offering a handful of options, within The GIMP, it's the principle way of accessing the program's functions. Right-clicking an image brings up a menu offering access to virtually everything you'll need while editing. SUSE Linux 9.1 includes the latest version of The GIMP, 2.0, and this includes a menu bar in the main image-editing window. This is considered sacrilege by many traditional The GIMP users, although it's undoubtedly useful for beginners. However, the right-click menu remains the most efficient way of accessing The GIMP's tools.

The main toolbar window, shown in Figure 21-1, is on the left. This can be considered the heart of The GIMP because, when you close it, all the other program windows are closed, too. The menu bar on the toolbar window offers most of the options you're likely to use to start out with The GIMP. For example, File ➤ Open will open a browser dialog box in which you can select files to open in The GIMP. It's even possible to create new artwork from scratch by choosing File ➤ New, although you should be aware that The GIMP is primarily a photo editor. To create original artwork, a better choice is a program like OpenOffice.org Draw.

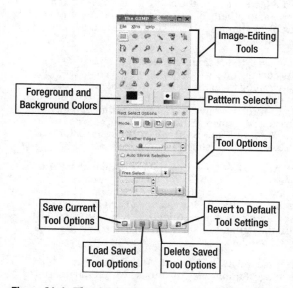

Figure 21-1. *The GIMP's main toolbar window*

Beneath the menu bar in the main toolbar window are the tools for working with images. Their functions are described in Table 21-1, which lists the tools in order from left to right, starting at the top left.

Table 21-1. *The GIMP Image-Editing Tools*

Tool	Description of Use
Rectangular selection tool	Click and drag to select a rectangular area within the image. This selected area can then be copied and pasted into a different part of the image or turned into a new layer.
Elliptical selection tool	Create an oval or circular selection area within the image, which you can then copy and paste.
Hand-drawn selection tool	Click and draw with the mouse to create a hand-drawn selection area. Your selection should end where it started. If not, The GIMP will draw a straight line between the start and end of the selection.

Table 21-1. *The GIMP Image-Editing Tools (Continued)*

Tool	Description of Use
Contiguous regions selection tool	Known as the "magic wand" in other image editors, this tool creates a selection area based on the color of the pixels where you click. For example, clicking on a red car hood will select most, if not all of the hood, because it is mostly red.
Color region selection tool	This tool works like the contiguous region selection tool, but will create a selection across the entire image based on the color you select. In other words, selecting a black T-shirt will also select a black signpost elsewhere in the picture if the shades are similar.
Shape selection tool	Another "magical" tool, the shape selector lets you create a selection by clicking on various points within an image, with the program joining the points together based on the color differences between the two points. This means that you can select the outline of a car by clicking a few points around the edge of the car and, provided the color of the car is different from the background, The GIMP will work out the color differences and select the car's shape automatically.
Path creation tool	This tool draws Bezier curves in order to create paths. Paths are akin to selections and can be saved for use later on in the image-editing process. Creating a Bezier curve is not too hard to do: just click and drag to draw a curve. Each extra click you make will define a new curve, which will be joined to the last one. To turn the path into a selection, click the button at the bottom of the toolbar.
Color picker	This lets you see the RGB, HSV, or CMYK values of any color within the image. Simply click the mouse within the image.
Zoom tool	Click to zoom into the image, right-click to see various zoom options, and hold down the Alt key while clicking to zoom out.
Measurer	This tool measures distances between two points (in pixels) and also angles. Just click and drag to use it. The measurements will appear at the bottom of the image window.
Move tool	Click and drag to move any selection areas within the image, as well as rearrange the positioning of various layers.
Crop tool	Click and drag to define an area of the image to be cropped. Anything outside the selection area you create will be discarded.
Rotate tool	This tool rotates any selections you make and can also rotate entire layers. It opens a dialog box in which you can set the rotation manually. Alternatively, you can simply click and drag the handles behind the dialog box to rotate by hand.
Scale tool	Known in some other image editors as "transform," this tool lets you resize the selection area or layer. It presents a dialog box where you can enter numeric values, or you can click and drag the handles to resize by hand.

Table 21-1. *The GIMP Image-Editing Tools (Continued)*

Tool	Description of Use
Shear tool	This tool lets you transform the image by shearing it. Slant a selection by clicking and dragging the corners of the selection area (if the selection area isn't square, a rectangular grid will be applied to it for the purposes of transformation).
Perspective tool	This tool lets you transform a selection by clicking and dragging its four corners and independently moving them without affecting the other corners. In this way, a sense of perspective can be emulated.
Flip tool	This tool flips a selection or image so that it is reversed on itself, either horizontally (click) or vertically (hold down Ctrl and click).
Text tool	Click on the image to add text.
Fill tool	Fill a particular area with solid color, according to the color selected in the color box below.
Gradient fill	This tool will create a gradient fill based on the foreground and background colors by clicking and dragging.
Pencil tool	This tool lets you draw individual pixels when zoomed in, or hard-edge lines when zoomed out. Simply click and drag to draw freehand, and hold down Shift to draw lines between two points.
Brush tool	This tool lets you draw on the picture in a variety of brush styles to create artistic effects. A brush can also be created from an image, allowing for great versatility.
Erase tool	Rather like the Brush tool in reverse, this tool deletes whatever is underneath the cursor. If layers are being used, the contents of the layer beneath will become visible.
Airbrush tool	This tool is also rather like the Brush tool, in that it draws on the picture in a variety of styles. However, the density of the color depends on the length of time you press the mouse button. Tap the mouse button, and only a light color will appear. Press and hold the mouse button, and the color will become more saturated.
Ink tool	This tool is like the Brush tool except that, rather like an ink pen, the faster you draw, the thinner the brush stroke is.
Pattern stamp	Commonly known as the clone tool, this is a popular image-editing tool. It is able to copy one part of an image to another via drawing with a brush-like tool. The origin point is defined by holding down Ctrl and clicking.
Blur/sharpen tool	Clicking and drawing on the image will spot blur or sharpen the image, depending on what settings are in use in the tool options area in the lower half of the toolbar.
Smudge tool	As its name suggests, clicking and drawing with this tool will smudge the image, rather like rubbing a still-wet painting with your finger (except slightly more precise).
Burn and dodge tool	This tool lets you spot lighten and darken an image by clicking and drawing on the image. The results depend on the settings in the tool options part of the window.

Directly beneath the image-editing tool icons, on the right, is an icon that shows the foreground and background colors that will be used when drawing with tools such as the Brush. To define a new color, double-click either the foreground (top) or background (bottom) color box. To the left is the pattern selector, which lets you choose which patterns are used with tools such as the Brush.

Beneath these icons, you'll see the various options for the selected tool. By using the buttons at the bottom of the window, you can save the current tool options, load tool options, and delete a previously saved set of tool options. Clicking the button on the bottom right lets you revert to the default settings for the tool currently being used (useful if you tweak too many settings!).

Next to the toolbar window is the Layers dialog box. This can be closed for the moment, although you can make it visible again later, if you wish.

Editing Images with The GIMP

After you've started The GIMP (and assigned it a virtual desktop), you can load an image by selecting File ➤ Open. The browser dialog box offers a preview facility, but this works only with images you've previously opened in The GIMP.

Once an image is opened, it's a good idea to alter the main program window's properties so it constantly stays on top of the desktop and doesn't disappear behind other windows. To do this, right-click its title bar, select Advanced, and then click Keep Above Others. After this, you will probably need to resize the image window so that it fits within the remainder of the screen. You can then use the Zoom tool (see Table 21-1) to ensure that the image fills the editing window, which will make working with it much easier.

You can save any changes you make to an image by right-clicking it and selecting File ➤ Save As. You can also print the image from the same menu.

Before you begin editing with The GIMP, you need to be aware of some essential concepts that are vital to understand in order to get the most from the program:

Copy, cut, and paste buffers: Unlike Windows programs, The GIMP lets you cut or copy many selections from the image and store them for use later. It refers to these saved selections as *buffers*, and each must be given a name for future reference. A new buffer is created by selecting an area using any of the selection tools, then right-clicking within the selection area and selecting Edit ➤ Buffer ➤ Copy Named (or Cut Named). Pasting a buffer back is a matter of right-clicking the image and selecting Edit ➤ Buffer ➤ Paste Named.

Paths: The GIMP paths are not necessarily the same as selection areas, although it's nearly always possible to convert a selection into a path and vice versa (right-click within the selection or path and look for the relevant option on the Edit menu). In general, the tools used to create a path allow the creation of complex shapes rather than simple geometric shapes, as with the selection tools. You can also be more intricate in your selections, as shown in the example in Figure 21-2. You can save paths for later use. To view the Paths dialog box, right-click the image and select Dialogs ➤ Paths.

Figure 21-2. *Paths allow for more elaborate and intricate selections, such as those that involve curves.*

■**Tip** Getting rid of a selection or path you've drawn is easy. In the case of a path, simply click on any other tool. This will cause the path to disappear. To get rid of a selection, simply select any selection tool and quickly click once on the image, being careful not to drag the mouse while doing so.

Layers: In The GIMP (along with most other image-editing programs), layers are like transparent sheets of plastic that are placed on top of the image. Anything can be drawn on each individual transparent sheet, and many layers can be overlaid in order to create a complicated image. Layers also let you cut and paste parts of the image between them. It's also possible to apply effects and transformations to a single layer, rather than to the entire image. The Layers dialog box, shown in Figure 21-3, appears by default, but if you closed it earlier, you can open it again by right-clicking the image and select Dialogs ➤ Layers. The layers can be reordered by clicking and dragging them in the dialog box. In addition, the blending mode of each layer can be altered. This refers to how it interacts with the layer below it. For example, its opacity can be changed so that it appears semitransparent, thereby showing the contents of the layer beneath.

■Tip To make sure the Layers dialog box is always visible, right-click the top of the Layers dialog box, click Advanced in the menu that appears, and then click Keep Above Others.

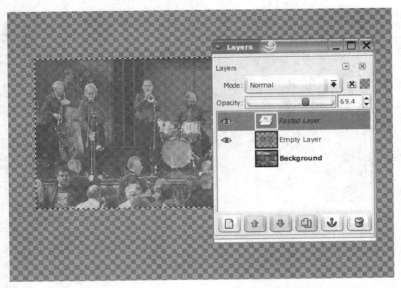

Figure 21-3. *The opacity of various layers can be set by clicking and dragging the relevant slider in the Layers dialog box.*

Making Color Corrections

The first step when editing most images is to correct the brightness, contrast, and color saturation. This helps overcome some of the deficiencies that are inherent in digital photographs or scanned-in images. To do this, right-click the image and select Layers ➤ Colors. You'll find a variety of options to let you tweak the image, allowing you a lot of control over the process.

For trivial brightness and contrast changes, selecting the Brightness/Contrast menu option will open a dialog box where clicking and dragging the sliders will alter the image. The changes you make will be previewed on the image itself, so you should be able to get things just right.

Similarly, the Hue/Saturation option will let you alter the color balance and also the strength of the colors (the *saturation*) by clicking and dragging sliders. By selecting the color bar options at the top of the window, you can choose individual colors to boost. Clicking the Master button will let you once again alter all colors at the same time.

The trouble with clicking and dragging sliders is that it relies on human intuition. This can easily be clouded by a badly calibrated monitor, which might be set too dark or too light. Because of this, The GIMP offers another handy option: Levels.

To access the Levels feature, right-click the image and select Layer ➤ Colors ➤ Levels. This presents a chart of the brightness levels in the photo and lets you set the dark, shadows, and highlight points, as shown in Figure 21-4. Three sliders beneath the chart represent, from left to right, the darkest point, the midtones (shadows), and the highlights within the picture. The first step is to set the dark and light sliders at the left and right of the edges of the chart. This will make sure that the range of brightness from the lightest point to the darkest point is set correctly. The next step is to adjust the middle slider so that it's roughly in the middle of the highest peak within the chart. This will accurately set the midtone point, ensuring an even spread of brightness across the image.

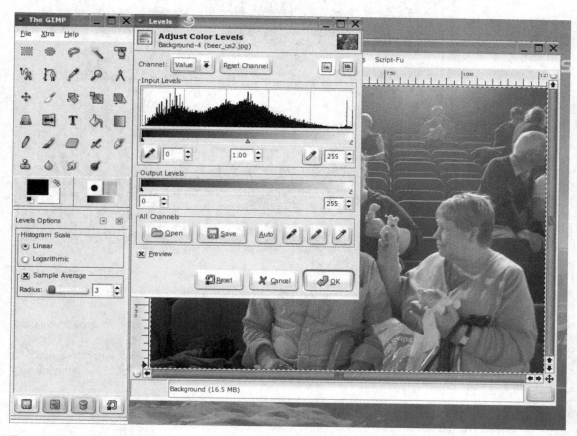

Figure 21-4. *The Levels function can be used to accurately set the brightness levels across an image.*

A little artistic license is usually allowed at this stage and, depending on the effect on the photo, moving the midtone slider a little to the left and/or right of the highest peak might produce more acceptable results. However, be aware that the monitor might be showing incorrect brightness/color values.

Cropping and Cloning

After you've adjusted the colors, you might want to use the Crop tool (see Table 21-1) to remove any extraneous details outside the focus of the image. For example, in a portrait of someone taken from a distance away, you might choose to crop the photo to show only the person's head and shoulders, as shown in Figure 21-5.

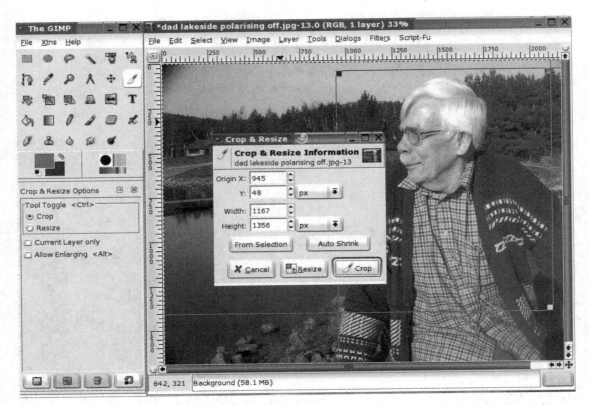

Figure 21-5. *You can use the Crop tool to remove any irrelevant details surrounding the subject of your photo.*

You might also want to use the Clone tool to remove facial blemishes. Start by using the Zoom tool to close in on the area. If the blemish is small, you might need to zoom in quite substantially. Then try to find an area of skin that is clear and that you can copy from. Hold down Ctrl and click in that area. Then click and draw over the blemish. The crosshair indicates the area you're copying from.

Sharpening

One final handy trick employed by professional image editors to give their photos a shot in the arm is to use the Sharpen filter. This has the effect of adding definition to the image and negating any slight blur caused by things such as camera shake or poor focusing. To apply the Sharpen filter, right-click the image and select Filters ➤ Enhance ➤ Sharpen.

As shown in Figure 21-6, a small preview window will show the effect of the sharpening on the image (you might need to use the scroll bars to move to an appropriate part of the image). Clicking and dragging the slider at the bottom of the dialog box will alter the severity of the sharpening effect. Too much sharpening can ruin a picture, so be careful. Try to use the effect subtly.

Figure 21-6. *Sharpening an image can give it a professional finish by adding definition.*

The Sharpen filter is just one of many filters you can apply in The GIMP, as explained in the next section.

Applying Filters

Like other image-editing programs, The GIMP includes many filters to add dramatic effects to your images with little, if any, user input. Filters are applied either to the currently selected layer or to a selection within the layer. To apply a filter, right-click the image and choose the relevant menu option. If you don't like an effect you've applied, you can reverse it by selecting Edit ➤ Undo, or by pressing Ctrl+Z.

The submenus offer filters grouped by categories, as follows:

Blur: These filters add various kinds of blur to the image or selection. For example, Motion Blur can imitate the effect of photographing an object moving at speed with a slow shutter. Perhaps the most popular blur option is Gaussian Blur, which has the effect of applying a soft and subtle blur.

Color: This option includes many technical filters, mostly of interest to image technicians or those who want to uncover and otherwise manipulate the color breakdown within an image. However, Filter Pack might appeal to the general user. This filter can quickly adjust the hue, saturation, and other values within the image. Also of interest is Colorify, which can tint the image to any user-defined color. Figure 21-7 shows an example of using the Colorify filter.

Figure 21-7. *The Colorify filter can be used to add a sepia-like effect to a picture.*

Noise: This collection of filters is designed to add speckles or other types of usually unwanted artifacts to an image. These filters are offered within The GIMP for their potential artistic effects, but they can also be used to create a grainy film effect—simply click Noisify.

Edge Detect: This set of filters can be used to automatically detect and delineate the edges of objects within an image. Although this type of filter can result in some interesting results that might fall into the category of "special effects," it's primarily used in conjunction with other tools and effects.

Enhance: The Enhance effects are designed to remove various artifacts from an image or otherwise improve it. For example, the Despeckle effect will attempt to remove unwanted noise within an image (such as flecks of dust in a scanned image). The Sharpen filter discussed in the previous section is located here, as is the Unsharp Mask, which offers a high degree of control over the image-sharpening process.

Generic: In this category, you can find a handful of filters that don't seem to fall into any other category. Of particular interest is the Convolution Matrix option, which lets you create your own filters by inputting numeric values. According to The GIMP's programmers, this is designed primarily for mathematicians, but it can also be used by others to create random special effects. Simply input values and then preview the effect.

Glass Effects: As the name suggests, these filters can apply effects to the image to imitate the effects that come about when glass is used to produce an image. For example, the Lens Effect filter will apply the same kind of distortion caused by various wide-angle lenses used on cameras, as shown in Figure 21-8.

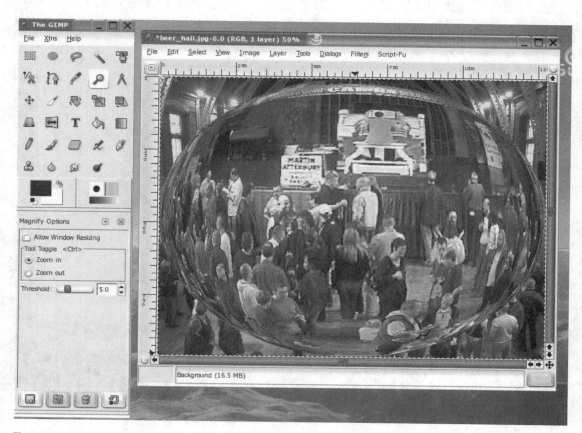

Figure 21-8. *The Glass Effects ➤ Lens Effect filter can be used to imitate a fish-eye lens.*

Light Effects: Here, you will find filters that imitate the effects that light can have on a picture, such as adding sparkle effects to highlights or imitating lens flare caused by a camera's lens.

Distorts: As the name of this category of filters suggests, the effects here distort the image in various ways. For example, Whirl and Pinch allow you to tug and push the image to distort it (to understand what is meant here, imagine the image is printed on rubber and then pinching or pushing the surface). This category also contains other special effects, such as Page Curl, which imitates the curl of a page at the bottom of the picture.

Artistic: These filters allow you to add painterly effects to the image, such as making it appear as if the photo has been painted in impressionistic brushstrokes, or simply making it appear as if the photo is painted on canvas by overlaying the texture of canvas onto the picture. Figure 21-9 shows an example of applying a filter for an oil painting effect.

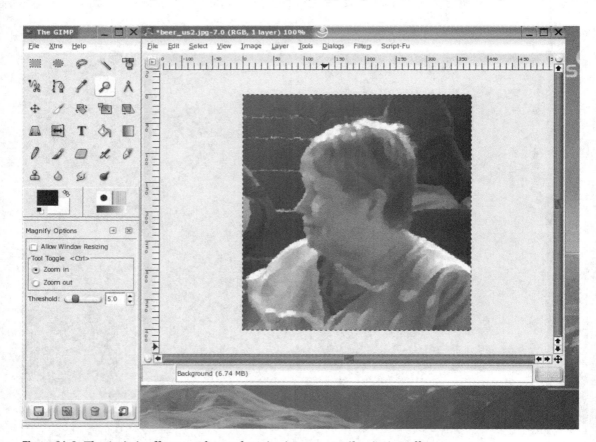

Figure 21-9. *The Artistic effects can be used to give images an oil painting effect.*

Map: These filters aim to manipulate the image by treating it like a piece of paper that can be folded in various ways and also stuck onto 3D shapes (a process referred to as *mapping*). Because the image is treated like it's a piece of paper, it can also be copied, and the copies placed on top of each other to create various effects.

Render: Here, you'll find filters designed to create new images from scratch, such as clouds or flame effects. They obliterate anything that was previously underneath on that particular layer or within that selection, and the original image has no bearing on what is generated by the filter.

Web: Here, you can create an image map for use in a web page. An *image map* is a single image broken up into separate hyperlinked areas, typically used on a web page as a sophisticated menu. For example, an image map is frequently used for a map where you can click to get more information about different regions.

Animation: These filters aim to manipulate and optimize GIF images, which are commonly used to create simple animated images for use on web sites.

Combine: Here, you'll find filters that combine two or more images into one.

Toys: These are so-called "Easter Eggs," which aren't designed to manipulate the image, but are present in the program as harmless animations for the user to enjoy. They're created by the programmers of The GIMP as a way of thanking you for using their program.

Tip The GIMP also includes Script-Fu, a scripting language akin to OpenOffice.org BASIC. Using Script-Fu, you can daisy-chain several commands together to produce a particular effect or to automate a particular image-editing process. There is little documentation available for Script-Fu. Try searching for "script-fu" using your favorite search engine for more information.

Summary

In this chapter, we took a look at image editing under SUSE Linux. This has involved an examination of one of the best programs available for the task under any operating system: The GIMP.

You learned how to start The GIMP and about some of the basic principles behind it. Next, we discussed some of the functions contained within The GIMP, including the image filters provided with the program.

In the next part of the book, we move on from multimedia to look at another core component of SUSE Linux: the OpenOffice.org suite, which provides word processing, spreadsheet, presentation, and other functions.

## PART SIX

Office Tasks

Making the Move to OpenOffice.org

You might be willing to believe that you can get a complete operating system for no cost. You might even be able to accept that this offers everything Windows does and much more. But one stumbling block many people have is in believing a Microsoft Office-compatible office suite comes as part of the zero-cost bundle. It's a step too far. Office costs hundreds of dollars—are they expecting us to believe that there's a rival product that is *free*?

Well, there is, and it's called OpenOffice.org. It comes preinstalled with SUSE Linux, as well as most other distributions, making it the Linux office suite of choice. It's compatible with most Microsoft Office files, too, and even looks similar and works in a comparable way, making it easy to learn. What more could you want?

Office Similarities

OpenOffice.org started life as a proprietary product called Star Office. Sun Microsystems bought the company behind it and released its source code in order to encourage community development. This led to the creation of the OpenOffice.org project, a collaboration between Open Source developers and Sun. This project has released several new versions of OpenOffice.org, and at the time of writing, has just released version 2. The version supplied with SUSE Linux 9.1 is 1.1.1.

Note For what it's worth, Sun still sells Star Office. This is based on the OpenOffice.org code, so it's effectively the same program. However, in addition to the office suite itself, Sun includes several useful extras such as fonts, templates, and the all-important technical support, which you can contact if you get stuck trying to undertake a particular task.

OpenOffice.org features a word processor, spreadsheet program, presentations package, drawing tool (vector graphics), web site creation tool, and several extras. As such, it matches Microsoft Office almost blow-for-blow in terms of core functionality. See Table 22-1 for a comparison of core packages.

Table 22-1. *How the Office and OpenOffice.org Suites Compare*

Microsoft Office	OpenOffice.org	Notes
Word	Writer	Word processor
Excel	Calc	Spreadsheet
PowerPoint	Impress	Presentations
Visio	Draw[1]	Technical drawing/charting
FrontPage	Writer[2]	Web site creation
Access	Writer/Calc[3]	Database

[1]*Draw is a vector graphics creation tool akin to Adobe Illustrator. Creating flow charts or organizational diagrams is one of many things it can do.*

[2]*Writer is used for word processing and HTML creation; when switched to Web mode, its functionality is altered appropriately.*

[3]*Writer and Calc must be coupled to a third-party database application such as MySQL or Firebird; however, SUSE Linux also comes with the Rekall relational database front end, which is discussed in Chapter 27.*

You should find the specific functionality within the packages is duplicated too, although some of the very specific features of Microsoft Office are not in OpenOffice.org. But OpenOffice.org also has its own range of such tools not yet found in Microsoft Office!

Unique OpenOffice.Org Features

Features unique to OpenOffice.org include the ability to export documents in PDF format across the entire suite of programs. These can then be read on any computer equipped with Adobe Acrobat Reader software. In addition, OpenOffice.org features powerful accessibility features that can, for example, help those with vision disabilities use the programs more effectively. For those who are technically minded, OpenOffice.org can be extended very easily with a variety of plug-ins, which allow the easy creation of add-ons using many different programming languages.

Although OpenOffice.org largely mirrors the look and feel of Microsoft Office, it adds its own flourishes here and there. This can mean that some functions are located on different menus, for example. However, none of this poses a challenge for most users, and OpenOffice.org is generally regarded as very easy to learn.

A Couple of Omissions

There are a couple of notable omissions from OpenOffice.org. There's no directly comparable Access replacement and no integrated Outlook replacement.

In terms of Outlook, we discussed in Chapter 11 how the Kontact application built into KDE offers an accurate reproduction, with e-mail, contacts management, and calendar functions all in one location. You'll find this on the K menu under the Office submenu. This isn't directly linked to OpenOffice.org, but it retains the SUSE Linux look, feel, and way of operating.

In terms of databases, SUSE Linux comes with Rekall, a relational database front end that is extremely similar to Access in that it provides a user interface for the quick creation of tables, forms, and queries (among other things). It makes setting up a database very easy. We explore this program in Chapter 27. Additionally, Writer and Calc include most of the tools needed to query a database, as well as create forms for data input, although this requires some knowledge of OpenOffice.org's scripting commands (OpenOffice.org BASIC).

File Compatibility

As well as core feature compatibility, OpenOffice.org is also able to read Microsoft Office files up to and including Office XP. The very latest version of Office, 2003, has an optional new XML file format that Microsoft has patented, so it's unlikely that OpenOffice.org will ever support it. On the other hand, the vast majority of people using Office have yet to upgrade to the very latest version, and those who have still use the older Office XP, 2000, and 97 file formats (these remain the default options for saving files within the suite).

For full file compatibility, you can always suggest to your colleagues that they, too, make the switch to OpenOffice.org. They don't need to be running SUSE Linux to do so. There are versions available that run on all Windows platforms, as well as on the Apple Macintosh. As with the SUSE Linux version, they're entirely free of charge. Indeed, for many people who are running versions of Office they've installed from "borrowed" CDs, OpenOffice.org offers a way to come clean and avoid pirating software.

Once your colleagues have made the switch, you can exchange files using OpenOffice.org's native format, or opt to save files in the Office file format. Figure 22-1 shows the file type options available in OpenOffice.org's word processor component's Save As dialog box.

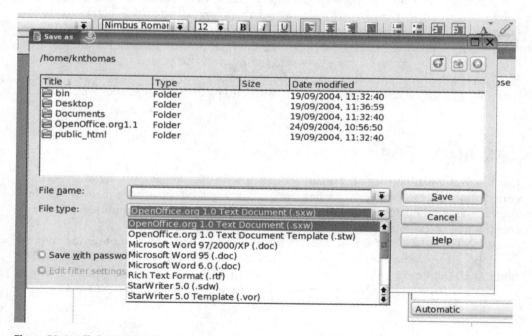

Figure 22-1. *All the OpenOffice.org components are fully compatible with Microsoft Office file formats.*

■**Note** OpenOffice.org also supports Rich Text Format (RTF) text documents and comma-separated value (CSV) data files, which are supported by practically every office suite program ever made.

When it comes to sharing files, there's another option: save your files in a non-Office format such as PDF or HTML. OpenOffice.org is able to export documents in both formats, and most modern PCs equipped with Adobe Acrobat or a simple web browser will be able to read them. However, while OpenOffice.org can open and edit HTML files, it can only export documents as PDF files, so this format is best reserved for files not intended for further editing.

IMPORTING AND EXPORTING FILES

There are some limitations that occasionally crop up when opening Microsoft Office files in OpenOffice.org. The first is that OpenOffice.org isn't compatible with Microsoft Office Visual Basic for Applications (VBA). It uses a similar but incompatible internal programming language. This means that Microsoft macros within a document probably won't work when the file is imported to OpenOffice.org. Such macros are typically used in Excel spreadsheets designed to calculate timesheets, for example. In general, however, only high-end users use VBA.

The second issue involves document protection. OpenOffice.org is unable to open any Office files that have a password, either to protect the document from changes or to protect it from being viewed. Theoretically, it would be easy for OpenOffice.org's programmers to include such functionality, but the laws of many countries make creating such a program feature illegal (it would be seen as a device to overcome copy protection).

The easiest solution is to ask whoever sent you the file to remove the password protection. For what it's worth, Office passwords are a fairly weak form of security compared to many other professional-level password solutions. In fact, OpenOffice.org's own form of password protection is a lot stronger. And that's another reason why you might suggest that your colleagues make the move to OpenOffice.org and abandon Microsoft Office.

The Right Fonts

One key to compatibility with the majority of Microsoft Office files is ensuring you have the correct fonts. This is an issue even when using Windows. It's very common to open an Office document to find the formatting incorrect because you don't have the fonts used in the construction of the document.

While there are a great many fonts in use on most Windows systems, there are a handful of core fonts that most people tend to rely on and which are default on most Windows installations: Arial, Tahoma, Verdana, Trebuchet MS, and Times New Roman (MS Comic Sans might also be included in that list, although it isn't often used within business documents).

There are various ways of getting hold of these fonts and installing them on your SUSE Linux system. Here we'll cover two methods: copying your fonts from Windows and installing Microsoft's TrueType Core Fonts.

Copying Windows Fonts

If you dual-boot SUSE Linux with Windows, you can simply use YaST2 to delve into your Windows partition's font folder and copy across every font you have available under Windows.

Note Installing Windows fonts under SUSE Linux is a legally gray area. Technically speaking, there's no reason why you shouldn't be able to use the fonts under SUSE Linux. Purchasing Windows as well as any software running on it should also have meant you purchased a license to use the fonts. But the license document for Windows XP makes no mention of font licensing, so the matter is far from clearcut.

Here are the steps for copying your fonts:

1. Assuming your Windows partition is automatically mounted under /Windows/C/, start the Control Center (K menu ➤ Control Center), and then click the System Administration icon on the left. Select the Font Installer icon.

2. In SUSE Linux, adding fonts affects the X server and therefore all users, so you'll need to click the Administrator Mode button at the bottom of the window and enter the root password.

3. Click the Add Fonts icon at the top of the screen (hovering the mouse over each icon shows a tooltip).

4. In the File Open dialog box that appears, browse to the fonts folder within your Windows partition. On most versions of Windows, this will be located at \Windows\Fonts\.

5. Once you've found your fonts cache, you can either select just the fonts you're interested in importing into SUSE Linux by holding down Ctrl and clicking, or select all of the fonts by clicking any font and then pressing Ctrl+A.

6. Click OK. The fonts will be copied across and imported for use under SUSE Linux.

Note that you might need to restart the X server (log out and then back in again) for the fonts to be usable.

Installing TrueType Core Fonts

If you don't want to undertake the font-copying maneuver, you can download and install Microsoft's TrueType Core Fonts. This package contains common Windows fonts, including Arial and Times New Roman.

SUSE Linux facilitates the installation of the Core Fonts bundle by making the package available via the YAST2 Online Update service, which you can use as follows:

1. Start Control Center (K menu ➤ Control Center), and then click the YAST2 Modules icon.

2. Click the Software icon, and then click Online Update.

3. Look in the Online Update Patch window (top left) for an entry mentioning Microsoft TrueType Core Fonts and select it, as shown in Figure 22-2.

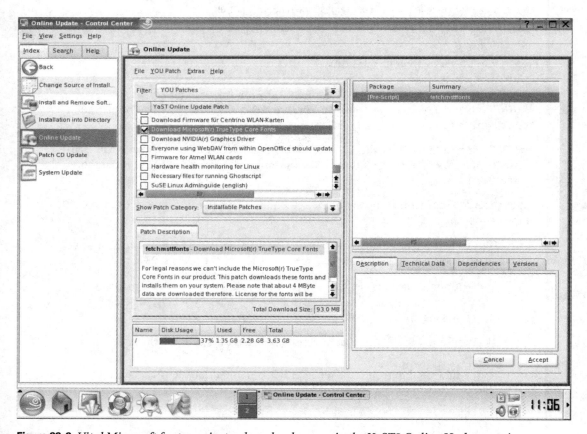

Figure 22-2. *Vital Microsoft fonts are just a download away via the YaST2 Online Update service.*

4. Click Accept in the bottom right of the window to download and install the fonts. Note that you should read and agree to the End User License Agreement that appears.

OTHER LINUX OFFICE SUITES

OpenOffice.org is widely regarded as one of the best Linux office suites, but it's not the only one. Its main open source competitor is KOffice. This tightly integrates into the KDE desktop and mirrors much of its look and feel. It includes a word processor, spreadsheet, presentations package, flow-charting tool, database-access tool, and much more. As with OpenOffice.org, in most cases, you can load and save Microsoft Office files. For more details, see its home page at www.koffice.org. It's available on the SUSE Linux DVD, too. Just search in the YaST2 Install or Remove Programs section.

In addition, there are several open source office applications that aren't complete office suites. For example, AbiWord is considered an excellent word processor that packs in a lot of features but keeps the user interface very simple. It's partnered by Gnumeric, a spreadsheet application that is developed separately (although both aim to be integrated into the GNOME desktop environment). For more details, see www.abisource.com and www.gnome.org/projects/gnumeric/, respectively.

If you don't mind paying for proprietary software, Hancom Office is extremely popular in Asian countries, and an English language version is also available. It offers a word processor, spreadsheet, presentations package, and more. A 30-day trial version and more details are available from http://en.hancom.com.

Summary

This chapter was a general introduction to OpenOffice.org, providing a global overview of what you can expect from the programs within the suite. In particular, we focused on the extent of the suite's similarities with Microsoft Office and discussed issues surrounding file compatibility with Microsoft Office. We also looked at how Windows fonts can be brought into SUSE Linux, which aids in successfully importing and creating compatible documents.

In the next chapter, you'll learn about the configuration options globally applicable to the suite, as well as common functions provided across all the programs.

CHAPTER 23

■ ■ ■

OpenOffice.org Overview

All the programs in the OpenOffice.org suite rely on a common interface, and therefore look and operate in a similar way. They are also configured in an identical way, and all rely on central concepts such as AutoPilots, which guide you through the creation of particular types of documents. In addition, many components within the suite are shared across the various programs. For example, the automatic chart creation tool within Calc can also be used within Writer.

In this chapter, we'll look at the OpenOffice.org suite as a whole, and explain how it's used and configured. In the following chapters, we'll examine some specific programs in the suite.

Introducing the Interface

If you've ever used an office suite, such as Microsoft Office, you shouldn't find it too hard to get around in OpenOffice.org. As with Microsoft Office, it relies primarily on toolbars, a main menu, and separate context-sensitive menus that appear when you right-click. In addition, OpenOffice.org provides floating palettes that provide quick access to useful functions, such as paragraph styles within Writer. These palettes remain on the screen at all times and appear above all other windows until they're closed. Figure 23-1 provides a quick guide to the OpenOffice.org interface.

Three main toolbars are universal across the suite, although the precise functions they offer vary from program to program:

Function bar: This provides quick access to global operations, such as saving, opening, and printing files. At the very left of the toolbar is the full name and path of the file currently being edited. The Function bar also provides a way to activate the various floating palettes, such as the Stylist, which offers quick access to text styles, and the Navigator, which lets you easily move around various elements within the document.

Object bar: This is the more traditional type of toolbar, which you may be familiar with from Microsoft Office. It offers functions specific to each component in the suite, with the aim of providing quick access to vital tools. For example, it includes a font-selection tool, as well as a drop-down list of font sizes. Generally speaking, the left side of the Object bar is similar throughout all the programs, offering font-related tools, while the right side of the toolbar provides functions specific to each program, such as currency-formatting tools within Calc.

Main toolbar: This toolbar runs down the left side of the screen and offers quick access to vital functions. Unlike the other two toolbars, it is tailored to each program in the suite, which means the functions on the Calc toolbar are different from those on the Writer toolbar, for example. Within Impress, the functions are largely related to drawing shapes and text boxes; in Calc, they relate to creating graphs and sorting or filtering cell ranges; and in Writer, they are geared toward producing text documents.

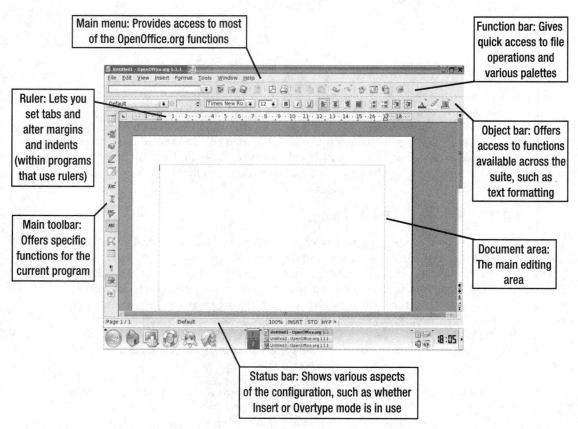

Main menu: Provides access to most of the OpenOffice.org functions

Function bar: Gives quick access to file operations and various palettes

Ruler: Lets you set tabs and alter margins and indents (within programs that use rulers)

Object bar: Offers access to functions available across the suite, such as text formatting

Main toolbar: Offers specific functions for the current program

Document area: The main editing area

Status bar: Shows various aspects of the configuration, such as whether Insert or Overtype mode is in use

Figure 23-1. *The OpenOffice.org interface*

Customizing the Interface

You can select which toolbars are visible on your screen, as well as customize those that are already there. You can also add new toolbars and customize the OpenOffice.org menus.

Adding Functions to Toolbars

The quickest way to add icons and functions to any toolbar is to right-click it and select the Visible Buttons entry on the menu. This will present a list of currently visible icons and functions, along with those that might prove useful on that toolbar. Any option already visible will have a check next to it.

However, practically any function may be added to a toolbar, including the options from the main menu. Simply right-click the toolbar and select the Customize option. You'll see a list of functions on the left, along with a list of which functions are currently in use on the toolbar on the right.

The list of functions on the left is extremely comprehensive and is arranged under broad categories, such as File, Edit, Format, and so on. For a definition of these categories, see Table 23-1. It's a mistake to think that these merely mirror the corresponding main menu options. They actually offer many more functions than those that are ordinarily visible. For example, under the Format category, you'll find entries related to specific functions, such as shrinking font sizes or setting a shadow effect behind text.

Table 23-1. *OpenOffice.org Customization Categories*

Category	Description
Application	These options relate to the specific OpenOffice.org application you're using. For example, if you select to customize a toolbar within Writer, the Application category menu will offer functions to start AutoPilots that will build word processor documents.
BASIC	Options under this category relate to the creation and playback of OpenOffice.org macros.
Controls	Under this heading, you'll find widgets that can be used in conjunction with formulas or macros, such as check boxes, buttons, text box creation tools, and so on.
Data	Here, you'll find a couple of options related to working with information sources, such as databases.
Documents	This category provides options specific to document control, such as those related to exporting documents as PDF files or simply saving files.
Drawing	Here, you'll find tools related to drawing objects, such as shapes and lines, and also tools for creating floating text boxes.
Edit	This category contains options related to cutting, pasting, and copying items within the document, as well as updating elements within it.
Format	Here, you'll find a range of options related largely to text formatting, but also some concerned with formatting other elements, such as drawings and images.
Frame	These options relate to any frames inserted into the document, such as how elements within the frame are aligned and how text is wrapped around the frame.

Table 23-1. *OpenOffice.org Customization Categories (Continued)*

Category	Description
Graphic	This category presents a handful of options related to manipulating bitmap graphics that are inserted into the document.
Insert	This category includes options related to inserting objects, such as sound, graphics, and elements from other OpenOffice.org documents.
Modify	These options relate to the drawing components within OpenOffice.org and let you manipulate images or drawings in various ways by applying filters.
Navigate	This category offers tools that let you move around a document quickly, such as the ability to quickly edit headers and footers, or move from the top of the page to the end very quickly.
Numbering	These are various options related to creating automatic numbered or bulleted lists.
OpenOffice.org BASIC Macros	Here, you can select from the various ready-made macros, which provide some of OpenOffice.org's functions.
Options	There are various options that relate to configuration choices in OpenOffice.org, allowing you to control how it works.
Table	Here, you'll find options related to the creation of tables.
Templates	In this category, you'll find options related to the creation and use of document templates.
Untitled {1,2,3} BASIC Macros	Here, you'll find any macros that you created or imported into OpenOffice.org.
View	This category offers options related to the look and feel of the suite, such as which items are visible within the program interface.
Invisible Separator	Selecting this option will insert a space between the icons on the toolbar.
Separator	This option will insert a small bar between the various icons on the toolbar.

To add a function to a toolbar, simply select the toolbar you want to add it to from the Toolbars drop-down menu on the right. Next, select the function on the left side of the Customize Toolbars dialog box, as shown in Figure 23-2, and then click the Add button. This will insert it above whichever entry is highlighted in the right column. To move the entry up and down, use the Move Up and Move Down buttons on the right side of the dialog box (entries already on the toolbar can also be moved in this way).

Many functions that can be added are automatically given a relevant toolbar icon, but you can choose another icon for a function by clicking the Icons button in the Customize Toolbars dialog box. You can also use this method to change an icon that already appears on a toolbar.

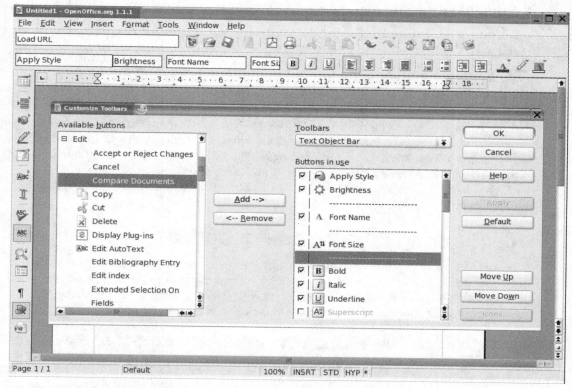

Figure 23-2. *Adding a new function to the toolbar is very easy within OpenOffice.org.*

Adding a New Toolbar

It's even possible within OpenOffice.org to add your own new toolbar. Here are the steps:

1. Right-click anywhere on the existing toolbars and select Configure.

2. Make sure that the Toolbars tab is highlighted in the dialog box that appears, and then click New. This will add a toolbar called User-defined No. 1.

3. To populate the toolbar with icons and functions, click it, and then click Customize. You will see the Customized Toolbars dialog box, as discussed in the previous section (see Figure 23-2).

4. Follow the procedure outlined in the previous section to add functions to your new toolbar.

If you don't perform steps 3 and 4 to customize the toolbar, the new toolbar will appear on screen, but it will be empty. You can customize it later by right-clicking it and selecting Customize.

Customizing Menus

You can also customize the OpenOffice.org menus. Just right-click within one of the toolbars and select Configure. Then select the Menu tab in the dialog box that appears.

Similar to the setup for customizing toolbars, the current menu options are listed at the top of the dialog box, and those that you can add are listed at the bottom, arranged under broad categories such as File, Edit, Format, and so on.

To add a menu option, select a position within the current menu on the list at the top of the dialog box, select the new function from the list at the bottom, and then click the New button at the top right of the dialog box. You can remove existing entries by highlighting them and clicking the Delete button. In addition, the up and down arrows allow you to alter the position of entries on the menu. You could move those you use frequently to the top of the menu, for example.

If you make a mistake, simply click the Reset button at the bottom right of the dialog box to return the menus to their default state.

Configuring OpenOffice.org Options

In addition to the wealth of customization options, OpenOffice.org also offers a range of configuration options that allow you to make it work exactly how you wish. These can be configured using the Options dialog box, as shown in Figure 23-3. To open this dialog box, selecting Tools ➤ Options from within any of the OpenOffice.org programs.

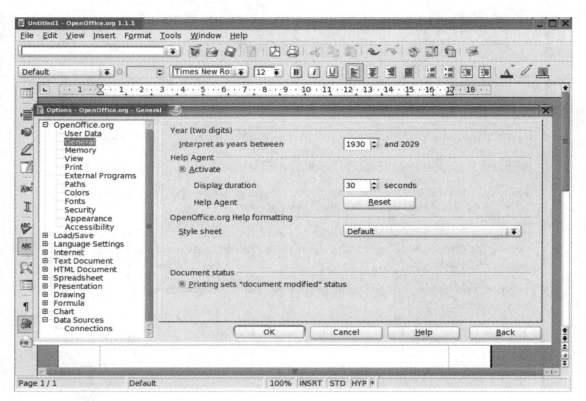

Figure 23-3. *OpenOffice.org's main configuration dialog box can be accessed by selecting Tools ➤ Options.*

A variety of options are offered, allowing you to tweak everything from the default file format to the colors used by default within the software. Table 23-2 explains the OpenOffice.org configuration options.

Table 23-2. *OpenOffice.org Configuration Options*

Option	Description
OpenOffice.org	
User Data	This is the personal data that will be added to the documents you create. You can leave this area blank if you wish.
General	This offers a handful of miscellaneous options, such as how to handle two-digit dates, when the help system should step in to offer tips, how the Help system should be formatted (such as in high resolution for people with vision problems), and whether printing a document is interpreted by OpenOffice.org as modifying it.
Memory	This entry relates to how much system memory OpenOffice.org can use. You can limit the number of undo steps, for example, and alter the cache memory used for holding graphical objects.
View	Here, you can alter the look, feel, and operation of OpenOffice.org. You can define whether the middle mouse button performs a paste operation (which is consistent with how SUSE Linux works), or whether it should perform a scrolling function, as with Windows. You can also alter elements such as whether icons appear in menus and fonts are previewed in the toolbar menu.
Print	This option lets you adjust how printing is handled within OpenOffice.org. The functions relate to those that can stop documents from printing incorrectly, such as reducing any transparency effects within the documents so on-page elements don't appear faint or completely disappear in the final output. (Note that specific print functions are handled within the Print dialog box when you actually print a document.)
External Programs	Here, you can select which programs are used when OpenOffice.org needs to call outside functionality. For example, you can select the browser program used for previewing web pages you might create.
Paths	This is where the file paths for user-configured and vital system tools are handled. Generally, there's little reason to edit this list, although you might choose to alter the default location where your documents are saved (simply double-click the My Documents entry to do this).
Colors	Here, you can define the default color palette that appears in the various programs in the suite.
Fonts	By creating entries here, you can automatically substitute fonts within documents you open for others on your system. If you don't have the Microsoft core fonts installed, this might prove useful. For example, you might choose to substitute Arial, commonly used on Microsoft Office documents, for Luxi Sans, one of the sans serif fonts used under SUSE Linux.
Security	This option controls which types of functions can be run within OpenOffice.org. For example, you can choose whether macros created by third parties should be run when you open a new document.
Appearance	Here, you can alter the color scheme used within OpenOffice.org, in a similar way to how you can alter the default SUSE Linux desktop color scheme. Individual elements within documents and pages can be modified, too.

Table 23-2. *OpenOffice.org Configuration Options (Continued)*

Option	Description
Accessibility	This option relates to features that might help people with vision disabilities to use OpenOffice.org. For example, you can define whether animated graphics are shown on the screen.
Load/Save	
General	Options here relate to how files are saved. You can select whether the default is to save in OpenOffice.org or Microsoft Office format. Choosing the latter is useful if you share a lot of documents with colleagues who are not running OpenOffice.org.
VBA Properties	This option relates to how Visual Basic for Applications (VBA) code is handled when Microsoft Office documents are opened. Specifically, it ensures that the code isn't lost when the file is saved again.
Microsoft Office	This option provides functions specifically needed to convert or open Microsoft Office files within OpenOffice.org.
HTML Compatibility	Here, you can set options that affect the compatibility of HTML files saved within OpenOffice.org.
Language Settings	
Languages	Here, you can set your local language so that documents are spell-checked correctly. In addition, Asian language support can be activated, which allows for more complex document layout options.
Writing Aids	Under this option, you can activate or deactivate various plug-ins designed to help format documents, such as the hyphenator or the spell-checking component. In addition, you can alter how the spell-checker works, such as whether it ignores capitalized words.
Internet	
Proxy	Here, you can let OpenOffice.org know about any proxy server you might need to go through in order to access the Internet.
Search	This option lets you set the search engines that tie in with OpenOffice.org's HTML editing modes.
Text Document	
General	Here, you can alter various options related to the editing of word processor documents, such as which measurements are used on the ruler (centimeter, inches, picas, etc.).
View	Under this option, you can configure the look and feel of the Writer program, such as which scroll bars are visible by default. You can also turn off the display of various page elements, such as tables and graphics.
Formatting Aids	This option lets you choose which symbols appear for "invisible" elements (such as the carriage return symbol or a dot symbol to indicate where spaces have been inserted) in Writer.
Grid	This controls whether page elements will snap to an invisible grid. You can also define the dimensions and spacing of the grid cells here.
Basic Fonts	This controls which fonts are used by default in the various text styles, such as for the default text and within lists.
Print	This option offers control over printing options specific to Writer, such as which page elements are printed (you might choose to turn off the printing of graphics, for example).

Table 23-2. *OpenOffice.org Configuration Options (Continued)*

Option	Description
Tables	Here, you can control how tables are created and how the user interacts with them within Writer. For example, you can control what happens when a table is resized, such as whether the entire table responds to the changes or merely the cell you're resizing.
Changes	This option lets you define how changes are displayed when the document tracking function is activated.
HTML Document	
View	Here, you can control the HTML editor component of OpenOffice.org (effectively an extension of Writer). You can control the look and feel of the HTML editor, including which elements are displayed on the screen.
Formatting Aids	As with the similar entry for Writer under Text Document, this option lets you view symbols in place of usually hidden text elements.
Grid	This lets you define a grid that on-screen elements are able to "snap to" in order to aid accurate positioning.
Print	Here, you can define how HTML documents created within OpenOffice.org are printed.
Tables	Similar to the Tables entry under Text Document, this controls how tables are created and handled within HTML documents.
Background	This lets you set the default background color for HTML documents.
Spreadsheet	
General	Here, you can modify miscellaneous options related to Calc, such as which measurement units are used within the program and how the formatting of cells is changed when new data is input.
View	This option relates to the look and feel of Calc, such as the color of the grid lines between cells and which elements are displayed on the screen. For example, you can configure whether zero values are displayed, and whether overflow text within cells is shown or simply truncated at the cell boundary.
Calculate	This option relates to how numbers are handled during certain types of formula calculations, such as those involving dates.
Sort Lists	This entry lets you create lists that are applied to relevant cells when the user chooses to sort them. Several lists are predefined in order to correctly sort days of the week or months of the year.
Changes	This option relates to the on-screen formatting for changes when the track changes function is activated.
Grid	This option lets you configure an invisible grid that stretches across the sheet, and also which page objects can be set to snap to the grid for correct alignment.
Print	This option relates to printing specifically from Calc, such as whether Calc should avoid printing empty pages that might occur within documents.
Presentation	
General	This option refers to miscellaneous settings within the Impress program, such as whether the program should always start with an AutoPilot wizard and which units of measurement should be used.
View	This option relates to the look and feel of Impress, and, in particular, whether certain on-screen elements are displayed.

Table 23-2. *OpenOffice.org Configuration Options (Continued)*

Option	Description
Grid	This controls whether an invisible grid is applied to the page and whether objects should snap to it.
Print	This option controls how printing is handled within Impress and, in particular, how items in the document will appear on the printed page.
Drawing	
General	This option relates to miscellaneous settings within the vector graphics component of OpenOffice.org, Draw.
View	Here, you can set specific preferences with regard to which objects are visible on the screen while you're editing with Draw.
Grid	This option relates to the invisible grid that can be applied to the page.
Print	This option lets you define which on-screen elements are printed and which are not printed.
Formula	
Settings	This option relates to miscellaneous settings within the Formula program. The Formula program lets you lay out mathematical formulas; it isn't directly linked to Calc.
Chart	
Default Colors	Here, you can set the default color palette that should be used when creating charts, usually within the Calc program.
Data Sources	
Connections	Via this option, you can set the connections OpenOffice.org should make with various database drivers, in order for OpenOffice.org to manipulate data from a database or act as a front end of a database.

Using OpenOffice.org Core Functions

Although the various programs within OpenOffice.org are designed for very specific tasks, they all share several core functions that work in broadly similar ways. In addition, each program is able to borrow components from other programs in the suite.

AutoPilots

One of the core functions you'll find most useful when you're creating new documents is the AutoPilot system, which you can access from the File menu. An AutoPilot guides you through creating a new document by answering questions and following a wizard-based interface. This replaces the template-based approach within Microsoft Office, although it's worth noting that OpenOffice.org is still able to use templates.

The AutoPilot usually offers a variety of document styles. Some even prompt you to fill in salient details, which it will then insert into your document in the relevant areas.

Help System

OpenOffice.org employs a comprehensive help system, complete with automatic context-sensitive help, called the Help Agent, which will appear if the program detects you're performing a particular task. Usually, the Help Agent takes the form of a light bulb graphic, which will appear at the bottom-right corner of the screen. If you ignore the Help Agent, it will disappear within a few seconds. Clicking it causes a help window to open. Alternatively, you can access the main searchable help file by clicking the relevant menu entry.

Object Linking and Embedding

All the OpenOffice.org programs are able to make use of Object Linking and Embedding (OLE). This effectively means that one OpenOffice.org document can be inserted into another. For example, you might choose to insert a Calc spreadsheet into a Writer document.

The main benefit of using OLE over simply copying and pasting the data is that the OLE item (referred to as an *object*) will be updated whenever the original document is revised. In this way, you can prepare a report featuring a spreadsheet full of figures, for example, and not need to worry about updating the report when the figures change. Figure 23-4 shows an example of a spreadsheet from Calc inserted into a Writer document.

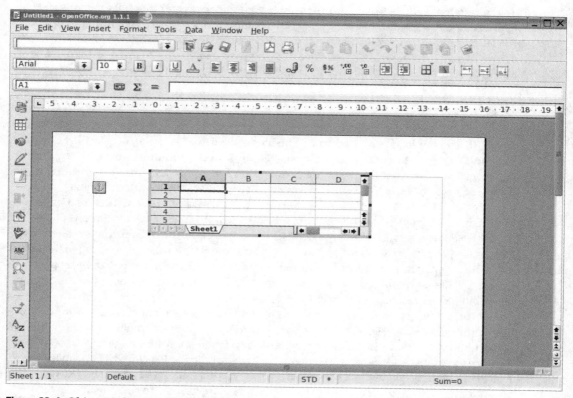

Figure 23-4. *Object Linking and Embedding (OLE) lets you incorporate one OpenOffice.org document into another.*

Whenever you click inside the OLE object, the user interface will change so that you can access functions specific to that object. For example, if you had inserted an Impress object into a Calc document, clicking within the object would cause the Calc interface to temporarily turn into that of Impress. Clicking outside the OLE object would restore the interface back to Calc.

You can explore OLE objects by selecting Insert ➤ Object ➤ OLE Object. This option lets you create and insert a new OLE object, as well as add one based on an existing file.

Creating Macros

OpenOffice.org employs a powerful BASIC-like programming language, which you can use to create your own functions. Although this language is called BASIC, it is several generations beyond the BASIC you might have used in the past. OpenOffice.org's BASIC is a high-level, object-orientated environment designed to appeal to programmers who wish to quickly add their own functions to the suite.

However, it's possible for any user to record a series of actions as a macro, which is then automatically turned into a simple BASIC program. This can be very useful if you wish to automate a simple, repetitive task, such as the insertion of a paragraph of text, or even something more complicated, such as searching and replacing text within a document.

To record a macro, select Tools ➤ Macro ➤ Record Macro. After you've selected this option, any subsequent actions will be recorded. All keyboard strokes and clicks of the mouse will be captured and turned automatically into BASIC commands. To stop the recording, simply click the button on the floating toolbar. After this, you'll be invited to give the macro a name. Once you've done so, click Save. You can then run your macro in the future by choosing Tools ➤ Macro ➤ Macro, selecting your macro in the list, and then clicking Run.

Saving Files

OpenOffice.org uses its own file format. The files end with an .sxc, .sxw, or .sxi file extension, depending on whether they've been saved by Calc, Writer, or Impress, respectively. The OpenOffice.org format is the best choice when you're saving documents that you are likely to further edit within OpenOffice.org. However, if you wish to share files with colleagues who aren't running SUSE Linux or OpenOffice.org, the solution is to save the files as Microsoft Office files. To save in this format, just choose it from the Save As drop-down list in the Save As dialog box.

Alternatively, you might wish to save the file in one of the other file formats offered in the Save As drop-down list. However, saving files in an alternative format might result in the loss of some document components or formatting. For example, saving a Writer document as a simple text file (.txt) will lead to the loss of all of the formatting, as well as any of the original file's embedded objects, such as pictures.

To avoid losing document components or formatting, you might choose to output your OpenOffice.org files as PDF files, which can be read by the Adobe Acrobat viewer. The benefit of this approach is that a complete facsimile of your document will be made available, with all the necessary fonts and on-screen elements included within the PDF file. The drawback is that PDF files cannot be loaded into OpenOffice.org for further editing, so you should always save an additional copy of the file in the native OpenOffice.org format. To save any file as a PDF throughout the suite, select File ➤ Export As PDF. Then choose PDF in the File Format drop-down box, as shown in Figure 23-5.

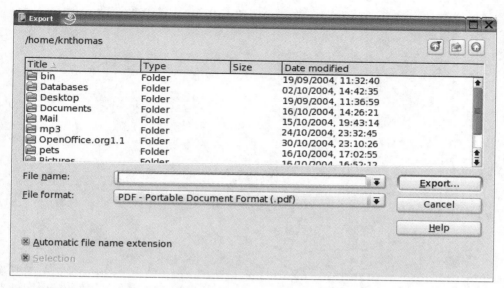

Figure 23-5. *All the programs in the suite can export files in Adobe PDF format.*

Summary

In this chapter, we looked at the configuration options provided with OpenOffice.org. You were introduced to the user interface, which is shared across all the programs within the suite, and learned how it can be customized. We also examined some common tools provided across the suite of programs, such as macro generation.

Over the following chapters, we will look at each major component of the suite, starting with Writer.

## CHAPTER 24

In Depth: Writer

The word processor is arguably the most popular element within any office suite. You'll be happy to know that OpenOffice.org's Writer component doesn't skimp on features. It offers full text-formatting functionality, along with powerful higher-level features such as mail merge.

In this chapter, we'll take a look at some of Writer's most useful features. As with all of the components in the OpenOffice.org suite, describing the features within Writer could easily fill an entire book. You should do some exploring on your own by clicking around to discover new features, as well as make judicious use of the help system.

Formatting Text

You can format text within Writer using several methods. Here, we'll look at using the Object bar, the context menu, and the Stylist palette.

The Object Bar

Formatting text is easy to do via the Object bar, which is just above the ruler and main document area. Using the toolbar buttons, you can select the type of font you wish to use, its point size, and its style (normal, bold, italics, and so on). The range of fonts is previewed in the Font drop-down list, making it easy to select the right typeface.

In addition, the Object bar lets you justify text so that it's aligned to the left or right margin, centered, or fully justified. You can also indent text using the relevant icons. As with elsewhere in SUSE Linux, a tooltip will appear over each icon when you hover the mouse cursor over it, as shown in Figure 24-1. To the right of the indentation buttons are tools to change the text background and foreground colors, and also a tool to create highlighter pen-style effects.

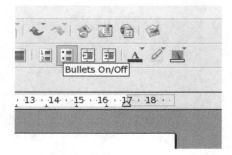

Figure 24-1. *When you hover your mouse over an icon, a tooltip appears to explain what it does.*

Context Menu

Rather than use the Object bar, you can format text using the context menu. Right-click the text you want to format, and a context menu will present options for the font, size, style, alignment, and line spacing. The context menu also allows you to create strike-through, outline, and shadowed text. If you create reports involving footnotes, you might be interested in the superscript and subscript options, also available through the context menu.

By selecting the Character option from the context menu, you get ultimate control over the font formatting. This will present a dialog box that includes every possible option, such as rotating the text and altering the individual character spacing.

■**Tip** The Character dialog box lets you create interesting typographical effects. The Paragraph dialog box has many options for formatting paragraphs. These tools open up the possibility of using Writer for simple desktop publishing work.

Selecting Paragraph from the context menu displays the Paragraph dialog box, as shown in Figure 24-2. This gives you control over paragraph elements, such as line spacing, indentation, and automatic numbering. Here, you will also find an option to automatically create drop caps, so you can start a piece of writing in style!

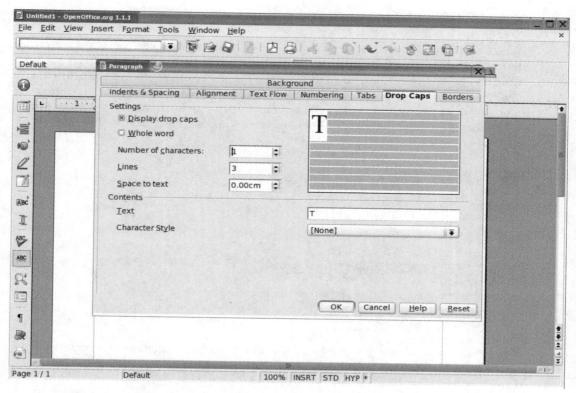

Figure 24-2. *Writer includes many elements found in desktop publishing packages, such as the ability to create drop caps.*

The Stylist Palette

When you first start Writer, you will probably notice the Stylist floating palette (this is rather confusingly labeled Paragraph Styles on the actual palette, and is shown/hidden by pressing F11). This palette offers a variety of predefined formatting styles that you can apply to selected text or enable before you begin adding text.

You can easily add your own text styles to the Stylist palette. Simply select some text that has the formatting applied, and then click the New Style from Selection button. You'll be invited to give the style a name, and when you click OK, it will then appear in the list.

Spell-Checking

Writer is able to automatically spell-check as you type. Any words it considers misspelled will be underlined in red. You can choose from a list of possible corrections by right-clicking the word and selecting from the context menu. If you're sure the word is spelled correctly but it doesn't appear to be in the dictionary, you can select Add ➤Standard.dic from the context menu, as shown in Figure 24-3. This will add the word to your own personal dictionary extension (other users won't have access to your dictionary and will need to create their own list of approved words).

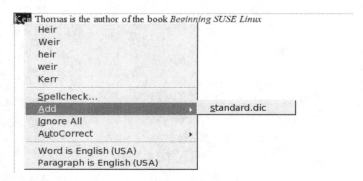

Figure 24-3. *Any words you're going to use frequently, but which Writer doesn't recognize, can be added to your personal dictionary.*

■**Tip** By default, the spell-checking component of Writer is set for US English. If you live outside the United States, or need to create documents for readers in other countries, you can choose a dictionary tailored to your locality or needs. To change the language, select Tools ➤Options. In the list on the left, select Language Settings, and then Languages. In the Default Languages for Documents list, select your local variation. This will then become the default for all new documents.

If you find live spell-checking invasive or distracting, you can deactivate it by selecting Tools ➤Spellcheck and removing the check next to Autospellcheck. Then, to spell-check the document, choose Tools ➤Spellcheck ➤Check. This will scan through the document and prompt you for corrections for words the program considers misspelled.

Inserting Pictures

Writer includes quite substantial desktop publishing-like functions, such as the ability to insert pictures into text documents and to have text flow around pictures.

Inserting any kind of graphic—a graph, digital camera photo, drawing, or any other type of image—is easy. Simply choose Insert ➤Graphics ➤From File.

Tip If you have a scanner and have correctly installed the XSane program (see Chapter 8), you can also scan pictures into Writer documents.

After you've inserted a picture, you can place it anywhere on the page. When you select the picture, a new toolbar appears. This toolbar contains various simple image-tweaking tools, such as those for altering the brightness, contrast, and color balance of the image. Additionally, by clicking and dragging the blue handles surrounding the image, you can resize it.

Graphics that are imported into Writer must be anchored in some way. In other words, they must be linked to a page element so that they don't move unexpectedly. By default, they're anchored to the nearest paragraph, which means that if that paragraph moves, the graphic will move, too. Alternatively, by right-clicking the graphic, you can choose to anchor it to the page, paragraph, or character it is on or next to, as shown in Figure 24-4. Selecting to anchor it to the page will fix it firmly in place, regardless of what happens to the contents of the surrounding text. The As Character option is slightly different from the To Character. When you choose As Character, the image will be anchored to the character it is next to, *and* it is actually inserted in the same line as that character, as if it were a character itself. If the image is bigger than the line it is anchored in, the line height will automatically change to accommodate it.

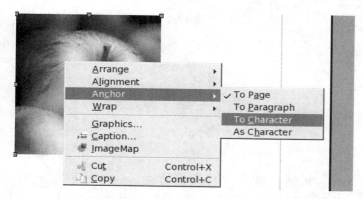

Figure 24-4. *A picture can be "anchored" to the page, paragraph, or a character. This affects how it responds to the paragraphs surrounding it.*

As you can see in Figure 24-4, the context menu also includes a Wrap option, which lets you set the type of text wrap you want to use. By default, No Wrap is selected, so the graphic will occupy the entire space on the page; no text is allowed on either side of it. Page Wrap is the best option if you're looking for a desktop publishing-style effect, because the text will wrap around both sides of the picture. Optimal Page Wrap causes the text to wrap down just one side of the picture, the side on which the picture is furthest from the edge of the page. Alternatively, if you wish the image to appear in the background of the page with text flowing across it, you can select the relevant option from the menu.

As always within OpenOffice.org, ultimate control is achieved by opening the relevant dialog box. You can set up how graphics are treated on the page by right-clicking the image and selecting Graphics. In the dialog box that appears, you can select the wrap effect, specify the invisible border around the wrap (which governs how close the text is to the image), and give the image a frame.

Working with Tables

Often, it's useful to present columns of numbers or text within a word processor document. To make it easy to align the columns, OpenOffice.org offers the Table tool. This lets you quickly and easily create a grid in which to enter numbers or other information. You can even turn tables into simple spreadsheets, and tally rows or columns via simple formulas.

To insert a table, click and hold the Insert icon on the Main toolbar (which runs down the left side of the screen). Then select the Insert Table icon and simply drag the mouse until you have a table of the correct size. Click to create it, as shown in Figure 24-5.

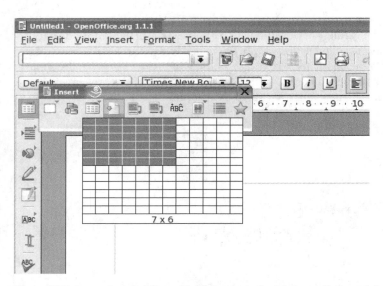

Figure 24-5. *Just select the Insert Table icon on the Main toolbar and drag the mouse to define the size of the table; click when you're finished.*

As with spreadsheets, tables consist of cells arranged into rows (running horizontally) and columns (running vertically). Altering the size of a column is easy. Just hover the mouse over the edge of a cell until it changes to a resizing cursor, and then click and drag. Altering a row's height is a matter of right-clicking within it, selecting Row ➤Height, and entering a value for the height.

■**Tip** An alternative way of resizing cells is to click in a cell and press the Enter key, which inserts a carriage return, too. Cells expand in size to fit their contents. If you don't want this to happen, select the entire table and click the Table:Fixed icon on the Object bar.

Once the cursor is within a table, you can move from cell to cell using the Tab key. Alternatively, you can move backward through the cells by pressing Shift+Tab.

To add more rows or columns, click the relevant icon on the Object bar. To split existing cells, select them and click the Split icon on the Object bar.

If you want to total figures within tables, click the Sum icon. This is similar to inserting a function in a spreadsheet. The table cell holds the formula for the sum, and clicking additional cells adds them to the sum.

■**Note** Only correctly formatted cells can be summed using the Sum icon on the Object bar. Cells with spaces or text within them cannot be added to the formula.

Tables come with their own paragraph styles, which are available on the left side of the Object bar. There are predefined styles for table headers, for example. By using the icons on the right side of the toolbar, you can alter the style of borders around each cell, as well as the background color for each cell.

Mail Merging

Mail merging refers to automatically applying a database of details, such as names and addresses, to a document, so that many personalized copies are produced. It's ordinarily used to create form letters for mailings.

OpenOffice.org makes the procedure very easy, but it requires a source document containing the data that is to be merged into the document. Unlike with Microsoft Word, there's no way of entering this data within Writer itself.

Unless you have enough knowledge of databases to connect one to OpenOffice.org (the program works with dBase and MySQL files, among others), you may want to output existing data in the form of a comma-separated value (CSV) text file. You can then import this file into OpenOffice.org Calc and save it in the OpenOffice.org spreadsheet file format, which Writer's mail merge function works very well with. Alternatively, you can just enter the data in a new spreadsheet document. When creating a data source from scratch, create the data headings (such as Name, Street, City, and so on) along the top of the spreadsheet document, and enter the data itself beneath those headings, as shown in Figure 24-6.

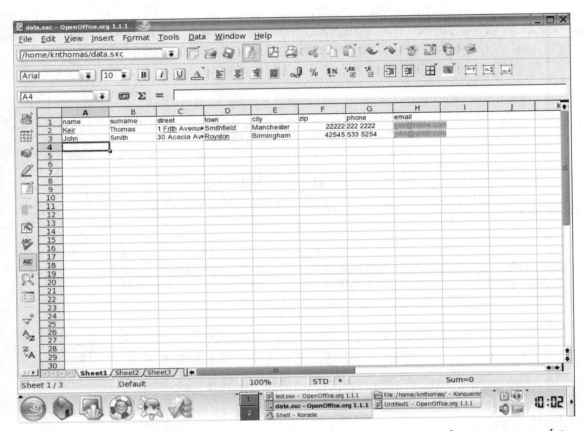

Figure 24-6. *You can quickly create mail merge data within a spreadsheet. Just make sure you create data headings at the top.*

To mail merge this or any other kind of data within Writer, follow this general procedure (this example uses spreadsheet data):

1. Select Tools ➤Mail Merge ➤Other External Data Source. Then click Settings.

2. In the Database type drop-down list, select Spreadsheet. In the Data Source URL text box, enter the path to the spreadsheet. You can click the ellipsis button (...), and then browse to the data source file.

3. Click OK, and then click the Field Assignment button to assign your data fields, so that Writer knows which fields contain the data you want to use. Just click the drop-down lists and select the relevant data heading, as taken from the spreadsheet, so that the two match up. Note that there's no need to match every data field within this dialog box. It's perfectly acceptable to leave some blank if they're not relevant to your document.

4. Next, you'll be invited to type a name by which OpenOffice.org can identify the merge data in future. The default name is usually okay.

5. Click the Create button. You'll be returned to your document, which now has a new floating palette.

6. As you compose your document, you can click within the floating palette to expand the tree next to the data source you just created, and then double-click each of your data headings (on the page, these are known as *merge fields*) to insert them into your document at the cursor.

7. When you're ready to perform the merge, click OK in the floating palette.

8. If you want to simply send the documents straight to the printer, simply click OK in the merge dialog box that appears, as shown in Figure 24-7. However, if you want to save the merged document as a new file, click the File button, and then enter a path for the file and specify a filename. The file can be named automatically after a database field (which you can select in the relevant drop-down list) or named manually by typing the relevant entry in the Manual Setting text field.

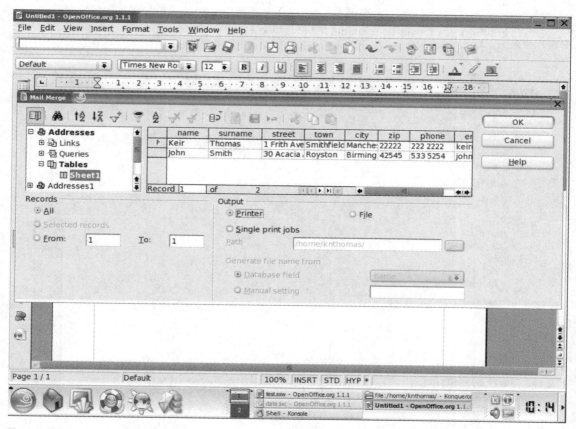

Figure 24-7. *The final mail merge stage is to create the personalized letters from the merged data.*

Adding Headers and Footers

You may want to add headers and footers to long documents to aid navigation. They appear at the top and bottom of each page, respectively, and can include the document title, page number, and other information. Headers and footers are created and edited independently of the main document.

As you might expect, inserting both headers and footers takes just a couple of clicks. Select Insert ➤Header or Footer, depending on which you wish to insert (documents can have both, of course). Writer will then display an editing area where you can type text to appear in the header or footer. For more options, right-click in the area, select Page, and then click the Header or Footer tab. Here, you can control the formatting and nature of the header or footer. Clicking the More button will let you apply borders or background colors.

You might wish to insert page numbers that will be updated automatically as the document progresses. OpenOffice.org refers to data that automatically updates as a *field*. You can insert a wide variety of fields by selecting Insert ➤Fields, as shown in Figure 24-8. For example, along with the page number, you can insert the document title and author name (which is read from the details entered into the Options configuration dialog box, accessed from the Tools menu). In addition, you can enter mail merge fields by clicking Other (see the previous section for a description of how to associate mail merge data with a document).

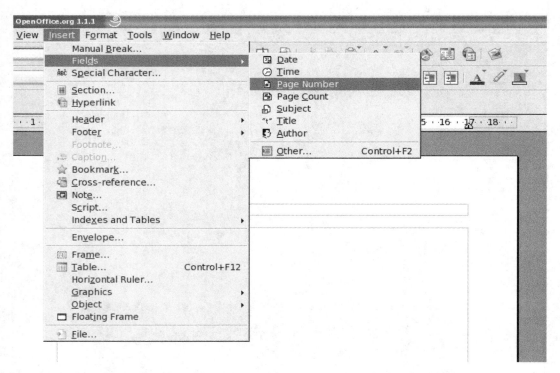

Figure 24-8. *Automatically updating data, such as page numbers, can be inserted into headers and footers.*

Summary

In this chapter, we've examined Writer, one of the core components of OpenOffice.org. We've looked at the some of the key tools, which enable quick and easy document creation. In particular, you've learned how to format text, use the spell-checking component, create and edit tables, and insert pictures into documents.

We also looked at some slightly more advanced capabilities, including mail merging data to create form letters and adding headers and footers to documents.

In the next chapter, we move onto another vital part of OpenOffice.org: Calc, the spreadsheet component.

■ ■ ■

## CHAPTER 25

In Depth: Calc

Calc is the spreadsheet component of OpenOffice.org. Like most modern spreadsheet programs, it contains hundreds of features, many of which few average users will ever use. However, it doesn't abandon its user-friendliness in the process and remains very simple for those who want to work on modest calculations, such as home finances or mortgage interest payments.

In this chapter, you'll learn about some of the best features of Calc, as well as the basics of spreadsheet creation.

Entering and Formatting Data

As with all spreadsheets, entering data into a Calc document is simply a matter of selecting a cell and starting to type. You can enter practically anything into a cell, but a handful of symbols are not allowed. For example, you cannot enter an equal sign (=) followed by a number and have it appear in a cell, because Calc will assume that this is part of a formula.

■**Tip** To enter any character into a cell, including an equal sign followed by a digit, precede it with an apostrophe ('). The apostrophe itself won't be visible within the spreadsheet and whatever you type won't be interpreted in any special way; it will be seen as plain text.

Entering a sequence of data across a range of cells can be automated. Start typing the sequence of numbers, then highlight them, and then click and drag the small handle to the bottom right of the last cell. This will continue the sequence. You'll see a tooltip window, indicating what the content of each cell will be. Figure 25-1 illustrates this process.

Cells can be formatted in a variety of ways. For trivial formatting changes, such as selecting a different font or changing the number format, you can use the Object bar. For example, to turn the cell into one that displays currency, click the Currency icon. You can also increase or decrease the number of visible decimal places by clicking the relevant Object bar icon.

For more formatting options, right-click the individual cell and select Format Cells from the menu. This displays the Format Cell dialog box, where you can change the style of the typeface, rotate text, place text at various angles, and so on. The Border tab of the Format Cell dialog box includes options for cell gridlines of varying thicknesses, which will appear when the document is eventually printed out.

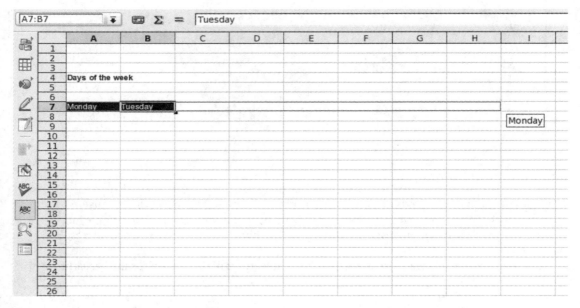

Figure 25-1. *You can automate the entering of data sequences by clicking and dragging.*

Deleting and Inserting Data and Cells

Deleting data is also easy. Just highlight the cell or cells with the data you want to delete, and then press the Delete key. You'll be asked exactly what kind of data you want to remove, and if you want to remove formatting as well or to leave it in place.

If you want to totally eradicate the cell along with its contents, right-click it and select Delete. This will cause the data to the sides of the cell to move in to fill the space.

To insert a new cell, right-click where you would like to it to appear and select Insert. The data in the cells surrounding the inserted cell will shift to make space for it.

Working with Formulas

Calc includes a large number of formulas. These can be applied principally to numerical data, but some also work with other kinds of data, too. This component is actually a continuation of the AutoPilot system, and some of the functions are available in other OpenOffice.org programs.

In addition to simple and complex math functions, there are a range of logical functions, as well as statistical and database tools. Certain formulas can also be used to manipulate text strings such as dates.

You can get an idea of the available functions by clicking the AutoPilot: Functions button on the Formula bar (just below the Object bar). This will bring up a categorized list of formulas, along with brief outlines of what function the formula performs. If you would like more details, use the help system, which contains more comprehensive descriptions of most of the formulas, complete with examples of the correct syntax.

You can reuse formulas simply by cutting and pasting them. Calc is intelligent enough to work out which cells the transplanted formula should refer to, but it's always a good idea to check to make sure the correct cells are referenced.

Using the AutoPilot

To use the AutoPilot to add a function, click the AutoPilot: Functions button on the Formula bar and select the desired type of formula from the Category drop-down list, and then double-click an entry in the Function list to select it. Following this, you'll be prompted to input the relevant figures or define the appropriate data sources. Next to each text-entry box is a "shrink" button, which temporarily hides the AutoPilot window, so you can select cells to be used within the formula.

Let's look at a quick example of using the AutoPilot to work out an average value of a number of cells.

1. Select the cell in which you want the result of the formula to appear.

2. Start the AutoPilot by clicking the AutoPilot: Functions button on the Formula bar. In the left-hand list of functions, double-click AVERAGE. The AutoPilot will then present a list of fields on the right-hand side of the dialog box, where you can enter the values to be averaged. Theoretically, you could type numeric values directly into these fields, but it's more likely that you'll want to reference individual cells from the spreadsheet.

3. Click and drag the top of the dialog box to move it so that the spreadsheet underneath is at least partially visible.

4. Click the cursor in the first field of the dialog box, and then click the first cell you want to include in the calculation. This will automatically enter that cell reference into the field.

5. Click the next field in the dialog box, and then click the next cell you wish to include.

6. Repeat step 5 until all the fields you wish to include have been added to the fields in the dialog box (up to 30 can be selected).

7. Once you've finished, click the Okay button. Calc will insert the formula into the cell you selected at the start, showing the result of the formula.

After you've added a formula with the AutoPilot, you can edit it manually by clicking it and overtyping its contents. Alternatively, you can use the AutoPilot once again, by clicking the button on the Function bar.

Summing Figures

To add the values of a number of cells, you could use the AutoPilot and select the Sum function, as shown in Figure 25-2. The procedure for choosing the cells is the same as described in the previous section.

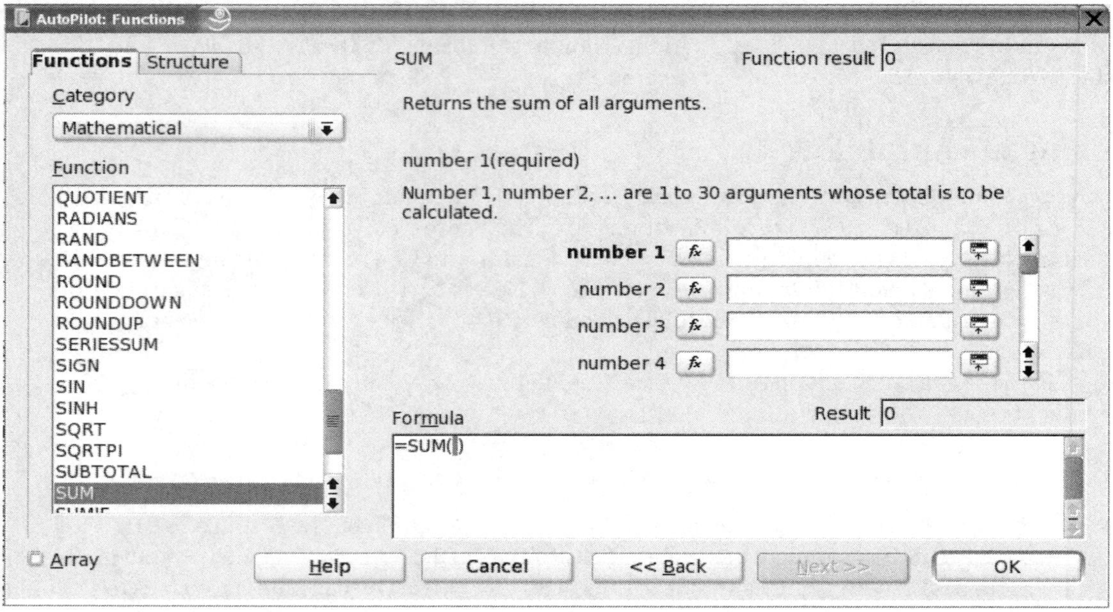

Figure 25-2. *Creating formulas is easy using the AutoPilot wizard.*

However, Calc provides a far easier method of creating the sum formula. Simply click the Sum icon (the Greek Σ character) on the Formula bar, and then select the cells you wish to include in the sum.

Tip You can select more than one cell by holding down the Ctrl key. You can select a range of cells in succession by clicking and dragging the mouse while pressing the Shift key.

Sorting Data

Within a spreadsheet, you may want to sort data according to any number of criteria. For example, you might want to show a list of numbers from highest to lowest, or rearrange a list of names so that they're in alphabetical order. This is easy to do within Calc.

Start by highlighting the range of data you wish to sort. Alternatively, you can simply select one cell within it, because Calc is usually able to figure out the range of cells you want to use. Then select Data ➤ Sort from the main menu. Calc will automatically select a sort key, which will appear in the Sort By drop-down list, as shown in Figure 25-3. However, you can also choose your own sort key from the drop-down menu if you wish, and you can choose to further refine your selection by choosing up to two more sort subkeys from the other drop-down menus.

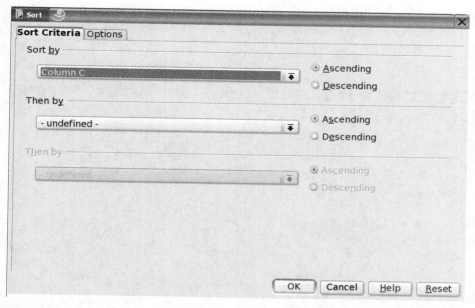

Figure 25-3. *Data can be sorted so that it's in alphabetical or numerical order.*

Creating Charts

Charts are useful because they present a quick visual summary of data. Calc produces charts through a step-by-step wizard, so it becomes very easy indeed. Here are the steps:

1. Highlight the data you want to graph. Be careful to include only the data itself and not any surrounding cells, or even the cell that contains the title for the array of data.

2. Click the Insert Object button on the Main toolbar. This lets you insert a variety of objects, but if you click it just once, Calc automatically assumes you want to insert a graph.

3. The cursor turns into a target with a small graph next to it. Click and drag on the spreadsheet itself to define the area of the graph. This can be any size. Also, you can resize it later.

4. The wizard will start. The first step is to define the range of cells to be used for the chart. By highlighting the cells before you started, you've already done this, so you can click the Next button. However, first make sure that the First Row As Label option is highlighted.

5. The next step is to choose the type of chart you wish to use. For most simple data selections, a bar graph is usually best. However, you might also choose to select a horizontal bar graph. Then click Next.

6. The wizard presents a subselection of graph types. You can also select whether gridlines are used to separate the various areas of the graph. Make your selections and click Next.

7. The last step allows you to give the chart a title and also choose whether you want a legend (a key that explains what the axes refer to) to appear next to it.

8. Click Create, and the chart will be created. Figure 25-4 shows an example.

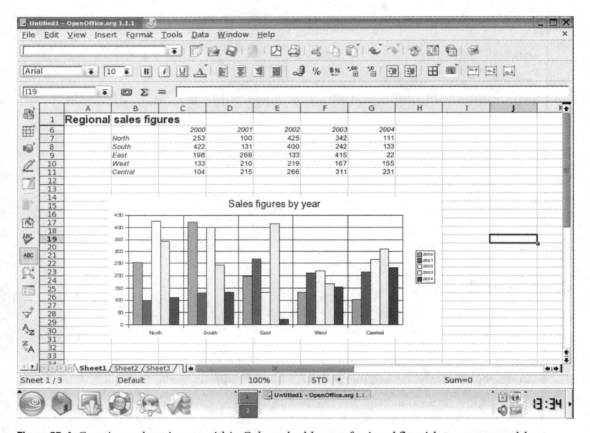

Figure 25-4. *Creating a chart is easy within Calc and adds a professional flourish to your spreadsheet.*

Once you've created a chart, you can alter its size by clicking and dragging the handles. You can also change various graphical aspects by double-clicking them. However, keep in mind that the graph is actually a picture, so the properties you edit are limited to changing the color and size of various elements.

The chart is linked to your data. Whenever your data changes, so will your chart. This is done automatically and doesn't require any user input.

Using Filters

The Filter function in Calc lets you selectively hide rows of data. The spreadsheet user then selects which of the rows of data to view from a drop-down list that appears in the cell at the top of the rows, as shown in the example in Figure 25-5.

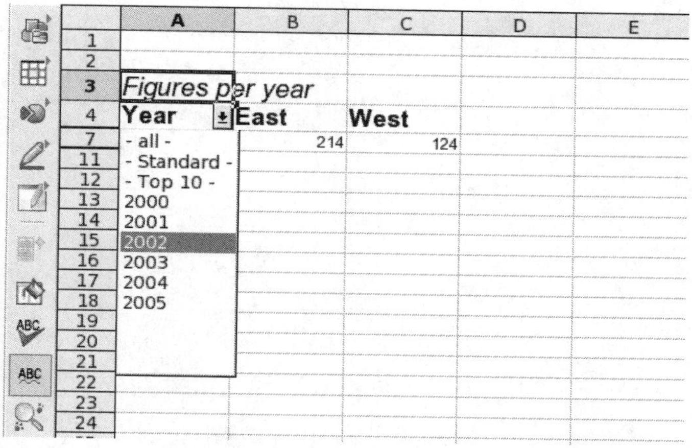

Figure 25-5. *Filters allow you to selectively hide or show rows of data in a spreadsheet.*

■**Note** A Calc filter is a little like an Excel pivot chart, especially when it's combined with an automatically generated chart.

Using filters in this way can be useful when you're dealing with a very large table of data. It helps isolate figures so you can compare them side by side in an easy-to-follow format. For example, you could filter a table of sales figures by year.

To use the Filter function, start by highlighting the data you wish to see in the drop-down list. Make sure the column header for the data is included, too. If you're using the Filter feature on a table of data, this selection can be any column within the table, although it obviously makes sense to use a column that is pertinent to the filtering that will take place. After you've selected the data to filter, select Tools ➤ Filter ➤ Autofilter. You should find that, in place of the column header, a drop-down list appears. When a user selects a various entry in the list, Calc will display only the corresponding row of the spreadsheet beneath.

To remove a filter, select Tools ➤ Filter ➤ Hide Autofilter.

Summary

In this chapter, we examined OpenOffice.org Calc. We looked at the basics of how data can be entered into a cell and how it can be formatted. Then you learned how to create formulas. This is easy to do with the AutoPilot function, which automates the task.

Next, you saw how to sort data in a spreadsheet. We also went through the steps for creating charts using a Calc wizard. Finally, we looked at creating data filters, which work rather like pivot charts in Microsoft Excel.

In Chapter 26, we move on to Impress, the presentations component of OpenOffice.org.

■ ■ ■

In Depth: Impress

Impress is the presentations package within OpenOffice.org. At first glance, it appears to be the simplest of the key OpenOffice.org components, and also the one that borrows most the look and feel from Microsoft Office. However, delving into its feature set reveals more than a few surprises, including sophisticated animation effects and drawing tools. Impress can also export presentations as Macromedia Flash-compatible files, which means that many Internet-enabled desktop computers around the world will be able to view the files, even if they don't have Impress or PowerPoint installed on their computers.

In this chapter, you'll learn about the main features of Impress, as well as the basics of working with presentations.

Creating a Presentation

As soon as Impress starts, it will offer to guide you through the creation of a presentation using a wizard. This makes designing your document a matter of following a few steps.

You'll initially be offered three choices: Empty Presentation, From Template, or Open Existing Presentation. When Impress refers to *templates*, it means presentations that are both predesigned and also contain sample content. There are only two templates supplied with Impress, so this option is somewhat redundant. However, you might choose to look at them later, if only to get an idea of what a presentation consists of and how it's made.

■**Tip** When you become experienced in working with Impress, you can create your own templates or download some from the Internet. To create your own template, simply select to save your document as a template in the File Type drop-down list in the Save As dialog box. Make sure you place any templates you download or create in the /opt/OpenOffice.org/share/template/english/presnt directory (you will need to be root user to do this and should make sure the file permissions are readable for all users).

The standard way of getting started is to create an empty presentation. This sounds more daunting than it actually is, because an AutoPilot will start, asking you to choose from a couple of ready-made designs, as shown in Figure 26-1. You'll also be given a chance to choose what format you want the presentation to take: whether it's designed primarily to be viewed on-screen or printed out.

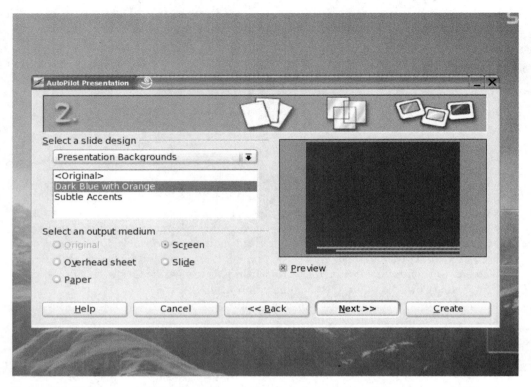

Figure 26-1. *The Impress AutoPilot guides you through the creation of a new presentation.*

After this, you'll be invited to choose the presentation effects, including the transition effect that will separate each slide when the presentation is viewed and the speed of the transition. If you wish, you can set the pause between slides, too, as well as the length of time each slide stays on the screen.

After clicking the Finish button in the wizard, Impress will start, and you'll be invited to choose a design for your initial slide. These are previewed on-screen. A variety of design templates are available, ranging from those that contain mostly text to those that feature pictures and/or graphs.

Depending on which template you choose, you should end up with a handful of text boxes on your screen. Editing the text in these is simply a matter of clicking within them. The formatting of the text will be set automatically.

■**Tip** You can move and shrink each text box by clicking the handles surrounding the box. To draw a new text box, select the relevant tool on the Main toolbar, which runs down the left side of the screen. Simply click and drag to draw a box of whatever size you want.

When the AutoPilot has finished and Impress has started, you'll notice a floating palette on the right side of the screen, as shown in Figure 26-2. This is called the Presentation palette and provides an easy way to add new slides to the presentation. You can also change the template that it's based on by clicking the Modify Slide Layout or Slide Design option, to alter either the slide's objects or the actual design, respectively.

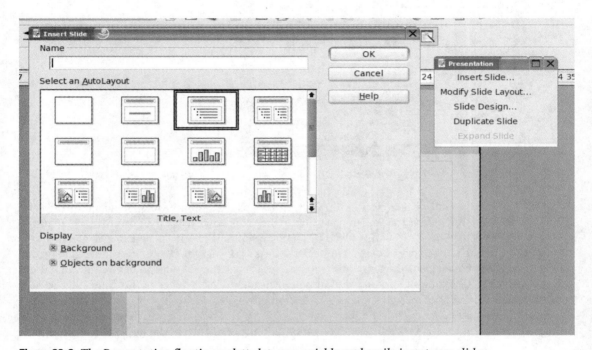

Figure 26-2. *The Presentation floating palette lets you quickly and easily insert new slides.*

Animating Slides

All elements within Impress can be animated in a variety of ways. For example, you might choose to have the contents of a particular text box fly in from the edge of the screen during the presentation. This can help add variety to your presentation, and perhaps even wake up your audience!

Setting an animation effect is simply a matter of clicking the border of the object you wish to animate so that it is selected, and then selecting Slide Show ➤ Effects. Then select from the categories listed in the Effects drop-down list. The Favorites category offers a good range, as shown in Figure 26-3.

Figure 26-3. *A wide variety of animation effects is available for on-screen elements.*

Each animation effect is thumbnailed, and it's usually possible to guess what the effect is from this. Simply select the effect you want. In the drop-down list at the bottom of the window, you can select the speed of the effect. (Selecting a slow animation speed can give you invaluable time to talk to your audience while the slide is being drawn.) By clicking the Extra button, you'll be able to tweak the animation. For example, click the Sound icon to give the animation a sound effect (although some come with them automatically). When you're finished, click the green check icon. This will apply the animation effect.

Note that the animation Effects dialog box is actually a palette, which will remain on your screen. This means you can select several other on-screen objects and apply effects.

Applying Fontwork

The Fontwork tool lets you take ordinary text and manipulate it in various ways, such as making it follow specific curved paths. It can be found on the Format menu and takes the form of a floating palette, as shown in Figure 26-4.

Fontwork can be applied to any existing text box or a new one you draw. At the top of the palette, you can select the path you want the text to follow. Don't worry about the angle of the curve, because you can alter that later. Once you click a path, the text will change instantly.

After this, you can set the profile you wish the text to use. The text itself can be made to slant while following the path or, if the path is vertical, can be made to align itself so it's upright.

The Fontwork palette also includes buttons for setting a shadow effect. You can control the color of the shadow, as well as its distance away from the text.

By clicking and dragging the text box, it can be further manipulated. For example, by shrinking the box, you can make the angle between the start and the end of the path more acute. Fontwork allows the creation of some interesting effects. Experiment with it to see the results.

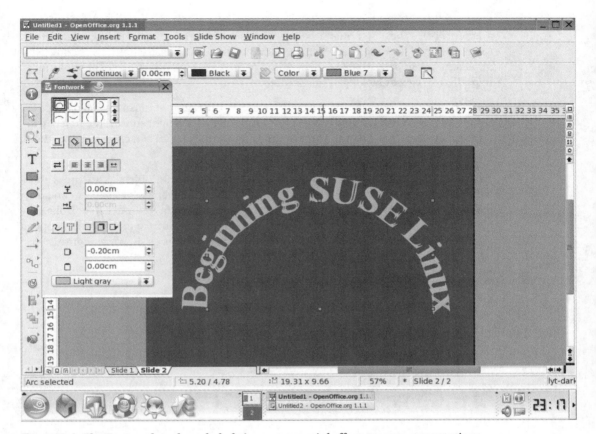

Figure 26-4. *The Fontwork tool can help bring some special effects to your presentations.*

Using 3D Effects

In addition to Fontwork effects, Impress includes a powerful 3D tool, which can give just about any on-screen element a 3D flourish. Start by creating a text box or shape using the Main toolbar on the left. Then select Format ➤ 3D Effects. This will open a floating palette window. Make sure your text box or shape is selected, and then simply double-click any of the 3D effects in the Favorites window. This will instantly apply the effect. Beneath the window are two icons that give you a choice of simply applying the 3D effect to the selection (the left icon), or applying the color and texture within the preview as well.

If you would like more control over the effect, you can click the icons at the top of the 3D Effects palette. These will let you construct your own effects, although if you've previously selected one of the ready-made designs (which is a good idea if you're new to the tool), it will be used as a template. There are five other configuration panels, which each affect not only the type of 3D effect, but also its lighting:

- **Geometry:** This defines how the 3D effect will look when it's applied to on-screen selections. For example, you can increase or decrease the rounded-edges value, and this will make any sharp objects on the screen appear softer when the 3D effect is applied.

- **Shading:** This affects not the actual texture of the 3D object, but instead alters its color gradient. This is best demonstrated in action, so select the various shading modes from the drop-down list to see the effect. In addition, you can choose whether a shadow is applied to the effect, as well as the position of the virtual camera (the position of the hypothetical viewer looking at the 3D object).

- **Illumination:** This lets you set the lighting effect. All 3D graphics usually need a light source because this helps illustrate the 3D effect; without a light source, the object will appear flat. Various predefined light sources are available. You can click and drag the light source in the preview window.

- **Textures:** This affects how the textures will be applied to the 3D object. A texture is effectively a picture that is "wrapped around" the 3D object. Clever use of textures can add realism to a 3D object. A map of the world applied to a sphere can make it look like a globe, for example, or you could add wood or brickwork textures to make objects appear as tabletops or walls. A variety of texture modes are available, as shown in Figure 26-5.

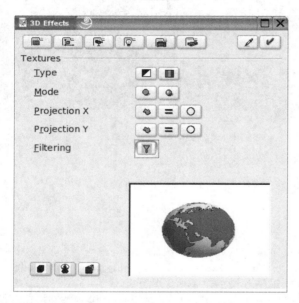

Figure 26-5. *You can apply textures to any object, basically meaning that pictures are wrapped around the item.*

- **Material:** This lets you apply various color overlays on the texture. This can radically alter the texture's look and feel, so it is quite a powerful option. To change the texture itself, right-click the object and select Area. This will present a list of predefined textures. Alternatively, you can select to use a color or pattern.

As with the other presentation effects, the best policy is simply to experiment until you're happy with the results.

Outputting a Presentation As Flash

If you plan to put your presentation online, or want to send it to a colleague who doesn't have Impress or PowerPoint installed, outputting your presentation as a Flash animation could be a good idea. The process is simple. Just select File ➤ Export, and then select Macromedia Flash (SWF) in the File Format drop-down list (SWF is the Flash file type, which stands for Shockwave Flash). No further configuration is necessary.

In order to play the file, it needs to be opened within a web browser that has the Flash player installed. This can be done by selecting File ➤ Open on most browsers, although you can also drag-and-drop the SWF file onto the browser window under Microsoft Windows. There shouldn't be much of a problem with compatibility. The Flash player is close to ubiquitous these days. If the web browser doesn't already have Flash installed, it's easy to download and install. When the Flash file is opened in a web browser, the presentation starts, as shown in Figure 26-6. You can progress through it by clicking anywhere on the screen.

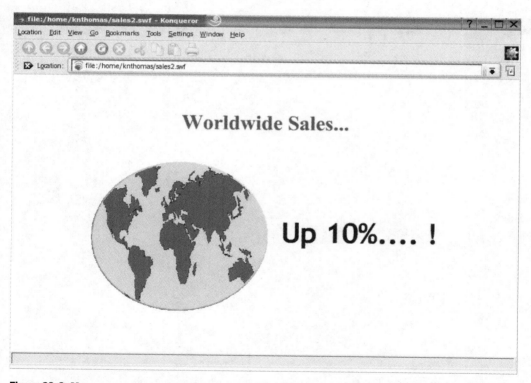

Figure 26-6. *You can save any presentation as a Flash animation, which can be played back in a suitably equipped web browser.*

Summary

In this chapter, we examined Impress, which is the presentations component within OpenOffice.org. We started by looking at how you can use the AutoPilot function to automate production of a basic Impress document. Then you saw how various effects can be added to the presentation, including 3D effects. Finally, we looked at how the presentation can be exported as a Shockwave Flash file for playback on virtually any web browser.

In the next chapter, we will explore the database component within SUSE Linux: Rekall.

## CHAPTER 27

In Depth: Rekall

OpenOffice.org includes a number of tools to both interface with database servers and perform tasks such as enter and edit data. However, for most day-to-day users who have humble needs, creating such a setup is too complicated. It requires some knowledge of how databases work on a technical level.

Perhaps because of this, SUSE includes Rekall within its Linux distribution. This tool is merely a front end for a database, but it includes a module that will automatically set up a database server, making the creation of databases as straightforward as it is with Microsoft Access. In fact, Rekall takes a similar design-based approach to the creation of tables and forms, so anyone who has previously created a database under Access will feel right at home.

As supplied with SUSE Linux and using the built-in database driver, Rekall lets you create relational databases. This is a type of database technology ideal for quickly creating catalogs of information, such as inventory lists. In addition to making database creation simple and quick, relational databases let you easily query data to produce reports tailored to individual needs. For example, you could use an inventory list database to produce a report showing all products added for a certain geographical region on a certain date.

In this chapter, we'll work through an example of using Rekall to create a simple database cataloging a collection of music. You can use the same techniques to create any kind of relational database.

Getting Started with Rekall

To start Rekall, select K menu ➤ Office ➤ Database. The first time you start this application, you'll need to make some setup choices. These define how the program will work in future.

SDI or MDI: The first choice is whether you want an SDI or MDI interface. These stand for Single Document Interface and Multiple Document Interface. The latter is used within programs like The GIMP image editor. Every on-screen element receives its own Panel button and effectively runs as a separate program. In contrast, MDI is the standard way of working within Windows. Every on-screen element is contained within a single window. Which choice you make is up to you, but MDI is probably best.

Scripting type: After this, you'll be asked what kind of scripting you want. These are fairly advanced functions that can help automate tasks. Macros are easiest to start with, but scripts offer more power. You might want to explore all of this later, but for the moment, choosing Prompt As Needed covers both bases.

Action confirmation: Next, you'll be asked what kind of database actions you want to confirm when Rekall is up and running. This is designed to help prevent accidents that might result in data being overwritten or deleted. The default is to have the confirmation options deactivated, but you might choose to select to confirm multiple deletions (or even single deletions, if you wish), by selecting that option in the drop-down list, as shown in Figure 27-1.

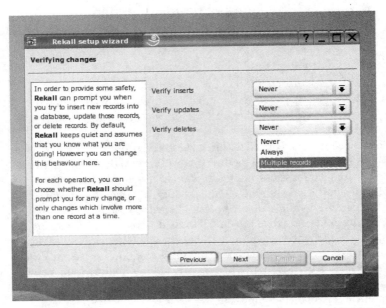

Figure 27-1. *To avoid accidents, you can make Rekall confirm the deletion of more than one data record at any one time.*

After you've completed the setup wizard, you'll be able to start using Rekall.

Setting Up a Database

To illustrate how Rekall works, we're going to set up a database for cataloging a music collection. This involves creating two key items: a table, which will store the data, and a form, for entering and viewing data. For this simple example, we'll create only one table and one form. More ambitious database projects may include many tables and forms, depending on their needs and size.

As with the other OpenOffice.org applications, the key to Rekall is its wizards, which walk you through practically any task. This includes setting up your database file, tables, and forms. We'll use a wizard now to set up a database.

1. In Rekall, select File ➤ New. You're asked whether you want to bypass the wizard and set up a database manually. You might want to choose this option after you have more experience with Rekall. For now, click Next to start the wizard.

2. The first choice to make is where Rekall should store its files, as shown in Figure 27-2. These aren't the database files, but rather the files Rekall uses to store its own data, such as any forms you create. You can store the files in your home directory or create a new directory beneath that for the database data. You'll also need to give this file a name. You should keep the filename short and avoid putting spaces into it. Click Next to continue.

Tip Instead of spaces in filenames, you can use an underscore (_). This can be found on the key next to the zero at the top of the keyboard.

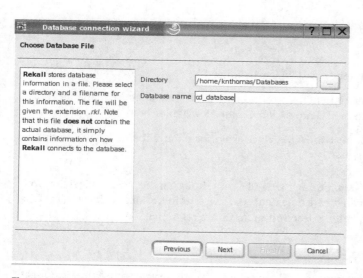

Figure 27-2. *The first step is to let Rekall know where you want to store its own files.*

3. You're asked where you want to store various kinds of database objects: in the database itself or in separate files. For our simple example, storing the data within the database itself means that there will be fewer files to lose, so select that option. Click Next.

4. The next choice is which database you want to connect to. This option isn't relevant to us, and there's only one option within SUSE Linux, which is Rekall XBase/XBSQL Driver. This means that you'll effectively generate database data files as and when you need them on your own hard disk, rather than connecting to a central server (which is how high-end databases work). Click Next.

5. Select the directory where these database files should be stored. Once again, you can select your home directory or the directory you created within it to hold your database files. Click Next.

6. Click Finish. You'll be told that, "The server lacks an object table." Click Yes to create one.

You should find yourself at a complicated-looking window with several options down the left side. Don't worry. The next steps are surprisingly simple. The first task is to create a table to hold your data.

■**Note** In the version of Rekall I used, the window that appeared at this stage was too small. Simply clicking and dragging its handles was enough to make it large enough to use.

Creating a Table

Once you've set up your database file, you're ready to add tables to it. We'll create one table to store data about CDs.

1. Click Tables on the left under the Objects heading.

2. Expand the entry on the right of the window that shows the database filename you entered previously, and then double-click Create New Table.

3. You're asked to give a name to the table. Once again, keep the name short but descriptive, and avoid using spaces.

After this, you'll be shown something that looks very similar to the Design View option within Microsoft Access. You can create data fields (known within Rekall as *columns*), set what type of data they contain, and enter a description for future reference.

Creating the Primary Key

The first field to create is the primary key. All tables need one of these because they uniquely identify each row of data. Doing so in Rekall is very simple. Just enter **PrimaryKey** into the first name box, select Primary Key from the Type drop-down list, and (if you wish) enter a comment in the Description box to remind yourself what the field does. Figure 27-3 shows the primary key entered in the table.

■**Note** The primary key automatically updates itself when new data is entered, so there's no need to set the field to do this, as with some versions of Microsoft Access.

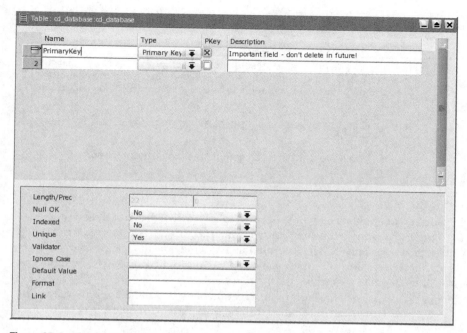

Figure 27-3. *The first step in making a table to hold your data is to create a primary key.*

Adding Columns

After setting up a primary key, you must enter columns for the data you want to enter. In our example of a CD database, we'll add columns to contain the artist information, the title of the CD, the year of release, notes, and an indication of whether the CD is scratched. You can add as many columns as you wish.

Along with the column name, you must specify its *data type*. For example, a Rekall table column might consist of nothing but whole numbers, so it would be a Number type. A column that holds text would be a Char type. Table 27-1 shows the various Rekall data types.

Table 27-1. *Data Types Within a Rekall Table*

Data Type	Description
Primary Key	A column that holds the number that identifies a particular row of data as being unique. Practically all databases must have a Primary Key column.
Foreign Key	Used in place of a primary key in some circumstances, particularly when interfacing with certain types of database servers. When creating simple databases with Rekall, this is not a data type you should use or worry about.
Bool	Stands for Boolean; used to define columns that hold one of two values: true or false. This data type is useful for creating check boxes in database forms.
Number	For whole numbers, without any decimal places. Numbers can range from minus two billion to plus two billion.
Float	For numbers that have (or might have) decimal places, such as 3.1415926.

Table 27-1. *Data Types Within a Rekall Table (Continued)*

Data Type	Description
Date	For columns that hold a date of some kind, whether that's a simple day and month or a day, month, and year (you will be able to choose the formatting of dates and times later). For what it's worth, years can go back to 1752 and up to 8000 AD.
Char	Short for characters; used to hold practically any amount of text, both letters and numbers.
Binary	Used to define a column that can contain files, such as images or multimedia files.

Why do you need to specify data types? Because it helps when the data is manipulated later on. For example, knowing that a field contains dates means that various tools can be created and used to manipulate the date information. In a similar fashion, if a data column can contain only numbers, then these numbers can be added, multiplied, and so on, without the worry of rogue letter characters jamming the formulas.

The principal data type we'll be using in the creation of our CD database is the Char type. This is designed to hold alphanumeric characters, and so is perfect for entering details about CDs such as titles and artist information.

So let's get started creating data columns.

1. Enter **Artist** in the second Name box. Then select Char from the Type drop-down list. If you wish, enter some details in the Description box (although you can leave the Description box blank).

2. Add a data column for the CD title named **Title** with a Char data type. You can move from text box to text box by pressing the Tab key.

3. Add a data column for the CD year named **ReleaseYr** with a Date data type.

Note Each data column name can contain only ten characters and must not have spaces in it. In addition, it cannot contain solely numbers and must contain at least one alphabetical character.

---

4. Add a data column for extra information about the CD named **Notes** with a Char data type.

5. Add a data column named **Scratched**. This will contain a true/false value pertaining to whether the CD is scratched, and therefore unplayable. Set its data type as Bool. This will mean that the column can hold only two possible types of data: true or false. Considering that the CD will either be scratched or not scratched, this is very useful for our purposes.

6. Click the floppy disk icon on the main Rekall window toolbar to save the table. Figure 27-4 shows the columns defined for our table.

Note Rekall doesn't automatically save tables, forms or other elements you create, as with Microsoft Access. You must click the Save icon or choose File ➤ Save every time you make a change.

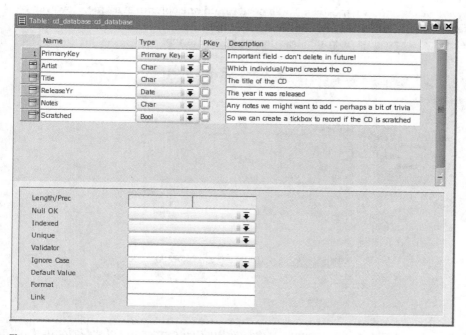

Figure 27-4. *Add data columns for every piece of data you want to store in your database.*

Creating a Form to Enter Data

Now that the table has been created, we need a means for entering and accessing the data. Rekall uses *forms* for this purpose. As the name might suggest, these are like the paper forms filled in by people whenever data needs to be collected, such as tax returns, job applications, and so on.

Designing a Form

When creating a Rekall database, you must first design the form from scratch. Once this is done, the same form can be used over and over again to enter new data. Once a data set has been entered (for example, details of a CD in our sample database), the data is saved into the database, and then the form cleared, ready for new data.

Let's get started.

1. Close the table-editing screen and return to the main Rekall window.

2. Click Forms on the left, and then double-click the entry on the right relating to the filename you entered earlier.

3. Select Create New Form with Wizard.

4. Select the table you created earlier. This will most likely be automatically selected, so click Next.

5. Select the data columns you created earlier, and then click the Add >> button so that they will be available on the form. You'll need to add one column at a time. However, be sure *not* to add the Primary Key data column. Figure 27-5 shows the columns added to the form. Click Next when you're finished adding columns.

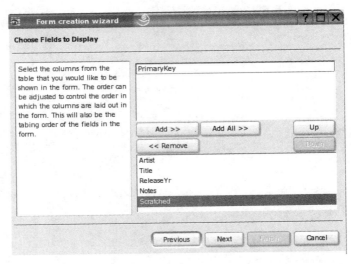

Figure 27-5. *Add all the data columns to the field, with the exception of the Primary Key.*

6. Now, you're invited to choose from various formats in which the data will be entered and displayed. For example, what format do you wants dates to be entered in? US or UK format? Just the year and month, or days as well? On the other hand, you can leave the drop-down lists alone if you prefer. Click Next when you're finished.

7. You're asked how many records you want on a page. A *record* refers to a complete entry in your database, so in our example, it refers to an entry relating to a single CD. In our case, it makes sense to have only one record per form.

8. The next step asks if you want any buttons on the page. These let the user move from record to record within the database, so they are very useful. Put ticks in both boxes.

9. The final step is to give the form a name, which can be anything provided it's kept short and doesn't include spaces. After you enter a name, click the Finish button.

Rekall will now open the form you've created. You can then use this to enter data.

Adding Elements to a Form

You'll notice your form isn't quite right. We wanted a check box to appear near the Scratched heading, but currently we have a text box. Fortunately, you can edit the form components to add new buttons and text boxes. Let's add a check box.

1. Close the form, and then right-click its entry in the main program window.

2. Select Design View from the menu that appears.

3. Select the Scratched box, right-click it, and select Delete. Then do the same for the actual data-entry text box.

4. Right-click in a blank spot on the form and select New ➤ New Check. This will bring up a Properties window with many options that can be edited.

5. Double-click the Control Name entry in the list and, in the text box, type the name of the data column you created to hold the data relating to whether the CD is scratched: **Scratched**. Your screen should look like Figure 27-6. Then click Accept.

6. Repeat step 5 with the Display Expression header, so that it, too, contains the name of the data column. Then click OK.

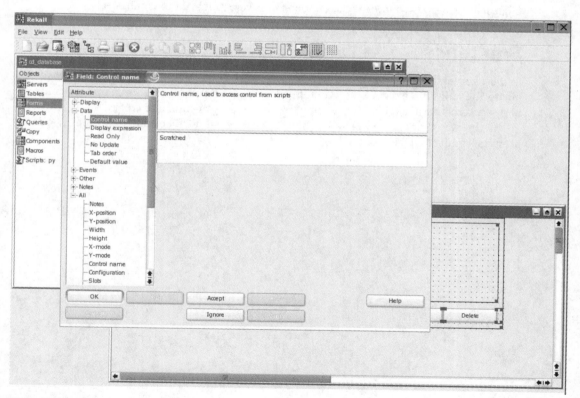

Figure 27-6. *Enter the name of the data column you created under the Control Name and Display Expression headings.*

7. This will have created a check box so large that it dominates the form. Click and drag one of its corner handles to shrink it.

8. The text box still needs something to identify it. It needs what's called a *label*. Right-click a blank spot within the form and select New ➤ New Label.

9. Once again, this will show a Properties dialog box with many choices, but all we're interested in is the Label Text entry. Double-click this and type in a suitable name for the check box, such as **Scratched?**. Click OK.

10. Like the added check box, the label takes up most of the space on the form. Click and drag the corner handles to shrink it down to the appropriate size. You can also click and drag it to the relevant spot on the form, as you can move the check box itself.

11. Click the Save icon, and then close the form design window.

12. Double-click the entry on the form so you can enter data. You should now find your check box works fine.

We've only scratched the surface of Rekall's power in this chapter. There are many more options, such as creating automated queries that can manipulate and search data in various ways. By clicking Help, you'll be able to read the Rekall manual, which is written in everyday English and doesn't assume the user understands very much about databases.

Summary

In this chapter, we looked at the Rekall database front end and how it can be used to easily create and edit simple databases. We stepped through an example of setting up a database table and creating a database form that users can employ to enter and edit data.

In the next chapter, we will look at how to run Microsoft Office and many other Windows programs under SUSE Linux.

CHAPTER 28

■ ■ ■

Running Microsoft Office under SUSE Linux

The title of this chapter might sound somewhat strange. How can a Windows program be run under SUSE Linux? The answer comes courtesy of the Wine project. Wine is an acronym for Wine Is Not an Emulator, which is a way of saying that the Wine software doesn't emulate Windows, but instead re-creates certain parts of it called the Application Programming Interface (API).

In theory, the vast majority of Windows program can be run using Wine. In this chapter, we'll begin with the steps for setting up Wine, and then walk through installing and running Microsoft Office 2000. Finally, you'll learn how to install Internet Explorer and other Windows software.

Installing and Configuring Wine

A version of Wine comes on the SUSE Linux DVD and, if you selected the default options when installing SUSE Linux, it should already be installed. You can test this by opening a Konsole window and typing `wine`.

This will also have the effect of automatically setting up Wine, such as writing its initial configuration file (no user input is required, and defaults are automatically selected). If you receive an error message to the effect that Wine isn't present, use the Install and Remove Software component of YaST2 to install it (select K menu ➤ Control Center, click YaST2 Modules, click Software, and then click Install and Remove Software).

Wine aims to re-create the Windows API layer within Linux. Although it's extremely successful in this task, the constantly updating nature of the Windows core software, as well as a few other technical issues, mean that some preparatory work is necessary before you attempt to install Windows programs.

■**Note** Not all Windows software works under Wine. Alternatively, some software might work partially and suffer from bugs in certain circumstances. There are no hard-and-fast rules about what works and what doesn't. In most cases, it's best to simply try to install the software to see if it works.

Installing DCOM95

The first task is to install the Windows DCOM95 package. This installs a handful of vital Microsoft system files necessary for running other Windows software. Technically speaking, installing Microsoft system files might seem to defeat the purpose of using Wine, which is to re-create the Windows files as free software, but installing and using the DCOM95 software simply saves a lot of time and effort. In some cases, it's the only way to get certain Windows programs to work.

At the time of writing, this file can be downloaded from `http://prdownloads` `.sourceforge.net/wine/dcom95.exe?download`. If you find this URL doesn't work, try using a search engine to look for the file.

After you've downloaded DCOM95, you must run the program via Wine with the following command:

```
WINEDLLOVERRIDES="ole32=n" wine dcom95.exe
```

You might then be surprised to see a Windows dialog box asking you to confirm the installing of DCOM95. Click Yes. The program will then work its way through setup.

■**Note** Don't worry about feedback on the console that appears during and after the DCOM95 installation. Wine is automatically set to debug mode, which means it feeds back a lot of information to the user, even if it doesn't encounter any genuine errors.

Editing the Wine Configuration File

Next, within Wine you must set the version of Windows you wish to emulate. Windows 98 is the best choice, because it's the most mature in terms of Wine emulation and also the lowest specification demanded by most recent Windows software (very few modern software titles install on Windows 95). To do this, you need to edit the Wine configuration file. This is contained within a hidden directory within your home directory, and can be accessed by typing the following:

```
vi ~/.wine/config
```

Alternatively, you can use any text editor, such as Kate. You can start Kate by selecting K menu ➤ Utilities ➤ Editor, or via the command line, by typing `kate ~/.wine/config`. Once the file is loaded into your editor, scroll down to the section headed [Version]. In that section, remove the semicolon before the following line:

```
;"Windows" = "win98"
```

So you're left with:

```
"Windows" = "win98"
```

Figure 28-1 shows the file after the change.

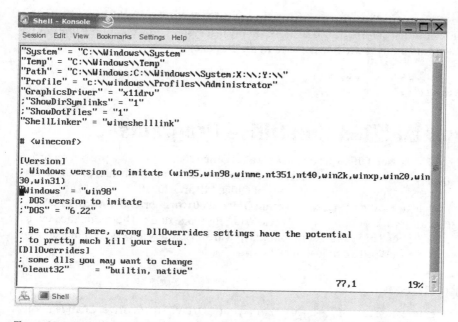

```
"System" = "C:\\Windows\\System"
"Temp" = "C:\\Windows\\Temp"
"Path" = "C:\\Windows;C:\\Windows\\System;X:\\;Y:\\"
"Profile" = "c:\\windows\\Profiles\\Administrator"
"GraphicsDriver" = "x11drv"
;"ShowDirSymlinks" = "1"
;"ShowDotFiles" = "1"
"ShellLinker" = "wineshelllink"

# <wineconf>

[Version]
; Windows version to imitate (win95,win98,winme,nt351,nt40,win2k,winxp,win20,win
30,win31)
"Windows" = "win98"
; DOS version to imitate
;"DOS" = "6.22"

; Be careful here, wrong DllOverrides settings have the potential
; to pretty much kill your setup.
[DllOverrides]
; some dlls you may want to change
"oleaut32"      = "builtin, native"
                                                    77,1              19%
```

Figure 28-1. *To get Windows programs working under Wine, some configuration is necessary.*

In addition, if you have a DVD-ROM drive rather than a CD-ROM drive, you should edit the lines that refer to where Wine should look for its virtual drive mappings. On my test system, this is under the [Drive M] heading. I replaced these lines:

```
"Path" = "/media/cdrom"
"Label" = "/media/cdrom"
```

with these:

```
"Path" = "/media/dvd"
"Label" = "/media/dvd"
```

After you've made the necessary changes, save the file and quit vi or Kate.

Editing the fstab File

It's also necessary to edit your fstab file so that hidden files on Windows CDs can be seen when the disc is mounted. Start by switching to root user and opening fstab in vi:

```
su
[enter root password]
vi /etc/fstab
```

Alternatively, you can edit the file in Kate, as described in the previous section.

Within the file, edit the line pertaining to your CD/DVD-ROM drive, adding nohide to the end of the list of options, before the 0 0 section. On my test system, this meant the line ended up looking like this (split over two lines here to fit on the page):

```
/dev/dvd      /media/dvd      subfs      fs=cdfss,ro,procuid,nosuid,nodev,exec,
iocharset=utf8,nohide      0 0
```

Installing and Running Office Programs

The best choice of Microsoft Office product to install is Office 2000. This has a proven record of installing and generally running well under Wine. It also uses file formats that are, to all practical purposes, unchanged in the very latest versions of Office (XP and 2003).

However, not all the software packages within Office 2000 work correctly. Word, Excel, and PowerPoint appear to work, but Microsoft Access and FrontPage don't. Therefore, the key to installing Office is to install only those components that are absolutely necessary. For example, if you only intend to use Word, then just install Word.

Installing Office

Start by inserting the Microsoft Office 2000 CD into your CD/DVD-ROM drive. Change to the relevant directory (such as /media/cdrom or /media/dvd), and then issue the following command:

```
wine SETUP.EXE
```

This will start the Microsoft Office installation wizard. Work your way through until you get to the point where you can choose which components to install. The following choices should result in a successful installation of Office:

- Word

- Excel

- PowerPoint

- All of the file filters

- The spell-checker component

Everything else should be deselected (made Not Available) so it's not installed, including Internet Explorer. After this, the installation should run smoothly.

Installing Internet Explorer at this stage will cause problems with the installation of Microsoft Office, so the easiest way to install Office under Wine is to deselect it. However, IE is often a prerequisite for many other Windows applications, so you'll learn how to install it using a different technique later in this chapter.

Once the Office installation has finished, select not to automatically reboot. Instead, return to the shell and type this:

```
wineboot
```

This is a Wine command that simulates a Windows reboot. After this, Office will continue its configuration and installation.

Running Office Programs

In order to install programs, Wine creates an entire pseudo file system in the hidden .wine directory in your system folder, within the fake_windows directory. Aside from being a subdirectory within it, this is entirely separate from your main file system, which is to say that no Windows programs will ever be installed outside this subdirectory. Therefore, running any programs you install is simply a matter of navigating to this folder and typing the name of the .exe file, preceding it with the wine command (and, because the path contains spaces, enclosing it within quotation marks).

For example, to run Microsoft Word, type the following:

```
wine "~/.wine/fake_windows/Program Files/Microsoft Office/word.exe"
```

Word will start, as shown in Figure 28-2.

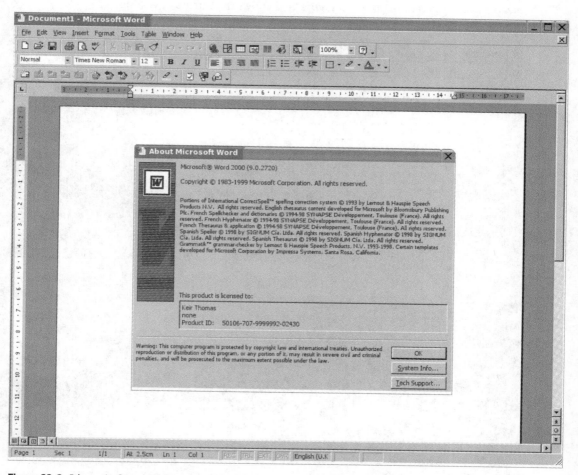

Figure 28-2. *It's entirely possible to run Microsoft Office programs under SUSE Linux using Wine.*

Alternatively, you can easily create a shortcut on the KDE menu or the desktop to run each program. See Chapter 10 for details on creating shortcuts.

Installing and Running Other Windows Programs

A lot of Windows applications will work under Wine. Installing them is usually a matter of typing this:

```
wine <programname.exe>
```

The main Wine web site offers a list of programs that are compatible with the software, along with reports from users as to the best way to get Windows software working. You can find this at http://appdb.winehq.org. Very nearly every mainstream Windows program can be made to work, although it may take a little extra effort.

In my tests, I managed to use Wine to install the popular WinZip archiving application, as well as the Winamp audio software and the ICQ instant messenger. (For Winamp, I needed to disable a few installation options.) Figure 28-3 shows the startup of WinZip.

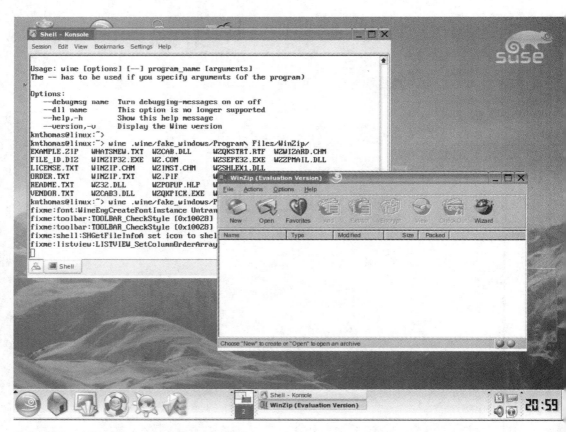

Figure 28-3. *Although it often takes a bit of effort, virtually any Windows application can be made to run under SUSE Linux.*

After some program installations, it's often necessary to reboot Windows. This doesn't mean you need to reboot SUSE Linux. Instead, as mentioned above, you can issue the following command:

```
wineboot
```

This will fake a Windows reboot within the console.

Installing Internet Explorer

Many modern Windows programs will not work unless the most recent version of Internet Explorer is installed. Therefore, this should be one of the first Windows programs you install.

At the time of writing, Internet Explorer had reached version 6 (IE6), Service Pack 1. Alas, installing IE6 is not easy under Wine. Because of this, Wine developer Mike Hearn has created a script that will install IE6 automatically. Simply head over to his site at http://bylands.dur .ac.uk/~mh/wine-ie/ and download the script..

■**Note** At the time of writing, Mike's script had been superceded by a newer version but you should still use the older version ("install-ie6.sh"), which can still be downloaded from his site, because it's designed to work with the older version of Wine supplied by default with SUSE Linux.

After it has downloaded, you'll need to use the chmod program to change its permissions to make it executable (using chmod is covered in Chapter 15), and then run it from the command line:

```
chmod +x install-ie6.sh
./install-ie6.sh
```

Then simply follow the installation wizard as usual. This will both download and install IE6, Service Pack 1. You need to make virtually no installation choices; everything is automated. On my test system, running the script brought up a few errors later in the installation process, but eventually Internet Explorer worked perfectly.

■**Caution** Make sure to read the EULA agreements of any software you install. For example, in order install IE6, you must have a license for a Windows product. If you don't have such a license, then it is illegal to install IE6, and you should quit the installation.

Installing Programs with Installers

If you plan to install programs created with the InstallShield program, which is used by many Windows programs as an installer, you may need to precede the wine command you use to run the installer program with the following:

```
WINEDLLOVERRIDES="ole32,oleaut32,rpcrt4=n" wine <programname.exe>
```

In addition, if you need to install Windows installation files with an `.msi` extension (which stands for Microsoft Installer), you'll first need to download and install the Windows Installer add-in. At the time of writing, this can be downloaded from `http://download.microsoft.com/download/WindowsInstaller/Install/2.0/W9XMe/EN-US/InstMsiA.exe`. However, if this link doesn't work, simply search for the program with the search engine of your choice. Then install it by typing this:

```
wine InstMsiA.exe
```

After installing the Windows Installer add-in, you'll need to edit your Wine configuration file again. Open the file for editing by typing this:

```
vi ~/.wine/config
```

Then add the following line at the bottom of the [DllOverrides] section:

```
"msiexec.exe" = "native, builtin"
```

CROSSOVER OFFICE

The developers behind Wine also produce a proprietary version of Wine called CrossOver Office. Technically speaking, this is actually no different from any other version of Wine except that a GUI-based front end is added to make installation of programs simpler. It also includes several scripts to overcome various incompatibilities between Windows programs and Wine. This makes it possible to install the very latest version of Office, for example. In addition, CrossOver Office also lets you use Internet Explorer-based plug-ins within Linux-based browsers.

You can learn more about CrossOver Office by visiting its official web site at www.codeweavers.com. CrossOver Office is available for a fee from CodeWeavers, but considering they are one of the major sponsors of the Wine project, this is an excellent way of investing in the community.

Summary

In this chapter, we looked at how the Wine suite of programs can be used to install and run various Windows programs under SUSE Linux, including Microsoft Office. Because using Wine is not without problems, we looked at how it should be configured, and then walked through the steps needed to install Microsoft Office 2000. Then you saw how to install other Windows programs, including Internet Explorer.

In Part Seven of the book, starting with the next chapter, we look at the techniques you need to know to keep your SUSE Linux system running smoothly.

## PART SEVEN

Keeping Your System Running

## CHAPTER 29

Installing Software

One of the fun things about running any operating system is the ability to expand it—to add in new software over time to improve your workflow or just for entertainment value.

Linux is blessed in this regard, because there are tens of thousands of software titles available to meet just about every need. However, if you've tracked down the ideal software title, there's just one barrier to overcome: actually installing it on your system.

Installing software under SUSE Linux isn't the same as with Windows. Users are afforded a lot more power over what happens to their system, but this comes at the expense of needing to take a little time to understand the terminology and techniques. That is what you'll learn in this chapter.

Software Installation Basics

Installing programs on Windows is relatively easy. If you wish to use the Winamp media player, for example, you can browse to the web site, download the installer .exe file, and install the software.

Although you might not realize it, a lot of work goes into making this seemingly simple task possible. Once the original software has been created by the programmers, it must be made into a form that you, the end user, can deal with. Before it's released for general consumption, the program has to be compiled and packaged.

Compiling is the process of turning the source code created by programmers into an actual file (or set of files) that can be used on a daily basis. On most systems, compiling source code involves a lot of number crunching. This takes time—whole days, in some cases— and this is why you cannot compile the source code every time you want to run the program.

Once the program files have been compiled, there needs to be a way they can be installed on various systems and easily transported across the Internet. Programs usually consist of many files. To make each program file individually available would mean that some are sure to get lost or corrupted, and the program wouldn't work. Therefore, the files are usually combined into a single archive file. In addition, third-party system files are added to ensure compatibility on all computers. Also, an extra program, called an *installer*, is added so that users can quickly get the files onto their system.

All of this means that, to be able to install a program like Winamp on Windows, all you need to do is download the installer .exe file and run it once. Then you can run Winamp. No more work is necessary.

Linux is a little more involved, largely because it never assumes that the user wants things kept simple, with limited options.

The Formats of Linux Installation Files

At the most basic level, Linux software is made available as source code. Unlike with Windows and a lot of the programs that run on it, where the source code is kept secret, the philosophical cornerstone of Linux is that source code should be shared.

Note Linux isn't the only operating system for which open-source programs are created and used. There are open-source projects for both Windows and Apple Macintosh, many of which are hosted at the `http://sourceforge.net` web site. Many other less widely used operating systems also rely on open-source software to a greater or lesser extent.

Linux software can come in several forms:

- **Source code:** When you attempt to download a program, you might simply find that the source code is all that's available from the developer's web site. You can then download and compile this on your own system. This isn't very hard to do. In most cases, any difficult work is handled via scripts (small programs that run through a chain of commands and, in the case of program installation, check the system for compatibility).

- **Binary files:** In other cases, you might find ready-made binary files are available. In other words, the programmer has taken his or her own source code and, as a service to users of the program, compiled it so that it's ready for use as soon as it's downloaded. Sometimes, these come with scripts to help you install them. However, in most cases, you simply put the files in a convenient location on your hard disk, and then run them from there. In other words, you install the program files yourself.

Note In both the case of source code and binary files, the files usually come in a *tarball*, which is a single archive file containing other files. A tarball isn't by definition compressed, but usually the `bzip2` or `gzip` tool is used to shrink the file to ease transportation across the Internet.

- **Self-installing binaries:** Some larger programs are made available as a self-installing binary. This comes very close to the way Windows works because, when it's run, a GUI-based installation wizard takes you through installation. If you download OpenOffice.org from the official web site (`www.openoffice.org`), for example, you'll end up with a single 80MB+ file, which you then simply run from the command line in this way.

- **RPM:** In many cases, you'll find that an RPM file is available. RPM stands for Red Hat Package Manager. RPM is a form of installation file technology created by Red Hat but also used on many other distributions, including SUSE Linux. RPM files are called *packages* because they package all the program files together in a convenient form. The entire system of using RPM files is often called *package management.*

Note The open-source nature of Linux encourages the sharing of programs and technologies among companies that are otherwise direct commercial competitors. This is why the RPM system is used on SUSE Linux, Red Hat, Mandrake Linux, and others.

Package Management

RPM is an entire system for managing programs within SUSE Linux. It can install programs, upgrade them, and uninstall them. It's a little like the Windows Add/Remove Programs applet on steroids, because it's very powerful and offers a great many configuration options. It's worth noting that RPM files don't include installer programs. Instead, the RPM software on the user's computer does the actual work of installing the program.

Once RPM is set up, which is done automatically when you install SUSE Linux, it creates a database of currently installed software, along with other information such as version numbers. Whenever you attempt to install a program, it's checked against the database for compatibility. This means that an RPM system is one that's tightly controlled. For example, no program is able to get onto your system unless the system files it needs are present. Installing two versions of the same program is often prohibited, thus avoiding compatibility problems.

Note In some cases, it's actually desirable to have two or more versions of the same program on your system, and the RPM system is able to cope with such an occurrence, too.

RPM mostly works with precompiled binary files, although RPM source files are also sometimes available, with the idea being that you can then compile the source code yourself. Additionally, special RPM files that are designed to be compiled into binary RPMs are available, but most ordinary users don't need to worry too much about these.

RPM isn't the only prepackaged installation file used under Linux. There are many others. Table 29-1 lists some of the more popular types. As a blanket rule, an installation package created for one distribution won't be compatible with another. You can find software that aims to convert packages between distributions, but this should be seen as a last resort. The first resort it to simply get a package specifically designed for your Linux distribution.

Table 29-1. *Linux Installation File Types†*

File Extension	Type of Installation File	Notes
.bin or .sh	Executable program	Usually a single file, which, in the context of installation files and when executed from the command line, starts an installation routine similar to that found in Windows.
.tar.gz	Compressed tarball	Collection of files in a tar archive, which also employs gzip compression. This extension usually indicates a source code file, but sometimes binaries are distributed this way, too.
.tar.bz2	Compressed tarball	Collection of files in a tar archive, which also employs the newer and more efficient bzip2 compression (although it's otherwise similar to .tar.gz files).
.deb	Debian	Installation file designed for use with the dpkg system; used on the Debian distro and those based on it, such as Linspire.
.tgz	Slackware	Usually indicates a Slackware program archive, although traditionally a tgz archive simply indicates a tarball that has been compressed with gzip.

Software Versions

Because most Linux software is open source, a curious thing happens when it comes to software versions. Rather than there being just one "official" version of a program, such as with most Windows software (where you must download the official version of the file), many individuals and organizations take the source code, compile it, and make their own RPMs available for others to use.

For example, virtually all the software installed with SUSE Linux has been compiled by SUSE itself and made into RPM files. This can be quite different from what might be "officially" available at the programmer's web site. In some cases, the source code is tweaked, so that notorious bugs are fixed or a different look and feel applied to the software so it integrates with the distribution. Often, the configuration files are changed so that the software works in the best way for the SUSE Linux system, such as integrating with other software packages. The programmer doesn't mind when such things happen, because this way of working is part and parcel of open-source software. In fact, the programmer is likely to encourage such tweaking.

Because of this, the first place to look if you want any additional software is not the developer's web site, but the SUSE DVD-ROM or SUSE's online update service. This way, you'll get an officially sanctioned SUSE release that will fit in with the rest of your system and won't require much, if any, additional work to get it up and running. As you can see in Figure 29-1, the SUSE DVD offers many programs to install on your system.

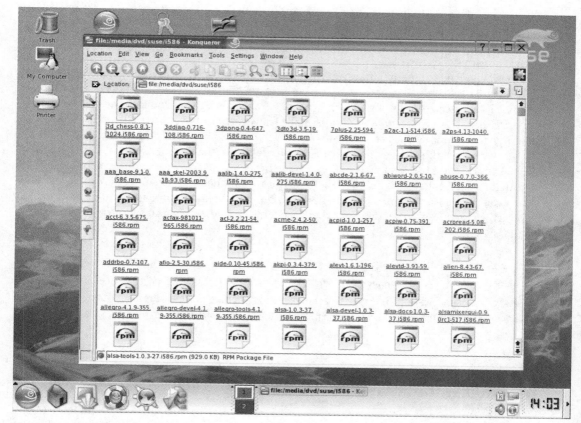

Figure 29-1. *The SUSE installation DVD is packed with prepackaged programs from SUSE.*

The trouble is that while SUSE Linux's collection of software is vast and covers most popular titles, it doesn't support *all* the software that's available. There's simply too much for SUSE to prepackage everything, so in some cases, you might be forced to go online and see what else you can uncover. Once again, this doesn't present huge challenges, because some individuals put together their own SUSE-compatible RPMs as a public service, and the original programmers of applications often make their own SUSE-compatible RPM available.

Adding and Removing Programs with YaST2

If there's a specific program you would like to install, the simplest and most efficient way is to use YaST2. YaST2 is able to handle all aspects of program installation, dealing with RPM files and managing the entire RPM system.

One of the best things about using YaST2 to install software is that it automatically takes care of *dependencies*. If any program needs additional software or library files, YaST2 will install these, too, and will confirm the additional selection of programs with you before writing anything to the hard disk.

Dependencies are something you'll come across on a regular basis when installing programs. Unlike many Windows programs, SUSE Linux installation packages ordinarily don't come complete with all the support files they need. It's anticipated that you'll either already have these installed or will install them separately. However, a RPM package will refuse to install unless these support files are present.

Because of this, when manually installing programs (that is, not using YaST2), a situation informally called "dependency hell" can arise. In such a case, the user attempts to install a program but is told that it needs other files. These other files are then found, downloaded, and an attempt made to install them, but then another error message appears saying that they, too, have their *own* set of dependencies! When installing by hand, this can take some time to resolve. YaST2 takes care of it automatically.

Note If a Linux program *does* come with the support files it needs, it will most likely be described as *statically linked*. However, this is rare. Most are *dynamically linked*, which means the program doesn't come with the required library files compiled into it, forcing the user to ensure the libraries are available elsewhere on the system.

Installing from the SUSE DVD

To use YaST2, select K menu ➤ Control Center, and then click the YAST2 Modules icon. Click the Software icon, and then click Install and Remove Software. Changes made to the software setup affect the entire system, so it's necessary to click the Administrator Mode button and enter your root password.

You'll then be able to search for any program by its name. This will query the database of programs that are available on the installation DVD, as show in Figure 29-2. You should make sure you insert your SUSE installation DVD, because the files will be read from the disc and installed.

If you're looking for a program to fulfill a particular need but don't know its name, you can enter a search term and put a check in the Description box beneath the Search field. For example, if you're looking for a web browser, you could enter "browser" as a search term. The results will be displayed on the right side of the screen. In using this function you're also searching the one- or two-sentence description of each application, but these are usually concise rather than verbose, so this shouldn't be seen as comprehensive way of finding what you want.

Once you've found the program you're looking for, put a tick in the box next to it, and then click the Accept button at the bottom right.

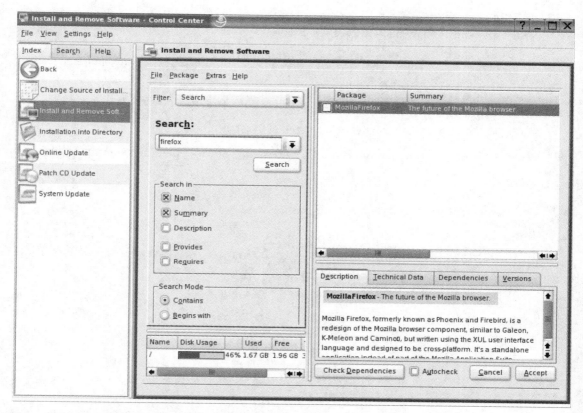

Figure 29-2. *You can search for programs on the DVD-ROM using the YaST2 program.*

Note If the box next to the application already has a tick in it, that program has been previously installed. You should check the K menu to see if it's present. If it doesn't appear to be, try opening a Konsole window and running the program from there by typing its name.

YaST2 also provides a user-friendly way to browse the programs you have installed as well as look at those that are available for installation, avoiding the need to keep searching for programs. Simply select Package Groups in the Filter drop-down list at the top of the YaST2 program window. This will show a similar grouping of programs that you saw when you first installed SUSE Linux, and it's a nice way to get acquainted with the programs you have installed on your system.

Installing from the SUSE FTP Archive

By default, YaST2 is set up to use the SUSE installation DVD as its source. However, it's also possible to add the main SUSE FTP archive as an installation source, which you might want to do if you have a fast connection to the Internet and/or you're not always going to have the DVD around to be able to install from.

To add the FTP site, be sure you're online (YaST2 will check the installation source to make sure it's valid), and then follow these steps:

1. Select K menu ➤ Control Center, click YaST2 Modules, click Software, and then click Change Source of Installation.

2. Click the Administrator Mode button and enter your root password.

3. Click the Add button in the lower half of the screen.

4. Select FTP from the list. In the dialog box that appears, enter the following details, as shown in Figure 29-3:

```
Server name: ftp.suse.com
Directory on server: pub/suse/i386/9.1/
```

Figure 29-3. *You may want to add the main SUSE FTP site as an installation source if you won't always have the DVD on-hand.*

5. Click OK.

6. You can then delete the DVD installation option, which should be at the top of the list. Select it and click the Delete button at the bottom of the screen.

7. Return to the Software screen of YaST2. When you first do this, you should find that there's a delay while YaST2 downloads the list of packages from the FTP site.

Depending on where you live, you might find the main SUSE FTP server a little slow. SUSE takes advantage of mirror servers that echo the content of its main site. You can find a list of these at www.suse.com/us/private/download/ftp/int_mirrors.html. Simply substitute the details in step 4 with those for a server local to you.

INSTALLING PROPRIETARY SOFTWARE

A lot of proprietary (closed-source) software, as well as some large open-source applications, come in the form of a single, large installable file. Usually, such programs have their own installation routine, just as with Windows, which runs either on the desktop or at the console.

Normally, such files will have .bin or .sh file extensions. However, in some cases, they might not have any file extension, although the filename will usually indicate that this is an installable file.

Installing such programs is easy. You can just execute them from the command line:

```
./<program name>
```

Don't forget that running any binary program within the current directory means you must precede the command with the dot and slash combination, in order to avoid having the shell search your path for the program. You should be aware that installation programs frequently lose their executable status during download. Therefore, the first thing to do in many cases is to change the file permissions so you can run the file:

```
chmod +x <program name>
```

Uninstalling Programs via YaST2

Removing programs using YaST2 is almost as simple as adding them. The procedure is undertaken from the same Install and Remove Software component within YaST2. Once again, you will need to search for the program, but this time, the results returned will be those that are already installed. You can tell this because each piece of software in the search results will already have a check in the box next to it.

Marking the software for deletion is simply a matter of unchecking the box until a trash can icon appears. You need to click twice for this to happen. Clicking only once selects the program for an update, which reinstalls the program (this is useful for attempting to fix programs that have gone wrong).

Once you've marked the software for deletion, click Accept, and YaST2 will attempt to uninstall that program. I use the word *attempt* deliberately, because the program might be part of a dependency chain. In this case, other programs rely on it, just like some programs need other packages in order to be installed. If there are dependencies, then the program cannot be uninstalled without further work, and YaST2 will present a dialog box offering solutions to fix the problems.

For example, you would encounter this problem if you tried to remove the Sane scanner program. The XSane program relies on this, as do various other system programs. Because of this, attempting to remove Sane will cause YaST2 to show an error dialog box along with three separate solutions, as shown in Figure 29-4: don't delete Sane, delete Sane as well as the programs that rely on it, or simply go ahead and delete just Sane (and risk problems in future).

There's no hard-and-fast rule in a dependency situation such as this, apart from the obvious: unless you have a pressing need to remove the program, you might as well let it stay on your system to avoid problems. Alternatively, you can try to find out about the programs that rely on the program you're trying to remove, and decide if they can go, too. However, be aware that removing these other programs might create additional dependency chains!

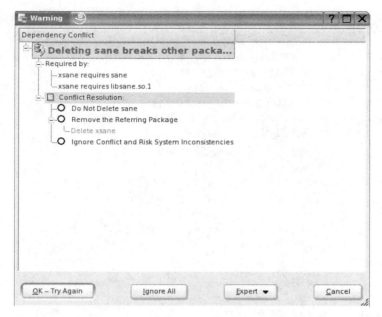

Figure 29-4. *If you try to remove a program that other programs need, YaST2 will offer various solutions.*

■**Caution** Unless you absolutely know what you're doing, you should definitely not choose to go ahead and delete a package when there are dependency problems. This is one of the quickest ways to damage your system. Apart from anything else, every time you try to add a program in the future using YaST2, you'll be presented with the same error dialog box reporting dependency problems, which will get annoying very quickly.

Installing Programs from the Shell

As you would expect, working at the shell offers the most control with regard to program installation. It's one of the only ways of installing packages that are considered "unofficial," which are usually RPM files that are not supplied by SUSE.

A variety of commands are available to handle program installation and maintenance. They let you interface directly with the RPM software, avoiding YaST2 completely if you wish (although bear in mind that YaST2 merely presents the RPM database in a user-friendly form and lets you administer it easily).

Understanding RPM Filenames

As discussed earlier, SUSE Linux uses RPM files for software installation. These are the files you'll usually be dealing with at the command line, and their filenames usually tell you everything you need to know about them. Here's one example:

```
mozilla-1.6-72.i586.rpm
```

At the beginning of the filename is the name of the program: the popular Mozilla web browser in this instance. Following this are the version numbers: 1.6-72. These aren't guaranteed to follow the version number conventions used by the developer of the software, although they're very similar in most cases. However, the numbers after the dash in a version number tend to refer to the build of the RPM, which indicates the specific version of the RPM file. Many different RPMs might be created from the same original software, so it's necessary to have such a way of telling the different RPMs apart.

After the name and version number is the platform the RPM file will work on. i586 indicates that this program will work on all 80586-compatible processors—anything including a Pentium chip and above. i586 refers to the numbering system used within CPU manufacturing.

In some instances, you might find packages stipulating i686, indicating that they're designed for a Pentium II processor and above. Also, many RPM files simply indicate i386, which means they'll work on any processor from the 80386 upwards, including the 486, Pentium, Pentium II, and all subsequent Intel, AMD, IBM, and other improvements.

Note SUSE produces a version of SUSE Linux that is optimized for the new 64-bit range of chips, such as the AMD Athlon 64. Unfortunately, RPM files compiled for use on these chips won't work on 32-bit systems, which includes the majority of computers in use today. Such files are usually marked with an x86_64 extension.

If you attempt to download an RPM file from an unofficial source, it's very likely the filename will indicate the Linux distribution it's designed to work with, too. For example, fc2 indicates that an RPM file is designed to work on Fedora Core 2. In the case of SUSE Linux, you might find suse91 added to the RPM filename. Alas, there are no rules regarding the naming of RPM files. Understanding the filenames is usually a case of applying common sense and understanding the conventions outlined here.

Tracking down RPM files for your specific distribution can sometimes be difficult, and you might be tempted to install one designed for a different Linux distribution. The question arises as to whether these will work. To answer this, you need to bear in mind that an RPM is more than just a collection of program files waiting to be installed. RPM files are able to change your current system configuration, too. Additionally, the RPM system can both delete and create files practically anywhere on your hard drive. Each RPM is tailored to an individual system. Not all distributions install day-to-day binary program files in the same location, as just one example, and this can cause obvious problems if an RPM is used on an incompatible system.

In many cases, you might find that an RPM for a different distribution from yours will seem to install correctly. However, it might not work. Because of this, if you cannot track down an RPM file for your distribution, the best solution is to compile from source, as discussed later in this chapter.

Using YaST at the Command Line

SUSE's officially prescribed way of installing an RPM at the shell is to use the following command (which, as with all these package installation commands, must be run as root):

```
yast -i mozilla-1.6-72.i586.rpm
```

This invokes the shell version of YaST2, YaST, to install the program, and the RPM file is expected to be in the directory from which the command is run. This simply installs the file without first checking for dependencies, so it's not a very good way to install software.

Specifying just a program name means that YaST will look to the DVD-ROM archive for the program. For example, typing the following:

```
yast -i mozilla
```

will cause YaST to try to install the RPM called Mozilla on the DVD-ROM, as shown in Figure 29-5. As with running YaST2 in GUI mode, this will also resolve any dependencies, so that everything you need will be automatically installed.

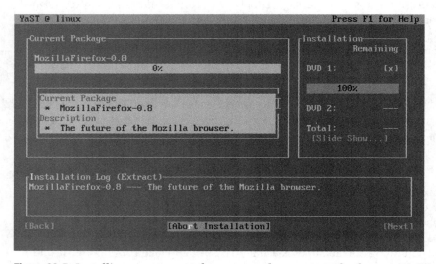

Figure 29-5. *Installing programs at the command prompt can be done via YaST.*

Because using YaST2 in this way is virtually identical to using the program in GUI mode, there's no real advantage to be had from running the program in command-line mode. Additionally, there are other clear disadvantages to using YaST2 for command-line program installation. For example, there's an almost complete lack of feedback, meaning that it can be hard to see whether something has worked or not.

In order to install at the command-line prompt, it's a much better idea to use the rpm command, as described next.

Using the rpm Command

The single rpm command administers practically the entire RPM system. However, it's never used on its own and is controlled by various command-line options. Consider the following example:

```
rpm -i mozilla-1.6-72.i586.rpm
```

The -i command option is used to tell the rpm command to install the specified file. If you're updating a file, you can use the -U option instead. In fact, using -U all the time is a good idea because, if the program isn't installed, rpm is clever enough to realize and will install the program instead.

You can try this yourself. You'll find the RPM for the Firefox web browser in the /suse/i586 directory of the SUSE installation DVD (remember that DVDs are usually mounted in the /media/dvd folder). You can use the following command to install it:

```
rpm -U /media/dvd/suse/i586/MozillaFirefox-0.8-44.i586.rpm
```

The trouble with running this command is that it will go through the process of installing the file, but it will give little, if any, feedback or indication of progress. Because of this, many people add the -v and -h command options. The -v specifies verbose output, meaning that more information is fed back to the user. The -h option simply causes rpm to indicate its progress with a progress bar consisting of hash symbols. Figure 29-6 shows an example.

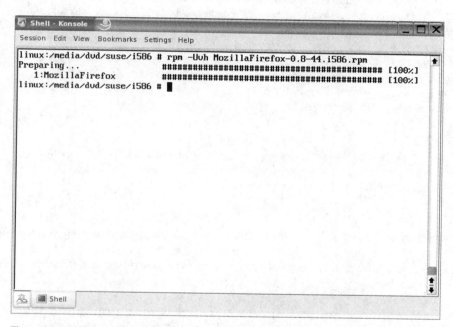

Figure 29-6. *The rpm command offers all the power you need to install software on SUSE Linux.*

Putting all this together, the standard command issued to install a program takes the following form (for the Firefox example):

```
rpm -Uvh MozillaFirefox-0.8-44.i586.rpm
```

After each installation, under SUSE Linux, you should run the following command:

```
SuSEconfig
```

This will register the new program with any necessary background services and also update any necessary configuration files. Because of this, it's a good idea to run the SuSEconfig program (discussed in Chapter 13) each time you use rpm. Note that this is specific to SUSE Linux and isn't necessary on other distributions.

RPM SECURITY

When installing programs, it's vital that some mechanism exists to prove that the RPM files utilized are genuine. By its very nature, open-source software is open to abuse. A nefarious individual could alter the source code of a program, implanting something such as a trojan routine that could steal data. After inserting the code, he could then compile and package the file as if it were the genuine article provided by SUSE. The simplest defense is to make sure that you download only from web sites you can trust, such as that of SUSE itself. However, you can also make use of the RPM GPG key system.

Every officially released RPM file from SUSE is signed with a GNU Privacy Guard (GPG) hashcode. This hashcode is unique to each file and is generated based on the contents of the RPM using a so-called secret key, which only SUSE knows. All secret keys have public key counterparts, and the SUSE RPM public key is added by default to all SUSE Linux installations. The public key can be used to confirm that the hashcode is correct, based on the contents of the file. This allows for a high degree of security.

RPM files also contain checksums that can be used to confirm that the file is complete and not missing files, or that it doesn't contain altered files. Checksums are the results of mathematical formulas applied to the file. If the file changes in any way, no matter how small, then the checksum will change, too.

To check any kind of RPM file for both checksum and GPG hashcodes, type the following:

```
rpm --checksig filename.rpm
```

The results should read OK for each category. Of course, this depends on whether the GPG public key from the organization that created the RPM file is known to your system. If it's not, then you will see an error.

You can import public keys from trusted online sources using the following command:

```
rpm --import ftp://mysite.com/publickey
```

Ordinarily, the key is imported directly from an online source, such as an FTP server, although it can also be from a text file on your own hard disk. But, once again, this file must be from a trusted source. If you intend to use a new online RPM file archive, for example, you should ensure you use the key offered on its server. You certainly cannot assume that a site you stumble across using a search engine will contain an authentic public key for another download source.

For various reasons, both GPG and checksum signing of RPM files are imperfect forms of security and can be overcome by crackers. One simple way of confirming any kind of installation file's integrity, not only RPM files, is to use a separate program to check its md5sum checksum figure. For example, you could download an installation file from a third-party source, and then check its md5sum against a list held on a server you can trust. Using md5sum is easy. Just type this:

```
md5sum filename
```

You should then compare the resulting figure to that contained in a list on an authentic server. These figures are usually contained in a text file called md5sums, or something similar. If the numbers are different, which is usually immediately apparent, this means that the file has been altered since the original checksum was created, and you should be suspicious.

Note that a different checksum doesn't necessarily mean a cracker has been at work. It might be that the file is simply corrupted, perhaps during download, for example. Often, simply downloading the file afresh solves the checksum problem.

Taking Care of Dependencies

If there are any problems with the installation of the program, the rpm command will let you know. The most common of these is the dreaded dependency failure, which occurs when additional software or libraries required by the program aren't present and therefore need to be installed, too.

For example, if you try to install the Epiphany web browser on the SUSE installation DVD, you receive the following error message:

```
error: Failed dependencies:
  mozilla = 1.6 is needed by epiphany-1.0.7-64
  libgtkembedmoz.so is needed by epiphany-1.0.7-64
```

The problem then becomes one of trying to track down the missing dependencies. In the case of Epiphany, the first one is easy enough to solve: you can list the directory specifying mozilla as a filter (using ls mozilla*) and see what comes up.

The best guess is that the main Mozilla program is what's needed. There's no rule for working this out; it just takes a little common sense. However, it's important to take note of the version number: 1.6. This is the lowest version of Mozilla that you can install in order to meet this particular dependency (version numbers later than that specified are usually okay, too).

The second dependency is more difficult to solve because its filename indicates that it's a library (it starts with lib and ends with an .so file extension). Library files are usually installed as part of a larger program or as part of a larger RPM containing many libraries. In most cases, it's very hard to find out if the RPM file in question contains the library file.

In such a situation, the quickest and easiest solution is to search the Web. For example, typing the library filename into the Google search box will bring up sites containing information about the library, as shown in Figure 29-7. By careful detective work examining and comparing the search results, you should be able to find out which RPM file on the DVD is likely to contain the library. If you do not get any joy after this, trying adding "RPM" to the search string as well.

Alternatively, if you have an archive of RPM files at your disposal, such as the SUSE installation DVD, you can query each of the RPM files in turn, looking at the files they contain, and searching for the library file. You can do this using the rpm command with the -q command option. The query command option is unusual because it has it *own* set of command options. Anything that appears after -q is considered a query option.

By default, -q queries installed RPM files (the main database). This is handy if you want to explore the list of installed programs (the -qa option will list *all* of the installed programs). To query an RPM file that's not installed, you need to add the -p command. Used together, the -qp options will merely tell you what program is contained within the specified RPM file—nothing more. You want a complete file listing, so add -l, and also -i, to return some additional information about the program contained in the file. Using all these command options together, plus specifying a wildcard so that all files are searched, and piping the command to less, you can create a scrollable list of files contained in every single RPM file in the archive:

```
rpm -qpli *.rpm |less
```

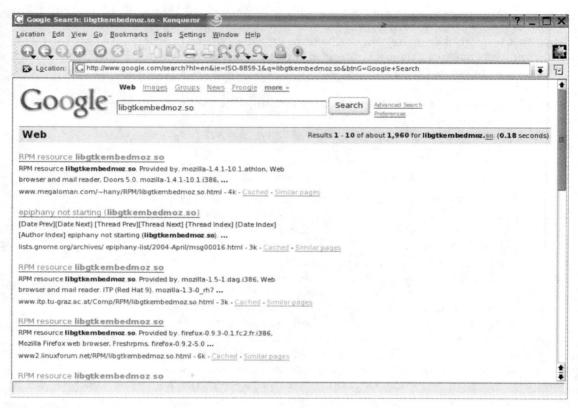

Figure 29-7. *When tracking down library dependencies, a good search engine like Google helps enormously.*

After this, you can use the search function within less. For this example, press the forward slash key, /, and type libgtkembedmoz.so to find the library file. However, the list of files will be *very* long, and you might need to wait a minute or two for the entire set of files to be queried and the results piped into less.

Once the file is located in the output, it's simply a matter of scrolling through the list of files to find the name of the RPM that owns it. In our example, it turns out that it is Mozilla itself that installs this particular system file, so all that is necessary is to install Mozilla to take care of both dependencies.

Using Advanced RPM Techniques

As well as querying files, there are other advanced ways of using the rpm command. More than one file can be specified for installation at the same time, for example. In order to install Epiphany, as in the example in the previous section, two separate RPM files need to be installed: Mozilla and Epiphany itself. Therefore, you can simply specify them on the same command line, like this:

```
rpm -Uvh mozilla-1.6-72.i586.rpm epiphany-1.0.7-64.i586.rpm
```

It doesn't matter in which order you list the RPMs. The rpm command is clever enough to put everything in order and install the packages in the right sequence.

Uninstalling an installed RPM file is just as easy as installing one. Simply specify the -e command option, like so:

```
rpm -e mozilla
```

In most cases, this is quick and simple. Note that there's no need to specify anything other than the main program name, unless there are a number of programs on the system with similar filenames. If this is the case, rpm will prompt you for more information. You can grep the output of rpm -qa to search for the exact package name.

Once again, when uninstalling RPM packages, you can specify more than one RPM file on the command line in order to overcome dependency problems. This is useful because removing a program is just as prone to dependency problems as installing programs.

As with most shell commands, rpm has a very long and interesting man page. This is well worth reading in order to get a complete understanding of how package management works.

Compiling from Source

Back in the old days of Unix, the *only* way to install software was from source code. This was because most people edited the source code themselves, or at least liked to have the option of doing so. Nowadays, innovations such as RPMs make life easier, but knowing how to compile a source file is a vital Linux skill to have. In some cases, it's your only option for installing a certain program.

Note For what it's worth, a program compiled on your own system will be faster than one compiled by a third-party for general users. However, whether this speed boost is noticeable is open for debate.

Before you can compile from source, you usually need two specific pieces of system software: the make program and the development (also referred to as devel) versions of any libraries you might need to run the application you want to install.

Note If you selected the C++ Compiler and Tools options during initial installation, you'll already have the make program.

Getting the Make Program and Devel Libraries

Getting the make program is best done via YaST2's software installation facility. Select K menu ➤ Control Center, click YaST Modules, click the Software icon, and then click Install and Remove Software. In the Filter drop-down list at the top of the screen, choose Selections. Then make sure there's a check in the C++ Compiler and Tools entry in the list on the left side of the screen, as shown in Figure 29-8. Then click the Accept button in the bottom right to install the software.

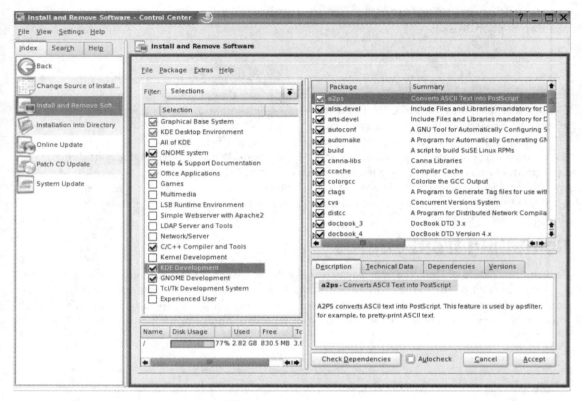

Figure 29-8. *To compile software, you'll need the C++ package set, as well as development versions of various software.*

The requirement of installing devel versions of libraries is a little more difficult to meet. For example, if you intend to compile from source a program that relies on components of KDE (or the QT libraries, which KDE itself relies on), you can select the KDE Development option in the YaST2 Install and Remove Software screen.

However, you won't really know which libraries a program installation routine requires until you see an error message pointing out they're not present! Generally speaking, however, selecting both the KDE and GNOME devel package options within YaST2 (as shown in Figure 29-8) is a good idea if you intend to compile any kind of Linux software from source, because it will invariably depend on one or the other.

Compiling and Installing a Program

Once you have the necessary system software, compiling a program is actually easier than you might think. In most cases, the programmer generates scripts that check your system and then creates a file specifically built to facilitate installation of the program on your system. In fact, in most cases, you can install a program by issuing three simple commands in sequence:

```
./configure
make
make install
```

In some cases, the programmer might also create a few brief text files outlining any specific options you might need to specify as command options with the `./configure` command, or anything else you should bear in mind. This information will most likely be included in text files named `README` and `INSTALL`.

As an example, we'll walk through installing an application from source. For demonstration purposes, I've chosen the KTag program, which is a prototype application designed to allow the easy editing of MP3 music artist and track information. At the time of writing, it's just reached version 0.5 and isn't yet included in the SUSE Linux default installation. The program's home page is integrated into the main KDE page at `www.kde.org`.

Decompressing the File

Once the program has downloaded, you end up with a file called `Ktag-0.5.tar.bz2`. You can see immediately that this is a tarball archive that has been compressed with `bzip2`, because it has a `.tar.bz2` file extension. Therefore, the first step is to decompress it with the following command:

```
tar -zxf Ktag-0.5.tar.bz2
```

I'll explain how the `tar` command works in the Chapter 32, which covers backup.

Checking the README and INSTALL Files

Decompressing the file creates a folder called `Ktag-0.5`. We switch into it and have a look around. In particular, we take a look at the `README` and `INSTALL` files to see if there's any specific advice. It turns out there isn't in this case, although some programs sometimes suggest you specify which operating system you're using as a command option when using the `./configure` command (keep in mind that the open-source nature of software used on Linux means it can also be installed on other versions of Unix, so this is often necessary).

Running configure

Because no special treatment is necessary, we press ahead with the first command, which can be run as an ordinary user:

```
./configure
```

This will quickly fill the console window with line after line of text as the `configure` script checks your system for compatibility, as shown in Figure 29-9. If it runs into a problem, such as a missing library file, you'll be told about it there and then. If such an error arises, you're back to the dependency problems, as described previously. You must then track down the specified dependencies. There's no need to install these from source. You can find and use an RPM file if that's most convenient.

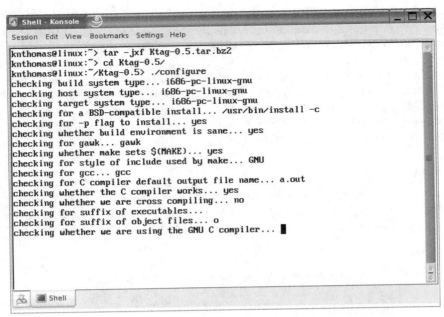

Figure 29-9. *The ./configure command will test your system for compatibility, so keep an eye on the output.*

If the configure script complains that it's missing a certain library file, you should install not only the library itself, but the additional version of the library marked devel. You can track down the devel file using YaST2, just like the standard version of the program.

Note Be aware that the configure script is very thorough and checks for components that the program you're trying to install might not even need. Because of this, you shouldn't worry if, as the text scrolls past, you see that various components are missing. Unless configure complains about it, it's not a problem.

If the configure script finds no problems, then you might not be informed of your good fortune. It will simply finish with a handful of lines mentioning that a make file has been created. This is what's needed for the next stage: compiling the program itself.

Compiling the Program

To compile the program, use the following command, again as an ordinary user:

```
make
```

Once again, the screen will rapidly fill with text, although this time there's no need to pay attention. This is merely the output of the compiler and doesn't mean much to anyone other than programmers. Depending on the complexity of the program and its size, this stage can take a long time to complete.

When it's finished, you once again won't be told much, unless something has gone wrong. Unless you're specifically informed of a failure, you should assume that everything has worked fine.

Installing the Program Files

The last command must be issued as root user because it copies the files to the various locations on the hard disk where they're going to reside:

```
su
<enter root password>
make install
```

This step should be finished relatively quickly and, again assuming that you don't receive an error message, you should find the program is installed and ready for use.

It's unlikely that compiling a program from source will undertake any user-friendly niceties such as creating a K menu entry. You'll need to do this by hand. To run the program, you can simply type its name from a shell prompt.

Summary

This chapter described how to install software under SUSE Linux. We've looked at how this differs from Windows software installation, and how the RPM package management system is designed to make life easier.

You learned how to use YaST2 to install software under the GUI, as well as both YaST and the rpm command to install software at the command-line prompt. Finally, we looked at how programs can be compiled from their source code, which is a fundamental process of all versions of Linux.

In the next chapter, we'll look at how the system of users under SUSE Linux can be administered.

CHAPTER 30

■ ■ ■

Managing Users

SUSE Linux was designed from the ground up to be a multiuser system. When it is deployed on huge mainframe computers, it's capable of serving hundreds, if not thousands, of users at the same time, provided there are enough terminal computers for them to log in. In a more domestic setting, such as when SUSE Linux is installed on a desktop PC, it usually means that more than one family member can have their very own account on the PC. Any files users create will be private, and users will also get their own desktop environment that is separate from that of the other users.

And even if you're the only person using your PC, you can still take advantage of SUSE Linux's multiuser capabilities. Consider creating user accounts for various aspects of your life—perhaps one for work and one for time spent browsing the Web. Each user account can be tailored toward each specific need.

In this chapter, you'll learn how to administer multiple user accounts.

Understanding User and Group Accounts

The concept of users and file ownership was explained in Chapter 15, but let's take a few minutes to recap and elaborate on some important points.

Each person who wishes to use SUSE Linux must have a user account. This will define what that user can and cannot do on the system, with specific reference to files. Because SUSE Linux is effectively one large file system, with even hardware devices seen as individual files (see Chapter 15), this means that user permissions lie at the heart of controlling the entire system. They can limit which user has access to which hardware and software, and therefore control access to various PC functions.

Each user also belongs to a group. Groups have the same style of permissions as individual users. Accessing a file can be denied to a user, depending on that person's group membership.

Note As in real life, a group can have many members and can be based around various interests. In a business environment, this might mean that a group is created for members of the accounting department, for example, or for the human resources department. By changing the permissions on files created by the group members, each group can have files only that group's members can access (although, as always, the root user can access all files).

On a default SUSE Linux system with just a handful of users, the group concept might seem somewhat redundant. However, the concept of groups is fundamental to the way SUSE Linux works and cannot be avoided. Even if you don't make use of groups, SUSE Linux still requires your user account user to be part of one.

In addition to actual human users, the SUSE Linux system has its own set of user and group accounts. Various programs that access hardware resources or particular sets of files normally use these. Setting up system users and groups in this way makes the system more secure and easier to administer.

The root user has power over the entire system. Root can examine any file and configure any piece of hardware. Root also belongs to its own unique group, also called root.

Because of its power, the root user can cause a lot of accidental damage, so it's rare for anyone to log in as root. Instead, you can switch to root user temporarily from an ordinary user account using the su command.

Although we talk of user and group names, these are only used for the end user's benefit. SUSE Linux uses a numerical system to identify users and groups. These are referred to as user IDs (UIDs) and group IDs (GIDs), respectively.

For various reasons, under SUSE Linux, all the GID and UID numbers under 1000 are reserved for the system to use. This means that the first non-root user created on a system during installation will probably be given a UID of 1000. In addition, any new groups created after installation are numbered from 1000 upwards, although the default group that standard users are added to by default has a GID of 100.

Note UID and GID information isn't important during everyday use, and most commands used to administer users and file permissions understand the human-readable usernames. However, knowing UIDs and GUIDs can prove useful when you're undertaking more complicated system administration.

Creating New Users and Groups

The easiest and quickest way of adding a new user or group is to use YaST2. Of course, you can also perform these tasks through the command line, as we explain later in this chapter.

Adding and Deleting Users and Groups with YaST2

Here are the basic steps for using YaST2 to add a new user:

1. Select K menu ➤ Control Center, click the YaST2 Modules icon, click Security and Users, and then click Edit and Create Users.

2. This requires root privileges, so click the Administrator Mode button and enter your root password.

3. You see a list of current ordinary (nonroot or system) users. To add a new user, click the relevant button at the bottom left of the screen.

4. You see a screen virtually identical to that presented during initial installation, as shown in Figure 30-1. Enter the full name of the new user (for your own reference), the new username, and the password.

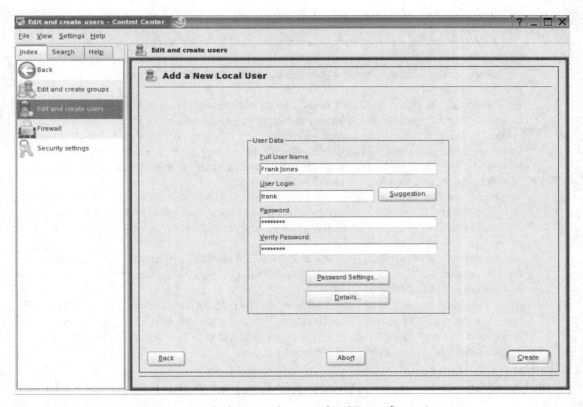

Figure 30-1. *Creating new users is easily done via the central YaST2 configuration program.*

5. If you want to set a password expiration time, click the Password Settings button. This can be useful if you want to create a user account that is valid for a limited period.

■Note Unlike under Windows NT, when a user account's password expires in SUSE Linux, the user won't then be prompted to enter a new password. The account will simply be disabled, at least until the root user steps in to reset the password. Also, the user won't be able to overcome the expiration by changing her password manually in advance. The expiration date applies to any password on the account.

---

6. If you want to manually enter a UID number, or adjust the groups to which the user belongs, click the Details button. As discussed earlier, by default, the user will belong to a handful of system groups that will give her access to particular hardware resources. You can see a list of these here. However, it's not advisable to change any default group memberships, because the user account could be seriously crippled when it comes to running programs on the system.

7. Click the Create button.

8. You're returned to the username list. Click the Finish button to confirm the changes.

When you're finished, the new user will be set up and will have her own directory within the /home/ directory.

Adding a new group is similarly easy. Simply click Edit and Create Groups on the left side of the YaST2 program window. You can enter a group name and add members from the list of current users. You can also manually specify a GID if you wish. Perhaps surprisingly, a group can also have a password. This comes into play when a user uses the newgrp command to temporarily switch group membership. If he tries to switch to a group that is password-protected, he will be prompted for the password first.

If you want to edit any of the user or group information, from the main Edit and Create Users or Edit and Create Groups screen, select the user or group you are interested in, and then click the Edit button. You can then change any of the details you previously entered. Click Next to return to the main administration screen.

To delete a user account, from the main Edit and Create Users screen, select the user you want to remove, and then click the Delete button. You'll be asked to confirm that you really want to go through with the deletion.

If you want to delete a group, you'll first need to remove all the members from the group. From the main Edit and Create Groups screen, select the group, click Edit, and uncheck all the boxes next to the users in the list. Then you can return to the main Edit and Create Groups screen, select the group, and click the Delete button.

Adding and Deleting Users and Groups at the Command Line

Creating new users at the command-line shell is easily done using the useradd command. This command can be run only by root. When switching to the root user, use the following command in order to adopt the root user's $PATH details and thereby access root-only commands:

```
su -
```

The command to add a user is normally used in the following way:

```
useradd -m <username>
```

The -m command option tells the command to create a home directory for the user (this is created from a template, so comes ready-made with SUSE-specific folders, configuration files, and so on). Used on its own, useradd merely updates system files with the new user's details and nothing else. There are several other useful command options, which can be discovered by a quick browse of the command's man page.

Creating a new user this way will automatically add him to the Users group—the default group that most ordinary users are added to under SUSE Linux. In addition, the command uses a range of skeleton settings that are applied to the account. In this way, the user will be added to the standard system groups necessary to access various pieces of hardware, and vital hidden system files for various pieces of software will be installed in his home directory, ready for use.

▓**Caution** Creating a new user won't automatically apply a password to the account. Anyone will be able to log in with the username by leaving the password field blank. Because of this, the first thing you should do is to use the `passwd` command to assign a password to the new account, as we discuss in a minute.

Perhaps unsurprisingly, deleting a user can be achieved with the `userdel` command. Used on its own, this sweeps the system files, removing any mention of the user. However, the command is normally used with the `-rf` command options. These cause the user's home directory to be removed, too, along with any files it might contain. The `-f` option means that the command won't stop with an error if it comes across any files in the home directory that are not owned by the user. Because of this, `userdel` is a powerful command and should be used with care!

Groups can be added using the `groupadd` command in much the same way as using the `useradd` command. The `-p` option can be added to set a password for the new group. The `groupdel` command removes the group.

Changing Passwords

On a default SUSE Linux installation, ordinary users are able to change their passwords at the shell. In fact, under SUSE Linux 9.1, as supplied with this book, using shell commands is the *only* way users can change their password, because there's no GUI tool that will do this job.

The command to change the user's password is simple:

```
passwd
```

The user will be asked to confirm his current password, and then to enter the new password twice, to confirm that it's been typed correctly.

There are various rules imposed on the creation of new passwords. For example, passwords over eight characters won't be accepted, and passwords that are too short also won't be accepted. If the user breaks any of these rules, she will be told at the command prompt and allowed to try again, as shown in Figure 30-2. Up to three attempts can be made before the program will quit.

The root user can use the `passwd` command to change anyone's password, as well as various other aspects relating to the user's login. All that's needed is to specify the user whose password is to be changed:

```
passwd frank
```

In this case, you won't be asked to enter the old password, because the user himself might have changed it. Instead, you'll simply be asked to enter the new password.

Just as when a regular user changes a password, the root user will see warnings if a password is too long, too short, or violates any of the other rules. However, the root user can override these warnings by simply retyping the password and thereby forcing it through.

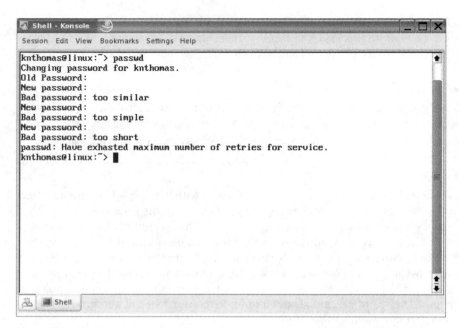

Figure 30-2. *Ordinary users can change their own passwords, but there are rules on size and style.*

A number of command options can be specified along with the `passwd` command when it is run as root user. For example, the `-l` option will lock the account so that it can't be accessed (the `-u` option will unlock it). The `-e` option will force the specified user to change his/her password the next time he logs in. He will be prompted to enter his old password and then told to choose a new one.

Sharing Root Powers via sudo

You may be wondering if it's always necessary to switch to root user in order to perform system maintenance. Although it's easy to type `su` to temporarily switch to root, it's also sometimes easy to forget that you're running as root user. Because of this, it can become very easy to make devastating mistakes.

For this reason, the `sudo` command was invented. Inserted before a command, this gives the user one-time root powers for that command only. When the command has finished running, the user returns to being an ordinary user. Technically speaking, the `sudo` command lets one user run a command as *any* other user. However, in most cases, it is used to temporarily gain root powers. (For more information, see the `sudo` man page.)

By default, under SUSE Linux, the `sudo` command works by asking for the root password. For example, typing the following:

```
sudo vi /etc/fstab
```

will cause a password prompt to appear. Once the root password has been entered, vi will run as if it were started by root.

On some other Linux systems, sudo is used in a different way, which trades system security for convenience. In such a case, sudo can be used to adopt root powers without the user needing to know the root password. Instead, the user's password is entered. This might seem like casting security concerns to the wind, and it's certainly something that should be adopted only on a system you know is secure, such as one that only you access or for which you know and trust the other users.

If you want to allow an ordinary user to use the sudo command without entering the root password, you must edit the /etc/sudoers file (as the root user). A special command has been created for this purpose: visudo. This loads the sudoers file into vi and checks that anything added to the file is correct. After the sudoers file is open, move the cursor down to the section headed User Alias Command, and enter something similar to the following (substituting the name of the user for <username>):

```
<username> ALL=(ALL) ALL
```

Then move down to the lines underneath the Defaults Specification section and type a hash before the lines beginning with Defaults targetpw and %users ALL=. Your file should look similar to Figure 30-3. Then save the file and exit vi.

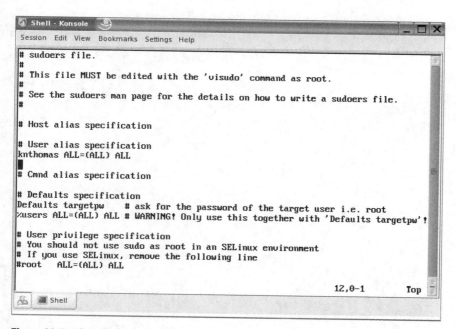

Figure 30-3. *The sudo command can give ordinary users root powers, but it must first be set up correctly.*

Summary

In this chapter, we looked at the principles behind user and group accounts under SUSE Linux. We've examined how user and group accounts can be created, edited, and deleted using the GUI, as well as the command-line prompt. We also looked at how passwords can be manipulated both by the root user and by the individual users themselves.

Finally, you learned how the sudo command can be used to run root-only programs, allowing users to avoid needing to switch to root user frequently.

In the next chapter, we'll look at how the system can be optimized. You'll also learn about several interesting and important system tools.

## CHAPTER 31

Optimizing Your System

There's always some extra performance to be squeezed out of a computer, regardless of whether it's old or new. Because SUSE Linux offers a high degree of control over your hardware and software setup, it's ideal for this purpose.

SUSE Linux is unique among Linux distributions in that, out of the box, it's already highly optimized. However, there are still many opportunities to generally speed things up and, in particular, reduce delays. While you shouldn't expect miracles from the techniques outlined in this chapter, they do allow a certain degree of system tuning, which can bring dividends, particularly on older systems.

Speeding Up Booting

Let's take a look at what happens when a SUSE Linux-equipped PC boots. First of all, the GRUB boot loader appears. This offers you a choice of booting into SUSE Linux, booting from a floppy disk, or booting into safe mode. If you dual-boot with Windows, this will also be listed among the options. Usually, there's a ten-second delay until the default choice is automatically selected, which will be to boot into SUSE Linux (on an unmodified system).

Immediately after this, the Linux kernel is booted. This takes around ten seconds, although it may take more or less time, depending on your system setup.

After this, the `init` script is started. This takes care of essential system components, such as making sure the hard disk partitions are mounted and available so that data can be loaded from disk.

When this has completed, the run-level `init` scripts are started. These start various background processes and programs that make SUSE Linux what it is. For example, the scripts start up various Internet services, which make it possible for you to go online. If run level 5 is in operation, the GUI is started up. The BASH shell is also loaded into memory, so that you're able to enter commands.

Once the GUI has started, it, too, has its own set of initiation processes. It needs to start its own set of programs, such as system tray applets, which provide handy functions like on-screen volume control. Once all that has finished, you can use the computer!

Because so much must take place for your system to come to life, booting SUSE Linux can take up to a minute or two, depending on your PC configuration. There's certainly some time that can be shaved from this.

Reducing the Boot Menu Delay

The first optimization area to look at is the boot menu delay. This can be reduced to just a few seconds, or even eradicated completely. As with all kinds of configuration within SUSE Linux, this is done via the YaST2 configuration program, as follows:

1. Select K menu ➤ Control Center, click the YaST2 Modules icon on the left, click the System icon, and then click Boot Loader Configuration.

2. This affects the entire system, so click the Administrator Mode button and enter your root password.

3. YaST2 displays a list of values that can be edited. The one that controls the length of time the boot menu appears is called Timeout. Double-click it and enter a lower value. If you enter a value of zero, as shown in Figure 31-1, the boot menu won't appear at all, although three seconds is probably long enough to give you the chance to make an alternative decision at boot time.

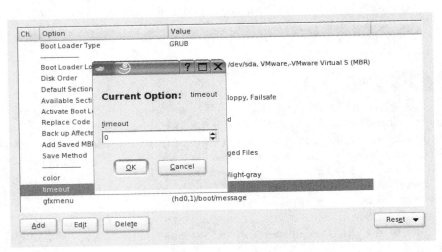

Figure 31-1. *Reducing the boot menu delay can speed up the time taken to start your system.*

4. Click OK to save your new setting.

Optimizing Run-Level Services

Adjusting the boot menu delay will shorten the boot time somewhat, but you can achieve a more dramatic change by editing which run-level services start. These are the programs that run in the background of your computer to provide the various essential bits and pieces you need for day-to-day use. Because SUSE Linux is designed to meet a diverse selection of needs, it starts up many run-level services, some of which you can safely remove. By trimming the run-level boot procedure in this way, you can speed things up, as well as leave your PC with more memory available.

Tip You can view the run-level boot process by pressing the F2 key when the system is booting up (when the SUSE logo and progress bar usually appear).

Once again, you can use YaST2 to edit the run-level services. Select K menu ➤ Control Center, click the YaST2 Modules icon on the left, click the System icon, and then click Runlevel Editor. YaST2 will display a list of all the run-level programs available on the system, as shown in Figure 31-2. Alongside each is a column showing if it's enabled in the current run level. There's also a brief description of what each service does, although some of these are complex and confusing. Some services have extra help messages that will appear beneath the list. Simply click the service to see if there's any more information available.

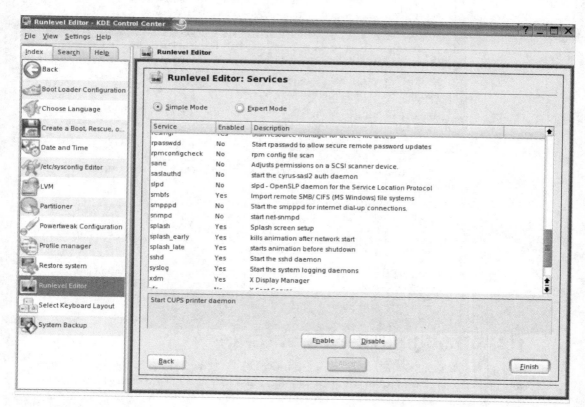

Figure 31-2. *Removing services makes for a speedier bootup, but remove only those that you're sure you can do without!*

Some run-level services are vital to the correct operation of SUSE Linux, so you should be very conservative in your choice of which services to remove. Make sure you won't need a service before getting rid of it. For example, if you don't use a printer on your PC, you can safely remove services related to printing. If you don't intend to use SSH to connect to other machines across the Internet, you can also remove the service relating to the SSHD program: the SSH daemon. If you don't access Windows file shares or printers across a network, you can remove all services relating to this.

Pruning services requires common sense and a gentle touch. If you're in doubt as to what a service does, leave things be! For guidance on services that can be safely removed, see Table 31-1.

Table 31-1. *Services That Can Be Safely Disabled*

Service	Notes
autofs	Automatically mounts file systems. This can be disabled if this functionality is not desired, although CD-ROMs, floppies, and other removable storage will then need to be mounted manually.
cups	Controls the printing service. If you don't intend to print, whether to a local printer or across a network, this service can be shut down.
fbset	Controls the frame buffer service that displays the colorful SUSE wallpaper during the boot process. This can safely be disabled if you can live without the decoration.
isdn	Used to configure and activate ISDN telephony devices. This can be deactivated if you're not using ISDN.
nfsboot	Used when booting from an NFS network mount. This can be disabled on the majority of desktop computers.
postfix	Starts the postfix mailer service. If you use an ISP or corporate SMTP mail server, this can be disabled, although you should first check Kmail's configuration to make sure its SMTP section isn't set up to use Sendmail or localhost.
smbfs	Allows the mounting of Windows/Samba (SMB) file or printer shares. This can be disabled if you never connect to such a network share.
splash	Makes the splash screen appear while booting. This can be safely disabled, along with splash_early and splash_late.
sshd	Starts the SSH daemon, which allows remote connections (see Chapter 34). This can be disabled if you never intend to connect to your PC remotely.

Optimizing Hard Disk Settings

The hard disk is one of the key elements in the modern PC. Because most of your PC's data must travel to and from it, speeding up your hard disk means that your entire PC will be faster.

SUSE Linux provides a powerful command-line tool that you can use to control every aspect of your hard disk: hdparm. This is a power-user's tool. Not only must you switch to root to use it, but you also must be careful not to mistype the commands. All changes are made instantly, so if you make a mistake, your system may crash, or at least suffer from serious problems. There's even the risk of data loss, although this is minimized by making sure that you have no other programs running at the same time you run hdparm.

The good news is that changes made via hdparm will last for only the current session, so there's no risk of permanent damage (any changes that are beneficial can be made permanent later).

In the context of optimization, hdparm lets you both benchmark the disk, as well as change various technical settings, such as the DMA access mode. These adjustments can bring speed boosts.

■**Note** The changes described here are designed to work with IDE hard disks only. This is the standard type of hard disk used in the majority of desktop PCs. If your computer is one of the small minority that uses SCSI hard disks, you should skip this section, because it does not apply to SCSI.

Benchmarking Your Hard Disk

Because experimenting with hdparm can cause crashes, and because its benchmarking feature needs almost exclusive access to the hard disk, hdparm is best run with as few as possible additional programs up and running. Therefore, first switching to run level 3 so that the GUI is deactivated is a good idea. Open a command-line shell prompt, switch to root, and type the following:

```
init 3
```

You'll then need to log in again, so do so (as an ordinary user). Once logged in, switch to root user again.

■**Note** Technically speaking, switching to run level 1 is an even better idea, because this will deactivate all unnecessary services. Run level 1 is akin to the Windows Safe Mode, except without the GUI. However, you want realistic benchmark results to test the changes you make via hdparm, and it's debatable whether the restricted confines of run level 1 will provide this.

Let's start by benchmarking your hard disk to see its performance based on the current settings. Type the following (assuming SUSE Linux is installed on the first hard disk in your system; if it's on the second hard disk, change /dev/hda to /dev/hdb):

```
hdparm -tT /dev/hda
```

This will benchmark your disk in two ways. The first tests the PC's memory throughput, measuring the data rate of the memory, CPU, and cache. The second actually tests the disk's data rate. The second test affects the outcome of the first, which is why the two are used together. Between them, these two methods of benchmarking present the standard way your disk is used on a day-to-day basis. Figure 31-3 shows an example of running these tests.

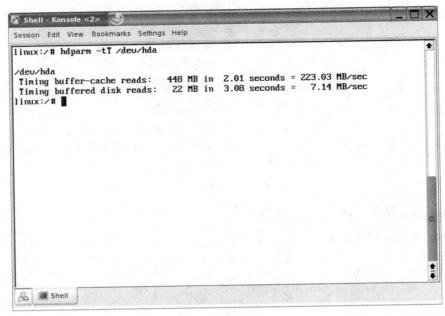

Figure 31-3. *Benchmarking your hard disk will let you see the results of any tweaks you make later.*

Make a note of the figures so that you can compare them to the results of these tests after you change hard disk settings.

Changing Hard Disk Settings

You can use hdparm to view your current hard disk settings by entering the following at the command prompt:

```
hdparm /dev/hda
```

On my test PC, these are the results I got:

```
/dev/hda:
 multcount    = 16 (on)
 IO_support   =  1 (32-bit)
 unmaskirq    =  1 (on)
 using_dma    =  1 (on)
 keepsettings =  0 (off)
 readonly     =  0 (off)
 readahead    = 256 (on)
 geometry     = 65535/16/63, sectors = 160086528, start = 0
```

Let's take a look at what these settings mean.

The Multcount Setting

The first, multcount, refers to how many sectors can be read from the hard disk at any one time. The theory is that the highest possible value here is best. Most modern hard drives support a value of 16, but some drives may support 32. You can find out by issuing the following command:

```
hdparm -i /dev/hda
```

Look in the line headed BuffType and at the value MultSect. On my test PC, the value is 16.

Ironically, although higher values are thought best, sometimes a lower value can speed up hard disk access. You can experiment with the multcount setting on your hard disk by using the -m hdparm command option:

```
hdparm -m8 /dev/hda
```

You can then follow this by another benchmark to see if there is an improvement:

```
hdparm -tT /dev/hda
```

On my test PC, a lower value does indeed bring dividends. With a multcount value of 16, the buffer-cache read value was 606 MB/sec. With a value of 8, it rises to 633 MB/sec!

The IO Support Setting

The IO_support line refers to the input/output (I/O) mode used by the hard disk controller. There are four possible settings: 0, to disable 32-bit support; 1 to enable 32-bit support; and 3 to enable 32-bit support with a special sync signal.

You can change the IO_support setting with the -c hdparm command option:

```
hdparm -m8 -c3 /dev/hda
```

Notice that this includes the previous multcount change. This is because testing a tweak in isolation could produce erroneous results. Any changes you make and intend to keep must be used alongside tweaks you've previously used.

After a benchmark to test the changes, my test PC shows that this tweak slows down disk access, although your PC might be different.

The Unmaskirq Setting

The third setting, umaskirq, allows SUSE Linux to attend to other tasks while waiting for your hard disk to return data. This won't affect hard disk performance very much, and generally it's a good idea for the health of your system to have it turned on, as it is by default.

The Using_dma Setting

The fourth setting refers to whether Direct Memory Access (DMA) is in use. Hard disks are sold on the basis of their DMA modes, such as UltraDMA Burst 2 and the like. DMA is considered an indicator as to the speed of a hard disk, but the truth is that, like any specification, it is only a guide.

You can tweak the DMA mode using a variety of options. The first, and most necessary, is the -d1 option, which actually activates DMA. After this, you can use the -X command option. On most modern PCs, this isn't necessary because the computer's BIOS defaults to the fastest DMA mode. However, specifying that DMA should be used *is* necessary.

Here's a chain of hdparm commands that, on my test PC, produced a marked improvement in hard disk access speed:

```
hdparm -d1 -m8 /dev/hda
```

All of the command options for hdparm are explained succinctly in its man page, and this is well worth reading if you would like to learn more.

Other Settings

The last three settings, above the summary of the geometry and sector information of the disk, are those you shouldn't change. The readahead setting controls how many hard disk blocks are loaded in advance. It doesn't affect the performance of modern IDE-based hard disks, because the drive electronics contain buffers that perform this task themselves.

The keepsettings setting refers to the ability of the drive to remember hdparm settings over a reboot. The readonly setting sets whether or not the hard disk is read-only (so that no data can be written to it). Changes to these settings are not advisable!

Making Your Disk Optimizations Permanent

When the PC is rebooted, any changes you've made with hdparm are lost. To make this command run during bootup, you can create a custom service and add it to the current run level. This sounds more complicated than it actually is.

The first thing to do is enter the changes into a simple text file. For example, you could use vi. Simply type the command (for example, hdparm -d1 -m8 /dev/hda) in the editor window, and then save the file with a name along the lines of disk_optimize. (Make sure you add a carriage return after the line when entering it in vi.)

The next step is to make the text file an executable file, which can be done with the following command:

```
chmod a+x disk_optimize
```

This effectively turns the file into a run-level script.

The next step is to save the file with all the other run-level scripts in the /etc/init.d/ folder:

```
cp disk_optimize /etc/init.d/
```

Finally, the script must be symbolically linked to the current run level, using the following command:

```
ln -s /etc/init.d/disk_optimize /etc/init.d/rc5.d/S99disk_optimize
```

This also changes the filename of the symbolically linked file to tell SUSE Linux when it should be run during bootup. A value of S99 means it will be run at the very end of the boot procedure. Any hard disk performance tweaking must take place as near as possible to the end of booting, because the changes it makes can negatively affect the startup of other services.

Prelinking

As we discussed in Chapter 29, a lot of SUSE Linux software relies on other pieces of code to work. These are sometimes referred to as *libraries*, which is a good indicator as to their purpose: to provide functions that programs can check in and out whenever they need them, as if they were borrowing books from a library.

Whenever a program starts, it must look for these other libraries and load them into memory so they're ready for use. This can take some time, particularly on larger and more complicated programs. Because of this, the concept of *prelinking* was invented. By a series of complicated tricks, the prelink program makes each bit of software you might run aware of the libraries it needs, so that memory can be better allocated.

Prelinking claims to boost program startup times by up to 50% or more, but the problem is that it's a hack—a programming trick designed to make your system work in a nonstandard way. Because of this, some programs are incompatible with prelinking. In fact, some might simply refuse to work unless prelinking is deactivated. At the time of writing, such programs are in the minority. However, keep in mind that prelinking can be easily reversed if necessary. Alternatively, you might want to weigh whether it's actually worth setting up prelinking in the first place.

If you decide to go ahead, you'll need to install the relevant software from the SUSE Linux installation DVD, so insert that in your computer drive first. Select K menu ➤ Control Center, click YaST2 Modules, click the Software icon, and then click Install and Remove Software. In the Search box, type prelink, as shown in Figure 31-4. In the list of results on the right, put a tick into the Prelinking box. Then click Accept to install the software.

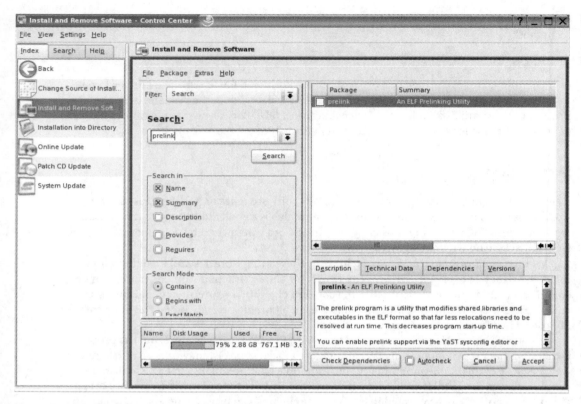

Figure 31-4. *The prelink program is able to shorten the time taken to start your applications.*

Once the software is installed, activating the prelinking function is easy.

1. Open a Konsole window (K menu ➤ System ➤ Terminal ➤ Konsole) and switch to root user (type su).

2. Navigate to the /etc/sysconfig/ directory and open the prelink file in a text editor.

3. Change the line that reads:

   USE_PRELINK="no"

   to

   USE_PRELINK="yes"

4. Run the SuSEconfig program (open a Konsole window and type SuSEconfig) to ensure system configuration files are up-to-date, including those that have been added relating to prelinking.

5. Issue the `prelink` command itself:

```
prelink -a
```

The `-a` command option is used with `prelink` to ensure all binary files are prelinked (according to the `/etc/prelink.conf` file, that is, which includes lists of notable exceptions). Prelinking can take some time to work through your system, and you might see some error messages. It's normally safe to ignore these.

Prelinking can also work on individual files if you specify a path:

```
prelink /usr/bin/cdrecord
```

This example will prelink just the `cdrecord` program.

Using the command on individual files can prove useful if you run into trouble after performing a prelinking sweep of your system, because you can use the `-u` command option to undo any prelinking:

```
prelink -u /usr/bin/cdrecord
```

Optimizing the Kernel

The kernel is central to SUSE Linux. In many ways, it *is* Linux. Most of the other software that composes the operating system can (and does) run just as well on any other version of Unix. The kernel is what makes Linux truly unique.

The Linux kernel handles all of the system's hardware I/O and provides a way of managing various aspects of your software setup. Because of this, optimizing it can bring performance dividends, although, as with other tweaks, the measure of the benefits depends on the nature of your system.

Optimizing the kernel is done by compiling your own kernel: taking the source code, adding in (or removing) the options you don't want or need, and then compiling the source code into a binary file. This usually has the effect of making the kernel smaller, freeing more memory, and also reducing the amount of clutter on your hard disk. In addition, some speed boosts come from choosing options specific to your system, such as matching the CPU that is in use.

As you might expect, compiling your own kernel requires significant knowledge of the way the kernel works and shouldn't be undertaken by beginners. There are a great many caveats and "gotchas." However, perhaps surprisingly, the actual task of compiling a new kernel is elementary and usually involves inputting a few commands.

I won't explain each of the configuration options involved in creating your own kernel. It's not an exaggeration to say that explaining such things could easily fill an entire book on its own. However, I will describe how to make simple changes that can improve the kernel's performance.

▪**Caution** Compiling your own kernel can be productive and educational, but be aware that it's not how SUSE Linux is designed to work. SUSE anticipates that you will use its precompiled kernel. This means that when you perform an update across the Internet, your homemade kernel will probably get replaced with a ready-made one, and you'll need to download the new sources and compile once again from scratch.

Downloading and Installing the Kernel Source Code

To compile your own kernel, you need to download the kernel source code. As with most components of SUSE Linux, this comes in a prepackaged RPM format and can usually be downloaded from the SUSE FTP site. You should avoid the temptation to download a kernel from the official Linux kernel site, www.kernel.org. The SUSE packaged version of the kernel has been tailored to run on your system, and it's therefore the best choice, even if it might lag a few version numbers behind the latest "official" release.

The first step is to find out the exact version number of the kernel currently in use so you can find the kernel source code RPM to match. Issue the following command at the command-line shell, when logged in as root:

```
cat /proc/version
```

On my test SUSE Linux system, which had been updated online since it was first installed, the kernel version number was 2.6.5-7.108-default.

You should download and install a matching source file in order to match the other system components and keep up with the security improvements in the latest release.

The source kernel can be downloaded directly from the SUSE FTP update site:

```
ftp://ftp.suse.com/pub/suse/i386/update/9.1/rpm/i586/
```

The source file will be named along the lines of kernel-source and will have the standard .rpm filename extension. Don't download files that have an .srpm extension, because they're designed for other uses. The RPM necessary for my test system was kernel-source-2.6.5-7.108.i586.rpm.

After you download the RPM, install it as the root user at the command-line shell, as shown in Figure 31-5:

```
rpm –Uvh kernel-source-2.6.5-7.108.i586.rpm
```

▪**Note** The Linux kernel is constantly being improved, and each major release is given a new version number. SUSE Linux 9.1, as supplied with this book, was one of the first Linux distros to incorporate version 2.6 of the kernel. Prior to this, most distros used version 2.4. The changes between the two are multiple, but are mostly hidden and not something you need to be concerned with. However, you should be aware that in the steps here, you're effectively compiling a 2.6 kernel. A 2.4 kernel will present compatibility issues with SUSE Linux 9.1. You can discover your kernel version by opening a Konsole window and typing uname -r.

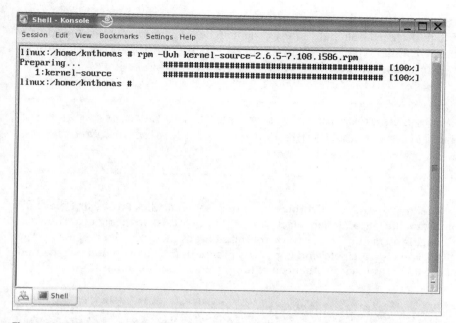

Figure 31-5. *By downloading and installing the kernel source, you can build your own optimized kernel.*

Configuring the Kernel

Ordinarily, you would now run the kernel configuration program and work your way through the hundreds of settings. However, SUSE kindly provides a ready-made configuration file that you can import and simply tweak in places. This is based on the configuration file used to create the ready-made binary kernels available from the main SUSE site. It's located in the /proc folder and is a compressed file called config.gz. You can copy it to the relevant folder, as well as base your configuration on it, by typing the following as root user:

```
zcat /proc/config.gz > /usr/src/linux/.config
cd /usr/src/linux
make oldconfig
```

After this, you can run the graphical configuration program, named xconfig (there are other GUI configuration programs, but xconfig is the most established and easiest to use). However, first you'll need to switch back to an ordinary user and issue the following command, which gives the root user permission to run programs via the GUI:

```
xhost +
```

Then switch back to root user and, making sure you're in the /usr/src/linux directory, issue the following command:

```
make xconfig
```

This will start the basic but functional graphical configuration program. On the left is a tree view of the settings that can be altered. At the top right of the program window are the options that can be changed, while helpful messages will appear at the bottom right. These should give you guidance in relatively plain English as to what each option does.

■**Tip** There are many guides to configuring the Linux kernel available on the Internet, including a very good one written by The Linux Documentation Project (TLDP). The guide is called *The Kernel Rebuild Guide* and can be found at `www.digitalhermit.com/linux/Kernel-Build-HOWTO.html`.

One option definitely worth configuring is the processor type. Click Processor Type and Features in the list on the left, and then select your CPU from the list on the right, as shown in Figure 31-6. Changing this setting will let the kernel take full advantage of your processor. (The ready-made SUSE kernels anticipate working on any processor from a Pentium upwards, and are thus unable to take advantage of architecture improvements in later chips.)

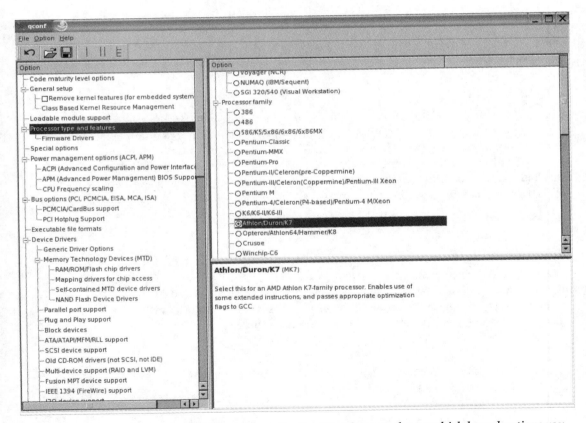

Figure 31-6. *SUSE provides a graphical configuration tool that lets you choose which kernel options you want to include.*

Feel free to look through the other options available in the kernel configuration list on the left. A tick in the option box indicates that the configuration choice will be compiled into the kernel program, which is to say it will be included in part of the large kernel file. A circle blob in the option box indicates that the function will be compiled as a *module*—a separate piece of code that is loaded only when needed. Because the default SUSE configuration file is designed to create a kernel that nearly every type of system can use, a lot of the options will be compiled as modules. There's no harm in this, apart from the fact that each module takes up some disk space.

If you're sure you won't need a particular function, you can remove the tick and/or blob from the option box. For example, in the section relating to network cards, you can do away with most choices if you either don't have a network card or if you know the make and model of the one in your machine. Don't forget to read the helpful guidance at the bottom right. This will tell you if some seemingly unnecessary options are actually vital for the correct operation of the kernel.

If you're not sure if something needs to be compiled into the kernel, consider including it as a module. When the kernel is up and running, modules are loaded and unloaded automatically by the kernel, without the user having to do anything, so this is a safe choice.

Once you're finished, select File ➤ Save, and then quit the program. After this, it's time to build your kernel.

RESCUING YOUR SYSTEM

Compiling a kernel from scratch is something that only an experienced user should undertake. Although the process is essentially simple, there are many factors that need to be kept in mind, and neglecting even the smallest detail can result in a system that is unable to boot.

If you cannot boot your system, you can reinstall one of the preconfigured SUSE kernels. Boot from the SUSE installation DVD and, on the boot menu, select Rescue System. After choosing your keyboard, a login prompt will appear. Enter root as the user (no password is necessary). You should then find yourself logged in to a SUSE Linux system.

Although you might appear to have an entire file system at your fingertips, you're actually accessing a RAM disk that is held in memory. Therefore, the next step is to create a mount directory and mount the SUSE Linux file system on your hard disk (the rescue system works in a RAM disk, so these changes aren't written to an actual hard disk):

```
mkdir SUSE
mount /dev/hda1 SUSE
```

This assumes that your SUSE Linux partition is the first on the disk (hda1). If it's the second or third, then you should substitute hda2 or hda3 as appropriate (you can view your hard disk partition list by typing fdisk -l). Then type the following command, which will make the SUSE folder the root of the file system. This will make it seem as if you have booted into the SUSE partition.

```
chroot SUSE
```

The last step is to restore a previous version of the kernel. If you've updated your system since installing SUSE Linux, you'll probably find an updated kernel in the /var/lib/YaST2/you/mnt/i386/update/9.1/rpm/ i586/ directory.

Continued

> To restore the kernel, a strange maneuver is necessary: the kernel must be uninstalled so that it can be rein-stalled. This is done with the following commands:
>
> ```
> rpm -e kernel-default
> rpm -Uvh <kernel filename>.rpm
> ```

Building and Installing the Kernel

Building the kernel involves issuing the following commands in sequence, waiting for each to complete before the next is issued:

```
make clean
make bzImage
make modules
```

This will take some time to work through, depending on the capabilities of your system. The command-line shell window will also fill with output, but there's no need to worry about this.

Once the commands have finished, the new kernel must be installed. The following commands, issued as root, will do the trick:

```
cp /boot/vmlinuz /boot/vmlinuz.old
cp /boot/initrd /boot/initrd.old
cp /usr/src/linux/arch/i386/boot/bzImage /boot/vmlinuz
cp /usr/src/linux/System.map /boot/
```

In addition, the kernel modules need to be installed, with the following command:

```
make modules_install
```

Also, you should make a new boot RAM disk with the following command:

```
mk_initrd
```

The boot RAM disk is necessary to load essential system drivers to help the kernel start.

Configuring the Boot Loader Menu

After this, you should configure the GRUB boot loader menu. An entry needs to be added for the old kernel. Why for the old kernel? Well, if the new kernel doesn't work for whatever reason, then having the old one as a backup will prove invaluable. It will let you boot your system and effect repairs, such as having another attempt at compiling a kernel!

Note The boot menu will already be configured to use your new kernel, because when you copied the files, you used the standard filenames for kernels under SUSE Linux. This means that the existing boot menu entry should be enough to boot the new kernel.

To add an entry for the old kernel, start YaST2 and select System, then Boot Loader Configuration. Then type the following beneath the first entry in the list (this assumes that the SUSE Linux partition is the first on your hard disk; if you dual-boot with Windows, it will most likely be the second, so you should replace /dev/hda1 with /dev/hda2):

```
title Old Linux kernel
    kernel (hd0,1)/boot/vmlinuz.old root=/dev/hda1
    initrd (hd0,1)/boot/initrd.old
```

Figure 31-7 shows this addition.

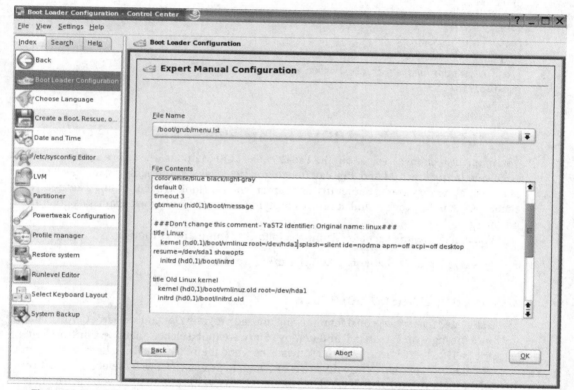

Figure 31-7. *Adding a boot menu entry for your old kernel will let you boot back into SUSE Linux if your new kernel doesn't work.*

Freeing Up Disk Space

After using SUSE Linux for some time, you might find that the disk begins to get full. You can keep an eye on disk usage using the following command at the command-line shell:

```
df -h
```

This will show the free space in terms of megabytes or gigabytes, and also expressed as a percentage figure.

If the disk does start to get full, there are a number of measures you can take to free up space.

Emptying the /tmp Folder

An easy way to regain disk space is to empty the /tmp folder. As with the Windows operating system, this is the folder in which temporary data is stored. Some applications clean up after themselves, but others don't, leaving behind many megabytes of detritus.

Because the /tmp folder is accessed practically every second the system is up and running, to empty it safely, it's necessary to switch to run level 1. This ensures few other programs are running and avoids the risk of deleting data that is in use. The following series of commands will switch to run level 1, empty the /tmp folder, and then reboot afterwards:

On a similar theme, don't forget to empty the desktop Trash. This can hold many megabytes of old data.

```
su -
[enter root password]
init 1
[log in as root and enter the password]
rm -rf /tmp/*
reboot
```

Empting the Cache of RPM Update Files

You might also choose to clear out the YaST2 cache of RPM update files. On a system that has been very frequently updated, this can free up many megabytes (possibly gigabytes) of space. However, as demonstrated earlier in this chapter when we looked at compiling a kernel, this cache can actually prove useful at times. Emptying it should be weighed against its potential advantages.

You can empty the cache by typing the following command as root:

```
rm -f /var/lib/YaST2/you/mnt/i386/update/9.1/rpm/i586/*.rpm
```

Removing Unused Software

If you still need disk space, consider removing unused programs. As you've learned, you manage software through YaST2's Install and Remove Software tool (select K menu ➤ Control Center, click the YaST2 Modules icon, click the Software icon, and then click Install and Remove Software).

The best way of managing software is to switch to Selection view, by selecting Selection from the Filter drop-down list. This lets you see which groups of programs you have installed, rather than viewing individual titles, which in themselves might not free up too much space. In Selection view, you might choose to deselect the Games group, for example. This will remove all the desktop games on the system. Alternatively, if you don't use any office programs on your system, you might choose to deselect the Office group.

▪**Caution** As always, removing software can create dependency problems, so you might find yourself limited in what software you can actually remove.

Adding Another Disk Drive

Another solution to the problem of running out of disk space is to add another hard disk drive, perhaps as a slave on the primary IDE channel. Using a new disk within SUSE Linux is very easy and can be done from the command-line shell.

Partitioning the Disk

Once the disk has been fitted, boot into SUSE Linux, open a command-line shell and switch to root user. You should then use the cfdisk command to initially partition the disk. Assuming that you've added the new disk as a slave on the primary channel, use the following command:

```
cfdisk /dev/hdb
```

Working out how SUSE Linux refers to the hard disks installed on the system isn't hard. Usually, they're given letters from a through to d. So, /dev/hda is the primary master, /dev/hdb is the primary slave, /dev/hdc is the secondary master, and /dev/hdd is the secondary slave. If your system uses SCSI drives, you'll find they're named /dev/sda, /dev/sdb, and so on.

The first thing to do within the cfdisk program is create a new partition. Use the cursor keys to highlight New, and then press Enter. The default partition size should automatically be all of the disk space, so press Enter again to confirm this. With the new partition created, highlight Quit on the menu. This will write the partition table. After this, you should reboot the system to ensure the new partition is made available.

When SUSE Linux is back up and running, open a command-line shell prompt again, switch to root user, and issue the following command (again assuming that the new hard disk is /dev/hdb):

```
mkfs -t reiserfs /dev/hdb1
```

Note that you need to specify the partition number in this instance. Because there's only one partition on the disk, this is number 1. Had you created two or more partitions, each would be numbered 1, 2, and 3 consecutively.

You've created a Reiser-formatted partition, because this is the preferred standard used within SUSE Linux. Other versions of Linux might use different file systems, such as ext3.

Configuring SUSE Linux to Use the Drive

Now the new drive is ready for use, but you need a way of making it available within the SUSE Linux file system. Therefore, you need to create a mount point and also configure the system so that the disk is mounted automatically at bootup.

As discussed in Chapter 15, creating a mount point is simply a matter of creating an empty folder. Therefore, you can create a directory in the root of the hard disk (or anywhere else) and call it something like second_disk.

Then you must edit the /etc/fstab file. All you need to do is add a line at the end of the file, such as this:

```
/dev/hdb1  /second_disk  reiserfs    default  1 1
```

Note that it's important that you add a carriage return after the line.

You can test your new hard disk by rebooting. When SUSE Linux returns, you should find that the new disk is available by accessing the /second_disk directory. You can check its capacity by typing df -h.

Summary

In this chapter, we looked at streamlining your installation of SUSE Linux. This involved speeding up the boot procedure by decreasing the boot menu delay and deactivating various unnecessary services that get loaded at boot time. We also looked at optimizing your hard disk settings to allow for greater efficiency in loading and saving files.

Additionally, we investigated prelinking programs so that they load faster, recompiling the kernel so that it's optimized for your system, freeing disk space by various means, and adding a second hard disk.

In the next chapter, you'll learn how to perform backups to safeguard your data.

CHAPTER 32

■ ■ ■

Backing Up Data

Every computer user knows that backing up data is vital. This is usually because every computer user has lost data at some point, perhaps because of a corrupted file or accidental deletion.

Some of the people behind Unix were highly aware of such occurrences, and built in several advanced and useful backup tools. These have been mirrored within Linux, with the result that creating and maintaining backups is easy. SUSE Linux adds its own tools, which make the procedure even easier, courtesy of the GUI.

However, regardless of the software available to use, the questions are which data should be backed up and where the archive file should be stored. These and other questions are answered in this chapter.

What Data Should You Back Up?

Data on your system can be classified into three broad types: program data, configuration data, and personal data. It's traditionally reasoned that backing up all types of data is inefficient and difficult, largely because it would mean backing up practically the entire hard disk. Because of this, you usually want to back up the latter two types of data: configuration and personal. The theory is that if your PC is hit by a hard-disk-wrecking disaster, you can easily reinstall the operating system from the CD/DVD. Restoring your system from backup is then simply a matter of ensuring the configuration files are back in place, so your applications work as you would like them to, and ensuring your personal data is once again made accessible.

Practically all the personal configuration data for programs you use everyday, as well as your personal data, is stored in your /home/ folder (although the configuration files for software used systemwide are stored in the /etc/ folder). If you take a look in your /home/ directory, you might think that previous sentence is incorrect. On a freshly installed system, the directory appears largely empty. However, most, if not all, of the configuration files are hidden; their directory and filenames are preceded with a period (.), which means that Linux doesn't display them during a standard directory listing.

To view hidden files and folders in Konqueror, select View ➤ Show Hidden Files. This can be quite an eye-opener when you see the masses of data you didn't even realize were there, as shown in the example in Figure 32-1. To view hidden files at the shell prompt, simply use the -a command option with the ls command:

```
ls -a
```

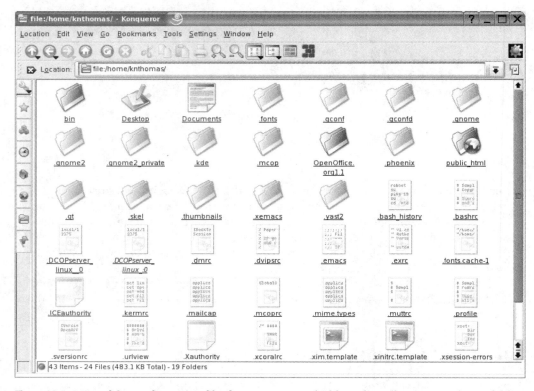

Figure 32-1. *Most of the configuration files for programs are hidden—literally—in your /home/ folder.*

The configuration files held in your /home/ folder relate solely to your user account. Any other users will have their own configuration files, entirely independent of yours. In this way, all users can have their own configuration settings for various applications, which can be backed up independently.

Under SUSE Linux, you can back up configuration data using the YaST2 System Backup tool and back up personal data using Konserve. Keep in mind that there's little point in making backups using either Konserve or the YaST2 System Backup tool if you leave the resultant archive files on your hard disk. For full backup protection, the archives should be stored elsewhere, such as on an external hard disk or CD/DVD-ROM. Consider using a program like K3b for burning backup discs.

Backing Up Data via YaST2

YaST2 includes a component designed to back up and restore vital system data, with the idea being that a restore operation can potentially take place later on a corrupted system (in this way, it's somewhat similar to Windows XP's System Restore, although it's not an incremental backup and must be activated manually). This tool is *not* designed to back up your personal data, which must be backed up separately, as explained in the next section.

As with most backup programs, the YaST2 System Backup component works on the principle of backup jobs, which it refers to as *profiles*. You can create a profile to back up a defined set of data (which is usually automatically defined by the program), and this can be run whenever necessary. It can then be restored should anything go wrong.

To back up data with YaST2, follow these steps:

1. To start the System Backup tool, start select K menu ➤ Control Center, click YaST2 Modules, click System, and then click System Backup.

2. Because backing up systemwide data requires root file permissions, click the Administrator Mode button, and then enter your root password.

3. Click the Profile Management button, and then click Add.

4. On the next screen, you have a choice of either saving the eventual backup file locally (to your PC's hard disk or a storage device attached to it) or saving it to a network address.

   - If you're working in a corporate environment on a networked computer, you might consider asking your system administrator if an NFS share is available. The network address must be an NFS location. NFS is a way of networking Unix computers together, designed to be simple to use. Be aware that NFS can be insecure, so make sure you adopt appropriate security measures.

   - If you choose to save the backup as a local file, the file can be saved to any kind of mounted file system, including a network mount or to a second hard disk. It's simply a matter of specifying the mount point as the save location. The filename for the backup must be an absolute path. For example, if you want to save the file in your /home/ directory, you'll need to type the complete path and filename (for example, /home/knthomas/mybackup).

■Note An *absolute path* is one that includes a complete description of the path from root, such as /home/knthomas. A *relative path* is one that merely indicates the path from the perspective of the current directory.

---

5. In the Archive Type box, you can select which type of archive file you wish to create. All the data from the backup will be contained in one file, which will be created automatically via the tar program (we'll discuss how this command works later in this chapter). The tar file can also be compressed, which is a good idea because it will save a lot of disk space. Linux uses two forms of compression: gzip and bzip2. The latter is more recent and offers better compression, but not all Linux systems support it, while virtually every Linux and Unix system will have gzip built in. The "tar with tar-bzip2 subarchives" choice is probably the best one for most desktop users.

6. Click the Next button after you've made your choices on this screen.

7. The next screen offers more backup choices, such as giving the backup archive a description for future reference. Clicking the Expert button lets you include the system areas of your hard disk, such as the master boot record and partition table. This can prove invaluable should your hard disk become corrupted. Click Next to continue.

8. Next, you need to select which files and folders you *don't* want to backup. The System Backup tool works on the basis of exclusion, as shown in Figure 32-2. You must define areas where the backup component won't search for files. Everywhere else is searched in order to uncover the configuration and updated files that will be backed up. The default choice is fine, so click OK.

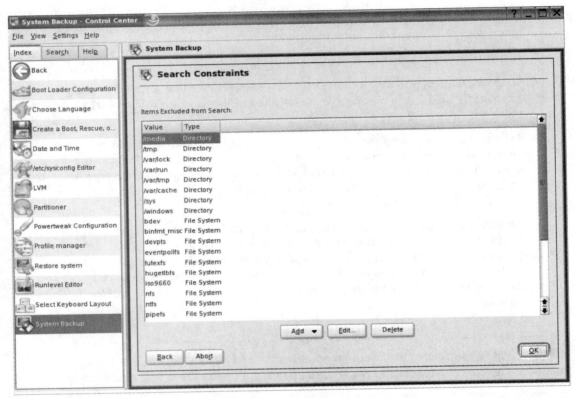

Figure 32-2. *The System Backup tool works on the basis of exclusion, so you must identify directories you don't want backed up.*

9. You return to the earlier screen, where you can highlight your new backup profile and click Start Backup.

Be aware that backing up data can take some time and, because files are being copied, can be system-intensive.

Backing Up Personal Data

SUSE Linux also includes the Konserve utility, which you can use to back up your personal data, but this isn't installed by default. To add it, simply navigate to the Install and Remove Software section within YaST2 and, in the Search field, enter konserve. When it appears in the list of results, put a tick in its selection box, and then click the Accept button to install it. (You'll need to insert the SUSE Linux installation DVD.)

Konserve is a simple backup program that will appear as an applet in your system tray to the right of the Panel. Once it's installed via YaST2, you'll need to log out and then back in again for it to appear on the K menu. Then you can use it to back up your personal data, as follows:

1. To start Konserve, select K menu ➤ System ➤ Desktop Applet ➤ Konserve. This will install Konserve into your system tray, where you can then right-click to configure it. Select the Wizard menu entry to have the program walk you through making backup choices.

2. The first step is to add a name for the backup profile. If you intend to make a daily backup, then a name like Daily Backup should do the trick.

3. You're prompted to enter the folder you wish to back up. For example, if you wish to back up your /home/ folder, type that here.

Note When it comes down to it, your /home/ folder is the only personal data on the system that you should back up. Everything else can be taken care of using the YaST2 System Backup tool.

---

4. You're prompted to enter a name and path for the backup file. Something sensible that you'll remember later is a good choice here. You need to precede the filename with the absolute path to the directory where the file will be stored, as shown in the example in Figure 32-3.

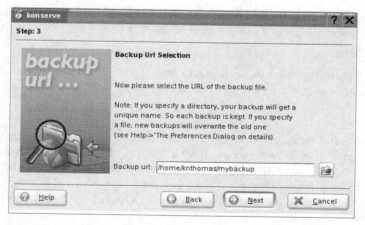

Figure 32-3. *Konserve is a simple but useful tool that you can use to back up personal data in your /home/ directory.*

5. You're invited to schedule your backups. This means that they take place automatically in the background, provided that Konserve is up and running (after you first run it, Konserve will automatically start each time you boot).

6. You're shown a confirmation of the backup details. Click Finish.

After you've configured Konserve, if you want to start the backup, right-click the Konserve system tray icon and select your job from the list.

You can also use Konserve to create instant backups of files. Simply click and drag them from a Konsole file browser window and drop them on the Konserve icon. The wizard will start, and it will already be using the file or folder as the source for the backup.

Making Backups from the Command Line

Although the GUI-based tools allow the uninitiated to make quick backups, all of these tools output tar files. The tar files, and the tar program that makes them, are one of the original carryovers from Unix. tar stands for Tape ARchive and refers to backing up data to a magnetic tape backup device. Although tar files are designed for backup, they've also become a standard method of transferring files across the Internet, particularly with regard to source files or other installation programs.

A tar file is simply a collection of files bundled into one. By default, the tar file isn't compressed, although additional software can be used to compress it. tar files aren't very sophisticated compared to modern archive file formats. They're not encrypted, for example, but this can also be one of their advantages.

■**Note** Linux comes with a couple more backup commands, which you might choose to use. They are cpio and pax. Both aim to improve on tar in various ways, but neither is broadly supported at the moment. Examine their man pages for more details.

Creating tar Files

Perhaps unsurprisingly, tar files are created at the console using the tar command. Usually, all that's needed is to specify a source directory and a filename, which can be done like so:

```
tar -cf mybackup.tar /home/knthomas/
```

This will create a backup called mybackup.tar based on the contents of /home/knthomas/. tar is automatically recursive so, in this example, it will delve into all subdirectories beneath /home/knthomas. The -c command option tells tar you're going to create an archive, and the -f option indicates that the filename for the archive will immediately follow. If you don't use the -f option, tar will send its output to standard output, which means that it will display the contents of the archive on the screen.

If you typed in a command like the preceding example, you would see the message "Removing leading '/' from member names." This means that the folders and files added to the archive will all have the initial forward slash removed from their paths. So, rather than store a file in the archive as:

```
/home/knthomas/Mail/file1
```

the file will be stored as:

```
home/knthomas/Mail/file1
```

The difference between the two forms concerns when the files are later extracted from the archive. If the files have the initial slash, tar will write the file to /home/knthomas/Mail/file1. If there's already a file of that name in that location, it will be overwritten. On the other hand, with the leading slash removed, tar will create a new directory wherever you choose to restore the archive. In this example, it will create a new directory called home, and then a directory called knthomas within that, and so on.

Because of the potential of accidentally overwriting data by specifying absolute paths in this way, a better way of backing up a directory is simply to change into its parent and specify it without a full path:

```
cd /home/
tar -cf mybackup.tar knthomas
```

When this particular archive is restored, it will simply create a new folder called knthomas wherever it's restored.

Compressing tar Archives

You can also compress the archive from within tar, although it actually calls in outside help from either bzip2 or gzip, depending on which you specify.

To create a tar archive compressed using bzip2, the following should do the trick:

```
tar -cjf mybackup.tar.bz2 knthomas
```

This will create a compressed backup from the directory knthomas. The -j command option passes the output from tar to the bzip2 program, although this is done in the background. Notice the change in the backup filename extension to indicate that this is a bzip2 compressed archive.

The following command will create an archive compressed with the older gzip compression:

```
tar -czf mybackup.tar.gz knthomas
```

This uses the -z command option to pass the output to gzip. This time, the filename shows it's a gzip compressed archive, so you can correctly identify it in the future.

Extracting Files from a tar Archive

Extracting files using tar is as easy as creating them:

```
tar -xf mybackup.tar
```

The -x option tells tar to extract the files from the maybackup.tar archive.

Extracting compressed archives is simply a matter of adding the -j or -z option to the -x option:

```
tar -xjf mybackup.tar.bz2
```

■Note Technically speaking, `tar` doesn't require the preceding hyphen before its command options. However, it's a good idea to use it anyway, so you won't forget to use it with other commands in the future.

Viewing tar Archive Information

To view the contents of a `tar` archive without actually restoring the files, use the `-t` option:

```
tar -tf mybackup.tar |less
```

This example adds a pipe into `less` at the end, because the listing of files probably will be large and will scroll off the screen. Just add the `-j` or `-z` option if the `tar` archive is also compressed.

In addition, you can add the `-v` option to all stages of making, extracting, and viewing an archive to see more information (chiefly the files that are being archived or extracted).

Typing `-vv` provides even more information:

```
tar -cvvf mybackup.tar knthomas
```

This will create an archive and also show a complete directory listing as the files and folders are added, including permissions.

Saving the File to a CD-R/RW

Once the `tar` file has been created, the problem of where to store it arises. As I mentioned earlier, storing backup data on the same hard disk as the data it was created to back up is foolish, since any problem that might affect the hard disk might also affect the archive. You could end up losing both sets of data!

If the archive is less than 700MB, it might be possible to store it on a CD-R or CD-RW. To do this from the command line, first the file must be turned into an ISO image, and then it must be burned.

To turn it into an ISO image, use the `mkiso` command:

```
mkiso -i backup.iso mybackup.tar.bz2
```

You can then burn the ISO image to a CD by using the `cdrecord` command. Before using this, you must determine which SCSI device number your CD-R/RW drive uses (all CD-R/RW or DVD-R/RW drives are seen as SCSI devices, even if they're not). Issue the following command (as root, since `cdrecord` must be run as root, no matter what it's doing):

```
cdrecord -scanbus
```

You should find the device numbers listed as three numbers separated by commas. To burn the backup image, all you need to do is enter a command in this format:

```
cdrecord dev=<dev number> speed=<speed of your drive> mybackup.iso
```

On a typical system, this will take the form of:

```
cdrecord dev=0,0,0 speed=24 mybackup.iso
```

Backing Up to a Tape Drive

The tar command was designed to back up to a tape drive. If you have one of these installed on your computer, writing data to it is very easy. However, you'll first need to know if your tape drive is supported by SUSE Linux. Most modern tape drives are made available as SCSI devices, even if they aren't actually SCSI. Therefore, you can scan the hardware bus for SCSI devices like so (once again running this command as root):

```
hwinfo -scsi
```

In the results, look for a line relating to your tape drive and, in particular, a line that begins Device file:. This will tell you where in the /dev/ folder the tape drive has been made available.

Once you have this information, it's simply a matter of adapting the tar commands discussed previously in order to direct the output of the tar command to the drive (the following assumes you've identified your tape drive as /dev/st0):

```
tar -cf /dev/st0 /home/knthomas
```

Extracting files is just as easy:

```
tar -xf /dev/st0
```

The tape itself can be rewound and erased using the mt command. See its man page for the various command options. Generally, the -f command option is used to specify the device to use (such as /dev/st0 in the previous example), and then a plain English word is used to tell the device what to do. These are listed in the man page.

The most useful commands are those that can rewind a tape and also erase it. To rewind a tape, type the following:

```
mt -f /dev/st0 rewind
```

To erase a tape, type this:

```
mt -f /dev/st0 erase
```

One particularly useful command that you can use if the tape becomes unreliable is the retension command, which winds the tape to the end and then rewinds it to the beginning:

```
mt -f /dev/st0 retension
```

Summary

In this chapter, we looked at making backups. First, you saw how to verify where your personal and other vital data is stored. Then we looked at how the YaST2 System Backup tool can be used to back up system configuration data. For personal data, you can use Konserve, as described in this chapter, which can arbitrarily back up files. Finally, you learned how to use tar at the command line to back up any kind of data.

In the next chapter, we'll look at how tasks can be scheduled to occur at various times under SUSE Linux.

## CHAPTER 33

Scheduling Tasks

In this book, you've learned about various tasks you can perform to keep SUSE Linux running smoothly. You may decide that you want some of these tasks to occur on a regular basis. For example, perhaps you want your home directory to be backed up every day, or perhaps you want to clean the /tmp folder to ensure that you always have enough free disk space. You could carry out each task individually, but human nature would no doubt step in, and you would forget, or you might perform the action twice, because you've forgotten that you've already done it.

As you might expect, SUSE Linux is able to automate the running of particular tasks. They can either be run periodically at scheduled times or as one-time tasks. Using SUSE Linux's scheduling features is explained in this chapter.

Scheduling with crontab

Under SUSE Linux, there's one main way of scheduling tasks: via the cron daemon. This works on behalf of the user in order to schedule individual tasks, and it is also used by the system in order to run vital system tasks, although a different way of working is used in each case.

For cron to run user-scheduled tasks, it reads a file called crontab. Each user has his or her own version of this, which is stored in the /var/spool/cron/tabs directory. You should use a special command to edit this file in vi (the text editor covered in Chapter 16), rather than edit it directly.

Note For systemwide tasks, a series of scripts are placed in the /etc/crontab/ directories, which contain subdirectories relating to whether the task is to run each day, week, month, and so on. The average user never needs to bother with systemwide cron jobs. These are handled by the internal system, and programs create their own entries as and when necessary.

The cron daemon starts at bootup and simply sits in the background while you work, checking every minute to see if a task is due. As soon as one comes up, it starts the task going, and then goes back to waiting.

Creating a Scheduled Task

Adding a scheduled task is relatively easily and is done via the shell. Entering the following command will cause your personal crontab file to be loaded into vi, ready for editing:

```
crontab -e
```

If this is the first time you've edited your crontab file, it will most likely be completely empty. However, don't be put off. Adding a new entry is relatively easy and normally takes the form of something like this:

```
01 12 15 * * tar -cjf /home/knthomas/mybackup.tar.bz2 /home/knthomas
```

Let's examine the line piece by piece. The first part—the numbers and asterisks—refers to when the task should be run. From left to right, the fields refer to the following:

- Minutes, from 0 to 59

- Hours, in 24-hour time, so from 0 to 23

- Day dates, for the day of the month, from 1 to 31 (assuming the month has that many days)

- Months, from 1 to 12

- Day, for a particular day, either from 0 to 6 (0 is Sunday), or specified as a three-letter abbreviation (mon, tue, wed, and so on)

In the example, the task is set to run at the first minute at the twelfth hour (midday) on the fifteenth day of the month. But what do the asterisks stand for? They're effectively wildcards and tell cron that every possible value applies. Because an asterisk appears in the month field, this task will be run *every* month. Because an asterisk appears in the day field, the task will be run every day.

You might have noticed a logical contradiction here. How can we specify a day if we also specify a date in the month? Wouldn't this seriously limit the chances of the task ever running? Yes, it would. If you were to specify sat, for example, and put 15 in the date field, the task would run on only the fifteenth of the month if that happened to be a Saturday. This is why the two fields are rarely used in the same crontab entry, and an asterisk appears in one if the other is being used.

After the time and date fields comes the command itself: tar. As you learned in the previous chapter, tar is designed to back up your personal data.

Only standard BASH shell commands can be used in the command section. cron isn't clever enough to interpret symbols such as the tilde (~) as a way of referring to your home directory. For this reason, it's best to be very thorough when defining a cron job and always use absolute paths.

Let's take a look at another example (shown in Figure 33-1):

```
59 23 * * 0-3 tar -cjf /home/knthomas/mybackup.tar.bz2 /home/knthomas
```

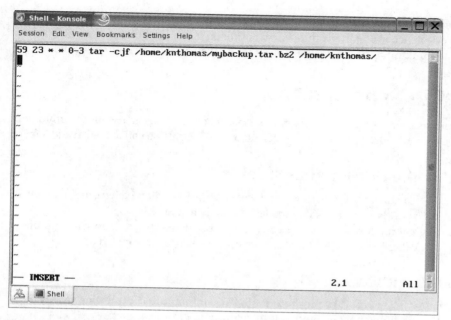

Figure 33-1. *Editing* crontab *lets you schedule tasks using the* vi *text editor.*

The first field says that this task will run at the fifty-ninth minute of the twenty-third hour (that is, one minute before midnight). The date and month field have asterisks, so this implies that the task should run every day and every month. However, the day field contains 0-3. This says that the task should run on only days 0 through to 3, or Sunday through Wednesday.

You can have as many cron entries as you like; simply give each a separate line. There's no need for them to be in date or time order. You can just add them as and when you see fit.

When you're finished, save the file and quit vi in the usual way (by entering :wq).

Note SUSE Linux is unusual among Linux distributions in that it doesn't make use of another form of task scheduling called anacron. anacron is designed to periodically schedule tasks, so that, for example, a task could be started every other day, regardless of the date. However, cron can be used to duplicate this functionality.

Editing crontab with the GUI

The SUSE Linux disk includes the vcron program, which provides a simple method of editing your crontab file using a GUI. You can also add at jobs, described in the next section, using the program. You can install vcron by searching for the program using the Install and Remove Software component of YaST2 (see Chapter 29).

Using the vcron program is similar to manually editing crontab. Click the Add button to add a scheduled job according to the time format outlined in the previous section. The only difference is that you can simply click radio buttons rather than typing dates and times manually.

Using at to Schedule Tasks

What if you quickly want to schedule a one-time-only task? For this, you can use the at command. This relies on a daemon that isn't activated by default on SUSE Linux, so you'll need to add it first.

Adding at to the Current Run Level

You can use YaST2 to add at to the current run level. Start YaST2, click System, and then click Runlevel Editor. The at daemon is called atd. Select it and click Enable.

This will start it at run levels 2, 3, and 5 every time the system is booted, until it's disabled. (Don't worry if YaST2 reports an additional service must be started to support atd.)

Adding a Job with at

Adding a job with at is very easy, largely because the at command accepts a wide variety of time formats. For example, the following will run a job at lunchtime tomorrow:

```
at noon tomorrow
```

It really is as simple as that!

Alternatively, you can specify a time, date, and even a year:

```
at 13:00 jun 25 2008
```

This will run the job at 1 PM on June 25, 2008. The various time and date formats are explained in the at command's man page.

Once the at command containing the date has been entered, you'll be presented with a mock shell prompt. Here, you can type the commands you want to run. Many shell commands can be entered, one after the other; just press Enter between them. Then press Ctrl+D to signal that you're finished editing. At this point, at will confirm the time and write the task into its list.

You can view the list at any time by typing atq. This will show a list of numbered jobs. You can remove any job by typing atrm, followed by its atq job number. For example, the following will remove the job numbered 9 in the atq list:

```
atrm 9
```

Summary

In this brief chapter, we looked at how you can schedule tasks under SUSE Linux, which is essentially making programs run at certain times. We examined the cron facility, which can schedule tasks to run periodically, and we also examined the at service, which can schedule one-time tasks to run at certain times.

In the final chapter of this book, we will look at how you can access your SUSE Linux computer remotely—theoretically, from any Internet-equipped location in the world.

CHAPTER 34

■ ■ ■

Accessing Linux Remotely

One area where Linux particularly excels is in its support for networking, including the Internet. If you wish to learn about how networks operate on a fundamental level, then Linux is an ideal choice, because it puts you in virtually direct contact with the technology.

The widespread integration and support for networking extends to several useful system tools, which let you access Linux across any kind of network, including the Internet. In fact, it's even possible to access a Linux machine running on a different continent, just as if you were sitting in front of it!

This chapter looks at the many ways you can access Linux remotely.

Using Secure Shell

The history of Unix has virtually always featured computers connecting to other computers in some fashion, whether they were dumb terminals connecting to a mainframe computer or Unix machines acting as nodes on the fledgling Internet. Because of this, a wide variety of techniques and protocols were invented to allow computers to communicate and log in to each other across networks.

However, while these still work fine over the modern Internet, the Internet presents a new threat to the privacy of your data. In theory, any data transmitted across the Internet can be picked up by individuals at certain key stages along the route. If the data isn't protected in any way, it can be read and privacy breached.

To counter such an occurrence, the ssh suite of programs was created. Although these programs started as open source, they gradually became proprietary. Therefore several newer open-source versions were created, including the one used on the majority of Linux distributions: OpenSSH.

The goal of the ssh program is to let you log in to a remote computer and initiate a shell session, as if you were sitting in front of it. However, it uses various techniques at both ends of the connection to encrypt not only the data passing between the two machines, but also the username and password. This creates a completely secure connection between the two machines.

■Note This chapter refers to *remote* and *local* machines. The *remote* machine is the computer you're connecting to across the network or Internet. The *local* machine is the one you're actually sitting in front of. These two terms are widely used within documentation describing networking.

Running an ssh Session

Initiating an ssh session with another machine is usually achieved by typing something similar to the following:

ssh knthomas@192.168.0.11

In other words, you specify the username you want to log in under, as well as the address of the machine. The example uses an IP address, but if there's a fully qualified domain name (FQDN) for that particular system, you could specify that instead. An FQDN is the portion of a URL that identifies the server it points to; that is, all of the URL, minus the http:// prefix. So if 192.168.0.11 were the IP address of the www.myserver.com server, then the FQDN would be www.myserver.com.

When you log in for the first time, you'll be told that, "The authenticity of the host <*host IP address*> can't be established," as shown in the example in Figure 34-1. This means that the remote computer's encryption key hasn't yet been added to your PC's store file. However, once you agree to the initial login, the encryption key will be added, and it can be used in the future to confirm that the remote computer you're connecting to is authentic.

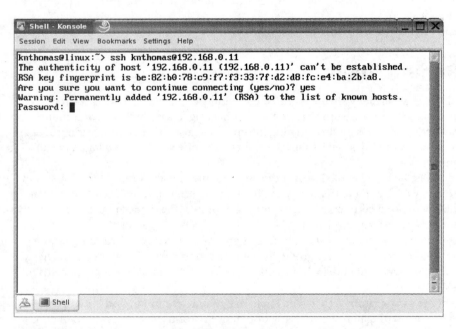

Figure 34-1. *When logging in via ssh for the first time, you'll need to confirm acceptance of the encryption key.*

After confirming that you want to make the connection, you'll be invited to enter the password for the user account under which you initiated the ssh connection. Once this is done, you should find yourself with a shell login on the remote computer. You can run the same commands as usual and perform identical tasks.

The machine you're logged in to will show no symptoms of being used remotely. This isn't like the movies, where what you type on your local machine is somehow mirrored on the remote machine for all to see. However, obviously, if a user of the remote machine were to view her network connections using something similar to the netstat command, then she would see another computer attached via ssh.

Managing Remote Sessions

Whenever you open any kind of shell to enter commands and run programs, you might have noticed that any commands you start running last only as long as the shell window is open. When the shell window is closed, any task running within it ends, too. This is because the shell is seen as the "owner" of the process, and when the owner dies, any processes it started also dies.

When using ssh to start a remote shell session, this also applies. Whenever you log out, any tasks you were running are ended. This can be annoying if, for example, you've started a lengthy download on the remote machine. Effectively, you must remain logged in via ssh until the download has finished.

To get around this, you can use the handy screen program. This isn't specifically designed to be an aid to remote logins, but there's no reason why it cannot be used in such a situation.

The screen program effectively starts shell sessions that stick around, even if the shell window is closed or the ssh connection is ended or lost. After logging in to the remote computer via ssh, you can start a screen session by simply typing the program name at the prompt:

```
screen
```

Note that, on SUSE Linux at least, there won't be any indication that you're running a screen session, so keep your wits about you.

You can run any commands from within screen. To detach from the screen session, press Ctrl+A and then Ctrl+D. You'll then be returned to the standard shell and can disconnect from your ssh session as usual. However, the screen session will still be running in the background on the remote computer. To prove this, you can log back in, and then type this:

```
screen -r
```

This will resume your screen session, and you should be able to pick up quite literally where you left off; any output from previous commands will be displayed.

To quit a screen session, you can either type exit from within it or press Ctrl+A, and then Ctrl+\ (backslash).

The screen program is very powerful. To learn more about it, read its man page. To see a list of its keyboard commands, press Ctrl+A, and then type a question mark (?) while screen is running.

Transferring Files with SFTP

What if you want to transfer files to and from the remote computer? The ssh program offers no way of copying files to the local computer's hard disk. You're limited to working within the confines of the remote machine. You could feasibly use the mail command-line program to e-mail the file to yourself, but that would hardly be the most elegant solution.

To transfer files, you need to use the sftp program. If you've ever used a shell-based ftp program, you'll feel right at home, because sftp isn't very different.

You can initiate a session by typing something similar to the following:

```
sftp knthomas@192.168.0.11
```

The same rules as logging in with ssh apply, both in terms of formatting the login command and also confirming the encryption key if this is the first time you've logged in.

The sftp commands are fairly basic. For example, to copy a file from the remote machine, simply type this:

```
get filename
```

This will copy the file into the directory you were in on the local machine before you started the sftp session.

By specifying a path after the filename, the file will be copied to the specified local directory:

```
get filename /home/knthomas/downloaded_files/
```

Sending files from the local machine to the remote machine is just as easy:

```
put filename
```

By specifying a path after the filename, you can ensure the file is saved to a particular remote path.

One useful thing to remember is that any command preceded by an exclamation mark (!, called a *bang* in Linux-speak) is executed on the local machine as a shell command. So, if you wanted to remove a file on the local machine, you could type:

```
!rm -rf filename
```

Simply typing a bang symbol on its own starts a shell session on the local machine, so you can perform even more tasks. When you're finished, type exit to return to the sftp program.

For a list of popular `sftp` commands, see Table 34-1.

Table 34-1. *sftp Commands*

Command	Function
cd	Change the remote directory
lcd	Change the local directory
get	Download the specified file
ls	List the remote directory
lls	List the local directory
mkdir	Create a directory on the remote machine
lmkdir	Create a directory on the local machine
put	Upload the specified file to the remote machine
pwd	Print the current remote directory
rmdir	Delete the remote directory
rm	Delete the remote file
exit	Quit `sftp`
!command	Execute the specified command on the local machine
!	Start a temporary local shell session (type `exit` to return to `sftp`)
Help	Show a list of commands

Using GUI Applications Remotely

The graphical subsystem of Linux, X, is designed to work across a network. If you run Linux on your desktop PC, X still works via a loopback network within your machine (meaning that network commands are sent out, addressed to the very same machine on which they originated). Because of this, it's possible to access a remote machine and run graphical applications on the local machine. The actual work of running the application is handled by the remote machine, but the work of displaying the graphics is handled by the local machine.

Configuring ssh for Running X Applications on a Remote Computer

Once again, the problem of unencrypted communications rears its ugly head. Simply connecting to a remote computer via X across the Internet means any confidential data might be intercepted along the route of the data. To solve this problem, you can configure `ssh` so that X applications on the remote computer can be run on the local machine via the `ssh` connection. This is a two-step procedure:

- First, on the local machine, you must configure the local X server so that it allows remote applications to run (technically speaking, you're allowing remote X connections). On many Linux installations this isn't necessary, but SUSE Linux deactivates this function as a security measure. However, it's easily reactivated by entering xhost +.

- After this, you must log in to the remote machine using ssh, but specify the -X flag, which will allow X traffic as well as ssh shell traffic to pass between machines:

```
ssh –X knthomas@192.168.0.11
```

When you're logged in, you can simply start any application by typing its name as usual. The only difference is that the program will appear on the screen of the local machine, rather than the remote machine, as shown in Figure 34-2.

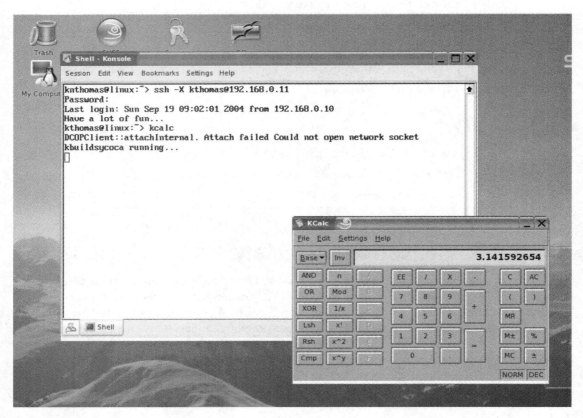

Figure 34-2. *You can run GUI programs on a remote machine across an* ssh *connection.*

Using X across the Internet or even a local network isn't very fast, and you can expect delays when you open menus or if the screen must frequently redraw. However, it can prove very useful.

Running the KDE Desktop Across an X Server

It's even possible to run the entire KDE desktop across an X server. On the local machine, switch to run level 3 (text-only mode) by typing the following as root user:

```
init 3
```

Then log in as an ordinary user and type this:

```
xinit
```

This will start a rudimentary X session, complete with an `xterm` shell window. You can then use the `ssh` command to log in to your remote machine, specifying that X communications should be allowed over the connection:

```
ssh -X knthomas@192.168.0.11
```

And then type the following:

```
startkde
```

This will make the remote computer's KDE desktop appear. Once again, it will be fairly slow to respond to mouse clicks and keyboard strokes, but it should be just about usable.

Using YaST2 Remote Administration

SUSE Linux includes its own system of allowing remote connections via the YaST2 Remote Administration module. This relies on TightVNC (VNC stands for Virtual Network Computing), a piece of software that simply mirrors the remote desktop on the local machine. This is less secure than running programs via `ssh` because, although the password is sent encrypted, the actual data isn't encrypted.

Remote Administration is also designed to be used by two people. The idea is that one person invites another to access his PC, perhaps to enact repairs. As such, each user must confirm the connection, so it's not ideal for those who simply want to access their PC while they're away from it.

To enable Remote Administration, you must first activate the service via YaST2. Start YaST2 and click Network Devices and Remote Administration. Click the radio button next to Allow Remote Administration, as shown in Figure 34-3.

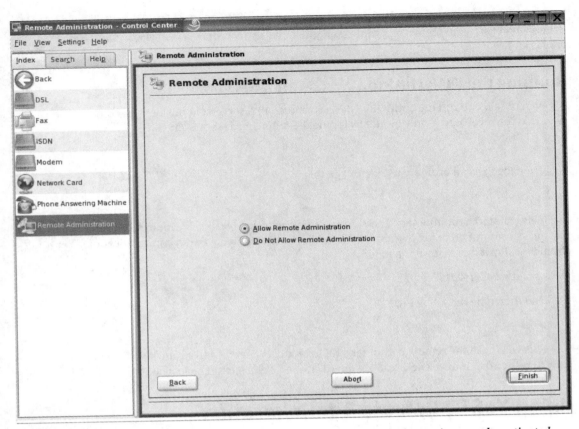

Figure 34-3. *Before inviting others to make a remote desktop connection, the service must be activated within YaST2.*

The next step is to create an invitation, which will allow the other user to connect to your computer. Select K menu ➤ System ➤ Remote Access ➤ Desktop Sharing. You will then have a choice of creating a personal invitation or sending one by e-mail. In the case of a personal invitation, the IP address of your computer will be displayed alongside a randomly generated password. You can then pass these to the other user, perhaps by a phone call, and he can use the details to connect. Selecting the e-mail option sends these details by e-mail to an address that you specify.

Once the invitation has been set up, your computer is ready for another computer to connect. On the other machine, the other user will need to be running SUSE Linux to be able to hook up. He should select K menu ➤ System ➤ Remote Access ➤ Remote Desktop Connection. He will then need to fill in the IP address you supplied earlier. However, the address must be preceded by vnc://, like this:

```
vnc://192.168.0.12:0
```

Back at your machine, a dialog box will appear asking you to agree to the remote connection, as shown in Figure 34-4. Once this happens, the remote user will be invited to enter the password, and the connection will be made. He will then have joint control over the desktop and will be able to move the mouse cursor and enter data via the keyboard.

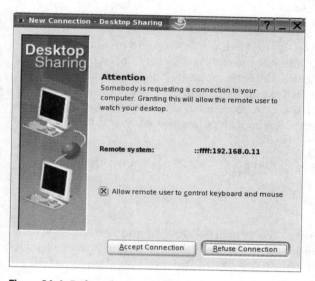

Figure 34-4. *Before the remote user can connect, you'll need to agree to that user having access.*

Configuring the Firewall for Remote Connections

For any kind of remote connection, the firewall on both the local and remote machine must be configured to allow the network traffic relating to the remote connection. If the computers are behind routers or firewall devices, these must be also be configured. Under SUSE Linux, this configuration is done by modifying the firewall component of YaST2.

Note For any other version of Linux, you'll need to examine the distribution's documentation to discover how to allow remote connections. For a router or firewall device, you should look within the documentation to see how "port forwarding" is set up.

To configure SUSE Linux's firewall, follow these steps:

1. Start YaST2 (select K menu ➤ Control Center ➤ YaST2 Modules) and click Security.

2. Click the Administrator Mode button and type your root password.

3. When the firewall configuration screen appears, click Next. This will show the configuration screen where the services you wish to allow through the firewall can be specified.

4. Make sure that SSH is checked. This will allow SSH and SFTP traffic.

5. To allow Remote Administration sessions, click the Expert button, just to the right of the line labeled Additional Services.

6. In the dialog box that appears, you can type in the individual port number of the application you wish to let through the firewall. You can also enter multiple ports in the input field by separating them with a space, and enter ranges by typing the first number, then a colon, and then the final number. For example, entering 22:40 indicates that ports 22 through 40 should be opened. In this case, you want to allow through port 5900, the standard port for VNC connections. So simply type this port number in the box and click OK.

7. Click Next, and then click Finish to restart the firewall with the new settings.

Summary

In this chapter, we looked at how you can access your SUSE Linux computer remotely across the Internet. We examined how you can access the computer as if you were sitting in front of it, using the ssh program. This allows you to start a command-line prompt and even run GUI programs on the remote computer.

In addition, we discussed how the screen program can be used to keep sessions alive across various logins, and how you can transfer files using the sftp program. Then we looked at how to use the YaST2 Remote Administration tool to share your desktop interface with a remote computer. Finally, you learned how to configure your firewall to allow remote connections.

PART EIGHT

Appendixes

■ ■ ■

Glossary of Linux Terms

This appendix provides brief explanations of common terms used in the Linux and Unix world. These include technical terms, as well as conventions used within the Linux community. Due to space limitations, this glossary is somewhat selective, but still should prove a lasting reference as well as a helpful guide for those new to Linux.

Cross-referenced terms are highlighted in italics.

Symbols

.

Symbol that, in the context of file management, refers to the current directory.

..

Symbol that, in the context of file management, refers to the parent directory of that currently being browsed.

/

Symbol that, in the context of file management, refers to the *root* of the file system; also separates directories in a path listing.

~

Symbol that, in the context of file management, refers to a user's home directory.

|

Pipe symbol; used at the *command prompt* to *pipe* output from one *command* to another.

>

Symbol that, when used at the *command prompt*, indicates output should *redirect* into a file.

<

Symbol that, when used at the *command prompt*, indicates a *command* should take input from a file (see *redirect)*.

#

Symbol that, when it appears on the *command prompt*, usually indicates the user is currently logged in as *root*.

$

Symbol that, when it appears on the command prompt, usually indicates the user is currently logged in as an ordinary user. (Note that *SUSE Linux* doesn't follow this convention and uses a right angle bracket instead (>). Additionally, some versions of *Linux/Unix* use the % sign instead of $.

?

Wildcard character indicating that any character can be substituted in its place.

*

Wildcard character indicating that zero or more characters can appear in its place.

*nix

Popular but unofficial way of describing the family tree that comprises *Unix* and its various clones, such as *Linux* and *Minix*.

A

administrator

Another word for the *root* user.

AIX

IBM's *proprietary* form of *Unix* that runs on the company's proprietary hardware, as well as *commodity* hardware based around AMD and Intel processors. Nowadays, IBM is slowly deprecating AIX in favor of *Linux*.

alias

Method of creating a user-defined *command* that, when typed, causes another command to be run or *string* to be expanded.

Apache

Popular *Open Source* web server software that runs on *Unix*, *Linux*, and other operating system platforms. Considered responsible in part for the rise in popularity of Linux in the late 1990s.

applet

Small program that, in the context of the *SUSE Linux* desktop, runs as part of a larger program and offers functions that complement the main program. The *KDE* desktop *Panel* incorporates several applets in its system tray area.

archive

Any file containing a collection of smaller files, compressed or otherwise (see also *tar*).

B

BASH

Bourne Again SHell. The most common *shell* interpreter used under *Linux* and offered as default on many Linux systems.

binary executable

Another way of referring to a program that has been compiled so that it can be used day-to-day. See also *compile*.

block device

How the *Linux kernel* communicates with a *device* that sends and receives blocks of data; usually your hard disk or removable storage device. See also *character device*.

BSD Unix

Berkeley Software Distribution Unix; form of *Unix* partially based on the original Unix *source code* but also incorporating recent developments. BSD is *Open Source* and free for all to use and share with practically no restrictions. There are various forms of BSD Unix, such as FreeBSD, NetBSD, and OpenBSD. BSD doesn't use the *Linux kernel*, but it runs many of the same programs. Some of the programs offered within the Linux operating system come from BSD.

bzip2

Form of file compression. Together with the older and less efficient *gzip*, it is a popular form of file compression under *Linux* and the equivalent to Zip compression under Windows. Files employing bzip compression are usually given a .bz2 file extension. See also *tar*.

C

C

Programming language in which much of the *Linux kernel* is written, as were later versions of *Unix* before it. C was created by some of the same people who created Unix, and its development mirrors that of Unix.

C++

Object-oriented programming language; originally designed to be an enhancement to *C*, but now seen as a popular alternative.

C#

Modern programming language, which uses similar syntax to *C*, created by Microsoft and re-created on *Linux* via the Mono project.

character device

How Linux refers to a *device* that sends/receives data asynchronously. For various technical reasons, this typically refers to the *terminal* display. See also *block device*.

checksum

Mathematical process that can be applied to a file or other data to create a unique number relative to the contents of that file. If the file is modified, the checksum will change, usually indicating that the file in question has failed to download correctly or has been modified in some way. The most common type of checksum program used under *Linux* is md5sum.

client

Shorthand referring to a computer that connects to a *server*.

closed source

The reverse of *Open Source* in which the *source code* is not available for others to see, share, or modify. See also *proprietary*.

code

See *source code*.

command

Input typed at the *shell* that performs a specific task, usually related to administration of the system and/or the manipulation of files.

command-line prompt

See *shell*.

commodity

In the context of hardware, describes PC hardware usually based around Intel or AMD processors that can be bought off the shelf and used to create sophisticated computer systems (as opposed to buying specially designed hardware). One reason for *Linux*'s success is its ability to use commodity hardware.

community

The general term for the millions of *Linux* users worldwide, regardless of what they use Linux for or their individual backgrounds. By using Linux, you automatically become part of the community.

compile

The practice of creating a binary file from *source code*. Usually achieved using the ./configure, make, make install series of commands and scripts.

config file

Configuration file; any file that contains the list of settings for a program. Sometimes it's necessary to edit config files by hand using programs like *vi* or *emacs,* but often the program itself will write its config file according to the settings you choose.

copyleft

The legal principle of protecting the right to share a creative work, such as a computer program, using a legally binding license. Copyleft also ensures future iterations of the work are covered in the same way.

cracker

Someone who breaks into computer systems to steal data or cause damage. The term is not necessarily linked to *Linux* or *Unix* but was created by the *community* to combat the widespread use of hacker in this sense. The word *hacker* has traditionally defined someone who merely administers, programs, and generally enjoys computers.

cron

Background *service* that schedules tasks to occur at certain times, specified in anything up to minute-by-minute resolution. It relies on the crontab file.

CUPS

Common Unix Printing System; set of programs that work in the background to handle printing under *Unix* and *Linux.*

curses

Library that lets software present a semigraphical interface at the *shell*, complete with menu systems and simple mouse control (if configured). The version of curses used under *Linux* and *Unix* is called ncurses.

CVS

Concurrent Versioning System; application that allows the latest version of software packages to be distributed over the Internet to developers and other interested parties.

D

daemon

See *service*.

Debian

Voluntary organization that produces *distributions* of *Free Software* operating systems, including *Linux*. Because it is a nonprofit organization run by passionate Free Software advocates, it is considered the most ethically sound of all Linux outfits. Many commercial *distros* use Debian as the basis for their software because of its claimed reliability and relative simplicity.

dependency

A way of referring to system files that a program requires in order to run. If the dependencies are not present during program installation, it will usually refuse to install.

device

Linux shorthand describing something on your system that provides a function for the user or that the system requires in order to run. This usually refers to hardware, but it can also describe a virtual device that is created to provide access to a particular Linux function.

directory

What Windows refers to as a folder; areas on a hard disk in which files can be stored and organized.

distribution

A collection of software making up the *Linux* operating system; also known as a *distro*. The software is usually compiled by either a company or organization. A distribution is designed to be easy to install, administer, and use by virtue of it being an integrated whole. Examples include *SUSE Linux*, *Red Hat*, and *Debian*.

distro

Shorthand for *distribution*.

documentation

Another way of describing written guides or instructions; can refer to online sources of help as well as actual printed documentation.

E

emacs

Seminal text editor and pseudo-shell beloved by *Unix* aficionados; can be used for programming tasks, simple word processing, and much more. This editor has cultural significance as one of the core pieces of software offered by *GNU Project, The*. Emacs was originally developed principally by *Stallman, Richard*. See also *vi*.

environment

Shorthand referring to a user's unique *Linux* configuration, such as variables that tell the *shell* where programs are located.

F

FAT32

File Allocation Table 32-bits; file system offered by Windows 98, Me, 2000, and XP. *Linux* can both read and write to FAT32 file systems. See also *NTFS* and *VFAT*.

FLOSS

Free, Libre, or Open Source Software; used within the *community* to describe all software or technology that, broadly speaking, adheres to the ethical approach of *Open Source* software and/or *Free Software*, as well as its legal guidelines.

FOSS

Free or Open Source Software; alternative term for *FLOSS*.

free

When used to describe software or associated areas of technology, "free" indicates that the project abides by the ethical (if not legal) guidelines laid down by *GNU Project, The*. It doesn't indicate that the software is free in a monetary sense; its meaning is quite different from "freeware."

Free Software

Software in which the *source code*—the original listing created by the programmer—is available for all to see, share, study, and adapt to their own needs. This differs from the concept of *Open Source* because the right of others to further modify the code is guaranteed via the *GPL* software license (or a compatible license). For various reasons, Free Software sometimes does not include the source code (although the software can still be legally decompiled), but this is rare.

G

gcc
GNU Compiler Collection; programs usually used when creating *binary executable* files from *source code*.

GID
Group ID; numbering system used by the operating system to refer to a *group*.

GIMP
GNU Image Manipulation Program; high-powered image-editing program that runs under *Linux, Unix,* and Windows. Often preceded by the definite article: "The GIMP."

GNOME
GNU Network Object Model Environment; a *GUI*-based desktop environment offering similar functionality to *KDE*. It uses the GTK+ *libraries* instead of the QT libraries used by KDE.

GNU
GNU's Not Unix; see *GNU Project, The.*

GNU/Linux
Another name for the operating system referred to as *Linux*. The name GNU/Linux gives credit to the vast quantity of *GNU Project, The* software that is added to the *Linux kernel* within a *distro* to make a complete operating system. As such, GNU/Linux is the preferred term of many *Free Software* advocates.

GNU Project, The
Organization created by *Stallman, Richard* in order to further the aims of *Free Software* and create the body of software comprising the *GNU* operating system.

GNU Public License
Software license principally created by *Stallman, Richard* in order to protect software *source code* against *proprietary* interests and ensure that it will always be shared. It does this by insisting that any source code covered by the GNU Public License (GPL) must remain licensed under the GPL, even after it has been modified or added to by others. The *Linux kernel*, as well as much of the software that runs on it, uses the GPL.

GPL
See *GNU Public License.*

grep

Global Regular Expression Print; powerful *shell command* that lets you search a file or other form of input using *regular expressions*. Because of the ubiquity of the grep program, many *Linux* and *Unix* users refer to searching as "grepping." To "grep a file" is to search through it for a *string*.

group

Collection of users under one heading (group name) to facilitate system administration.

GRUB

GRand Unified Bootloader; boot manager program that offers a menu from which you can choose which operating system you wish to boot. It's needed to load the *kernel* program and thereby initiate the *Linux* boot procedure.

GUI

Graphical User Interface; describes the software that provides a graphical system to display data and let you control your PC (usually via a mouse).

guru

One who is experienced and knowledgeable about *Linux*/*Unix* and is willing to share his or her knowledge with others. In a perfect world, every *newbie* would have his or her own guru.

gzip

One of the two preferred forms of file compression used under *Linux*. Files employing gzip compression usually have a .gz file extension. See also *bzip2*.

H

hack

Ingenious and/or extremely efficient solution to a problem, particularly within the programming world.

hacker

Term used within the *community* to describe anyone who enjoys computers and possesses some skill therein, either in a professional capacity or as a hobby. This term is distinct from connotations of maliciously breaking into computers propagated by the media. See also *cracker*.

host

Shorthand referring to any computer that acts as a *server* to another computer. See also *client*.

HP-UX

Hewlett-Packard's *proprietary* form of *Unix* designed to work on its own hardware platform.

Hurd

Kernel being developed by *GNU Project, The*. It's not associated with the *Linux* kernel in any way.

I

inode

Part of the usually invisible file system structure that describes a file, such as its ownership permissions or file size.

init

The program that is automatically run after the *kernel* has finished loading, and therefore early in the boot procedure. It's responsible for effectively starting the operating system.

init.d

Collection of startup *scripts* that make up the components of a *run level*. Found under the *SUSE Linux* systems at /etc/init.d/. *Symbolic links* to selected init.d scripts are contained in folders within /etc/init.d that are named after *run level* numbers, such as rc0.d, rc1.d, rc2.d, and so on.

initrd

Initial RAM disk; system used by the *Linux kernel* to load *modules* that are essential for the kernel to be able to boot, such as disk controllers.

ipchains

Now deprecated component of version 2.2 of the *Linux kernel* that allows the creation of network security setups, such as firewalls or port-forwarding arrangements. Note that some *distros* still prefer to use ipchains. See also *iptables*.

iptables

Component of versions 2.4 and 2.6 of the *Linux kernel* that allows powerful network security setups. Chiefly used in the creation of firewalls, but can be used for more elementary arrangements such as network address translation (NAT) routers.

J

job

How the *BASH shell* refers to a running program in order to facilitate administration by the user.

journaling

File system technology in which integrity is maintained via the logging of disk writes.

K

K menu

Menu system akin to the Start menu under Windows. It runs under *KDE* and allows the quick launching of programs. This menu is usually located on the very left of the *Panel* and, under *SUSE Linux*, indicated with a green gecko icon.

KDE

K desktop environment; *GUI* and set of additional programs that run on top of *X* to provide such things as graphical file browsing, window management, program/file icons, and mouse-driven control over your system.

kernel

Essential but ordinarily invisible set of programs that run the computer's hardware and provide a platform on which to run software. In the *Linux* operating system, the kernel is also called Linux, after its creator, *Torvalds, Linus*.

kernel panic

Error message that appears when the *kernel* program in *Linux* cannot continue to work. In other words, a polite way of indicating a crash or, more often, a problem arising from user misconfiguration. This is most often seen when booting up after making incorrect changes to the system.

kludge

Community slang describing an inelegant way of making something work, usually not in a way that is generally accepted as being correct. Pronounced "kloodge."

Konqueror

Integrated file manager and web browser used within *KDE*.

Konsole

Program that runs a *shell* under *KDE*.

L

LAMP
Acronym describing a series of programs that work together to provide a complete *Linux*-based web-hosting environment. Stands for *Linux*, *Apache*, *MySQL*, and Perl or PHP (the last two in the list are scripting languages).

LGPL
Lesser GPL; version of the *GPL* in which some use restrictions are slackened at the expense of various freedoms laid down by the main GPL. The LGPL is ordinarily used for *library* files.

library
General term referring to code that programs need to run and that, once in memory, is frequently accessed by many programs (leading to the phrase "shared library"). The most common and vital library is glibc (GNU C Library), created by *GNU Project, The* and the fundamental building block without which *Linux* couldn't operate. *KDE* relies on the QT libraries, among others.

link
File system method of assigning additional filenames to a file; also known as a "hard link." See also *symbolic link*.

Linux
You mean you don't know by now? Linux is what this book is all about. It is a *kernel* program created by *Torvalds, Linus* in 1991 to provide an inexpensive operating system for his computer, along with other components. These days, Linux is used to describe the entire operating system discussed in this book, although many argue (perhaps quite rightly) that this is inaccurate, and use the term *GNU/Linux* instead.

local
Shorthand referring to the user's PC or a device directly attached to it (as opposed to *remote*).

localhost
(1) Network name used internally by *Linux* and software to refer to the *local* computer, distinct from the network.

(2) The default name given to a Linux-based PC when no other name is defined during installation.

M

man page

Documentation accessible from the *shell* that describes a *command* and how it should be used.

Minix

Operating system that is a rough clone of *Unix*, created by Professor Andrew Tanenbaum. It was the inspiration for *Linux*.

module

Program code that can be inserted or removed from the *kernel* in order to support particular pieces of hardware or provide certain kernel functions. Drivers under Windows perform the same function.

mount

To add a file system so that it is integrated (and therefore accessible) within the main file system; applies to external file systems, such as those available across networks, as well as those on the *local* PC, such as the hard disk or CD/DVD-ROMs.

Mozilla

Organization founded by Netscape to create *Open Source* Internet software, such as web browsers and e-mail clients; originally based on the Netscape *source code*. At the time of writing, it produces the Mozilla, Firefox, and Camino web browsers, the Thunderbird e-mail and Usenet client, the Bugzilla bug-tracking software, and more.

MySQL

Popular and powerful *Open Source* database application. See also *LAMP*.

N

newbie

Term used to describe anyone who is new to *Linux* and therefore still learning the basics. It's not a derogatory term! See also *guru*.

NFS

Network File System; reliable and established method of sharing files, printers, and other resources across a network of *Unix*-based operating systems. See also *Samba*.

NTFS

NT File System; file system offered by Windows NT, 2000, and XP. It can be read by *Linux*, but usually writing is prohibited because it is considered unsafe. See also *FAT32*.

O

OpenOffice.org

Open Source office suite project created with the continuing input of Sun Microsystems and based on code Sun contributed to the Open Source *community*. Its commercial release is in the form of Star Office (although Star Office has several *proprietary* components added).

Open Source

Method and philosophy of developing software whereby the *source code*—the original listing created by the programmer—is available for all to see. The term also applies to a community of users. Note that Open Source is not the same as *Free Software*; describing software as Open Source doesn't imply that the code can be shared or used by others (although this is often the case).

P

Panel

Toolbar at the bottom of the *KDE* desktop on which program icons reside, as well as the Taskbar and system tray.

partition

Subdivision of a hard disk into which a file system can be installed.

PID

Process ID; the numbering system used to refer to a *process*.

pipe

Method of passing the output from one *command* to another for further processing. Piping is achieved within the *shell* by typing the | symbol.

POSIX

Portable Operating System Interface; various technical standards that define how *Unix*-like operating systems should operate and that the *Linux* operating system attempts to adhere to.

PPP

Point-to-Point Protocol; networking technology that allows data transfer across serial connections like telephone lines. In other words, it's the technology that lets you connect to your Internet service provider using a modem. Controlled under *SUSE Linux* using Kppp.

process

The way the system refers to the individual programs (or components of programs) running in memory.

proprietary

Effectively, software for which a software license must be acquired, usually for a fee. This usually means the *source code* is kept secret, but it can also indicate that the source code is available to view but not to incorporate into your own projects or share with others.

R

Red Hat

Well-known company that produces *distributions* of *Linux*. See also *SUSE Linux* and *Debian*.

redirect

To send the output of a *command* into a particular file. This also works the other way around: the contents of a particular file can be directed into a command. Redirection is achieved within the *shell* using the left and right angle brackets (< and >), respectively.

regex

See *regular expression*.

regular expression

Powerful and complex method of describing a search *string*, usually when searching with tools such as *grep* (although regular expressions are also used when programming). Regular expressions use various symbols as substitutes for characters or to indicate patterns.

remote

Indicates a computer or *service* that is available across a network, including but not limited to computers on the Internet (as opposed to *local*).

root

(1) The bottom of the *Linux* file system directory structure, usually indicated by a forward slash (/).

(2) The user on a *Unix* system who has control over all aspects of hardware, software, and the file system.

(3) Used to describe a user who temporarily takes on the powers of the root user (via the sudo command, for example).

RPM

Red Hat Package Manager; system used to install and administer programs. An RPM file, which has an .rpm extension, contains either the *binary executable* files that make up the program or the *source code*. In addition, it contains several *scripts* that check the operating system for compatibility, such as whether you have the correct *dependencies*, and installs the files on the hard disk.

RTFM

Read the f***ing manual/*man page*; exclamation frequently used online when a *newbie* asks for help without having undertaken basic research.

run level

Describes the current operational mode of *Linux* (typically what services are running). Run level 3 is text-only, although a *GUI* can be started manually. Run level 5 has a GUI started as part of the boot procedure. Run level 1 is single-user mode (a stripped-down system with minimal running services). Run level 6 is reboot mode; switching to it will cause the computer to terminate its processes and then reboot.

S

Samba

Program that recreates under *Unix* or *Linux* the Microsoft *SMB*-based system of sharing files, printers, and other computer resources across a network. It allows Linux to become a file or printer server for Linux and Windows computers, and also allows a Linux client to access a Windows-based server.

SaX2

SUSE Advanced X configuration tool, version 2; *GUI*-based software by which the keyboard, mouse, display and other aspects of *X* can be configured.

scalable

Term describing the ability of a single computer program to meet diverse needs, regardless of the scale of the potential uses. The *Linux kernel* is described as being scalable because it can run supercomputers, as well as handheld computers and home entertainment devices.

script

Form of computer program consisting of a series of *commands* in a text file. Most *shells* allow some form of scripting, and entire programming languages such as Perl are based around scripts. Shell scripts are usually created to perform trivial tasks or ones that frequently interact with the user. Shell scripts have the advantage that they can be frequently and easily modified. The *Linux* boot process relies on several complex scripts to configure essential system functions such as networking and the *GUI*. See also *init*.

server

(1) Type of computer designed to share data with other computers over a network.

(2) Software that runs on a computer and is designed to share data with other programs on the same PC or with other PCs across a network.

service

Background program that provides vital functions for the day-to-day running of *Linux*; also known as a *daemon*. Services are usually started when the computer boots up and as such are constituent parts of a *run level*.

shell

Broadly speaking, any program that creates an operating environment in which you can control your computer. The SUSE desktop can be seen as a shell, for example. However, it's more commonly understood within *Unix* and *Linux* circles as a program that lets you control the system using *commands* entered at the keyboard. In this context, the most common type of shell in use on Linux is *BASH*.

SMB

Server Message Block; network technology for sharing files, printers, and other resources. See *Samba*.

Solaris

Form of *Unix* sold by Sun Microsystems; runs on *proprietary* hardware systems as well as on *commodity* systems based on Intel and AMD processors.

source code

The original program listing created by a programmer. Most programs that you download are precompiled—already turned into *binary executables* ready for general use—unless you specifically choose to download and *compile* the source code of a program yourself.

SSH

Secure SHell; program that lets you access a *Linux/Unix* computer across the Internet. SSH encrypts data sent and received across the *link*.

SSL

Secure Sockets Layer; form of network data transfer designed to encrypt information for security purposes. It's used online for certain web sites and also within *Linux* for certain types of secure data exchange.

Stallman, Richard M.

Legendary *hacker* who founded *GNU Project, The* and created the concept of *copyleft*, as well as the software license that incorporates it: the *GPL*. See also *Torvalds, Linus*.

standard error

Linux and *Unix* shorthand for the error output provided by a *command*.

standard input

Linux and *Unix* shorthand for the *device* usually used to provide input to the *shell*. For the majority of desktop PC users, this refers to the keyboard.

standard output

Linux and *Unix* shorthand for the *device* usually used to display output from a *command*. For the majority of desktop PC users, this refers to the screen.

string

A word, phrase, or sentence consisting of letters, numbers, or other characters that is used within a program and is often supplied by the user.

SUSE Linux

Company owned by Novell that produces its own *distribution* of *Linux*. A version of SUSE Linux is provided with this book.

SVG

Scalable Vector Graphics; vector graphics technology. SVG is actually an XML markup language designed to create 2D graphics, increasingly used for *Linux* desktop icons.

swap

Area of the hard disk that the *Linux kernel* uses as a temporary memory storage area. Desktop or *server* Linux differs from Windows in that it usually requires a separate hard disk *partition* in which to store the swap file.

symbolic link

Type of file akin to a Windows shortcut. Accessing a symbolic link file routes the user through to an actual file. See also *link*.

sysadmin

Systems administrator; a way of describing the person employed within a company to oversee the computer systems. In such an environment, the sysadmin usually is the *root* user of the various computers.

System V

Variant of *Unix* used as a foundation for modern forms of *proprietary* Unix.

T

tainted

Describes a *kernel* that is using *proprietary modules* in addition to *Open Source* modules. Can also refer to insecure software.

tar

Tape Archive; software able to combine several files into one larger file in order to back them up to a tape drive or simply transfer them across the Internet. Such files are usually indicated by a .tar file extension. Note that a tar file isn't necessarily compressed; the *bzip2* and *gzip* utilities must be used if this is desired.

TCP/IP

Transmission Control Protocol/Internet Protocol; standard protocol stack used by most modern operating systems to control and communicate across networks and also across the Internet (as opposed to NetBEUI, commonly available on older versions of Windows, and IPX/SPX, used on Novell's NetWare operating system).

terminal

Another word for *shell*.

TeX

Method and set of programs for typesetting complex documents. Invented prior to word processors and desktop publishing software, and now considered a specialized tool for laying out scientific texts. An updated version of the program called LaTeX is also available.

Torvalds, Linus

Finnish programmer who, in 1991, created the initial versions of the *Linux kernel*. Since then, he has taken advantage of an international network of volunteers and staff employed by various companies who help produce the kernel. Torvalds himself contributes and oversees the efforts.

tty

TeleTYpewriter; shorthand referring to underlying *Linux* virtual *devices* that allow programs and users to access the *kernel* and thereby run programs.

Tux

The name of the penguin character that is the *Linux* mascot. The original Tux graphic was drawn by Larry Ewing.

U

UID
User ID; numbering system used by the operating system to refer to a *user*.

Unix
Seminal operating system created as a research project in 1969 by Kenneth Thompson and Dennis Ritchie at Bell Labs (later AT&T). Because it was initially possible to purchase the *source code* for a fee, subsequent revisions were enhanced by a variety of organizations and went on to run many mainframe and minicomputer systems throughout the 1980s, 1990s, and up to the present. Nowadays, Unix is fragmented and exists in a variety of different versions. Perhaps most popular is its *Open Source* rendition, *BSD Unix,* which has seen many developments since the source code was first released. This means that BSD Unix no longer exists but has instead diversified into a number of separate projects. *Proprietary* versions are also available, including *Solaris, HP-UX,* and *AIX.*

user
The way the operating system refers to anyone who accesses its resources. A user must first have a user account set up, effectively giving that user his or her own private space on the system. In addition to actual human users, an average *Linux* system has many other user accounts created to let programs and *services* go about their business. These are usually not seen by human users.

V

variable
A changeable value that stores a certain data type (such as a number, date, or *string*), remembering it for future reference by the system or *script* it is defined by. Variables defined by and for the *Linux kernel* are vital to it.

verbose
Command option that will cause it to return more detailed output (or, in some cases, to return actual output if the command is otherwise "quiet"); usually specified by adding the -v command option.

VFAT
Virtual File Allocation Table; technical name of Microsoft's FAT file system offered under Windows and also on removable storage devices such as flash memory cards.

vi
Arcane text editor and pseudo-shell beloved by *Unix* aficionados that can be used for creation of text files or for creating programs. Traditionally, Unix users either love or hate vi, often in preference to *emacs.*

W

Wine
Wine Is Not an Emulator; software that re-creates the Windows Application Programming Interface (API) layer within *Linux* and lets users run Windows programs.

workspace
X terminology referring to a *GUI* desktop.

X

X
Short for X Window; software that controls the display and input devices, thereby providing a software foundation on top of which desktop managers like *KDE* are able to run.

X11
Version 11 of the *X* software, currently in use on most desktop *Linux* systems.

XFree86 Project
Organization that creates *X* software and, in particular, a set of programs called XFree86. At one time, every *distribution* of *Linux* used XFree86 software, but most now use similar software from the Xorg organization.

xinetd
The *service* responsible for starting various network servers on the computer.

XMMS
Audio player program.

xterm
Simple program that allows you to run a *shell* under *X*. This program has the advantage of being available on most *Linux* systems that offer a *GUI*.

Y

YaST2
Yet Another Setup Tool, version 2; principle system configuration tool within *SUSE Linux* by which hardware is configured, software installed, and system preferences configured.

■ ■ ■

BASH Command Index

Thi s appendix provides a whistle-stop tour of commands that can be used at the BASH shell. This is a highly selective listing, which is to say it is a guide to commands that see day-to-day use on average desktop systems. In a similar fashion, although some command options are listed, they're strictly limited to those that receive regular deployment.

The descriptions of each command are deliberately simple. It's important to note that the quantity of space a command is given is not an indication of its importance or usefulness. To this end, commands in the list with an asterisk after their name offer far more than the brief description here hints at. In such cases, I strongly advise you to refer to the command's man page for more information.

Various conventions are used in the list:

- **Italics:** You should substitute your own details wherever italicized words appear.

- **$:** Commands that can and might be run by ordinary users are preceded with a dollar sign ($).

- **#:** Commands that require root privileges, or that are ordinarily run by root, are preceded with a hash (#).

Commands that present dangers to the system through misuse are clearly marked. Such commands should not be used without research into the command's usage and function.

Command	Notes/Command Options	Example of Typical Use
$ alias	Create or display command aliases	alias *list*='l'
$ apropos	Search man pages for specified words/phrases	apropos *"word or phrase"*
$ bzip2	Compress specified file (replaces original file with compressed file and gives it .bz2 file extension) -d: Decompress specified file -k: Don't delete original file -t: Test; do a dry run without writing any data	bzip2 *myfile*
$ bzip2recover	Attempt recovery of specified damaged .bz2 file	bzip2recover *myfile.tar.bz2*

Command	Notes/Command Options	Example of Typical Use
$ cal	Display calendar for current month (or specified month/year)	cal *4 2005*
$ cat	Display a file on screen or combine and display two files together	cat *myfile*
$ cd	Change to specified directory	cd */usr/bin*
$ cdparanoia *	Convert CD audio tracks to hard disk files -B: Batch mode; convert all tracks to individual files -S: Set CD read speed (2, 4, 8, 12, and so on; values relate to CD-drive spin speed; used to avoid read errors)	cdparanoia –S 8 –B
# cdrecord *	Burn audio or CD-R/RW data discs (the latter usually based on an ISO image; see mkisofs) -dev=: Specify the drive's device number (can be discovered by running cdrecord with the --scanbus option) --scanbus: Scan to see which CD-R/RW drives are present and return device numbers	cdrecord *dev=0,0,0 –speed=16 -v myfile.iso*
-speed=:	Specify the write speed (2, 4, 6, 8, and so on) -v: Verbose output; obligatory for feedback on cdrecord's progress	
# cfdisk *	DANGEROUS! Menu-based disk-partitioning program	cfdisk */dev/hda*
# chgrp	Change group ownership of a file/directory -R: Recursive; apply changes to subdirectories	chgroup *mygroup myfile*
# chkconfig	Administer or display services that comprise current run level	chkconfig *servicename* on
$ chmod	Change permissions of a file/directory (where a=all, u=user, g=group, r=read, w=write, x=executable) -R: Recursive; apply to subdirectories --reference=: Copy permissions from specified file	chmod a+rw *myfile*
$ chown	Change file ownership to specified username -R: Recursive; apply to subdirectories	chown *username myfile1*
# chroot	Change the root of the file system to the specified path	chroot */home/mydirectory*

Command	Notes/Command Options	Example of Typical Use
# chvt	Switch to the specified virtual terminal (equivalent of holding down Ctrl+Alt and pressing F1–F6)	chvt *3*
$ clear	Clears terminal screen and places cursor at top	clear
$ cp	Copy files -r: Recursive; copy subdirectories and the files therein -s: Create symbolic link instead of copying	cp *myfile1 directory/*
$ crontab	Edit or display the user's crontab file (scheduled tasks) -e: Edit the crontab file (create/amend) -l: List crontab entries -r: Delete the crontab file -u: Specify a user and edit their crontab file	crontab -e
$ date	Display the date and time	date
$ df	Display free disk space within file system -h: Human readable; display sizes in KB, MB, GB, and TB, as appropriate -l: Restrict to local file systems, as opposed to network mounts	df -h
$ diff	Display differences between specified files -a: Consider all files text files (i.e. don't halt when asked to compare binary files) -i: ignore lowercase and uppercase differences	diff *myfile1 myfile2*
$ diff3	Display differences between three specified files	diff3 *myfile1 myfile2 myfile3*
$ dig	Look up IP address of specified domain	dig *mysite.com*
# dmesg	Display kernel message log	dmesg
# dosfsck *	Check and repair MS-DOS–based file hard disk partition (see also fsck) -a: Repair without asking user for confirmation -r: Repair file system asking user for confirmation when two or more repair methods are possible -v: Verbose; display more information	dosfsck -rv */dev/hda4*

Command	Notes/Command Options	Example of Typical Use
$ du	Show sizes of files and folders in kilobytes -h: Human readable; produce output in MB, GB, and TB -s: Summary; display totals only for directories rather than for individual files	du -h /home/myuser
$ eject	Eject a removable storage disk -t: Close an already open tray	eject /media/dvd-rom
$ emacs *	Start the emacs text editor program	emacs myfile
$ ex *	Start a simple text-editor program used principally within shell scripts	ex myfile.txt
$ exit	Log out of shell (end session)	exit
$ fdformat	Low-level format a floppy disk (this won't create a file system; see also mkfs)	fdformat /dev/fd0
# fdisk *	DANGEROUS! Hard-disk partitioning program -l: List partition table	fdisk /dev/hda
$ fg	Brings job running in background to foreground	fg 1
$ file	Display information about specified file, such as its type	file myfile
$ find *	Find files by searching directories (starting in current directory) -maxdepth: Specify the number of subdirectories levels to delve into, starting from 1 (current directory) -name: Specify name of file to search for -type: Specify file types to be returned; -type d returns directories and -type f returns only files	find -name "myfile"
$ findsmb	Search network for Windows file sharing (SMB) computers	findsmb
$ free	Display information about memory usage -m: Show figures in MB -t: Total the columns at bottom of table	free -m
# fsck *	Check file system for errors (usually run from rescue disc)	fsck /dev/hda1
$ ftp *	FTP program for uploading/downloading to remote sites	ftp ftp.mysite.com
$ fuser	Show which processes are using a particular file or file system -v: Verbose; detailed output	fuser -v myfile

Command	Notes/Command Options	Example of Typical Use
$ grep *	Search specified file for specified text string (or word) -i: Ignore uppercase and lowercase differences -r: Recursive; delve into subdirectories (if applicable) -s: Suppress error messages about inaccessible files, etc.	grep "phrase I want to find" myfile.txt
# groupadd	Create new group	groupadd mygroup
# groupdel	Delete specified group	groupdel mygroup
$ groups	Display groups the specified user belongs to	groups myuser
$ gzip	Compress files and replace original file with compressed version -d: Decompress specified file -v: Verbose; display degree of compression	gzip myfile
# halt	Initiate shutdown procedure, ending all processes and unmounting all disks -p: Power off system at end of shutdown procedure	halt -p
# hdparm *	DANGEROUS! Tweak hard disk settings	hdparm /dev/hda
$ head	Print topmost lines of text files (default is first 10 lines) -n: Specify number of lines (such as -n 5)	head myfile.txt
$ help	Display list of common BASH commands	help
$ history	Display history file (a list of recently used commands)	history
$ host	Query DNS server based on specified domain name or IP address -d: Verbose; return more information -r: Force name server to return its cached information rather than query other authoritative servers	host 65.19.150.100
$ hostname	Display localhost-style name of computer	hostname
$ id	Display username and group info of specified user (or current user if none specified)	id myuser

Command	Notes/Command Options	Example of Typical Use
# ifconfig *	Display or configure settings of a network interface (assign an IP address, subnet mask, and activate/deactivate it)	ifconfig *eth0 192.168.0.10* netmask *255.255.0.0* up
	down: Disable interface (used at end of command chain)	
	netmask: Specify a subnet mask	
	up: Enable interface (used at end of command chain)	
$ info *	Display info page for specified command	info *command*
# init	Change current run level	init *3*
$ ispell *	Program that spellchecks specified file	ispell *myfile.txt*
	-b: Back up original file (provided original file is altered and subsequently saved)	
$ jobs	Display list of jobs running in background	jobs
# kernelversion	Display kernel version number	kernelversion
$ kill	Kill specified process	kill *1433*
$ killall	Kill process(es) that have specified name(s)	killall *processnumber*
	-i: Confirm before killing process	
	-v: Verbose; report if and when successful	
$ last	Display details of recent logins, reboots, and shutdowns	last
$ ldd	Display system files (libraries) required by specified program	ldd */usr/bin/program*
$ less	Interactively scroll through a text file	less *myfile.txt*
	-q: Quiet; disable beeps when end of file is reached or other error encountered	
	-i: Ignore case; make all searches case-insensitive unless uppercase letters are used	
$ ln	Create links to specified files, such as symbolic links	ln -s *myfile1 mfile2*
	-s: Create symbolic link (default is hard link)	
$ look	Spell-check specified word (or part of word)	look *word*
	-f: Ignore uppercase and lowercase	
$ lpr	Print file (send it to the printer spool/queue)	lpr *myfile.txt*
	-V: Verbose; print information about progress of print job	

Command	Notes/Command Options	Example of Typical Use
$ lpstat	Display print queue	lpstat
$ ls	List directory	ls -h *mydirectory*
	-a: List all files, including hidden files	
	-d: List only directory names rather than their contents	
	-h: Human readable; print figures in KB, MB, GB, and TB	
	-l: Long list; include all details, such as file permissions	
	-m: Show as comma-separated list	
# lsmod	Display currently loaded kernel modules	lsmod
$ lsof	Display any files currently in use	lsof -u *username*
	-u: Limit results to files used by specified user	
$ mail *	Program that can send and also receive mail	mail *user@mydomain.com*
	-s: Specify subject prior to creating new mail	
$ man	Display specified command's manual	man *command*
$ mc *	Semigraphical file-browsing program based on Norton Commander	mc
$ md5sum	Display MD5 checksum (normally used to confirm a file's integrity after download)	md5sum *myfile*
# mkfs *	DANGEROUS! Create specified file system on specified device (such as a floppy disk)	mkfs -t *vfat* */dev/fd0*
	-t: Specify type of file system	
$ mkisofs *	Create ISO image file from specified directory (usually for burning to disc with cdrecord)	mkisofs -o *isoimage.iso* -R -J -v *mydirectory*
	-o: Options; this must appear after command to indicate that command options follow	
	-apple: Use Mac OS extensions to make ensuing disc readable on Apple computers	
	-f: Follow symbolic links and source actual files	
	-J: Use Joliet extensions (make ISO compatible with Windows)	
	-R: Use Rock Ridge extensions (preferred Linux CD-ROM file system)	
	-v: Verbose; display more information (-vv for even more info)	
# modinfo	Display information about kernel module	modinfo *modulename*

Command	Notes/Command Options	Example of Typical Use
# modprobe	Insert specified module into the kernel, as well as any others it relies on -k: Set module's autoclean flag so it will be removed from memory after inactivity -r: Remove specified module as well as any it relies on to operate	modprobe *modulename*
$ more	Interactively scroll through text file (similar to less)	more *myfile.txt*
# mount *	Mount specified file system at specified location -o: Specify command options, such as rw to allow read/write access; various types of file systems have unique commands	mount */dev/hda4 /mnt*
$ mv	Move (or rename) specified files and/or directories -b: Back up files before moving -v: Display details of actions carried out	mv *myfile mydirectory/*
$ netstat *	Show current network connections	netstat -a
$ nice	Run specified command with specified priority -n: Specify priority, ranging from the highest priority of -20, to 19, which is the lowest priority	nice -n *19*
$ nohup	Run specified command and continue to run it, even if user logs out	nohup *command*
$ passwd	Change user's password	passwd
$ ping	Check network connectivity between local machine and specified address -w: Exit after specified number of seconds (such as -w 5)	ping *mydomain.com*
$ printenv	Display all environment variables for current user	printenv
$ ps *	Display currently running processes a: List all processes (note that command options don't require preceding dash) f: Display ownership of processes using tree-style graphics u: Limit results to processes running for and started by current user x: Include processes in results not started by user but running with the user ID	ps aux
$ pwd	Display current directory	pwd
# reboot	Reboot computer	reboot

Command	Notes/Command Options	Example of Typical Use
$ renice	Change a process' priority while it's running (see nice)	renice 19 10704
$ rm	Delete single or multiple files and/or directories	rm -rf mydirectory
	-r: Recursive; delete specified directories and any subdirectories	
	-f: Force; don't prompt for confirmation before deleting (use with care!)	
# rmmod	Delete module from kernel	rmmod modulename
# route *	Add and create (or view) entries in routing table (see ifconfig)	route add default gw 192.168.1.1
# rpm *	Red Hat Package Manager; installs specified RPM package(s)	rpm -Uvh packagename
	-e: Uninstall specified package	
	-h: Graphically indicate progress when installing/upgrading	
	-i: Install package	
	--nodeps: Ignore dependency errors (use with care!)	
	-qa: Display listing of installed packages	
	-qp: Display details of specified package	
	-U: Upgrade package (will install if package not already installed)	
	-v: Verbose; display detailed output	
# runlevel	Display current run level	runlevel
# sax2 *	Configure X (keyboard, mouse, and display); note that this is a SUSE Linux-specific GUI tool	sax2
	-V: Specify initial resolution and refresh rate (such as -V 800x600@60)	
$ screen *	Program that runs pseudo shell that is kept alive regardless of current user login	screen
	-ls: Display list of currently running screen sessions	
	-R: Reattach to already running screen session or start new one if none available	
$ sftp *	Secure Shell FTP; like FTP but running over an ssh connection (see below)	sftp username@192.168.1.14
$ shred	Overwrite data in a file with gibberish, thereby making it irrecoverable	shred -fv myfile
	-u: Delete file in addition to overwriting	
	-v: Verbose; show details of procedure	
	-f: Force permissions to allow writing if necessary	

Command	Notes/Command Options	Example of Typical Use
$ sleep	Pause input for the specified period of time (where s=seconds, m=minutes, h=hours, d=days)	sleep *10m*
$ smbclient *	FTP-style program with which you can log in to a SMB (Windows)-based file share	smbclient *//192.168.1.1/*
$ sort	Sort entries in the specified text file (default is ASCII sort)	sort *myfile.txt* -o *sorted.txt*
$ ssh *	Log in to remote computer using secure shell	ssh *username@192.168.1.15*
$ startx	Start GUI session when in run level 3 (at shell login)	startx
$ su	Temporarily log in as specified user; log in as root if no user specified -: Adopt user's environment variables, such as $PATH	su -
$ sudo	Execute specified command with root privileges (provided the facility has been set up)	sudo *command*
# SuSEconfig	Update system according to settings in SuSE Linux-specific config files	SuSEconfig
$ tac	Display specified text file but in reverse (from last to first line)	tac *myfile.txt*
$ tail	Display final lines of specified text file -n: Specify number of lines to display (such as -n4)	tail *myfile.txt*
$ tar *	Combine specified files and/or directories into one larger file, or extract from such a file -c: Create new archive -j: Use bzip2 in order to compress (or decompress) files -f: Specifies filename (must be last in chain of command options) -r: Add files to existing archive -x: Extract files from existing archive -z: Use gzip to compress (or decompress) files	tar -zcf *myfile.tar.gz mydirectory*
$ tee	Display piped output and also save it to specified file	ls -lh| tee *listing.txt*
$ top *	Program that both displays and lets the user manipulate processes	top
$ touch	Give specified file current time and date stamp; if it doesn't exist, create a zero-byte file with that name	touch *myfile*

Command	Notes/Command Options	Example of Typical Use
# traceroute	Discover and display network path to another host	traceroute *192.168.1.20*
$ umask	Set default permissions assigned to newly created files	umask u=rwx,g=r,o=
# umount	Unmount a file system	umount */media/cdrom*
# useradd	Add new user -m: Create home directory for user	useradd -m *username*
# userdel	Delete all mention of user in system configuration files (effectively deleting the user, although files owned by him/her might remain) -r: Remove user's home directory	userdel -r *username*
$ unalias	Remove specified alias -a: Remove all aliases (use with care!)	unalias *command*
$ uname	Display technical information about current system -a: Display all basic information	uname -a
$ unzip	Unzip a Windows-compatible Zip file -l: Display archive content but don't actually unzip	unzip *myfile.zip*
$ uptime	Display uptime for system, as well as CPU load average and logged-in users	uptime
$ vi *	Text editor program	vi
$ wc	Count the number of words in a file	wc *myfile.txt*
$ whatis	Display one-line summary of specified command	whatis *command*
$ whereis	Display information on where a binary command is located, along with its source code and man page (if applicable) -b: Return information only about binary programs	whereis -b *command*
# xf86config *	Command-line program that configures X system, including mouse, keyboard, and display	xf86config
$ xhost	Configure which users/systems can run programs on the X server +: When followed by a username and/or system name, gives the user/system permission to run programs on the X server; when used on its own, lets *any* user/system use the X server -: Opposite of above	xhost +

Command	Notes/Command Options	Example of Typical Use
$ xinit	Start elementary GUI session (when in run level 3)	xinit
# yast2 *	Start the YaST2 program -i: Install specified RPM	yast2
$ zip	Create Windows-compatible compressed Zip files -r: Recursive; includes all subdirectories and files therein -u: Updates Zip with specified file -P: Encrypts Zip with specified password -v: Verbose; display more information -#: Set compression level (from 0, which is no compression, to 9, which is highest)	zip -r *myfile*.zip *mydirectory*
$ zipgrep	Searches inside Zip files for specified text string	zipgrep *"search phrase" myfile.zip*

INDEX

See Appendix A, "Glossary of Linux Terms," and Appendix B, "BASH Command Index," for comprehensive information about terminology and commands, respectively.

Numbers

3D effects, applying in Impress presentations, 349–350

3D graphic cards, using, 113–115. *See also* graphics cards

15- and 17-inch monitors, standard resolutions for, 71

Symbols

- (dash), indicating file type with, 213

--- (three dashes), relationship to permissions, 215

- code, file type associated with, 214

! (bang or shriek), using with command history in BASH shell, 258

! command in sftp, function associated with, 441

$ command in vi, effect of, 234

* (asterisk)

    decoding in Windows passwords, 31

    using as wildcards, 259

. (period) before directory and filenames, meaning of, 423

/ (forward slash), removing from paths, 428

/ command in vi, effect of, 234

? (question mark) wildcard, effect of, 259

? command in vi, effect of, 234

[] (square brackets), using with grep, 240

\ (backslash) versus / (forward slash), 163

_ (underscore), using with Rekall databases, 355

| (pipe), using with command output, 259–260

> (angle bracket), using to redirect output, 261

.⁴ command in vi, effect of, 234

' (apostrophe), appearance in Calc spreadsheets, 337

/ (slash) versus \ (backslash), 163

A

-a option, using with ls command, 423

AbiWord word processor. *See also* word processing programs

    features of, 309

    web address for, 144, 309

absolute paths, relationship to backups, 425

"access denied" error message, occurrence of, 212

access permissions, for root and ordinary users, 119–120

Accessibility configuration option in OpenOffice.org, description of, 318

ACPI (Advanced Configuration and Power Interface)

    support for, 142

    incorrect operation of, 184

action confirmation, configuring for Rekall, 354

administrators. *See* root accounts

Adobe Acrobat

    accessing, 160

    using with OpenOffice.org, 322–323

Agfa scanners, lack of support for, 111

Airbrush tool in The Gimp, description of, 289

albums, using with Digikam software, 110

Alcatel SpeedTouch DSL modem, installing driver for, 93–94

alias command in BASH shell, example of, 471

aliases, creating, 203

▉C

■M

forums.apress.com

FOR PROFESSIONALS BY PROFESSIONALS™

JOIN THE APRESS FORUMS AND BE PART OF OUR COMMUNITY. You'll find discussions that cover topics of interest to IT professionals, programmers, and enthusiasts just like you. If you post a query to one of our forums, you can expect that some of the best minds in the business—especially Apress authors, who all write with *The Expert's Voice*™—will chime in to help you. Why not aim to become one of our most valuable participants (MVPs) and win cool stuff? Here's a sampling of what you'll find:

DATABASES
Data drives everything.

Share information, exchange ideas, and discuss any database programming or administration issues.

INTERNET TECHNOLOGIES AND NETWORKING
Try living without plumbing (and eventually IPv6).

Talk about networking topics including protocols, design, administration, wireless, wired, storage, backup, certifications, trends, and new technologies.

JAVA
We've come a long way from the old Oak tree.

Hang out and discuss Java in whatever flavor you choose: J2SE, J2EE, J2ME, Jakarta, and so on.

MAC OS X
All about the Zen of OS X.

OS X is both the present and the future for Mac apps. Make suggestions, offer up ideas, or boast about your new hardware.

OPEN SOURCE
Source code is good; understanding (open) source is better.

Discuss open source technologies and related topics such as PHP, MySQL, Linux, Perl, Apache, Python, and more.

PROGRAMMING/BUSINESS
Unfortunately, it is.

Talk about the Apress line of books that cover software methodology, best practices, and how programmers interact with the "suits."

WEB DEVELOPMENT/DESIGN
Ugly doesn't cut it anymore, and CGI is absurd.

Help is in sight for your site. Find design solutions for your projects and get ideas for building an interactive Web site.

SECURITY
Lots of bad guys out there—the good guys need help.

Discuss computer and network security issues here. Just don't let anyone else know the answers!

TECHNOLOGY IN ACTION
Cool things. Fun things.

It's after hours. It's time to play. Whether you're into LEGO® MINDSTORMS™ or turning an old PC into a DVR, this is where technology turns into fun.

WINDOWS
No defenestration here.

Ask questions about all aspects of Windows programming, get help on Microsoft technologies covered in Apress books, or provide feedback on any Apress Windows book.

HOW TO PARTICIPATE:
Go to the Apress Forums site at **http://forums.apress.com/**.
Click the New User link.

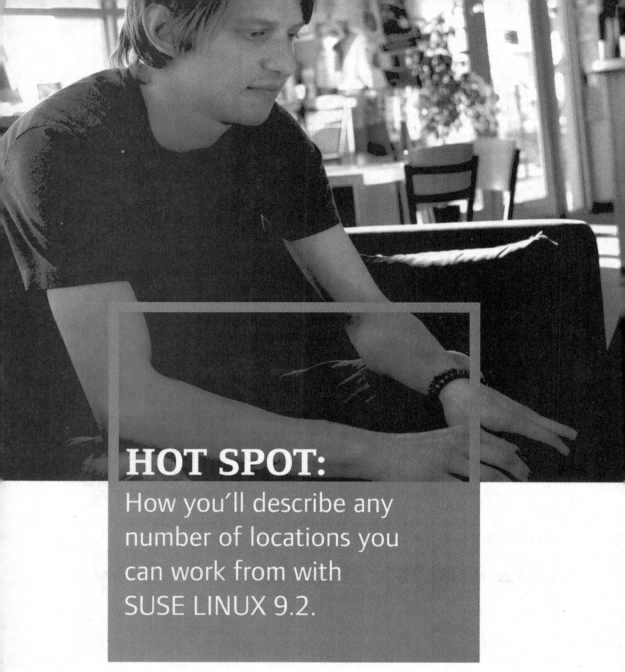

HOT SPOT:

How you'll describe any number of locations you can work from with SUSE LINUX 9.2.

SUSE LINUX Professional 9.2 isn't just fast, secure, and loaded with 1,000 popular open source application. It's also stacked with new mobility features that quickly connect you to wireless networks and synchroniz with your Bluetooth, cell phone, PDA, and other devices. Being mobile doesn't mean you can't be connecte For more information, please visit www.novell.com/suselinux. ⊕ **WE SPEAK YOUR LANGUAG**

Recommended retail price is $ 89.95/£ 64.95. For a list of our resellers, please visit www.suse.de/en/company/resellers/index.html.

Novel